OLD LONDO
Hyde Park to Bloom

THE
'VILLAGE LONDON'
SERIES
from
THE ALDERMAN PRESS

THE VILLAGE LONDON SERIES

Other titles already published in hard back are:

VILLAGE LONDON Volume I
VILLAGE LONDON Volume II
LONDON RECOLLECTED Volume I
LONDON RECOLLECTED Volume II
LONDON RECOLLECTED Volume III
LONDON RECOLLECTED Volume IV
LONDON RECOLLECTED Volume V
LONDON RECOLLECTED Volume VI
VILLAGE LONDON ATLAS

Other titles already published in paperback:

VILLAGE LONDON Pt. 1 West and North
VILLAGE LONDON Pt. 2 North and East
VILLAGE LONDON Pt. 3 South-East
VILLAGE LONDON Pt. 4 South-West

OLD FLEET STREET
CHEAPSIDE AND ST. PAUL'S
THE TOWER AND EAST END
SHOREDITCH to SMITHFIELD
CHARTERHOUSE to HOLBORN
STRAND to SOHO
COVENT GARDEN and the THAMES to WHITEHALL
WESTMINSTER to ST. JAMES'S
HAYMARKET to MAYFAIR
HYDE PARK to BLOOMSBURY

The above ten titles are extracts from the hardback edition of London Recollected.

OLD LONDON

Hyde Park to Bloomsbury
by
EDWARD WALFORD

THE ALDERMAN PRESS

British LIbrary Cataloguing in Publication Data

Walford, Edward, *1823–1897*
   Old London: Hyde Park to Bloomsbury
   1. London, history
   I. Title
942.1

ISBN 0-946619-38-7

This edition published 1989

The Village Press Ltd.,
7d Keats Parade,
Church Street,
Edmonton,
London N9 9DP.

Printed and bound in Great Britain
by Redwood Press, Yeoman Way,
Trowbridge, Wiltshire

CONTENTS.

CHAPTER XXX.
HYDE PARK.

CHAPTER XXXI.
HYDE PARK (continued).

CHAPTER XXXII.
OXFORD STREET AND ITS NORTHERN TRIBUTARIES.

CHAPTER XXXIII.
OXFORD STREET.—NORTHERN TRIBUTARIES (continued).

CONTENTS.

CONTENTS.

CHAPTER XL.

THE BRITISH MUSEUM (continued).

CHAPTER XLI.

BLOOMSBURY SQUARE AND ITS NEIGHBOURHOOD.

CHAPTER XLII.

RED LION SQUARE AND ITS NEIGHBOURHOOD.

CHAPTER XLIII.

QUEEN SQUARE, GREAT ORMOND STREET, &c.

CHAPTER XLIV.

RUSSELL AND BEDFORD SQUARES, &c.

CHAPTER XLV.

GORDON AND TAVISTOCK SQUARES, &c.

LIST OF ILLUSTRATIONS.

CHAPTER XXX.

HYDE PARK.

" The show shop of the metropolis, Hyde Park."—Pierce Egan.

HAVING travelled to the northern end of Park Lane, and exhausted our store of information respecting the fashionable district which lies on our right hand, we must now retrace our steps as far as Apsley House and Hyde Park Corner, and ask our readers to accompany us into that most famous of recreation-grounds, and chief of the " lungs of London," which all the world, to this day, persists in calling " the Park," as if we had no other park in our metropolis—no doubt because, in the Stuart times, and even later, it was the only park really open to the people at large. We shall find that, in spite of the absence of houses and mansions, and, therefore, of actual inhabitants, it is almost as rich in historical recollections as any other part of London.

In the days of the Roman occupation of England, as Mr. Larwood remarks, in his " History of the London Parks," " the site of the future Hyde Park lay in the far west, in the midst of virgin forests, which for more than ten centuries after continued to surround London to the north and the west. Wild boars and bulls, wolves, deer, and smaller game, a few native hunters, swine-herds, and charcoal-burners, were, in all probability, the only inhabitants of those vast wildernesses." If May Fair had any other inhabitants at that time, it is probable that they were painted savages.

In remote ages the tract of land now enclosed as the Park was bounded on the north by the Via Trinobantina—one of the great military roads—now identified with Oxford Street and the Uxbridge Road. On the east ran another Roman way, the old Watling Street, which crossed the other at Tyburn, and sloped off to the south-east, in the direction of Park Lane. On the west and south its limits were not equally well defined. Under the Saxon kings, it would appear that the Manor of Eia, of which it formed a part, belonged to the Master of the Horse; and Mr. Larwood most appropriately observes, " Could the shade of that old Saxon revisit the land which he held when in the flesh, no doubt he would be satisfied, for nowhere in the world could he now find finer horses and better riders than those we daily see in Rotten Row."

About the time of Domesday Book, the manor of Eia was divided into three smaller manors, called, respectively, Neyte, Eabury, and Hyde. The latter still lives and flourishes as a royal park, under its ancient name, no doubt of Saxon origin. The manor of Neyte became the property of the Abbey of Westminster, as did also that of Hyde, which remained in the hands of the monks until seized upon by King Henry, at the time of the Reformation. Of the manor of Hyde we know that its woods afforded to the monks both fire-wood and shelter for their game and water-fowl; and there is extant a document, in which William Boston, the abbot, and the rest of the Convent of Westminster, with their entire assent, consent, and agreement, handed over to his Majesty " the seyte, soyle, circuyte, and precincte of the manor of Hyde, with all the demayne lands, tenements, rentes, meadowes, and pastures of the said manor, with all other pro-fytes and commodities to the same appertayning and belonging, which be now in the tenure and occupation of one John Arnold."

" Henry's main object in appropriating this estate," observes Mr. Larwood, " seems to have been to extend his hunting-grounds to the north and west of London. As we have already seen, the king had previously purchased that plot of ground which afterwards became St. James's Park. Marylebone Park (now the Regent's Park and sur-rounding districts) formed already part of the royal domain; and thus the manor of Hyde, connected

with these, gave him an uninterrupted hunting-ground, which extended from his palace of West-minster to Hampstead Heath. That some such idea existed in the royal mind appears from a proclamation, for the preservation of his game, issued in July, 1536, in which it is stated that, 'As the King's most royal Majesty is desirous to have the games of hare, partridge, pheasant, and heron preserved, in and about the honour of his palace of Westminster, for his own disport and pastime, no person, on the pain of imprisonment of their bodies, and further punishment at his Majesty's will and pleasure, is to presume to hunt or hawk, from the palace of Westminster to St. Giles'-in-the-Fields, and from thence to Islington, to Our Lady of the Oak, to Highgate, to Hornsey Park, and to Hampstead Heath.' It was, probably, also about this period that the manor of Hyde was made into a park, that is, enclosed with a fence or paling, and thus became still better adapted for the rearing and preserving of game. And here it may be fit to observe, that its extent at that time, and for long after, was much greater than it is at present, reach-ing as far as Park Lane to the east, and almost up to the site of Kensington Palace to the west."

As soon as the church manor was thus turned into a royal park, it was a matter of course for the king to appoint a ranger. The first who held the post was George Roper—perhaps of the same family with William Roper, the worthy husband of good Sir Thomas More's daughter. On his death, two rangers or keepers were appointed, and a lodge assigned to each; the one lived not far from what now is Hamilton Place; and the other near the centre of the park, " in a building "—if Mr. Lar-wood's surmise is correct—" afterwards known as the Banqueting House, or the Old Lodge, and which was pulled down at the formation of the Serpentine." Queen Elizabeth gave one of the rangerships to her friend and favourite, Nicholas, Lord Hunsdon, with the handsome salary of " four-pence a day, together with herbage, pannage, and browsage for the deer." In Peck's " Desiderata Curiosa " is the following account, which may, perhaps, cause a smile, particularly if we notice that two men are paid for the same office, the one for holding it and the other for " exercising " it—in another word, for discharging its duties :—

	£	s.	d.
Hyde Park, annual fee of keeper ...	12	13	4
For exercising the said office ...	12	13	4
Keeper of Hyde Park ...	6	6	8
For his necessaries and costs ...	17	3	4
Keeper of the ponds (there)...	10	5	0
Keeper of St. James' Park ...	6	1	8

Hyde Park, as in the time of Henry VIII.,

says the author above quoted, "was still used as a hunting-ground in the reigns of Edward VI., Queen Elizabeth, and King James." In 1550 we find the boy-king, Edward VI., hunting in it with the French ambassadors. In January, 1578, John Casimir, Count Palatine of the Rhine, Duke of Bavaria, and a general in the service of the Dutch, paid a visit to Queen Elizabeth, lodged in Somerset House, and was by her Majesty made Knight of the Garter. Amongst the entertainments given to this princely visitor was that of hunting at Hampton Court, and shooting in Hyde Park, on which last occasion the old chroniclers relate that the duke "killed a barren doe with his piece from amongst three hundred other deer." Again, an entry in the accounts of the Board of Works for the year 1582 contains a payment "for making of two new standings in Marybone and Hyde Park for the Queen's Majesty and the noblemen of France [i.e., the Duke of Anjou, Elizabeth's intended husband, and his court] to see the hunting." No doubt, these were the "princely standes" to which Norden alludes, in his mention of Hyde Park in 1596, in his "Survey of Middlesex and Hertfordshire." "Perhaps the queen herself, at times, here followed the pursuit of her patroness Diana, for we know that her Majesty took pleasure in hunting. On such occasions the sport would conclude, according to the established law of the chase, by one of the huntsmen offering a hunting-knife to the queen, as the first lady of the field, and her '*taking say*' of the buck—*i.e.*, plunging the knife in its throat with her own fair and royal hand. Again, the pools in the Park must have been a favourite haunt of the heron (which Henry VIII. includes among the game to be preserved in the neighbourhood of his palace), and other water-fowl, and there the queen may have 'cast her hawk' on summer afternoons. We can imagine her riding here on an 'ambling palfrey' through the forest glades, accompanied by the fiery Essex, the courtly Burleigh, the manly Raleigh, or that arch plotter and scheming villain, Leicester, whose name . . . ought to have been for ever connected with a certain spot north-east of the Park, where Tyburn gallows stood."

Before the end of Elizabeth's reign the second rangership was given to Lord Hunsdon's son, Sir Edward Carey. He was a brother of the Countess of Nottingham, whose name is so well known to history in connection with the romantic episode of Lord Essex and the ring. In his time, some forty acres of land on the southern side, not far from Knightsbridge, were added to the park, and fenced in with rails. "No cattle," writes Mr. Larwood, "were allowed to enter this enclosure, as it was reserved for the deer to graze in; and the grass growing within it was to be mown for hay, on which to feed the deer in winter. The exact locality of these forty acres," he adds, "is not stated; but it is not improbable that it was this very fence that was pulled down by the Londoners on their Lammas crusade in 1592."

Mr. Larwood writes: "King James I., as everybody knows, was a 'mighty hunter before the Lord.' Frequently, no doubt, the dryads and hamadryads of the Park must have witnessed his sacred Majesty in that famous costume which he wore when on his journey from Scotland to England to ascend the throne—'a doublet, green as the grass he stood on, with a feather in his cap and a horn by his side.' Then the clear echoes, nestling in the quiet nooks and corners of the ancient forest, were awakened by the merry blasts of the horn, the hallooing of the huntsmen cheering the dogs, and the 'yearning' of the pack, as they followed the hart to one of the pools where it 'took soil,' and was bravely dispatched by his Majesty. After that followed the noisy 'quarry,' in which, of course, 'Jowler' and 'Jewel,' the king's favourite hounds, obtained the lion's share. When the hunt was over, his Majesty would probably adjourn to the Banqueting House, which stood in the middle of the Park, and refresh himself with a deep draught of sack or canary; and in the cool of the evening, as, returning home to Whitehall, the king crossed over 'the way to Reading' (now Piccadilly), he might see, in the far blue distance, the little village of St. Giles' nestled among the trees, the square steeple of old St. Paul's, and the smoking chimneys of his good citizens of London, whilst the faint evening breeze wafted towards him the sweet silvery sound of Bow bells ringing the curfew."

The next keeper of whom we read, under James I., was Robert Cecil, Earl of Salisbury, with whom, three years later, we find associated Sir Walter Cope, the same person who built the centre and the turrets of Holland House. During their joint keepership various improvements were made in the Park; grants of money were made for planting trees and repairing lodges, fences, palings, pond-heads, &c.; which show that it was then quite a rural park. In 1612 Sir Walter Cope resigned his rangership in favour of his son-in-law, Henry Rich, subsequently created Earl of Holland. This nobleman, it may be remarked, cut but a poor figure in history. In early life he was employed abroad to negotiate the marriage of Charles I. with Henrietta Maria; but after the outbreak of the Civil War he fought at one time on the side of the Parliament, and then again for the King, and being taken prisoner by the Roundheads, was executed.

In the first year of Charles's reign a strange scene was witnessed in the Park. The young queen, Henrietta Maria, just wedded, went through it barefoot, and clad in sackcloth, to Tyburn gallows, an event of which we shall have to speak more fully in our account of Tyburnia.

In the reigns of our early Stuart kings there was in Hyde Park a large number of pools or ponds, all communicating with each other, and variously given as ten, eleven, and twelve. They were fed by a small stream, the West Bourne, which, rising on the western slope of Hampstead, passed through Kilburn and Bayswater, and then intersected the Park, which it quitted at Knightsbridge on its way to join the Thames at Millbank and Chelsea. These pools used to supply the western parts of London with water, until a complaint was made that they were drained so much that there was no water for the deer. This at least, was stoutly asserted by the keepers, and as stoutly denied by the citizens, who petitioned the king to allow the supply to continue. But Charles I. preferred the

A LONDON DANDY OF 1646. (*See page* 383.)

word of his keepers to the petition of his loyal and faithful subjects; he chose rather to see his subjects than his favourite deer lacking water, and so he rejected the petition—a step which much increased his unpopularity at the time.

During the early part of the Civil Wars in the time of Charles I., Hyde Park was largely used for exercising the "trained bands," as the regular forces of the City were called. This body of men was first enrolled—or, as the phrase went, "drawn forth in arms"—on the side of the monarch; yet, subsequently, the citizens supported the popular cause, and it was principally by their aid that the House of Commons obtained its decided preponderancy. So early as November, 1642, within three months after Charles had set up his standard at Nottingham, the "trained bands" were marched

out to join the Earl of Essex, on the heath near Brentford, "where," says Clarendon, "they had indeed a full army of horse and foot, fit to have decided the title of a crown with an equal adversary." In the further progress of the war, several auxiliary regiments, both of foot and horse, were raised by the City; and to a part of these forces, joined to two regiments of the "trained bands," "of whose inexperience of danger," remarks the historian just quoted, "or any kind of service beyond the easy practice of their postures in the Artillery Garden, men had till then too cheap an estimation," the Parliament army was indebted for its preservation in the first battle of Newbury, "for they stood as a bulwark and rampire to defend the rest, and, when their wings of horse were scattered and dispersed, kept their ground so steadily," that Prince Rupert himself, who charged them at the head of the choice royal horse, "could make no impression upon their stand of pikes, but was forced to wheel about." The same historian designates London as "the devoted city" of the Commons, and their "inexhaustible magazine of men."

"In April, 1660," says Mr. Allen, in his "History of London," "about six weeks before the restoration of Charles II., and when the artful management of General Monk had disposed the citizens to countenance the measures he was pursuing in favour of royalty, a muster of the City forces was held in Hyde Park: the number of men then assembled amounted to about 18,600—namely, six regiments of 'trained bands,' six auxiliary regiments, and one regiment of horse; the foot regiments were composed of eighty companies, of two hundred and fifty men each; and the regiments of cavalry of six troops, each of one hundred men. The assembling of this force was judged to have been highly instrumental to the success of the plan for restoring the monarchy. Within a few months afterwards the king granted a commission of lieutenancy for the City of London, which invested the

HYDE PARK ON SUNDAY. *From a Print published in 1804. (See page 399.)*

commissioners with similar powers to those possessed by the lords-lieutenants of counties ; and by them the 'trained bands' were new-modelled, and increased to 20,000 men ; the cavalry was also increased to 800, and divided into two regiments of five troops, with eighty men in each. The whole of this force was, in the same year, reviewed by the king in Hyde Park."*

The Act of Parliament which ordered the sale of the Crown lands, after the execution of Charles I., excepted Hyde Park from its provisions, and it became the subject of a special resolution of the 1st of December, 1652, "That Hyde Park be sold for ready money." The Park at that time contained about 621 acres, and the sale realised £17,068 2s. 8d. The purchasers of the three lots were Richard Wilson, John Lacey, and Anthony Deane.

As soon as the king was brought back to Whitehall, Hyde Park very naturally again became what it had been before the Puritan episode—the rendezvous of fashion and pleasure. The sales of the Park to individuals, which we have mentioned, were treated as null and void ; Hyde Park became again royal property, and was open to the public once more. The king appointed his brother, the Duke of Gloucester, to the office of keeper ; he, however, held it only two months, and after his death it was granted to James Hamilton, one of the Grooms of the Bedchamber, whose name, as we have already seen, survives in Hamilton Place. This place, and other houses about Hyde Park Corner, had been erected during the Protectorate by the then proprietors, and it is uncertain what compensation or tenant-right they obtained for the outlay. Mr. Hamilton was killed in battle, in 1673 ; and as Charles II. had thrown open St. James's Park to the public, and it was rightly judged that one Ranger could superintend both parks, it is scarcely a matter of surprise to find that his successor, Mr. Harbord, an ancestor of Lord Suffield, was styled Ranger of St. James's Park, the latter taking precedence, as being not only royal property, but the residence of the merry king and his court. It was by Mr. Hamilton's advice that the Park was first enclosed with a brick wall, and re-stocked with deer, the enclosure of the herd being on Buckdean Hill, on the side farthest from the City, and, therefore, the most quiet and retired. This wall stood till the reign of George II., when it was replaced by a more substantial one, six feet and a half high on the inside, and eight feet high on the outside. A horse belonging to a Mr. Bingham leaped this wall in 1792 ;

this feat, it appears, was done for a wager. The wall was removed in the time of George IV., and an iron railing was substituted. Colonel Hamilton also made a speculation in the growth of apples for cider on an enclosure at the north-west corner, but with what result we are not informed.

But to return to the time of Charles II. The Park was then open ground, with the exception of such fences as were put up for the purposes of pasturage ; but in 1664 the Surveyor-General observes in a report that "the king was very earnest with him for walling Hyde Park, as well for the honour of his palace and great city as for his own disport and recreation." Ten years after, a portion of it was so well fenced in as to be replenished with deer. In 1642, a large fort, with four bastions, had been erected at Hyde Park Corner, and another to the south, called Oliver's Mount, the memory of which remains in Mount Street. This latter work was erected by popular enthusiasm, the ladies of rank not only encouraging the men, but, as we have had occasion to remark in a previous chapter, carrying the materials with their own hands. In a note by Nash to the second canto of the second part of "Hudibras," Lady Middlesex, Lady Foster, Lady Anne Waller, and others, are celebrated for their patriotic exertions as serious volunteers in this emergency. Since that period, the military performances in Hyde Park have been of a mimetic character.

In Evelyn's "Diary," under date the 11th of April, 1653, we read :—"I went to take the aire in Hide Park, when every coach was made to pay a shilling, and horse sixpence, by the sordid fellow who had purchased it of the State, as they were called." And in the "Character of England in a Letter to a Nobleman in France," published in the year 1659, it is described as "a field near the town, which they call Hide Park ; the place is not unpleasant, and which they use as our course, but with nothing of that order, equipage, and splendour ; being such an assembly of wretched jades and hackney-coaches as, next a regiment of carrmen, there is nothing approaches the resemblance." The writer adds that "the Parke was used by the late king and nobility for the freshness of air, and the goodly prospect, but it is that which now (besides all other exercises) they pay for hire in England, though it be free for all the world besides ; every coach and horse which enters buying his mouthful, and permission of the publican who has purchased it, for which the entrance is guarded with porters and long staves." It was, therefore, the Restoration which gave the people the free entrance to the Park, but with the entire reservation of the

---

* Strype's Stow, ii., p. 572.

royal rights, as shown in several ways; not the least curious being the obligation of Mr. Hamilton, the Ranger, to deliver to the Lord Steward, or to the Treasurer of the Household, "one-half of the pippins or red streaks, either in apples or cider, as his Majesty may prefer, the produce of the trees he is authorised to plant in fifty-five acres of the north-west corner of the Park, on the Uxbridge Road."

Pepys' "Diary" is invaluable for the minuteness with which he describes London life during the first nine years of the reign of Charles II., and from him we learn much incidentally about the Park and its frequenters. "Gaiety, jollity, and merry life," it has been well observed, "beam through his pages, which rustle with silk and velvet, and sparkle with gold lace and jewellery." A crowd of gay dissolute people still move through them with the same restless flutter which animated them when in the flesh, two hundred years ago and more. By his help we get peep after peep into that bygone world, and obtain a full view of the manners, fashions, and pleasures of those past generations; and we cannot do better than follow him whenever he shows his merry face in the Park. Early in June, 1660, within a few days after the Restoration, Pepys hears from friends that the two royal Dukes of York and Gloucester "do haunt the Park much;" but he has not as yet seen them there with his own eyes. It is not until the 9th of the month that the little Clerk of the Admiralty has had the happiness of seeing his Majesty there face to face, a sight which, he tells us, was "gallantly great." Again, on the 3rd of July, Pepys records his sight of the king's presence there, to which Evelyn adds, "and abundance of gallantry."

Both Evelyn and Pepys, in their "Diaries," bear frequent witness to the gay appearance which the Park presented after the Restoration, especially on May Day. The former tells us that on the 1st of May, 1661, he went to the Park to take the air, and that "there was his Majesty and an innumerable appearance of gallants and rich coaches, being now a time of universal festivity and joy." Our friend Pepys, however, was not a spectator of these gay doings in the Park, he having been ordered away, on his official duties to Portsmouth; much to his personal regret, as he does not forget to tell us.

When Pepys and Evelyn speak thus of the Park, they must not be understood to mean its whole circumference, but simply an inner circle in the centre of its northern half, generally known as "the Ring," round which it was the fashion to ride

and drive. It was on account of this circular movement that Lady Malapert, in the old comedy of *The Maid's Last Prayer*, calls the "Ring" a "dusty mill-horse drive."

Sometimes this "Ring" was called "the Tour;" and in this sense Pepys uses the word. Thus we have the following entry in his "Diary," under date of the 31st of March, 1668:—"Took up my wife and Deb, and to the Park, where being in a hackney (coach), and they undressed, was ashamed to go into the Tour, but went round the Park, and so with pleasure home."

In the above reign, it seems, horse and foot-races were of frequent occurrence here. Evelyn, under date May 20, 1658, even tells us that he "went to see a coach-race in Hide Park;" and Pepys, in his "Diary," August 10, 1660, records how that he went "with Mr. Moor and Creed to Hyde Park, by coach, and saw a fine foot-race three times round the Park, between an Irishman and Crow, that was once my Lord Claypole's footman." This was followed by a horse-race, and in the interval which occurred between the two performances a milk-maid went about, crying "Milk of a red cow!" which the humbler spectators partook of—the "quality" meanwhile sipping "sillabub with sack in it." The ladies, we are further told, wagered scarlet stockings and Spanish scented gloves on their favourite steeds.

"Hyde Park," says Pennant, "was celebrated by all our dramatic poets in the late century, and in the early part of the present (18th), for its large space railed off in form of a circle, round which the *beau monde* drove in their carriages, and in their rotation, exchanging, as they passed, smiles and nods, compliments or smart repartees." This large space was also, very suitably, the place in which coaches were displayed when first introduced by persons of fashion and "quality." Taylor, the water-poet, tells us that one William Boonen, a Dutchman, was the first who introduced the use of such vehicles into England. The said Boonen was Queen Elizabeth's coachman, and the date of their first appearance in London may be fixed at about 1564. Taylor quaintly observes, "Indeed, a coach was a strange monster in those days, and the sight of them put horse and man into amazement." The introduction of "glass-coaches" is fixed by the "Ultimum Vale of John Carleton," published in 1663. "I could wish her coach, which she said my Lord Taffe bought for her in England and sent it over to her, made of the new fashion, with glasses, very stately."

The railed-off space above mentioned was called the "Ring," and is often spoken of by the poets of the eighteenth century as the central resort of fashion. It was probably on his way hither that Cromwell once had a most narrow escape from sudden death. He was, as the story has been often told, driving his own coach in the Park; his horses ran away and were uncontrollable; the stern Protector, much to the delight of any Royalist who might have been present on the occasion, was thrown off the coach-box, and fell upon the pole between the wheelers, and his feet becoming entangled in the harness, he was dragged along for a considerable distance. He does not, however, appear to have suffered much beyond the necessary fright and a few bruises. On this accident the following lines were written by the old rhyming cavalier, Cleveland :—

" The whip again ! away ! 'tis too absurd
    That thou shouldst lash with whip-cord now, but sword.
  I'm pleased to fancy how the glad compact
  Of hackney-coachmen sneer at the last act.
  Hark how the scoffing concourse hence derives
  The proverb, 'Needs must go when the devil drives.'
  Yonder a whisper cries, ''Tis a plain case,
  He turned us out to put himself i' the place;
  But, God-a-mercy, horses once for aye
  Stood to 't, and turn'd him out as well as we.'
  Another, not behind with his mocks,
  Cries out, ' Sir, faith you were in the wrong box.'
  He did presume to rule because, forsooth,
  He 's been a horse commander from his youth :
  But he must know there 's a difference in the reins
  Of horses fed with oats and fed with grains.
  I wonder at his frolic, for be sure
  Four hamper'd coach-horses can fling a *brewer ;*
  But ' Pride will have a fall,' such the world's course is,
  He who can rule three realms can't guide four horses ;
  See him that trampled thousands in their gore,·
  Dismounted by a party but of four.
  But we have done with 't, and we may call
  This driving Jehu, Phaeton in his fall.
  I would to God, for these three kingdoms' sake,
  His neck, and not the whip, had given the crack."

It would be interesting, as Mr. Thomas Miller remarks, in his " Picturesque Sketches of London," to know whether the Lord Protector remembered the uncomplimentary wish contained in the last couplet when the old royalist afterwards had to petition Cromwell for his release from Yarmouth Gaol. If he remembered it, and yet released the writer, he must have had, at all events, a forgiving disposition. Cromwell's fall from his coach-box is likewise commemorated in one of the poems of Sir John Birkenhead, entitled " The Jolt." Cromwell had received from the German Count of Oldenburg a present of six German horses, which he attempted to drive, with his own hands, in Hyde Park, when "the political Phaeton" met with the accident above mentioned. Sir John Birkenhead

was not slow to perceive the benefit of such an event, and more than hints how unfortunate for the country it was that the fall was not a fatal one. During the dominion of Cromwell, Sir John was forced to "live by his wits," which meant nearly to starve. On the Restoration, he was made one of the Masters of Requests, with a handsome salary.

But to pass on to the Restoration and the times of Charles II. "Hardly," writes Mr. Larwood, "were the members of the royal family safely lodged in the palaces of Whitehall and St. James's, when they commenced their round of amusements, Hyde Park forming part of the programme. Both Charles and his brother James were of active habits, fond of open air and exercise ; both also found a still more powerful attraction in the Park, for it was the gathering place of all those matchless beauties which still live on the canvas of Lely and Kneller. All Grammont's equivocal heroines, and all their more virtuous and not less beautiful sisters, were daily there, fluttering in the sunshine, and dazzling alike both king and subjects. There were Lady Castlemaine, *la belle* Hamilton, *la belle* Stewart, and *la belle* Jennings, the Countesses of Chesterfield and Southesk, Lady Denham and Mrs. Lawson, Mrs. Middleton, Mrs. Bagot, Miss Price—in a word, that entire galaxy of ladies whose beauty, as Pope says, was an excuse for the gallantries of Charles, and an apology for his Asiatic court. These, in fact, were

' Those days of ease, when now the weary sword
    Was sheath'd, and luxury with Charles restor'd,
  In every taste of foreign courts improv'd,
  All by the king's example lived and lov'd.'

" There still remained some of the picturesque elegance of the Spanish costume which had been in vogue in the reign of Charles I., though it was gradually spoiled more and more by an invasion of exaggerated French fashions. But there was one great and charming novelty, the new riding garb— the *Amazone*, as it was called—the nondescript attire from which the present *habit* is descended. Till then ladies had worn the usual walking-dress on horseback ; it was left for the beautiful flirts of Charles's reign to introduce the ' habit.' It was this novelty which puzzled good Pepys so much, when he, for the first time, saw the ladies ' with coats and doublets with deep skirts, just for all the world like men, and their doublets buttoned up the breasts, with periwigs and with hats, so that, only for a long petticoat dragging under their men's coats, nobody would take them for women in any point whatever.' "

The following description of Hyde Park is from

the Memoirs of Count Grammont in the reign of Charles II. :—"Hyde Park, every one knows, is the promenade of London : nothing was so much in fashion, during the fine weather, as that promenade, which was the rendezvous of magnificence and beauty : every one, therefore, who had either sparkling eyes, or a splendid equipage, constantly repaired thither, and the king [Charles II.] seemed pleased with the place."

Our portrait of the "London dandy" (page 378) of the middle of the seventeenth century, the greater part of whose time probably was spent in the Park, shows the exact dress of the fashionable young men of the time ; the long locks of hair, hanging down from the temples on either side the face, with tasty bows of ribbon tied at the ends, were called by the ladies "love-locks ;" and Prynne, in his zeal, thought this so prominent a folly that he wrote a quarto volume to prove "The Unloveliness of Love-locks." Prynne, however, himself did not kill the fashion, which died a natural death at the end of the reign of Charles I. The stars and half-moons seen on the young man's face are ornamental patches of dark sticking plaster, a mode of embellishment which is in favour with the ladies occasionally, even in the reign of Victoria, as serving to show off a fair white skin. Among the absurdities of the age to which our illustration refers, it would be difficult to find one more ridiculous than that of gentlemen who are not riders wearing spurs on their boots, as part of their walking dress. The spur forms a conspicuous object in the dress of the dandy of 1646 ; and we learn that it was considered the very height of fashion to have the spurs made so as to rattle or jingle as the wearer walked along, like Apollo, with his rattling arrows, in the first book of Homer's "Iliad."

The "dandies" of that period, however, did not have it all their own way, or assert an entire monopoly to the Park, as a place intended only for promenading and flirtations, for we read that during the plague of August and September, 1665, a large number of the poorer inhabitants of London, who could not escape into the country, brought thither their household goods, and setting up tents, formed in the Park a sort of camp, which is described to the life in a ballad or broadside of the day, preserved in a volume of London songs in the British Museum. But in spite of all these precautions for safety, the plague pursued them thither, and those who died were buried as quickly as possible upon the spot :—

" We pitch'd our tents on ridges and in furrows,
 And there encamped, fearing th' Almighty's arrows.

But oh ! alas ! what did this all avail ?
Our men, ere long, began to droop and quail.
Our lodgings cold, and some not us'd thereto,
Fell sick and dy'd, and made no more adoe.
At length the plague amongst us 'gan to spread,
When every morning some were found stark dead.
Down to another field the sick were ta'en,
But few went down that ere came up again.
But that which most of all did grieve my soul,
To see poor Christians dragg'd into a hole."

It must have been with great satisfaction that the poor creatures thus encamped in Hyde Park learned that, by the end of October, the plague had disappeared, and that they were able to return to their homes in London.

The gay circle of "the Ring" being shorn of its old frequenters, in the year of the great plague, no doubt the grass grew where the horsemen and carriages had stirred the dust as often as spring and summer came round. During part of that fatal and fearful summer, however, a regiment of the Guards was quartered in the Park, under the command of Monk, Duke of Albemarle, who, like Lord Craven, refused wholly to quit the doomed city. Two years later, on St. George's Day, the Merry Monarch and the Knights of the Garter, we are told by Mr. Larwood, had the "ridiculous humour" of keeping on their robes all the day, and in the evening made their appearance in "the Ring," still wearing their insignia—cloaks, coronets, and all. The Duke of Monmouth and another noble lord indulged even in a further freak, for thus apparelled they drove about the Park in a hackney coach.

On the re-appearance of the company in the Park, after the plague and the "great fire," we soon come again across the lively figure of Pepys, who, on the 3rd of June, 1668, writes :—"To the Park, where much fine company and many fine ladies ; and in so handsome a hackney I was that I believe Sir W. Coventry and others who looked on me did take me to be in one of my own, which I was a little troubled for ; so to the Lodge and drank a cup of new milk, and so home." In the reign of Charles II. the Lodge here spoken of by Pepys stood in the middle of the Park, and was used for the sale of refreshments ; it was sometimes called Price's Lodge, from the name of Gervase Price, the chief under-keeper.

"Like everything connected with the Park," writes Mr. Larwood, "it is frequently mentioned by the dramatists of that reign. For instance, in Howard's *English Monsieur* (1674) :—'Nay, 'tis no London female ; she's a thing that never saw a cheesecake, a tart, or a syllabub at the Lodge in Hyde Park.' In Queen Anne's time it was more generally called the Cake House, or Mince-pie

House; and, according to the fashion which still continued to prevail, the beaux and belles used to go there to refresh themselves. The dainties which might be obtained there in the reign of George II. are thus enumerated in a little descriptive poem of the period :—

> " ' Some petty collation
> Of cheesecakes, and custards, and pigeon-pie puff,
> With bottle-ale, cider, and such sort of stuff.' "

worthy diarist was a frequent stroller in the Park, and his pages, therefore, contain numerous indications of the doings of the fashionable world in his time ; he not only brings before us, in brilliant colours, some of the most famous beauties and court gallants, but also gives us an account of the gentle flirtations of the king himself and his more favoured dames.

Mr. Harrison Ainsworth is but recording the

GROUP OF OLD TREES IN HYDE PARK.

The Lodge was a timber and plaster building, and was taken down in the early part of the present century."

As far back as the reign of Elizabeth we find that cheesecakes were to be had at a house near the Serpentine, while branch establishments existed at Hackney and Holloway for the retail of these dainties, and, from the northern heights, persons were employed to cry them in the streets.

Our friend Pepys, in his "Diary," under date May, 1669, describes a visit, with his wife and some friends, to the Park, where, doubtless, they ate cheesecakes before going "thence to the 'World's End,'" a noted drinking-house, which we shall have occasion to mention hereafter, when we reach the neighbourhood of Knightsbridge. The

actual state of things in the reign of Queen Anne, when he writes, in his historical romance of " St. James's :"—" Well may we be proud of Hyde Park, for no capital but our own can boast aught like it. The sylvan and sequestered character of the scene was wholly undisturbed, and, but for the actual knowledge of the fact, no one would have dreamed that the metropolis was within a mile's distance. Screened by the trees, the mighty city was completely hidden from view, while, on the Kensington road, visible through the glade which looked towards the south-west, not a house was to be seen. To add to the secluded character of the place, a herd of noble red deer were couching beneath an oak, that crowned a gentle acclivity on the right, and a flock of rooks were cawing loudly on the summits of the high trees near Kensington Gardens."

As far back as the year 1731, the author of the "Critical Review," chalking out a plan of London improvements, pointed to Hyde Park as "a place possessed of every beauty and convenience which might be required in the situation of the royal palace of the British king." In 1766, a Mr. John Gwynne proposed to build in the Park a palace

cost of the erection. The whole of the building was to extend from Knightsbridge to Bayswater, and to be relieved by occasional breaks. This design was much approved by the notorious Lord Camelford, who was then at Rome, where he saw Soane's drawings, and who became a warm friend and patron of the young architect when subsequently he settled in London."

Mr. Larwood also gives a map of Hyde Park,

THE CAKE-HOUSE, HYDE PARK.   *From a Drawing in the Crace Collection.*   (*See page 383.*)

with a circuit round it of one mile in circumference. In 1779, a correspondent of the *St. James's Chronicle*, writing under the *nom de plume* of "Possible," enumerates several large buildings which he considered ought to be erected in London; "amongst them," he observes, "a palace in Hyde Park is also much wanted." Towards the end of the last century, the subject was again broached by Sir John Soane, "who," writes Mr. Larwood, "in the gay morning of youthful fancy, full of the wonders he had seen in Italy, and inspired by the wild imagination of an enthusiastic mind, proposed, without regard to expense or limit, to erect a royal habitation in the Park. It was to consist of a palace, with a series of magnificent mansions, the sale of which was calculated to defray the entire

about the year 1736 or 1737. It shows the turnpike and gallows at Tyburn, and a double row of walnut-trees, with a wide gravel-walk between, runs from north to south, parallel to the Park Lane. In the centre of this avenue is a circular reservoir, belonging to the Chelsea Waterworks, and from which not only Kensington Palace and the suburb were supplied, but also "the new buildings about Oliver's Mount" (now Mount Street) "and the northern parts of Westminster." Mr. Larwood tells us that the machinery used for forcing the supply was at that time so primitive, that the water had to be conveyed to the houses on the high ground near Grosvenor Square by means of a mill turned by horses. It may interest our readers to learn that this avenue was standing till about the year 1810, when most of the trees, being much decayed, and in danger of being blown down whenever the wind was high, were cut down, their wood being destined to make stocks for the muskets of our infantry. In this map the "Ring" is marked with a large circle, apparently about 150 yards to the north of the east end of the Serpentine. Round the "Ring" stands a square of large trees, a few of which may, perhaps, still be standing. There is a small brook, which runs into the Serpentine, near the present boat-house, from the neighbourhood of the Uxbridge Road; and two small ponds of water are marked towards the south-east corner—one nearly where the statue of Achilles now stands, and the other nearer to the rear of Apsley House. The map shows also the two roads running parallel to the Serpentine on the south, marked respectively as "The King's Old Road, or Lamp Road," and "The King's New Road;" the former corresponding nearly with the Rotten Row of our time, and the latter running, as now, inside the Park, close to the Knightsbridge Road and Kensington Gore. On the north of the Serpentine there is, apparently, no regular road, except for about a hundred yards from the eastern end, where it bends to the north, away from the water, towards the "Ring."

The cutting down of trees needlessly, in the neighbourhood of London, is a sin. Evelyn, in his "Book of Forest Trees," as Dr. Johnson more than once reminds us in his "Letters," tells us of wicked men who cut down trees, and never prospered afterwards. It is to be hoped that a like fate awaited those persons who caused the destruction of the walnut-tree avenue mentioned in the preceding paragraph.

The "Ring," of which we have already spoken, was a place of fashionable resort down to the reign of George II., when it was partly destroyed in the formation of the Serpentine River. It is often alluded to in old plays and novels, and is described by a French traveller, in 1719, as being "two or three hundred paces in diameter, with a sorry kind of balustrade, or rather with poles placed upon stakes, but three feet from the ground, and the coaches drive round this. When they have turned for some time round one way, they face about and turn t'other. So rolls the world." * Another foreigner, who lived in England at the end of the seventeenth century, in speaking of the "Ring," says : "They take their rides in a coach in an open field where there is a circle, not very large, enclosed by rails. There the coaches drive slowly round,

some in one direction, others the opposite way, which, seen from a distance, produces a rather pretty effect, and proves clearly that they only come there in order to see and to be seen. Hence it follows that this promenade, even in the midst of summer, is deserted the moment night begins to fall, that is to say, just at the time when there would be some real pleasure in enjoying the fresh air. Then everybody retires, because the principal attraction of the place is gone." †

Pepys, in his "Diary," under date of 4th April, 1663, writes how that he "saw the king in one coach and Lady Castlemaine in another, in the Ring in Hyde Park, they greeting one another at every turn."

The origin of this "Ring" is unknown; Mr. Larwood suggests that "it may have been a remnant of the garden attached to the Banqueting House, or it may simply have been made by the two speculating citizens who hired the ground from Anthony Dean, Esq., and levied toll on the gates." Remnants of it were still traceable at the beginning of this century, on the high ground directly behind the farm-house. A few very old trees are even now to be found on that spot. Some of these are indeed ancient enough to have formed part of the identical trees round which the wits and beauties drove in their carriages, and, as Pennant says, "in their rotation exchanged, as they passed, smiles and nods, compliments or smart repartees." Plain as it was, it must have been a pleasant spot on a summer's afternoon. Situated on an upland space of ground, one may imagine the pleasurable prospect from hence when all around was open country, and nothing intercepted the view from the Surrey hills to the high grounds of Hampstead and Highgate. One can easily imagine how delightful it must have been for the ladies who "came in their carriages from the hot play-house and the close confined streets of the City, to be fanned by soft winds which blew over broad acres of ripening corn, flowering clover, and newly-mown hay, or rustled through the reeds and willows on the banks of the pools."

Walker, in "The Original," in 1835, speaks of the "Ring" as being still traceable round a clump of trees near the foot-barracks, and inclosing an area of about ninety yards in diameter, and about forty-five yards wide. "Here," he adds, "used to assemble all the fashion of the day, now diffused round the whole park, besides what is taken off by the Regent's Park."

In the merry days of our later Stuart sovereigns

---

* Misson's "Memoirs and Observations in his Travels through England.' 1719.

† "Lettres sur les Anglais et les Français." Cologne, 1727.

no equipage in the "Ring" was thought complete unless drawn by six grey Flanders mares, and the owner's coat-of-arms emblazoned conspicuously on the panels. Thus we read in "The Circus, or the British Olympus," professedly a satire on the "Ring:"—

> "Manlius through all the city doth proclaim
> His arms, his equipage, and ancient name;
> For search the Court of Honour, and you'll see
> Manlius his name, but not his pedigree.
> What then? This is the practice of the town;
> For, should no man bear arms but what's his own,
> Hundreds that make the 'Ring' would carry none;
> And that would spoil the beauty of the place."

Mr. Larwood, who quotes these lines, adds his own opinion that the "Manlius" here intended was none other than "Beau Fielding," who pretended to be a cadet of the noble house of the Earl of Denbigh, which is sprung, as every reader of the "Peerage" knows, from the Hapsburgs, cousins to the ancient Emperors of Germany. He gives the following version of the story to which allusion is made in the above verses:—"On the strength of his name he ventured to have the arms of Lord Denbigh painted on his coach, and to drive round the 'Ring,' as proud as the jackdaw with the purloined peacock's feathers. At the sight of the immaculate coat-of-arms on the plebeian chariot all the blood of all the Hapsburgs flew to the head of Basil, fourth Earl of Denbigh; in a high state of wrath and fury he at once procured a house-painter and ordered him to daub the coat-of-arms completely over, and before all the company in the 'Ring.' The beau seems to have thought with Falstaff that 'the better part of valour is discretion;' and as the insult had not been offered to his own arms, he judged it wise to bear it rather than to resent it." From this same satire we may glean a few other illustrations of the way in which the frequenters of the Park, towards the end of the seventeenth century, conducted themselves. For instance, it appears that the beaux bought fruit in the Park, and there, as in the theatres, amused themselves with breaking coarse jests with the orange and nosegay-women, and other female hawkers. Thus we read in the same poem:

> "With bouncing Bell a luscious chat they hold,
> Squabble with Moll, or Orange Betty scold."

The same practice is also alluded to in another satire, Mrs. Manley's "New Atlantis," where a Mrs. Hammond is represented buying a basket of cherries and receiving a *billet-doux* from the "orange-wench." Again, in Southerne's play of the *Maid's Last Prayer* (1693), Lady Malapert says, "There are a thousand innocent diversions more whole-some and diverting than always the dusty mill-horse driving in Hyde Park." But her airy husband is of a different opinion: "O law!" says he, "don't prophane Hyde Park: is there anything so pleasant as to go there alone and find fault with the company? Why, there can't a horse or a livery 'scape a man that has a mind to be witty; and then, I sell bargains to [*i. e.* 'chaff'] the orange-women." It was with such refined amusements, such a delicate way of displaying their wit, that the beaux of that period, like Sir Harry Wildair, acquired the reputation of being "the joy of the play-house, the life of the Park."

During the reign of Queen Anne, the "Ring" held its place as the resort of all the fashion and nobility, even in winter. "No frost, snow, or east wind," writes the *Spectator*, in 1711, "can hinder a large set of people from going to the Park in February, no dust nor heat in June. And this is come to such an intrepid regularity, that those agreeable creatures that would shriek at a hind-wheel in a deep gutter, are not afraid in their proper sphere of the disorder and danger of seven crowded Rings." In the *Tatlers*, *Spectators*, and in the plays of the period, there are constant allusions to the brilliant crowds who frequented the "Ring," around which a full tide of gaudily dressed ladies were whirled day by day. As Mr. Larwood happily remarks:—"It was an endless stream of stout coachmen driving ponderous gilt chariots lined with scarlet, drawn by six heavy Flanders mares; and running footmen trotting in front, graced with conical caps, long silver-headed canes, and quaintly cut silk jackets loaded with gold lace, tassels, and spangles. In those coaches appeared all the beauty and elegance of the kingdom, outvieing each other in splendour and extravagance; for daughters of Eve were scarce who thought, like Lady Mary Wortley Montagu, that 'All the fine equipages that shine in the Ring never gave me another thought than either pity or contempt for the owners that could place happiness in attracting the eyes of strangers.'"

It was in the "Ring" that a curious incident occurred in the life of Wycherley, which Pope related to Spence. "Wycherley was a very handsome man. His acquaintance with the famous Duchess of Cleveland commenced oddly enough. One day as he passed that duchess's coach in the 'Ring,' she leaned out of the window, and cried out loud enough to be heard distinctly by him, 'Sir, you're a rascal; you're a villain.' Wycherley from that instant entertained hopes. He did not fail waiting on her the next morning; and, with a very melancholy tone, begged to know how it was possible for him to have so much disobliged her grace. They were very good friends from that time."

In the days of George II., the machinery used for watering the fashionable drive in Hyde Park was very primitive indeed. "On account of the numerous coaches which drive round in a small circle," observes a German writer, Z. Conrad von Uffenbach, in his "Remarkable Journey through Europe," "we are greatly troubled by the excessive dust. When the heat and dust are very great, however, a man drives round with a barrel of water in a cart; and the tap is taken out of the barrel, so that as he goes on the water runs out into the road, and moistens it, and so lays the dust."

From the time of Cromwell down to the present day the history of Hyde Park is little more than a record of five events, of which from time to time it has been the scene—reviews of the troops and volunteers, encampments, duels, highway robberies, and executions. For a full catalogue of these matters, equally minute and monotonous, we must be content to refer our readers to the pages of Mr. Jacob Larwood's "Story of the London Parks." It will be enough for our purpose to enumerate here a few of the principal occurrences.

The earliest occasion on which the Park was used for a review, so far as we can learn, was in March, 1569, when the Ranger, Lord Hunsdon, caused Elizabeth's pensioners to muster before the Virgin Queen, his men all "well appointed in armour, on horseback, and arrayed in green cloth and white," the Tudor livery, as may be learnt from sundry pictures in the galleries at Windsor Castle and Hampton Court Palace.

Commencing then with the first year of the reign of Charles II., Stow tells us how, only a few months after his accession, the king here reviewed his "trained bands," 20,000 strong and upwards, in the presence of "divers persons of quality, and innumerable other spectators," and how in the following March (1661) the Park witnessed a muster of archers shooting with the long bow. This exercise had always been a favourite with the English people; and a writer named Wood, in his "Bowman's Glory," especially mentions the fact, that so great was the delight, and so pleasing the exercise, that three regiments of foot soldiery laid down their arms to come and see it.

Again in 1662, Charles reviewed here his troops, including the handsome Life Guards, whom he had formed in Holland. Their array was picturesque, and their gallant appearance pleased the people, who were sick of the dull Puritanical troopers. The *Kingdom's Intelligencer* thus describes the scene:

"It was a glorious sight, . . . and, with reverence be it spoken, worthy those royal spectators who came purposely to behold it; for his sacred Majesty, the Queen, the Queen-mother, the Duke and Duchess of York, with many of the nobility, were all present. The horse and foot were in such excellent order that it is not easy to imagine anything so exact; which is the more creditable if you consider that there were not a few of that great body who had formerly been commanders, and so more fit to be guard of the person of the most excellent king in the world."

Again, in July, 1664, we read in Pepys' "Diary" of another grand review of the Guards in the Park, the troops, horse and foot, being four thousand; but the diarist, in the honesty of his heart, speaks rather doubtfully of their real value as troops. In 1668 there was a similar display, in order to do honour to the Duke of Monmouth, who had been appointed Colonel of the Life Guards. Pepys was present on this occasion too, and gives us a picture of the duke in "mighty rich clothes;" but he saw no reason to change his former opinion of the men, though he owned, that he "indeed thought it mighty noble."

In January, 1682, there was another review of the Guards in the Park, in the presence of Charles, and of the ambassadors of the Sultan of Morocco. "The soldiers," says Mr. Larwood, "were gallantly, and the officers magnificently accoutred. After they had gone through their various exercises, to the great admiration of the ambassadors, the Moorish followers of their Excellencies would show what they could do; and though their performances were very different from the military exercises of Western nations, they proved themselves good and active horsemen. Whilst riding at full speed, with their lances they took off a ring, hung up for the purpose, and performed various other surprising feats."

An encampment, it would appear from one of Pope's letters, was formed in Hyde Park about the year 1714. At all events, he writes from the West-end to a lady friend, probably Martha Blount:— "You may soon have your wish to enjoy the gallant sights of armies, encampments, standards waving over your brother's corn-fields, and the pretty windings of the Thames stained with the blood of men. . . . . The female eyes will be infinitely delighted with the camp which is speedily to be formed in Hyde Park. The tents are carried there this morning, new regiments, with new cloaths and furniture, far exceeding the late cloth and linen designed by his Grace (the Duke of Marlborough) for the soldiery. The sight of so many gallant fellows, with all the pomp and glare of war yet undeformed by battles, those scenes which England has for many years beheld only on stages, may possibly invite your curiosity to this place."

In another letter to the Hon. Robert Digby, he thus describes the effect produced by the encampment on West-end society :—" The objects that attract this part of the world are quite of a different nature. Women of quality are all turned followers of the camp in Hyde Park this year, whither all the town resort to magnificent entertainments given by the officers, &c. The Scythian ladies that dwelt in the waggons of war were not more closely attached to the baggage. The matrons, like those of Sparta, attend their sons to the field, to be the witnesses of their glorious deeds ; and the maidens, with all their charms displayed, provoke the spirit of the soldiers. Tea and coffee supply the place of Lacedæmonian black broth. This camp seems crowned with perpetual victory, for every sun that rises in the thunder of cannon, sets in the music of violins. Nothing is yet wanting but the constant presence of the princess to represent the *mater exercitûs.*"

In June, 1799, King George III. here reviewed 12,000 volunteers. Of those reviewed on that day, at all events, two survived to take an active part, to the extent, at least, of shouldering a musket and attending drill, in the volunteer movement on its revival in 1858—the late Mr. C. T. Tower, of Weald Hall, Essex, and Mr. James Anderton, of Dulwich, Surrey.

At these reviews there was always a goodly concourse of spectators present, of whom the larger half were ladies, true then, as now, to Ovid's well-known line—

"They come to see, but also to be seen."

If we may believe Lord Lansdowne, there was among these lady frequenters of the Park on such occasions one whose name is now forgotten, though she was doubtless the "belle of the season" in her day. He calls her only Mira, and we have, alas ! no clue to the secret of Mira's parentage. Was she the daughter of a duke or a marquis ? or was she one of the maids of honour who attended in the train of royalty ? Alas ! we cannot tell. But we can quote Lord Lansdowne's lines entitled "Mira at a Review of the Guards in Hyde Park," as certainly not out of place :—

> "Let meaner beauties conquer singly still,
> But haughty Mira will by thousands kill:
> Through armèd ranks triumphantly she drives,
> And with one glance commands a thousand lives.
> The trembling heroes nor resist nor fly,
> But at the head of all their squadrons die."

The following anecdote is vouched for by Lady C. Davies, in her "Recollections of Society :"—Marshal Soult attended a review in Hyde Park in 1838, and his stirrups happening to break, a saddler, named Laurie—the same who became afterwards Alderman Sir Peter Laurie—being asked to supply others, sent the identical stirrups which had been used in the Waterloo campaign by Napoleon I."

On the 23rd of October, 1760, George II. held his last review. The king, we are told, "entered the grand pavilion, or tent, under the Kensington Garden wall," where were also present the Prince and Princess of Wales, the Duke of York, Princess Augusta, and some other of the young princesses, besides a host of noblemen. As soon as the review was over, says *Read's Weekly Journal* of October 25, 1760, "some pieces of a new construction, of a globular form, were set on fire, which occasioned such a smoke as to render all persons within a considerable distance entirely invisible, and thereby the better enabled in time of action to secure a retreat." The brave old king had been in bad health for some days previously, and within forty-eight hours after the review he was dead.

We must say a few words respecting some of the duels—many bloody and fatal ones—that have been fought in Hyde Park. The barbarous practice of duelling, no doubt, came down by tradition from the era of the Normans, if not from that of our Anglo-Saxon forefathers. From whatever race it came, it was a national stain and disgrace for centuries. In the reigns of Charles II. and James II. the mania for duelling was at its height, and, indeed, it could scarcely pass away as long as gentlemen wore their swords in every-day life as part of their costume. John Evelyn remarks, in 1686 : "Many bloody and notorious duels were fought about this time. The Duke of Grafton killed Mr. Stanley, brother to the Earl of Derby, indeed upon an almost insufferable provocation. It is to be hoped," he adds, "that his Majesty will at last severely remedy this unchristian custom."

The story of the duel between Lord Mohun and the Duke of Hamilton, which was fought here on the 15th of November, 1712, is thus told by Sir Bernard Burke, in his "Anecdotes of the Aristocracy :"—

"This sanguinary duel, originating in a political intrigue, was fought early one morning at the Ring, in Hyde Park, then the usual spot for settling these so-called affairs of honour. The duke and his second, Colonel Hamilton, of the Foot Guards, were the first in the field. Soon after, came Lord Mohun and his second, Major Macartney. No sooner had the second party reached the ground, than the duke, unable to conceal his feelings, turned sharply round on Major Macartney, and remarked, 'I am well assured, sir, that all this is by your contrivance, and therefore you shall for him, at this very moment the attention of the colonel was drawn off to the condition of his friend, and, flinging both the swords to a distance, he hastened to his assistance. The combat, indeed, had been carried on between the principals

THE STATUE OF ACHILLES. (See page 395.)

have your share in the dance; my friend here, Colonel Hamilton, will entertain you.' 'I wish for no better partner,' replied Macartney; 'the colonel may command me.' Little more passed between them, and the fight began with infinite fury, each being too intent upon doing mischief to his opponent to look sufficiently to his own defence. Macartney had the misfortune to be speedily disarmed, though not before he had wounded his adversary in the right leg; but, luckily with uncommon ferocity, the loud and angry clashing of the steel having called to the spot the few stragglers that were abroad in the Park at so early an hour. In a very short time the duke was wounded in both legs, which he returned with interest, piercing his antagonist in the groin, through the arm, and in sundry other parts of his body. The blood flowed freely on both sides, their swords, their faces, and even the grass about them, being reddened with it; but rage lent them that

A MEET OF THE FOUR-IN-HAND CLUB. (*See page* 400.)

almost supernatural strength which is so often seen in madmen. If they had thought little enough before of attending to their self-defence, they now seemed to have abandoned the idea altogether. Each at the same time made a desperate lunge at the other; the duke's weapon passed right through his adversary, up to the very hilt; and the latter, shortening his sword, plunged it into the upper part of the duke's left breast, the wound running downwards into his body, when his grace fell upon him. It was now that the colonel came to his aid, and raised him in his arms. Such a blow, it is probable, would have been fatal of itself; but Macartney had by this time picked up one of the swords, and stabbing the duke to the heart over Hamilton's shoulder, immediately fled, and made his escape to Holland. Such, at least, was the tale of the day, widely disseminated and generally believed by one party, although it was no less strenuously denied by the other. Proclamations were issued, and rewards offered, to an unusual amount, for the apprehension of the murderer, the affair assuming all the interest of a public question. Nay, it was roundly asserted by the Tories, that the Whig faction had gone so far as to place hired assassins about the Park to make sure of their victim, if he had escaped the open ferocity of Lord Mohun, or the yet more perilous treachery of Macartney.

"When the duke fell, the spectators of this bloody tragedy, who do not appear to have interfered in any shape, then came forward to bear him to the Cake-House, that a surgeon might be called in, and his wounds looked to; but the blow had been struck too home; before they could raise him from the grass, he expired. Such is one of the many accounts that have been given of this bloody affair, for the traditions of the day are anything but uniform or consistent. According to some, Lord Mohun shortened his sword, and stabbed the wounded man to the heart while leaning on his shoulder, and unable to stand without support; others said, that a servant of Lord Mohun's played the part that was attributed, by the more credible accounts, to Macartney. This intricate knot is by no means rendered easier of untying by the verdict of the jury, who, some years after, upon the trial of Macartney for this offence, in the King's Bench, found him only guilty of manslaughter.

"Lord Mohun himself died of his wounds upon the spot, and with him his title became extinct; but the estate of Gawsworth, in Cheshire, which he had inherited from the Gerards, vested by will in his widow, and eventually passed to her second daughter, Anne Griffith, wife of the Right Hon. William Stanhope, by whose representative, the Earl of Harrington, it is now enjoyed."

In "Crowle's Illustrated Pennant," now in the British Museum, there is a small drawing of the above duel; and there is also engraved in fac-simile, in Smith's "Historical and Literary Curiosities," a letter of Dean Swift to Mrs. Dingley, describing it. The Dean thus writes concerning this duel :—

"Before this comes to your Hands, you will "have heard of the most terrible accident that "hath almost ever happened. This morning at 9 "my man brought me word that D. Hamilton had "fought with Ld. Mohun and killed him and "was brought home wounded. I immediately "sent him to the Duke's house in St James' Square, "but the Porter could hardly answer him for tears, "and a great Rabble was about the House. In "short they fought at 7 this morning. The Dog "Mohun was killed on the spot, and well (when) "the Duke was over him, Mohun short'ning his "sword stabb'd him in at the shoulder to the heart. "The Duke was help'd towards the Cake-house "in the Ring in Hide Park (where they fought) "and dyed on the grass before he could reach the "House, and was brought home in his Coach by "8 while the poor Dutchess was asleep. Mac- "kartney, and an Hamilton were seconds and "fought likewise, and are both fled. I am told, "that a footman of Ld. Mohun's stabb'd D. "Hamilton, and some say Mackartney did so too. "I am infinitely concerned for the poor Duke "who was an honest good natured man, I loved "him very well and I think he loved me better."

Lord Mohun was a notorious profligate; he had frequently been engaged in duels and midnight brawls,* and had been twice tried for murder. The only remark made by his widow, when his corpse was brought home, was an expression of high displeasure that the men had laid the body on her state-bed, thereby staining with blood the rich and costly furniture! The Duchess of Hamilton, who was a daughter of Digby, Lord Gerard of Bromley, continued a widow until her death, in 1744. We have some scanty notices of this lady in Swift's "Journal and Correspondence." The dean visited her on the morning of the fatal occurrence, and remained with her two hours. "I never saw so melancholy a scene," he says. Two months afterwards, he was again on a visit to the duchess, but the tables were turned. She never grieved, but raged, and stormed, and railed:

* See Vol. III., p. 161.

"She is pretty quiet now, but has a diabolical temper."

A noteworthy duel took place in Hyde Park, in 1762, between John Wilkes, the witty agitator, and Samuel Martin, a rather truculent member of Parliament. Martin, in his place in the House of Commons, had alluded to Wilkes as a "stabber in the dark, a cowardly and malignant scoundrel." Wilkes prided himself as much upon his gallantry as upon his wit and disloyalty, and lost no time in calling Martin out. The challenge was given as soon as the House adjourned, and the parties repaired at once to a copse in Hyde Park with a brace of pistols. They fired four times, when Wilkes fell, wounded in the abdomen. His antagonist, relenting, hastened up and insisted on helping him off the ground; but Wilkes, with comparative courtesy, as strenuously urged Martin to hurry away, so as to escape arrest. It afterwards appeared that Martin had been practising in a shooting gallery for six months before making the obnoxious speech in the House; and soon after, instead of being arrested, he received a valuable appointment from the ministry.

Wilkes was the cause of another rather amusing than tragical duel in this park several years later. One Captain Douglas, discussing the great demagogue's merits and demerits in a coffee-house, spoke of him as a scoundrel and a coward; and, turning to the company, he added that these epithets equally applied to Wilkes's adherents. A Rev. Mr. Green took up Wilkes's cause, and pulled Captain Douglas's nose, saying he would back Wilkes against a Scot any day. They at once repaired to the Park, though it was late in the evening. The duel was fought with swords, and finally the parson militant ran the captain through the doublet, whereupon the honour of both gentlemen was asserted to be saved, and they left the field of combat, satisfied.

Richard Brinsley Sheridan, in 1772, repaired to Hyde Park with Captain Matthews to fight a duel; but finding the crowd too great, they went to the Castle Tavern, Covent Garden, instead, and there fought with swords. The quarrel was about the beautiful Miss Linley, the singer, to whom Sheridan was already secretly married. Both were severely cut, but neither was seriously wounded.

In 1780 a duel was fought here between the Earl of Shelburne and Colonel Fullarton; and three years later Lieutenant-Colonel Thomas and Colonel Gordon met here in deadly combat, when the former was killed. In 1797 Colonel King and Colonel Fitzgerald fought, the cause of dispute being a lady, a near relation of the former, who had been wronged by his antagonist; Fitzgerald was killed. It will scarcely be credited, that as recently as 1822 a duel was fought here between the Dukes of Bedford and Buckingham.

Mr. Harrison Ainsworth, in his historical romance of "St. James's," describes one of the duels which were fought in Hyde Park in the reign of Queen Anne. He pictures the parties as striking off in the direction of Kensington Gardens, and keeping on the higher ground till they reach a natural avenue of fine trees, chiefly elms, sweeping down to the edge of a sheet of water which has since been amplified into the Serpentine. He states that "about half way down the avenue were two springs celebrated for their virtues, to which, even in those days, when hydropathy was unknown as a practice, numbers used to resort to drink, and which were protected in wooden frames;" and that "at a later period the waters of the larger spring, known as St. Anne's well, were dispensed by an ancient dame who sat beside it with a small table and glasses. . . . A pump," he adds, "now occupies the spot, but the waters are supposed to have lost none of their efficacy." We shall have occasion to mention these springs again.

It is pleasant to pass from these records of bloodshed to the more enlivening accounts of the festivities and rejoicings that took place here in consequence of the Peace in 1814, and the visit of the Allied Sovereigns. Mr. Cyrus Redding describes, with the pen of an eye-witness, the review of the Scots Greys in Hyde Park in the presence of their Majesties. "It was amusing," he writes, "to see the activity of the other princes and of the Duke of Wellington in their movements, and the incapacity of the Prince Regent to keep up with them. Already grown unwieldly and bloated, he was generally left behind in the royal excursions, being too bulky and too Falstaff-like to move about as they did." He describes the Emperor Alexander of Russia as "affable, easy, and good-humoured;" the King of Prussia as being "as milk-and-water as his courtiers and his enemies could have desired;" and the King of Belgium (then simply aide-de-camp to one of their Majesties), as "lodging *au deuxième* in Marylebone Street."

Again, after the battle of Waterloo, the Park was made the centre of the rejoicings for the peace. Mr. Redding tells us how "a mock naval engagement on the Serpentine river in Hyde Park was presented on the occasion. Boats rigged as vessels of war were engaged in petty combat, and one or two filled with combustibles were set on fire in order to act as fire-ships. First a couple of frigates engaged. Then the battle of the Nile was im-

tated.   Later at night the fireworks commenced.
I was as close to them as any one could well be
placed.   There was a painted castle externally
made of cloth.   This mock fort gave out a pretended cannonade, amid the smoke of which, the
scene shifting, changed the whole into a brilliant
temple, with transparent paintings, to represent a
temple of Peace, quite in a theatrical way.   This
elicited shouts of admiration from the people.

" The newspapers made merry with these pro-
ceedings, of which the Prince Regent was said to
have been the designer.   They were worthy of the
Prince's taste, extravagant and puerile as it was.
One of the papers said, that two watermen, each
with a line-of-battle ship on his head proceeding

up Constitution Hill to the Serpentine, had been
met by their reporter that morning.   Another stated
that a corps of Laplanders, not to exceed three
feet six in height, had been reviewed for the purpose of sending them to man the Prince Regent's
fleet in Hyde Park, but that they were declared to
be eleven inches five lines too tall."

We may conclude this chapter by remarking
that the fresh air of the neighbourhood of Hyde
Park a century ago was proverbial ; for Boswell
writes to thank one of his friends for the offer
of the use of his apartments in London, but to
decline them on the ground that " it is best to
have lodgings in the more airy vicinity of Hyde
Park."

CHAPTER XXXI.

HYDE PARK (*continued*).

" Now in Hyde Park she flaunts by day,
All night she flutters at the play."
Foundling Hospital for Wit, vol. i., 1771.

Rural Aspect of the Park, and Purity of the Air—Extent of the Park, and Names of the Principal Entrances—The Chelsea Waterworks, and the
Duke of Gloucester's Riding-house—Mineral Waters—The Statue of Achilles—Rotten Row—The " Drive"—Anecdote of Lord Chesterfield
—Horace Walpole attacked by Robbers in the Park—The Park as a Lounge for Effeminate Gallants—" Romeo" Coates and his Singular
Equipage—The Park as a Place for the display of the " Newest Fashions"—Miss Burdett-Coutts and the " Irrepressible Stranger"—
The " Four-in-hand" and the " Coaching" Clubs—The Serpentine—The Royal Humane Society—The Swimming Club—A Favourite
Place for Suicides—Proposal for a World's Fair—The Apple-stall Keeper and the Government—The " Reformer's Tree"—The Marble Arch.

THE entrance into Hyde Park from the west end of
Piccadilly, at "the Corner," is, as we have already
seen, imposing and magnificent in the extreme.
" The park itself," writes Mr. James Grant, " is in a
fine, open, and airy situation ; and what with the
trees in Kensington Gardens, and the handsome
houses on the east, north, and south, presents a
remarkably interesting and pleasant view.   Its
attractions, indeed, altogether are so great that no
other place in the vicinity of London can bear a
moment's comparison with it.   I question if there
be many such places in the world."   At the beginning of the present century, however, it wore
a different appearance from that of to-day.   For
instance, from a print of 1808, it is clear that on
the left, inside the entrance at Hyde Park Corner,
was the under-keeper's lodge, a wooden structure.
At the bottom of an old view of Kensington Palace,
among the topographical illustrations belonging to
George III., is the following inscription :—" The
avenue leading from St. James's through Hyde Park
to Kensington Palace is very grand.   On each side
of it landthorns (*sic*) are placed at equal distances,
which being lighted in the dark seasons for the

conveniency of the courtiers, appear inconceivably
magnificent."

Hyde Park far surpasses that of St. James's in
pure rural scenery.   Its trees may not be greener
or leafier, but there is in its appearance less of art
and more of nature, and this is evidenced by the
beauty—artificial as it is—of the Serpentine river.

The air here, though not equal in purity to that
on Epsom Downs, or even Hampstead Heath, is
fresh enough, as compared with that of close-packed
rooms in the centre of London.   " Taking three
of Dr. Smith's London tests," observes a writer in
Once a Week, we find that while the air of the
Court of Chancery shows ·20 of carbonic acid, and
that of the pit of the Strand Theatre ·32, the air
of Hyde Park shows only ·03."   The parks, therefore, may well be called the " lungs of London."

The Park reaches from Piccadilly as far westwards as Kensington Gardens, and it lies between
the roads leading to Kensington and Bayswater,
the former a continuation of Piccadilly, and the
latter of Oxford Street.   It originally contained a
little over 620 acres ; but by enclosing and taking
part of it into Kensington Gardens, and by other

grants of land for building between Park Lane and Hyde Park Corner, it has been reduced to a little under four hundred. It has eight principal entrances. The first (as already mentioned) is at Hyde Park Corner; it consists of a triple archway, combined with an iron screen, and was erected from the designs of Mr. Decimus Burton, in 1828. In Park Lane is Stanhope Gate, opened about 1750; and also Grosvenor Gate, which was erected by a public subscription among the neighbouring residents, and named after Sir Richard Grosvenor. At the north-east corner of the Park, at the western end of Oxford Street, is Cumberland Gate, now adorned with the "Marble Arch," of which we shall have more to say presently. In the Bayswater Road is the Victoria Gate, opposite Sussex Square. The entrances on the south side are the Albert Gate, Knightsbridge, nearly opposite the road leading into Lowndes Square; the Prince of Wales's Gate, near the site of the old "Half-way House," and close by the spot whereon stood the "Great Exhibition" of 1851; whilst further westward is the Kensington Gate.

At a very early period, the Park was fenced in with deer-palings. In the reign of Charles II. these were superseded by a brick wall, which again, in the reign of George IV., gave place to an open iron railing. As late as the year 1826 the south side was disfigured by two large erections—the one a riding-house, and the other an engine-house belonging to the Chelsea Water-works Company. The former building, known as the Duke of Gloucester's Riding House, was built in 1768, but pulled down in 1820, having served as the head-quarters of the Westminster Volunteer Cavalry during the war against Napoleon. Its site was afterwards occupied for a time by an exhibition of a picture of the Battle of Waterloo, painted by a Dutch artist, which enjoyed a season's popularity as one of the sights for "country cousins" in London, and is now in the Royal Museum of the Pavilion, near Haarlem, in Holland. The licence of the Chelsea Water-works Company terminated towards the end of the reign of William IV., when the engine-house opposite Grosvenor Gate was taken down, and the circular space which it occupied was turned into a basin, with a fountain in the centre. This was filled up about the year 1860, and the place converted into a circular Dutch garden.

The enclosure at the north-west corner was well planted with trees, and stocked with cows and deer, and had a keeper's lodge. Sir Richard Phillips writes thus, in "Modern London," published by him in 1804:—"Beneath a row of trees,

running parallel with the keeper's garden, are two springs, greatly resorted to: the one is a mineral, and is drunk; the other is used to bathe weak eyes with. At the former, in fine weather, sits a woman, with a table, and chairs, and glasses, for the accommodation of visitors. People of fashion often go in their carriages to the entrance of this enclosure, which is more than a hundred yards from the first spring, and send their servants with jugs for the water, or send their children to drink at the spring. The brim of the further spring is frequently surrounded by persons, chiefly of the lower orders, bathing their eyes. The water is constantly clear, from the vast quantity which the spring casts up, and is continually running off by an outlet from a small square reservoir."

Of the recent improvements in this park, Walker speaks thus, in his "Original," in 1835:—"The widened, extended, and well-kept rides and drives in Hyde Park, with the bridge, and the improvement of the Serpentine, form a most advantageous comparison with their former state."

We have already described Apsley House, the residence of the great Duke of Wellington. "No stranger," writes Mr. T. Miller, in his "Picturesque Sketches in London," "would ever think of entering Hyde Park without first casting a look at Apsley House, the abode of 'the Duke;' and if he did, the statue of Achilles, which seems stationed as if to point it out, would remind him where he was."

The statue here mentioned stands on a gently sloping mound in the Park, facing the entrance, about a hundred yards north of Apsley House. It was executed by Sir Richard Westmacott in 1822. The figure is said to have been copied from one of the antique statues on the Monte Cavallo at Rome. The statue appears as if in the act of striking. On the pedestal is this inscription:—"To Arthur, Duke of Wellington, and his brave companions in arms, this statue of Achilles, cast from cannon taken in the battles of Salamanca, Vittoria, Toulouse, and Waterloo, is inscribed by their countrywomen." This statue, which was erected by a subscription among the ladies of England as a monument in honour of the military successes of the Duke of Wellington, is open to grave objections, besides the fact that the figure is undraped. From the first it was made the subject of very uncomplimentary remarks in English circles of refinement and discrimination, and a rather sharp controversy was carried on as to its merits and demerits, both before and after it was set up.

The author of a "Tour of a Foreigner in England," published in the year 1825, remarks:

"The important monuments of London seem to be chiefly consigned to Mr. Westmacott. This artist excels in grace and harmony of contour. He ought, perhaps, to devote himself wholly to the representation of nymphs. His 'Achilles,' which has been erected as a monument to the Duke of Wellington, is merely a colossal Adonis. Westmacott would have succeeded better in representing the youthful hero grouped with the daughters of King Lycomedes. Who would believe that this gladiator Achilles could ever have deceived set up, and excited at first something like wonder, then an ignorant or canting clamour, because it was undraped; but it has been from the first moment regarded by those who knew anything about art matters as a work of truly magnificent execution, and one of the noblest productions of modern art. With respect to its popular or vulgar name, it has no one distinctive trait of the Homeric Achilles, but that is immaterial; it is enough that we have before us a colossal representation of the human

BRIDGE OVER THE SERPENTINE. (*See page* 404.)

this gladiator Achilles could ever have deceived Deidamia and her companions under the disguise of a female? This colossal statue, which is erected in Hyde Park, as a monument to the Duke of Wellington, represents Achilles raising his shield. The illusion is somewhat forced. The ladies who subscribed for the monument affirm that the artist did not consult them respecting this allegorical statue; and that it was completed before the subscription was set on foot. A great outcry has been raised against the undraped figure of Achilles."

In a work entitled "Cities and Principal Towns," Westmacott's statue of "Achilles" is thus dealt with :—" The bronze colossus in Hyde Park, commonly called 'The Achilles,' was a novelty when figure in the full play of muscle and energetic grandeur of outline. It is a copy, as everybody knows, from a figure forming part of one of two groups on the Quirinal Hill. There it is grouped with a horse against, it is supposed, the original intention. This may be; but still it is quite clear that its detachment has essentially weakened the effect. There is a want of object, and a vagueness. The English sculptor, Mr. Westmacott, to supply this want— *this mancanza*—has placed upon the left arm a shield, from the evidence and authority of shield-straps on the arm of the original. The small dimensions of Mr. Westmacott's shield, so far short of the "orbicular" shields of Homer, which, turned behind, touched with their borders, in walking, the nape of the neck and the heels, negative the supposition of an Achilles in his mind ; and it may be questioned whether, by introducing it at all, he has not rather disenchanted the spectator of the power to supply much more effectually the vagueness of attitude and action, by still grouping the figure, in his imagination, as it is grouped on the Quirinal. As to the straps on the arm, they are far from proving that a shield had ever before been placed upon them. The ancient sculptors addressed them-

was the turning of the road near Grosvenor Gate. The Gloucester riding-house was then rapidly disappearing ; and that long useless pile would, it was asserted, make way for a plantation of young trees extending to the canal or basin. The esplanade on the south side of the Serpentine river was then nearly completed. "The gravel terrace," added the writer, "from its width, will no doubt become a fashionable promenade for the beaux and belles in the summer months."

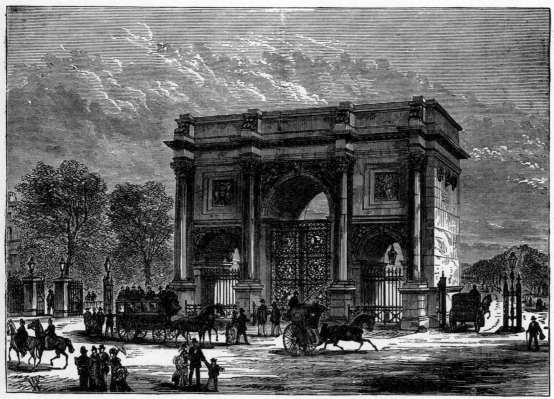

THE MARBLE ARCH. (*See page* 405.)

selves by signs and suggestions of this kind to the imagination ; and Mr. Westmacott had better, we think, have imitated them in this, as he has rivalled them in other graces. This grand production of English art is unfavourably placed ; and as to its destination and inscription, they set language at defiance."

In a newspaper paragraph of January 29th, 1825, we read that public curiosity was excited by the preparations for erecting here a temple for the exhibition of the long-talked-of painting, "The Battle of Waterloo." The ground marked out was in advance of the statue of Achilles, viewing it from the Piccadilly Gate, and to the west of the figure ; it adjoined the foot-path by the side of Rotten Row. Another object of attraction at that time

The part of the Park near the statue of Achilles, between it and "The Row," is, during the London season, what the "Ring" was in the old Stuart times, the very maze and centre of fashion. "Here," writes Mr. Thomas Miller, "the pride and beauty of England may be seen upon their own stage, and on a fine day in 'the season' no other spot in the world can outrival in rich display and chaste grandeur the scene which is here presented." Out of the "season," however, Hyde Park is a dull place enough. Tom Hood the elder thus speaks of it in the dull days of November :—

"No Park, no 'Ring,' no afternoon gentility,
    No company, and no nobility,
      No warmth, no cheerfulness, no healthful ease !"

Lord Byron, in "Don Juan," canto 13, if our

readers remember, says of Rotten Row, when out of season, that it—

> " Sleeps from the chivalry of this bright age."

And R. B. Sheridan, in his prologue to *Pizarro*, talks of the horse seen cantering along its sand and gravel in May or June as—

> " The hack Bucephalus of Rotten Row."

It has been suggested that the name itself is a corruption of *Route du roi* (the king's road); but Mr. John Timbs says, " the name *Rotten* is traced to *rotteran*, to muster; a military origin which may refer to the Park during the Civil War." Mr. Peter Cunningham, in his " Handbook of London," contents himself with just mentioning this place, as the part of Hyde Park, on the south of the Serpentine, most crowded with equestrians in the height of the London season; but he is wholly silent as to the derivation of its name. The " Row " is about a mile and a half in length, and is laid down with a fine loose gravel, mixed with tan, so that the fair equestrians and their friends can gallop over it without much danger from a fall.

There is extant a most amusing ballad which illustrates the character of the Park and its company shortly after the Restoration, entitled " News from Hyde Park," from which we quote the following stanzas; it is printed at length in the " History of the Parks : "—

> " One evening, a little before it was dark,
>   Sing tantararara tantivee,
> I call'd for my gelding and rid to Hide Parke,
>   On tantararara tantivee :
> It was in the merry month of May,
> When meadows and fields were gaudy and gay,
> And flowers apparell'd bright as the day,
>   I got upon my tantivee.
>
> " The Park shone brighter than the skyes,
>   Sing tantararara tantivee,
> With jewels, and gold, and ladies' eyes
>   That sparkled and cry'd, Come see me :
> Of all parts of England, Hide Park hath the name
> For coaches and horses, and persons of fame :
> It looked at first sight like a field full of flame,
>   Which made me ride up tantivee.
>
> " There hath not been seen such a sight since Adam's,
>   For perriwig, ribbon, and feather.
> Hide Park may be termed the market of Madams,
>   Or Lady-Fair, chuse you whether;
> Their gowns were a yard too long for their legs,
> They shew'd like the rainbow cut into rags,
> A garden of flowers, or a navy of flags,
>   When they all did mingle together."

One of the most constant frequenters of the Park, or more especially of the " Drive," about the middle of the last century, was Lord Chesterfield, " the man of the graces," on whom we have already peeped in at Chesterfield House, in May

Fair. * That nobleman late in life had a severe fall from his horse, which took fright whilst drinking at one of the little ponds in the Park.

A few days before his death, one of his friends expressed some astonishment at meeting his lordship again there, considering the precarious state of his health. " Why," replied Chesterfield, " I am rehearsing my funeral;" alluding to his own dark-coloured chariot drawn by four horses, and the string of fashionable carriages which followed behind. Thus Chesterfield remained to the last a seeker after the vanities of this world. His constant endeavour was to be more young and more frivolous than was becoming his age. His days were employed in parading in the Park among youth and fashion, his nights at " White's," gaming and pronouncing witticisms amongst " the boys of quality." The consequence was, as we find from his own letters, that his old age was one of fretfulness and disappointment. He was always attempting to keep up his former reputation, and found it constantly sinking under him.

Here Horace Walpole, as he tells us, was robbed, in the winter of 1749, by the fashionable highwayman, Maclean. He writes : " One night, in the beginning of November, as I was returning from Holland House by moonlight, about ten o'clock, I was attacked by two highwaymen in Hyde Park, and the pistol of one of them going off accidentally, razed the skin under my eye, left some marks of shot on my face, and stunned me. The ball went through the top of the chariot, and if I had sat an inch nearer to the left side, must have gone through my head." Such were the perils of the parks, within half a mile of Piccadilly, in the reign of the second George ! Maclean was the son of an Irish dean, and had once kept a grocer's shop in or near Welbeck Street; but losing his only child, of whom he was very fond, he sold off his business and " took to the road," and lived in town lodgings in St. James's Street, " over against White's Club," and in country apartments at Chelsea, whilst carrying on his depredations. He was hung at Tyburn in the year following, when some of the brightest eyes of ladies of high birth were in tears at his loss. Thus Soame Jenyns writes, in his " Modern Fine Lady "—

> " She weeps if but a handsome thief is hung."

It is clear that a hundred years ago " The Park " was the lounge of indolent and effeminate gallants ; for a writer in the *London Magazine* for 1773 mentions, in terms of ill-disguised contempt, " our emaciated youth, who, shattered by green tea and

---

* See *ante*, p. 353.

claret, drag their delicate and enervated forms at noon through the Park where their ruddy forefathers were wont to exhibit their manly forms."

Among the eccentric characters who figured in "The Park" in the days of the Regency, was a certain Mr. Coates, a wealthy planter from the West Indies, who made a sudden appearance in London, performing "for one night only," at the Haymarket Theatre, in *Romeo and Juliet*. We have already informed our readers * how ludicrously he played "Romeo" on this occasion, so as to be called "Romeo Coates" ever afterwards. His love of notoriety did not end at the Haymarket. He had built for him a singular shell-shaped carriage,. in which he drove two fine white horses about the Park almost daily. His harness and every available part of the vehicle was blazoned all over with his self-assumed heraldic device, a cock crowing ; and wherever he went his appearance was heralded by half the *gamins* of London running by his side, and crying "Cock-a-doodle-doo!" Eventually, having been the fun and sport of the West-end for a season or two, "Romeo" Coates left London and settled at Boulogne, where he induced a fair lady to become the partner of his existence, in spite of the ridicule of the world.

Hyde Park has always been the chief ground for exhibiting the "newest fashions" among the upper ten thousand ; and here, during "the season," a good opportunity is afforded to the stranger of seeing the aristocratic world *en masse*, and of noting the ever varying cut of fashionable attire. Our lady readers will doubtless be amused at the excess to which the belles of even the Georgian era went in the matter of adornment, when we tell them that we read in a newspaper of January, 1796, under the title of "The Height of Fashion," that Lady Caroline Campbell "displayed in Hyde Park the other day a feather four feet higher than her bonnet !"

From a poetic effusion printed in 1808, Sunday would appear to have been the great day for the *beaux* and *belles* of the middle classes, and the City in general, to "do" the Park. Here we read :—

> " Horsed in Cheapside, scarce yet the gayer spark
> Achieves the Sunday triumphs of the Park ;
> Scarce yet you see him, dreading to be late,
> Scour the New Road, and dash through Grosvenor Gate ;
> Anxious, yet timorous, too, his steed to show,
> The bold Bucephalus of Rotten Row.
> Careless he seems, yet, vigilantly shy,
> Woos the stray glance of ladies passing by ;
> While his off-heel, insidiously aside,
> Provokes the caper which he seems to chide."

* See *ante*, p. 225.

Captain Gronow says of the Park that, as lately as 1815, it looked a part of the country. Under the trees grazed not only cows, but deer, and the paths across it were few and far between. As you gazed from an eminence, no rows of monotonous houses reminded you of the vicinity of a large city, and its atmosphere was then "much more like what God made it than the hazy, grey, coal-darkened half-twilight of the London of to-day. The company, which then congregated daily about five, was composed of dandies and women in the best society ; the men mounted on such horses as England alone could then produce. The dandy's dress consisted of a blue coat with brass buttons, leather breeches, and top-boots ; and it was the fashion to wear a deep, stiff white cravat, which prevented you from seeing your boots while standing. All the world watched Brummell to imitate him, and order their clothes of the tradesman who dressed that sublime dandy. One day a youthful beau approached Brummell, and said, ' Permit me to ask you where you get your blacking?' 'Ah!' replied Brummell, gazing complacently at his boots, 'my blacking positively ruins me. I will tell you in confidence ; it is made with the finest champagne !'

" Many of the ladies used to drive into the Park in a carriage called a *vis-à-vis*, which held only two persons. The hammer-cloth rich in heraldic designs, the powdered footmen in smart liveries, and a coachman who assumed all the gravity and appearance of a wigged archbishop, were indispensable. The equipages were generally much more gorgeous than at a later period, when democracy invaded the Park and introduced what may be termed a 'brummagem society,' with shabby-genteel carriages and servants. The carriage company consisted of the most celebrated beauties, amongst whom were conspicuous the Duchesses of Rutland, Argyle, Gordon, and Bedford ; Ladies Cowper, Foley, Heathcote, Louisa Lambton, Hertford, and Mountjoy. The most conspicuous horsemen were the Prince Regent, always accompanied by Sir Benjamin Bloomfield ; the Duke of York, and his old friend, Warwick Lake ; the Duke of Dorset on his white horse, the Marquis of Anglesey with his lovely daughters, Lord Harrowby and the Ladies Ryder, the Earl of Sefton and the Ladies Molyneux, and the eccentric Earl of Morton on his long-tailed grey. In those days 'pretty horse-breakers' would not have dared to show themselves in Hyde Park ; nor did you see any of the lower or middle classes of London society intruding themselves into regions which, by a sort of tacit understanding, were then given up exclusively to persons of rank and fashion. Such was the

Park and the 'Row' little more than half a century ago."

Some amusing sketches of scenes in Hyde Park during "the season," with an essay on its equipages and throng of loungers that pass idly along the "Row," from the pen of Mr. Cyrus Redding, appeared in the columns of the *Pilot* newspaper in the hey-day of its early prosperity.

In 1823 it was the fashion for the fops of the London season to take a morning stroll in Hyde Park, and then to re-appear there from about five to seven in the afternoon. At that time, however, it was the east side of the Park, parallel to Park Lane, between Cumberland Gate and Hyde Park Corner, Piccadilly, which formed the centre of attraction, the "Drive" and the "Row" at that date not extending westwards. So changeable is custom or fashion, however, that, some twelve or fourteen years later, to have put in an appearance in the Park before the afternoon would have been considered vulgar; now once more it is the custom of the most fashionable persons to take a morning ride in the "Row."

It is hinted by Mr. James Grant in his "Travels in Town," that it was in the "Drive" in Hyde Park that Miss (now Lady) Burdett-Coutts first caught a glimpse of the irrepressible stranger who persecuted her life, and who interpreted an accidental smile as an encouragement to his attentions.

In spite of all rival attractions elsewhere, an afternoon's lounge in the Park during the summer months is still a delightful recreation to a country cousin, for there he will see a splendid assortment, not only of female beauty and lovely dresses, but also of equine symmetry and magnificent "turns out;" and it need hardly be said that the sight of the annual meets of the "Four-in-Hand Club," and "The Coaching Club," near the powder magazine at the north-west end of the Serpentine, is one well worth taking a little trouble to see. To such perfection has the coaching revival of late years been brought, that the present generation has fairly eclipsed not only that of its fathers, but that of its grandfathers. "Not in the most palmy days of the bygone coaching era," observes a writer in the *John Bull*, "when every country gentleman could keep a four-in-hand, and many drove their own coaches, were there to be seen such 'turns out' as now display themselves almost daily." Never were so many first-class animals put to such work, and never were "the ribbons" more artistically handled. Even the "butterfly" coaches which make country trips from London daily during the season are so horsed, so turned out, and so driven, as to be far in advance, in style and appearance, of

the best stages of the olden time. And it must be owned that this revival of coaching skill is by no means an unhealthy symptom of the age.

The vehicles formerly used by the "Four-in-Hand Club" are described as of a hybrid class, "quite as elegant as private carriages, and lighter than even the mails." They were horsed with the finest animals that money could procure; and, in general, the whole four in each carriage were admirably matched—grey and chestnut being the favourite colours. "The master generally drove the team, often a nobleman of high rank, who commonly copied the dress of a mail-coachman. The company usually rode outside; but two footmen in rich liveries were indispensable on the back seat, nor was it at all uncommon to see some splendidly-attired female on the box." Mr. Timbs, in his "Club Life of London," mentions, perhaps, one of the finest specimens of good "coachmanship," as performed by Sir Felix Agar. He had made a bet, which he won, that he would drive his own four-horses-in-hand up Grosvenor Place, down the passage into Tattersall's Yard (which was formerly close by Hyde Park Corner), around the pillar which stood in the centre of it, and back again into Grosvenor Place, *without either of his horses going at a slower pace than a trot.* In our chapter on Piccadilly we have spoken at some length of the good old custom of stage-coaching, and also of its recent revival; so that nothing further need be said here.

Having thus described the general features of the Park, and given these few sketches from its historical annals, it is time that we said something about the lake—or river, as it is called—which forms its chief ornament.

The Park is deeply delved, and abundantly supplied with springs which have been renowned for ages. "Many persons," says a writer in the *Lancet* of October 21st, 1848, "every morning drink of these wells, or have the water brought home for their daily use. A part is conveyed by pipes to Buckingham Palace for drinking purposes, and to Westminster Abbey, the Dean of which still holds a spring, formally granted by one of our Edwards to the Abbots of Westminster. In 1663 Charles II. granted to Thomas Hawes of Westminster all the springs, waters, and conduits in the Park to hold for ninety-nine years, rendering to the Exchequer 6s. 8d. per annum."

It was in 1730 that Queen Caroline, the Consort of George II., being a woman of taste, and of great activity, took into her head the idea of improving and embellishing the Park by forming the several ponds and pools and the brook of Westbourne into one large sheet of water. She consulted the Surveyor-General of Woods and Forests, a gentleman of the name of Withers, who gave to the Serpentine its present shape, the slight bend which it makes in the centre being thought sufficient to justify the name at a time when no ornamental water was allowed in landscape gardening, except perfectly straight and square after the Dutch fashion.* The works were commenced in the October of the year mentioned above; and apparently the Serpentine was intended only as part of a larger plan, including the erection of a new royal palace in Hyde Park, of which we have already spoken. At all events, we read in the *London Journal* of September 26th, 1730: "Next Monday they begin the Serpentine River and Royal Mansion in Hyde Park. Mr. Ripley is to build the house, and Mr. Jepherson to make the river, under the direction of Charles Withers, Esq." The old Lodge in the centre of the Park had to be sacrificed. "Two hundred men," Mr. Larwood tells us, "were employed on the work. A dyke or dam was thrown across the valley of the Westbourne, and with the soil dug out of it was raised a mound at the south-east end of Kensington Gardens, on the summit of which was placed a small temple, revolving on a pivot, so as to afford shelter from the winds." The cost of the works was £6,000, including a sum of £2,500 paid to the Chelsea Waterworks Company to induce them to forego their right of carrying water-pipes through the Park. "The king believed that it was all paid out of the queen's own money, and good-humouredly refused to look at her plans, saying he did not care how much money she flung away of her own revenue. He little suspected the aid which Walpole furnished her from the royal treasury; and it was only at the queen's death that this little trick of Walpole's policy came to light, for then it appeared that £20,000 of the king's money had been expended by her Majesty upon these various improvements."

Considerable alterations and improvements have been effected in the Serpentine at different periods. It originally received the water of a stream which had its rise in the neighbourhood of Hampstead; but as this stream was for many years the Bayswater sewer, the result was that we had about fifty acres of stagnant water and other matters, the depth varying from one to thirty feet. To remedy this state of things the Bayswater sewer was cut from

the Serpentine in 1834, and the loss of water, or rather of sewerage, which the river sustained in consequence was supplied from the Thames by the Chelsea Waterworks Company. The accumulation of putrid matter, nevertheless, still remained for many years in the bed of the river; but in the end it became absolutely necessary, in consequence of the effluvia arising from it during the hot weather, to remove the mud deposits, and to take means for ensuring a constant stream of pure water throughout.

It sounds absurd to our ears, but it is nevertheless true, that in the reign of George IV. Mr. John Martin suggested the following "plan for bringing to London a current of pure water, and, at the same time, materially beautifying the metropolis." He proposed that a stream should be brought from the Colne (the water of which is excellent), to be taken about three-quarters of a mile to the north-east of Denham, near Uxbridge, and to be conveyed, by a somewhat circuitous route, following on the whole the course of the Grand Junction Canal, to the reservoir at Paddington. He calculated that the elevation of the reservoir would ensure the distribution of the water, without the aid of a steam-engine, to all the western end of the metropolis, except the highest parts of Paddington and Marylebone. In order to combine other objects of utility, as well as ornament, with that of affording a supply of wholesome beverage, Mr. Martin proposed that a large bath should be formed, near the great reservoir, capable of containing one thousand persons, with boxes for the bathers; and he had marked out upon a map a route by which he proposed to carry the stream under Grand Junction Street and the Uxbridge Road into Kensington Gardens and the Serpentine, diversifying its course with occasional falls and pieces of ornamental water. From Hyde Park he would carry it underground to the gardens of Buckingham Palace, where "the stream might be made to burst out as from a natural cavern, and spread itself into an ornamental water." Passing under Constitution Hill into the Green Park, and "giving motion and wholesomeness to the water stagnant there," he proposed that the current should be conveyed under the Mall into the ornamental water then formed or forming in St. James's Park, at the two extremities of which he would place fountains. Finally, he suggested that the stream might flow into the Thames at Whitehall Stairs. Although Mr. Martin's plan does not appear to have received the attention it perhaps deserved, thanks to the Board of Works we have now something very nearly approaching what he had proposed.

---

* Lord Bathurst, the friend of Pope, is said to have been the first person who ventured on a departure from this tasteless style, in a rivulet which he widened into a sheet of water at his seat of Ritchings, near Colnbrook.

This sheet of water—something belying its name, it must be owned—is almost straight, instead of being what a stranger might expect to find it—a meandering stream, wandering hither and thither in graceful curves "at its own sweet will."

water is the favourite resort of the lovers of skating, for whose safety the Royal Humane Society has erected on the north side a neat classic edifice as a receiving-house. It is kept well supplied with boats, ladders, ropes, and everything necessary to

OLD OUTFALL OF THE SERPENTINE AT KNIGHTSBRIDGE, IN 1800. (*From the Crace Collection.*)

The Serpentine has been frequently frozen over so strongly as to realise Virgil's description of a real English frost in his days, when it might be said of its water—

"Undaque ferratos a tergo sustinet orbes,
  Puppibus illa prius, patulis nunc hospita plaustris."

In the winter of 1814 a fair was held on the ice; and in 1825 a Mr. Hunt for a wager drove a coach and four horses across the Serpentine during a severe frost. In severe winters this fine sheet of

the resuscitation and comfort of those who may be suddenly immersed. The building stands on the site of an older one, which had been erected in 1794 upon ground presented by George III. It was erected in 1834, from the designs of Mr. J. Bunning, the first stone being laid by the Duke of Wellington. Over the Ionic entrance is sculptured the obverse of the society's medal—a boy striving to rekindle an almost extinct torch by blowing it, together with the legend, "Lateat scintillula

TYBURN TURNPIKE, 1820. (*See page 407.*)

forsan" (Perchance a spark may be concealed). The Royal Humane Society, whose chief offices are in Trafalgar Square, was founded in 1774, by Drs. Goldsmith, Towers, Heberden, and others; and its receiving-houses in the parks cost about £3,000 a year. This society, which is supported by voluntary contributions, publishes accounts of the most approved and effectual methods for recovering persons apparently drowned or dead; and suggests and provides suitable apparatus for, and also bestows rewards on all who risk their lives in, the preservation or restoration of human life. Its records show that during the past thirty years upwards of 7,000 persons have been granted the society's honorary rewards for exertions in saving life; and that about 16,000,000 persons have bathed and skated in the royal parks and gardens of the metropolis under the care of the society's officers. In that large number accidents in which life was in danger were very numerous, and nearly all were rescued by the society.

Early in the morning in the summer months the Serpentine is much frequented by bathers; and 12,000 have been known to indulge in the luxury of a bath in one summer day. This, as may be seen from the Report of the Royal Humane Society in 1849, was before the purification of its waters had been effected!

We must not omit to mention here the Serpentine Swimming Club, whose members have done much to ensure the safety of bathers in these waters. In connection with this club, a handsome silver challenge cup is contested for over a distance of 100 yards. The trophy has to be won three times in succession by the same swimmer before he can substantiate his claim to retain it as his absolute property, and is contested on the first Tuesday in each month "all the year round."

Close by the receiving-house are the boat-houses where boats are let for hire; and the brightly-painted craft being extensively patronised during the summer, a pleasing and animated scene is presented on the water. The boats were introduced here in 1847, but that was not the first occasion on which a craft had scudded the waters of the Serpentine, for towards the close of the last century the ingenious and inventive Lord Stanhope here launched a model of a steamboat made by his own hands or under his own superintendence. How little did he expect at that time that his son would live to see the day when steam and a pair of paddle-wheels would carry a large ship across the broad Atlantic!

Like "Rosamond's Pond" in St. James's Park, of which we have already spoken in a former chapter,* the Serpentine is a favourite place for suicides, and frequently the spot selected by those unfortunate individuals who may have determined upon ending their existence. Here Harriet Westbrook, the unhappy first wife of the poet Shelley, drowned herself in December, 1816.

Somewhat oddly placed, in juxtaposition with the Royal Humane Society's house, is the great Government store of gunpowder. In this magazine it is stated that upwards of one million of ball and blank ammunition are kept ready for immediate use. Spanning the river near its western extremity, and at the point where it joins Kensington Gardens, is a handsome stone bridge of five arches, which was built from the designs of Sir John Rennie. The view of London from this point is much admired.

In 1840 it was proposed by Mr. T. S. Duncombe, then M.P. for Finsbury, that an annual fair should be held in Hyde Park; but the proposition was defeated in the House of Commons. Mr. Raikes, in mentioning the subject in his "Journal," remarks that it would have been "a source of endless riot and disorder among the lower classes, attended with much injury to the localities. It would," he adds, "indeed be preposterous, when all sober men are anxious to abolish Bartholomew Fair in the City, to institute another scene of the same description in the fairest part of the metropolis, and close to the palace." Little did Mr. Raikes or Mr. Duncombe anticipate that, in a few years later—namely, in 1851—the broad piece of ground south of the Serpentine would become the scene of one of the greatest "fairs" the world has ever seen. The Crystal Palace, or "temple of industry and the arts," was indeed frequently spoken of as the "World's Fair." Our notice of this exhibition, together with that of the Prince Consort's Memorial which now marks its site, we must reserve for a future chapter, when dealing with South Kensington and the various Industrial Exhibitions, of which the Great Exhibition of 1851 may be considered the parent.

Some little amusement and excitement, too, was caused in Parliament, in 1850–1, by an old woman named Anne Hicks, who, having been allowed to hold an apple-stall at the east end of the Serpentine, had by sheer importunity contrived to surround herself with a small hovel, and to convert that again into a cottage. When preparations were being made for holding the World's Fair in the Park, it became important to remove this cottage; but Anne Hicks refused to give up possession, and

---

* See *ante*, p. 49.

was turned out at last only by force. Her grievance was brought before Parliament, but it was explained that she had no legal rights as against the Crown, and the agitation died away, the poor old woman receiving a small compensation. " Many foreigners were in England at the time," writes Mr. Chambers in his " Book of Days," "and the matter afforded them rather a striking proof of the jealousy with which the nation regards any supposed infraction of the rights of private persons by the Government, even in so small a matter as an apple-stall."

In our time the walk by the " Lady's Mile"—as " Rotten Row" is sometimes called—is frequented by the leaders of fashion ; but of late the centre of the Park has come to be looked upon by certain of the working classes as a privileged spot wherein to vent their grievances—real or imaginary—against " the powers that be," and much damage has at times been done by these unruly and disorderly assemblages. On one occasion, in the year 1866, during Mr. Walpole's career as Home Secretary, when the park gates were closed against them, and the right of holding a political meeting in the Park was refused, the mob even went so far as to break down the railings in Park Lane, at the same time doing considerable damage to the shrubs and flowers.

Many of our readers will remember Lord Byron's description of the Park in one of the later cantos of " Don Juan :"—

" Those vegetable puncheons
Call'd parks, where there is neither fruit nor flower
Enough to gratify a bee's slight munchings;
But, after all, they are the only ' bower,'
In Moore's phrase, where the fashionable fair
Can form a slight acquaintance with fresh air."

Thanks to various Chief Commissioners of Public Works and Buildings, it can no longer be said with truth that our parks are wholly destitute of flowers, at least ; for all along the south, the east, and the north of the drives in Hyde Park there are beds of the gayest geraniums and roses in the summer, and in the spring there are brilliant displays of tulips and hyacinths to gladden the eyes of the Londoners.

Cumberland Gate, which, as we have said, stands at the north-eastern corner of the Park, at the western end of Oxford Street, was erected about 1744, at the expense of the inhabitants of Cumberland Place and its neighbourhood, and took its name after the " Butcher" Duke of Cumberland, the hero of Culloden. It was at first com-

monly called Tyburn Gate, from the gallows which stood close by. The original gateway was a mean brick building, comprising an arch with side entrances, and had wooden gates. Here took place, in August, 1821, a disgraceful conflict between the people and the soldiery at the funeral of Queen Caroline, when two persons were killed by shots from the Horse Guards on duty. In the following year the unsightly brick arch and wooden gates were removed, and in their place some handsome iron gates were set up, at a cost of nearly £2,000 ; but in 1851 these gates were removed in order to make room for the marble arch (see page 397) which now occupies the site, and the iron gates placed on each side of it.

The marble arch had, up to that time, stood in front of the chief entrance to Buckingham Palace, bearing the royal banner of England, and carrying the imagination back to that age of chivalry, the departure of which was lamented by Edmund Burke. The arch, which was adapted by Mr. Nash from the Arch of Constantine at Rome, was not included in the design for building the new front of Buckingham Palace. It cost £80,000 ; the metal gates alone cost £3,000. It was originally intended to have been surmounted by an equestrian statue of George IV., by Sir Francis Chantrey. The material is Carrara marble, and it consists of a centre gateway and two side openings. On each face are four Corinthian columns, the other sculpture being a keystone to the centre archway, and a pair of figures in the spandrils, a panel of figures over each side entrance, and wreaths at each end ; these were executed by Flaxman, Westmeath, and Rossi. The centre gates are bronzed, and ornamented with a beautiful scroll-work, with six openings, two filled with St. George and the Dragon, two with " G. R.," and above, two lions *passant gardant*. They were designed and cast by Samuel Parker, of Argyll Street, and are said to be the largest and most superb in Europe, not excepting those of the Ducal Palace at Venice, or of the Louvre at Paris. The frieze and semicircle intended to fill up the archway—the most beautiful part of the design—were unfortunately mutilated in the removal, and could not be restored.

Of Tyburn toll-gate, which stood nearly opposite Cumberland Gate, and at the corner of the Edgware Road and Cumberland Place, and also of the old gallows which stood a little beyond, we shall have to speak in future chapters.

CHAPTER XXXII.

OXFORD STREET, AND ITS NORTHERN TRIBUTARIES.

" Inter fœmineas catervas."—Horace.

Oxford Street in the Last Century—Figg's Theatre—Great Cumberland Place—Lady Buggin, afterwards Duchess of Inverness—Walpole's Musings on Popularity—Hyde Park Place—Charles Dickens' Last Residence in London—The Portman Family—Edgware Road—Bryanston Street—Spanish and Portuguese Jews' Synagogue—Upper Seymour Street and its Noted Residents—Old Quebec Street—Quebec Chapel— The Cripples' Nursery—Upper Berkeley Street—The West London Jewish Synagogue—St. Luke's Church, Nutford Place—The "Yorkshire Stingo"—The Christian Union Almshouses, John Street—Crawford Street—Homer Street—The Cato Street Conspiracy—St. Mary's Church, Bryanston Square—Montagu and Bryanston Squares—Gloucester Place—Portman Square and its Distinguished Residents—Montagu House and the "Blue-Stocking" Club—Mrs. Montagu and the Chimney-sweepers—Difference between Montagu Matthew and Matthew Montagu—Anecdote of Beau Brummell—John Elwes, the Miser—Baker Street—Madame Tussaud's Exhibition of Waxwork—The Baker Street Bazaar—Royal Smithfield Club—Portman Chapel—Roman Catholic Chapel of the Annunciation—York Place—Cardinal Wiseman— Orchard Street.

HAVING turned our backs on the fashionable part of London, and reached Tyburn, we may fairly ask for our readers' pardon if, startled and alarmed at the sights which meet us there, we now seek to travel eastwards, retracing our steps towards Bloomsbury by way of Oxford Street, and noting down, as we pass along, all that there is of interest to be told about its northern tributaries. We shall thus be able to look in upon Mrs. Montagu, in Portman Square, to find Lord and Lady Hertford dispensing the hospitalities of their great house in Manchester Square, and to see how the "princely" Duke of Chandos is getting on, not with bricks and mortar, but with marble and cement, in Cavendish Square, before we find ourselves once more in the dull regions which "fashion" has agreed to leave to artists and lawyers. With these few words by way of preface, we proceed along our way.

Oxford Street follows the line of the Via Trino-bantina, one of the military roads of the Romans, which bounded the north side of what is now Hyde Park, and continued thence to Old Street (Eald Street), in the north of London. Oxford Street extends from the north-east corner of Hyde Park to the junction of Tottenham Court Road with High Street, St. Giles's, where, as we have already stated, the village pound of St. Giles's formerly stood.* The thoroughfare was formerly called the "Ux-bridge Road," "Tyburn Road," and subsequently "Oxford Road," as being the highway to Oxford. Hatton, in 1708, describes it as lying between "St. Giles's pound east, and the lane leading to the gallows west." In a plan published in the above year, the "Lord Mayor's Banqueting House" is shown as standing at the north end of Mill Hill Field, and at the north-east corner of the bridge across Tyburn Brook, which is now covered over by part of Stratford Place. Pennant tells us how that "the Lord Mayor and his brethren of the City used to repair to a building called the City Banqueting House, on the north side of Oxford

Street, on horseback, attended by their ladies in waggons, to inspect the conduits, and then to par-take of their banquet." A view of the old house, as it appeared in 1750, is given on page 408.

In Ralph Aggas' map of London, published in 1560, it is almost needless to say, the space to the north of Oxford Street, then "the way to Ux-bridge," was open country, with fields and hedges, and dotted irregularly with trees; and in Vertue's plan, about a century later, the only building seen between the village of St. Giles's and Primrose Hill is the little solitary church of Marylebone, and still further away in the fields is the little church of St. Pancras, "all alone, old, and weatherbeaten."

Mr. Peter Cunningham says it "is somewhat uncertain when the thoroughfare was first formed into a continuous line of street, and in what year it was first called Oxford Street." Mr. J. T. Smith, in his "Book for a Rainy Day," tells us that "on the front of the first house, No. 1, in Oxford Street, near the second-floor windows, is the following inscription cut in stone: 'OXFORD STREET, 1725.'" This, however, no longer exists. Lysons, in his "Environs of London," remarks that "the row of houses on the north side of Tybourn Road was completed in 1729, and it was then called Oxford Street. About the same time most of the streets leading to Cavendish Square and Oxford Market were built, and the ground was laid out for several others." There is, it appears, says Mr. Cunning-ham, "good reason to suppose that it received its present name at a still earlier date; for a stone let into the wall of the corner of Rathbone Place is inscribed: 'RATHBONE PLACE, OXFORD STREET, 1718.'" In a "Tour through Great Britain, by a Gentleman," published in 1825, it is stated that "A new Bear Garden, called Figg's Theatre, being a stage for the gladiators or prize-fighters, is built on the Tyburn Road. N.B.—The gentlemen of the science taking offence at its being called Tyburn Road, though it really is so, will have it called the Oxford Road." Of Figg's theatre we shall have more to say in a subsequent chapter.

---

* See Vol. III., p. 200.

Facing us at the Marble Arch is Great Cumberland Place, formerly Great Cumberland Street, extending northward from Oxford Street to Bryanston Square. This thoroughfare was commenced about the year 1774, and, like the gate opposite leading into the Park, was named after the Duke of Cumberland, the hero of Culloden. On the east side the houses form a semicircle, the original design having been for a complete circus. Here, in 1826, at No. 5, was living Lady Buggin, the widow of Sir George Buggin, and afterwards the morganatic wife of the Duke of Sussex, when she was styled Lady Cecilia Underwood. In 1840 she was created Duchess of Inverness. She died at Kensington Palace, where she had resided for many years, in 1873.

At No. 3 lived for some time at the commencement of this century, Earl Cathcart, K.T., a distinguished general in the army, and colonel of the 2nd Life Guards. His lordship was Commander-in-Chief of the military forces in the expedition to Copenhagen, and died in 1843.

Here is a public-house bearing a portrait-sign of the Duke of Cumberland. Horace Walpole, in 1747, looking upon this sign, and remembering how such signs had everywhere superseded those of Admiral Vernon, the Duke of Ormonde, and other heroes, muses in his agreeable though cynical style on the fleeting nature of popularity, and compares glory itself to a sign-board!

At the western end of Oxford Road stood Tyburn Turnpike (see page 403), whose double gates commanded the Uxbridge and the Edgware Roads, which here branch off, divided by Connaught Terrace. Of the neighbourhood which lies beyond this point, and which is popularly known as "Tyburnia" (just as the district south of Hyde Park is "Belgravia" in common parlance), we shall have more to say hereafter. At present we shall keep ourselves entirely to the eastward of the Edgware Road, and treat it briefly and cursorily.

Hyde Park Place is the name given to a row of mansions overlooking the Park, and built on the right and left of the entrance to Great Cumberland Place. Here, at No. 5, the house of his friend Mr. Milner-Gibson, Charles Dickens, in the spring of 1870, became for a few months a resident, being obliged to stay in London in order to give his farewell readings at St. James's Hall, though his medical advisers in vain dissuaded him from the attempt. Here he wrote more than one number of "Edwin Drood." He left this house at the end of May for the rest and quiet of Gadshill, where he died suddenly on the 9th of the following month.

The moment that we pass to the north of Oxford Street, we find ourselves in far different latitudes from those in which we have lately been travelling. Owing to the comparatively modern period from which the streets and squares hereabouts date, we no longer have the friendly guidance of the honest old chroniclers, Stow and Strype, or even Pennant; and we no longer have before our eyes that *embarras de richesse* under which we laboured in selecting our materials in treating of the Strand and Whitehall, Pall Mall or Piccadilly. All to the north of Oxford Street was quite a *terra incognita* in the Stuart days, and there are no contemporary notices from the pens of Pepys and Evelyn to enliven our pages. We must, therefore, be grateful for even small mercies, and pick up with a thankful heart such scanty crumbs of information as may be found in stray magazines and books of anecdote biography. There is one advantage, however, and that is, that we shall move over the ground at a somewhat quicker pace.

We may remark, *en passant*, that the names of most of the streets and squares in this vicinity are synonymous with the names of the ground landlords, and, in some cases, of their county residences; such, for instance, as Wyndham Street and Place, Orchard Street, Berkeley Street, Portman Square, Bryanston Street and Square, and Blandford Street. These names, of course, were given with reference to the family and estates of the sole landowner of the district of which we are about to speak in this chapter—namely, Edward Berkeley Portman, Viscount Portman, of Bryanston, near Blandford, in Dorsetshire, who was for many years M.P. for Dorset, and for a short time M.P. for Marylebone. The Portmans were a family of distinction in Somerset in the reign of Edward I., but its most distinguished member was Sir William Portman, Lord Chief Justice of England, who died in 1555.

On turning round the corner into the Edgware Road, we notice that there are two houses on our right hand with balconies and verandas, nearly opposite to Connaught Square. These balconies were built in order to accommodate the sheriffs and other officials who were bound to be present at the executions of criminals, who, during the seventeenth and eighteenth centuries, were "turned off" on the gallows which stood about fifty yards on the other side of the road, occupying the site of one of the houses in Connaught Place, or, according to Mr. Peter Cunningham, of a house in Connaught Square. Of this gallows, and of those who suffered the extreme penalty of the law there, we shall have plenty to tell our readers hereafter.

In the early part of the present century the Edgware Road was void of any connected row of houses beyond those already mentioned; but there were one or two public-houses at the corners of rural cross-roads. At one of these, which stood near the corner of Oxford and Cambridge Terrace, it is said that a messenger of Charles I., who was travelling with dispatches *incognito*, had his saddle ripped open, and was robbed of its contents.

At the time of which we speak, Nutford Place and the other streets which connect Edgware Road

its architecture. The vestibule leads to stone stairs on either side, leading up to the ladies' gallery; while the floor of the synagogue will accommodate about 150 male worshippers.

Upper Seymour Street, the next turning, leading across Great Cumberland Place into Portman Square, was so named after the family of the Seymours, from whom the Portmans descend. Among the distinguished residents of this street have been

THE LORD MAYOR'S BANQUETING-HOUSE, OXFORD ROAD, IN 1750. *From the Crace Collection.* (*See page* 406.)

with Bryanston Square did not exist; and a gentleman then residing still further north in Chapel Street well remembered that from his back drawing-room windows he could see the troops being reviewed in Hyde Park by George III.

Bryanston Street, the first turning in Edgware Road, and extending eastward to Portman Street, was, like the square bearing the same name, so called, as we have shown above, from Bryanstone, in Dorsetshire, the seat of Lord Portman, the ground landlord. The street, which simply consists of some well-built private houses, has no history attached to it to require special mention.

In Upper Bryanston Street is a synagogue, erected for the use of the Spanish and Portuguese Jews residing at the West-end. It is Saracenic in

"Tom" Campbell, the author of the "Pleasures of Memory," who resided at No. 10 whilst editing the *New Monthly Magazine,* and who here lost his wife. The Corsican General, Paoli, who stood as sponsor to the first Emperor Napoleon, lived for some time at the first house, at the corner of Edgware Road. In Croker's "Boswell" appears a letter from Boswell to Lord Thurlow, dated from "General Paoli's, Upper Seymour Street, Portman Square, 24th June, 1784." According to Mr. Peter Cunningham, it was in the drawing-room of No. 45 in this street, in 1820, then the residence of Lady Floyd, that the late distinguished statesman, Sir Robert Peel, was married to Julia, youngest daughter of General Sir John Floyd, Bart.

Connecting the south side of Seymour Street

with Oxford Street, and running parallel with Cumberland Place, is old Quebec Street, which commemorates the capture of Quebec by General Wolfe, in 1759, and probably dates its erection from about that time. Quebec Chapel, so named from the street in which it is situated, is a chapel of ease to Marylebone. It is a square, ugly edifice, dating from 1787, with no pretensions to ecclesiastical fitness, and has been described as nothing

is the West London Synagogue, for the congregation of Jewish "dissenters." The building, though monumental in character, is erected on leasehold land belonging to the Portman estate, and was built in the year 1870. The main portion of the structure occupies back land, and the exterior is consequently unseen from the surrounding streets; but the stone entrance-front in Upper Berkeley Street forms a fitting entrance.

MRS. MONTAGU'S HOUSE, PORTMAN SQUARE. (*See page* 413.)

but a "large room with sash-windows." Among its ministers have been the amiable and accomplished Dean of Canterbury, Dr. Henry Alford; Dr. Goulburn, afterwards Dean of Norwich; and Dr. Magee, who here first acquired the popularity as a preacher which he carried to so great a height as Bishop of Peterborough.

At No. 14 in this street is a charitable institution bearing the name of the Cripples' Nursery. It was established in 1861, and consists of a home, with religious instruction and medical aid, for infant cripples. This charity has a branch establishment at Margate.

Connecting Edgware Road with the north side of Portman Square is Upper Berkeley Street. In this street, close by the corner of Edgware Road,

The synagogue is constructed of brick, and was erected from the designs of Messrs. Davis and Emanuel, at an expense of about £20,000. The edifice is a domical structure, Byzantine in character, and a square in plan. It has a wide gallery along the two sides and western end, the ceiling consisting of a large central dome, and four small domes in the angles, and four great arches covering the side spaces. This ceiling is supported by four piers of clustered columns of Devonshire marble with carved capitals. At the east end of the building is a domed semi-circular recess, or apse, in which is placed the organ and choir, and in the centre of this apse is placed the ark, which has been constructed of inlaid marble-work. A peculiar feature in this building is the placing of the choir at the east end of the building, facing the congregation, and concealing them from the view of the congregation by a screen of marble containing open-work grilles of gilded metal. The decoration is somewhat peculiar. The highest class of decorative art —namely, subject painting, or figure sculpture—is necessarily absent, the Jews, so far as their religious buildings are concerned, reading literally the Second Commandment.

Many special objects in the building were presented to the synagogue by the wealthier members of the congregation, the ark especially being the gift of the ladies of the Goldsmid family. It may be added that the founders of the congregation of Jewish dissenters, by whom this building was erected, left the orthodox Jewish body some thirty years ago, through just such a communal quarrel as caused old Isaac D'Israeli to leave the religion of his fathers. Starting with a small room in Burton Street, their numbers increased, until about twenty years ago they built for themselves a small synagogue in Margaret Street, and since that time the further increase of their congregation rendered necessary the erection of the building now under notice.

In this street Cyrus Redding occupied lodgings during the greater part of his career as sub-editor of the *New Monthly*. It was then on the very verge of the country, the town ending at Connaught Place, or thereabouts, as we have already stated.

Proceeding on our way along the Edgware Road, we pass Nutford Place and Queen Street, both of which terminate in Seymour Place. In Nutford Place is St. Luke's Church, a large Gothic edifice, with a tower ornamented with pinnacles, erected in gratitude for the exemption of this district from the visitation of the cholera in 1849.

The western end of Marylebone Road, between the bottom of Lisson Grove and the top of Oxford and Cambridge Terrace, forms of necessity what we may call our " north-west passage," in reference to this portion of our work. The chief object of interest in this neighbourhood, on the south side of the Marylebone Road, is the celebrated " Yorkshire Stingo" tavern. At the early part of the present century there were tea-gardens and a bowling-green attached to this rural inn, which was much crowded on Sundays, when an admission-fee of sixpence was demanded at its doors. For that a ticket was given, to be exchanged with the waiters for its value in refreshments—a plan very commonly adopted even then in such places of resort, in order to exclude the " roughs " and lower orders, and such as would be sure to stroll about

without spending anything, because they had no money to spend. It was from this house that the London omnibuses commenced running, in 1829, when first introduced by Mr. Shillibeer.

In John Street, through which we commence our return towards Oxford Street, are the Christian Union Almshouses, for the relief of thirty-eight poor and aged persons, in "full communion with some Protestant church." The almshouses were erected in 1832, and are supported by voluntary contributions.

Extending from John Street to Queen Street is a short thoroughfare called Horace Street. This, it is said, was formerly known as Cato Street, a view of which, as it appeared in 1820, has already been given in this work.* A loft over a stable in this thoroughfare, in the early part of the year 1820, formed the head-quarters of Thistlewood and some other assassins, who designed to murder the leading members of the then Administration. This is known to history as the Cato Street Conspiracy. The building contained but two rooms, which could only be entered by a ladder. The conspirators having mustered to the number of twenty-four, they took the precaution of placing a sentinel below, whilst they prepared for their dreadful encounter. We have already given an account of this affair in treating of Grosvenor Square, the intended scene of the massacre.† Mr. R. Rush, who was residing in London at the time of its occurrence as Minister from the United States, speaks of the conspiracy in the following terms, in his " Court of London : "—

"The assassination plot has continued to be a prevailing topic in all circles since its discovery and suppression. It has caused great excitement, it may almost be said some dismay, so foul was its nature, and so near did it appear to have advanced to success. Thanks were offered up at the Royal Chapel, St. James's, for the escape of those whose lives were threatened. Different uses are made of the events, according to the different opinions and feelings of the people in a country where the press speaks what it thinks, and no tongue is tied. The supporters of Government say that it was the offspring of a profligate state of morals among the lower orders, produced by publications emanating from what they called the 'cheap press,' which the late measures of Parliament aimed at putting down ; and added, that it vindicated the necessity and wisdom of those measures. The opponents of Government, who vehemently resisted the measures, insisted in reply, that it was wrong to suppress, or even attempt to interfere with, such publications, since, if every irritated feeling, however unjust might be deemed its causes, were not allowed vent in that way, it would find modes more dangerous."

We learn from Mr. Rush that the convicted prisoners confessed that it was their design, on getting to Lord Harrowby's house, that one of their number should knock at the door with a note in his hand, under pretence of desiring that it should be sent in to his lordship, doing this in such a manner as to cause no suspicion among the passers-by. The rest of the band, from twenty to thirty in number, were to be close at hand, but divided into small groups, so as to be better out of view. The servant who opened the door was to be knocked down by the bearer of the note, when the whole of the band were to rush forward, enter the house, and make for the dining-room, and there have massacred the whole of the ministers and guests, not sparing even the servants if they offered resistance. It is satisfactory to know that this daring gang stood convicted, out of their own lips, of a cool and deliberate murder in design and intention, and that they were not hung without richly deserving their sentence. The conspirators, as we have already mentioned,* were imprisoned in the Tower, and were the last State prisoners lodged there.

Thistlewood was a Lincolnshire man, by birth a gentleman, but reduced by gambling and bill transactions. Cyrus Redding, who met him at Paris, thus speaks of him in his "Recollections:"—" His countenance bespoke indomitable determination. I cannot forget it. He had been subjected to a long imprisonment by Lord Sidmouth, I forget on what account. His unscrupulous character, when driven to extremity, no doubt made him capable of the most revolting crimes." Mr. T. Raikes, in his "Journal," gives the following account of the execution of this villain and his associates:—" It was a fine morning, and the crowd in the Old Bailey was, perhaps, greater than ever was assembled on such an occasion; all the house-tops were covered with spectators; and when we first looked out of the window of the sheriffs' room, there was nothing to be seen but the scaffold, surrounded by an immense ocean of human heads, all gazing upon that one single object. At length the procession issued from the debtors' door, and the six culprits came on, one after the other, and were successively tied up to the gibbet. Thistlewood came first, looking as pale as

death, but without moving a muscle of his features or attempting to utter a word, except that when the rope had been adjusted round the neck of him who was next to him, he said, in a low tone to him, 'We shall soon know the grand secret.' Ings, the butcher, appeared in a great state of excitement, almost as if under the influence of liquor; he gave several huzzas, and shouted out to the crowd, 'Liberty for ever!' twice or thrice; but it was evidently a feint to try to interest the bystanders. The last in this odd rank was a dirty-looking black man, who alone seemed to be impressed with a sense of his awful situation; his lips were in continual motion, and he was evidently occupied in silent prayer. At this moment one of the gentlemen of the press, who had posted himself in the small enclosure close to the foot of the scaffold, looked up to Thistlewood with a paper and pencil in his hand, and said, 'Mr. Thistlewood, if you have anything to say, I shall be happy to take it down and communicate it to the public.' The other made him no answer, but gave him a look. As they were about to be launched into eternity, a well-dressed man on the roof of one of the opposite houses got up from his seat, and looking at Thistlewood, exclaimed, in a very loud but agitated voice, 'God bless you! God Almighty bless you!' Thistlewood slowly turned his head to the quarter whence the voice came, without moving his body, and as slowly reverted to his former position, always with the same fixed impassible countenance. The caps were then pulled down, the drop fell, an after some struggles they all ceased to live. The law prescribed that their heads should be severed from their bodies, and held up to public view as the heads of traitors. The executioner had neglected to bring any instrument for the purpose, and we in the sheriffs' room were horrified at seeing one of the assistants enter, and take from a cupboard a large carving-knife, which was to be used instead of a more regular instrument. When we were able to leave the prison, which was not for some time on account of the immense crowd, I drove to Seymour Place, found —— at breakfast, and gave him an account of the scene."

At the east end of John Street, and extending thence to Baker Street, is Crawford Street, out of which on either side branch a number of small courts and streets which we need not particularise, with one or two exceptions. The first turning on the left in this thoroughfare, running northward into Marylebone Road, is a small street called Homer Row. At the angle of this street and Marylebone Road stands a handsome Gothic edifice of red brick, with stone facings, and with a high-pitched roof and bell turret. This is a Roman Catholic church, dedicated to the Holy Rosary; the mission was commenced in 1855, and the church built in 1870. The ground floor of the edifice is used as a schoolroom.

Passing along Crawford Street, we cross Seymour Place, which forms a direct communication between Marylebone Road and Seymour Street, near its junction with the Edgware Road. Wyndham Place, the next turning eastward on the right, leads into Bryanston Square, on its north side; opposite, on the north side of Crawford Street, is St. Mary's Church, chiefly noticeable for its lofty semi-circular portico, supported by Corinthian columns, above which rises a graduating spire, surmounted by a cross. It was built in 1823, from the designs of Sir Robert Smirke. Here, in 1838, Miss Letitia E. Landon, the author of "Zenana," and other poetical works, and better known in literary circles by her initials, "L. E. L." was privately married, by her brother, to Mr. George Maclean, Governor of Cape Coast Castle, the scene of her early death. A former vicar of this church was the Rev. J. H. Gurney, celebrated for his zeal in education.

Upper Montagu Street, together with Old and New Quebec Streets, forms a direct line of communication, through Montagu Square, between the Marylebone Road and the western portion of Oxford Street. Montagu Square and also Bryanston Square, which is immediately contiguous to it on the west side, were, according to Mr. John Timbs, "built on Ward's Field, and the site of 'Apple Village,' by David Porter, who was once chimney-sweeper to the village of Marylebone." It has been the fashion to decry these two squares as scarcely deserving of the name. Thus, a writer in the *Builder* says, "They are mere oblong slips with houses built in dreary uniformity; they are fortunately out of the way, and few people see them." Bryanston Square, however, certainly does not deserve such criticism. In it resided for many years Mr. Joseph Hume, the economical M.P.; and also Sir Francis Freeling, many years Secretary of the General Post Office.

Gloucester Place, the next turning eastward of Montagu Street, extends from Marylebone Road to the north-west corner of Portman Square; it consists of well-built private houses. Making our way down Gloucester Place, we enter Portman Square, one of the most aristocratic of London neighbourhoods. It was formed, or rather commenced, about the year 1764, on land once belonging to the Knights of St. John of Jerusalem. According to Mr. Peter Cunningham, it is described in the last lease granted by the Prior of that Order

as "Great Gibbet Field, Little Gibbet Field, Hawkfield, and Brock Stand; Tassel Croft, Boy's Croft, and twenty acres Furse Croft, and two closes called Shepcott Hawes, parcel of the manor of Lilestone, in the County of Middlesex." The north side of the square was first built, and it was nearly twenty years before the whole was finished. This square takes its name from that of the proprietor of the land upon which it is built—namely, William Henry Portman, of Orchard-Portman, in Somersetshire, who died in 1796, and was the ancestor of the present Lord Portman. According to Lambert, who wrote in the year 1806, it is "one of the largest and handsomest squares in the metropolis;" though he complains of the want of correspondence—*i.e.*, of uniformity—in the houses which surround it.

Portman Square was built on high ground, with an open prospect to the north, which gave it a name as a peculiarly healthy part of London. Mrs. Montagu, whom we have already mentioned at Hill Street, Berkeley Square, but whose name is, more than any other, particularly associated with this square, called it the Montpelier of England, and said she "never enjoyed such health as since she came to live in it." It is one of the largest and handsomest squares in London for its general effect, but the houses have no architectural character; and the central enclosure is laid out as a shrubbery. They were, however, built with due consideration for the requirements of the wealthy, and were inhabited by a large number of the "quality" at their first building. In 1822 the following members of the nobility were living in the square:—Lord Clifford, Lord Teignmouth, Earl of Beverley, Lord Lovaine, Lord Kenyon, Lord Petre, Earl Manvers, Earl of Scarbrough, Duke of Newcastle, Countess of Pomfret, Lady Owen, Earl Nelson, Dowager Duchess of Roxburghe, Earl of Cardigan, Dowager Countess of Clonmell, and the Dowager Countess of Harcourt. In this same year lived, at No. 5, Mr. Thomas Assheton Smith, of Tedworth, who might truly be called the pattern and type of the old English sportsman.

No. 12 was the town-house of the late Duke of Hamilton, who married the daughter of William Beckford, the author of "Vathek," and who took a pride in showing on his walls some of the finest paintings in the collection of that connoisseur, which he inherited in right of his wife. At No. 6 lived General Sir John Byng, afterwards Field-Marshal the Earl of Strafford.

Early in the present century No. 40 was the residence of the Right Hon. Hugh Elliot; and Lord Garvagh, the possessor of the celebrated

"Aldobrandini Madonna" of Raffaelle, now in the National Gallery, lived at No. 26 for many years.

Sir William Pepperell, the eminent loyalist and royalist, of Rhode Island, in North America, and formerly the richest subject of the Crown in that country, died at his house here, in December, 1816. He was created a baronet in recognition of his loyalty and losses, and a handsome pension was settled on his title. But his son dying before him, his title became extinct, and his pension was not continued to his daughters.

M. Otto, the French ambassador at the Court of St. James's, was living in Portman Square at the time of the short-lived Treaty of Amiens. Peace had long been wished for by the people, and the preliminaries were signed at Lord Hawkesbury's office in Downing Street, on the 1st of October, 1801. On the arrival in London of General Lauriston, first aide-de-camp to Napoleon, with the French ratifications, he was greeted with enthusiastic cheers by a vast concourse of people. Some of the men took the horses from his carriage, and drew him to M. Otto's house with tumultuous expressions of joy.

A very curious print is in existence showing the illumination of M. Otto's house in celebration of this event. On the front was a row of large oil-lamps forming the word "Concord," and on either side were the initials "G. R.," for "George III.," and "R. F.," "République Française"—the first time, no doubt, and probably the last, on which those two names stood united. This illumination was somewhat unfortunate, for a London mob, unwittingly, interpreted "Concord" into "Conquered." All the ambassador's windows were smashed in consequence. When the word "Concord" was removed, its place was supplied by "Amitié;" but the stupid mob read this as "Enmity," and insisted on its removal also. Mr. Planché, who was present, writes: "The storm again raged with redoubled fury. Ultimately, what ought to have been done at first was done: the word 'Peace' was displayed, and so peace was restored to Portman Square for the evening."

The chief interest of Portman Square, however, centres in the large house—lately rebuilt or re-cased with red brick—standing by itself in a garden at the north-west corner; this was originally built for the once celebrated Mrs. Montagu, of "Blue-stocking" notoriety, whose memory has of late years been revived by Dr. Doran, by the publication of some of her letters in a volume entitled, "A Lady of the Last Century." As we have stated in a previous chapter, this distinguished lady re-

moved hither from Hill Street, Berkeley Square, a few years after the death of her husband, Edward Montagu, of whose family Lord Rokeby is the head.

Elizabeth Robinson—for such was Mrs. Montagu's maiden name—was born at York, in 1720, and, as we learn from Dr. Doran's interesting book, she was a lively girl, loving fun and pursuing learning, so that the Duchess of Portland nicknamed her *La petite Fidget*. In 1742 she married Edward Montagu, M.P., a mathematician of eminence, and a coal-owner of great wealth, after which event she became more sober, and told her friend the duchess that her "fidgetations" were much spoiled. She became a power in the literary world, and was the founder, or, at all events, one of the chief leaders, of the celebrated "Blue-Stocking Club." Her house in Hill Street, as we have already shown, became a favourite resort of statesmen, poets, and wits; and the young aspirant for fame felt that he had his foot on the first rung of the ladder when he was invited to her table. Indeed, her name will be known to all our readers as emphatically "the Englishwoman of letters" of the eighteenth century, for in that respect she stood unrivalled. Let us look for a moment at her as portrayed in 1776, by the pen of Sir N. W. Wraxall. He writes: "At the time of which I speak, the 'Gens de Lettres,' or 'Blue Stockings' as they were commonly termed, formed a very numerous, powerful, and compact phalanx in the midst of London. . . . Mrs. Montagu was then the Madame du Deffand of the English capital; and her house constituted the central point of union for all those persons who were already known, or who sought to become known, by their talents and productions. Her supremacy, unlike that of Madame du Deffand, was indeed established on more solid foundations than those of intellect, and rested on more tangible materials than any which her 'Essay on Shakespeare' could furnish her. . . . Impressed, probably from the suggestions of her own deep knowledge of the world, with a deep conviction of that great truth laid down by Molière, which no man of letters ever disputed, that '*Le vrai Amphytrion est celui chez qui l'on dine,*' Mrs. Montagu was accustomed to open her house to a large company of both sexes, whom she frequently entertained at dinner. A service of plate, and a table plentifully covered, disposed her guests to admire the splendour of her fortune, not less than the lustre of her talents. She had found the same results flowing from the same causes during the visit which she made to Paris, after the Peace of 1763, where she displayed to the astonished *literati* of that metropolis the extent of her pecuniary as well as of her mental resources. As this topic formed one of the subjects most gratifying to her, she was easily induced to launch out on it with much apparent complacency. The eulogiums lavished on her repasts, and the astonishment expressed at the magnitude of her income, which countenance bespoke intelligence, and her eyes were accommodated to her cast of features, which had in them something satirical and severe, rather than amiable and inviting. She possessed great natural cheerfulness, and a flow of animal spirits; loved to talk, and talked well on almost every subject; led the conversation, and was qualified to

MADAME TUSSAUD. (*See page* 419.)

appeared prodigiously augmented by being transformed from pounds sterling into French livres, seemed to have afforded her as much gratification as the panegyrics bestowed upon the 'Essay on the Genius and Writings of Shakespeare.'

"Mrs. Montagu, in 1776, verged towards her sixtieth year; but her person, which was thin, spare, and in good preservation, gave her an appearance of less antiquity. From the infirmities often attendant on advanced life she seemed to be almost wholly exempt. All the lines of her preside in her circle, whatever subject of discourse was started; but her manner was more dictatorial and sententious than conciliating or diffident. There was nothing feminine about her; and though her opinions were usually just, as well as delivered in language suited to give them force, yet the organ which conveyed them was not musical. Destitute of taste in disposing the ornaments of her dress, she nevertheless studied or affected those aids more than would seem to have become a woman professing a philosophic mind intent on higher

MARYLEBONE IN 1740. (*From an Old Print.*)

pursuits than the toilet. Even when approaching to fourscore, this female weakness still accompanied her ; nor could she relinquish her diamond necklace and bows, which, like Sir William Draper's 'blushing riband,' commemorated by 'Junius,' formed of evenings the perpetual ornament of her emaciated person. I used to think that these glittering appendages of opulence sometimes helped to dazzle the disputants whom her arguments might not always convince, or her literary reputation intimidate. That reputation had not as yet received the rude attack made on it by Dr. Johnson at a subsequent period, when he appears to have treated with much irreverence her 'Essay on Shakespeare,' if we may believe Boswell. Notwithstanding the defects and weaknesses that I have enumerated, she possessed a masculine understanding, enlightened, cultivated, and expanded by the acquaintance of men as well as of books. Many of the most illustrious persons in rank no less than in ability, under the reigns of George II. and III., had been her correspondents, friends, companions, and admirers. Pulteney, Earl of Bath, whose portrait hung over the chimney-piece in her drawing-room, and George, the first Lord Lyttelton, so eminent for his genius, were among the number. She was constantly surrounded by all that was distinguished for attainments or talents, male or female, English or foreign ; and it would be almost ungrateful in me not to acknowledge the gratification derived from the conversation and intercourse of such a society."

Lord Bath thought there never was a more perfect being than Mrs. Montagu, and Edmund Burke was inclined to agree with him. Hannah More describes her as combining "the sprightly vivacity of fifteen with the judgment and experience of a Nestor ; " and Cowper, after he had read her "Essay on the Genius of Shakespeare," no longer wondered that she stood "at the head of all that is called learned."

Boswell tells us that when Reynolds, Garrick, Johnson, Goldsmith, and a knot of literary friends were dining with him in Old Bond Street in 1769, and mention was made of Mrs. Montagu's "Essay on Shakespeare" by Reynolds, who remarked that it "did her honour," Dr. Johnson replied, sharply, "Yes, sir, it does *her* honour, but it would do honour to nobody else. . . . I will venture to say that there is not one sentence of true criticism in her book." And yet the burly doctor was not above accepting the hospitality of the lady of whom he spoke thus lightly ; but then it must be remembered that it was Mrs. Montagu who made the witty and most truthful remark, that "were an

angel called upon to give the *imprimatur* to Dr. Johnson's works, they would not have to be curtailed by a single line."

On another occasion, as his biographer informs us, Johnson had formed one of a party one evening at Mrs. Montagu's, where a splendid company had assembled, consisting of the most eminent literary characters. "I thought," adds Boswell, "he seemed highly pleased with the respect and attention that were shown him ; and asked him, on our return home, if he was not 'highly *gratified* by his visit.' 'No, sir,' said he, 'not highly *gratified ;* yet I do not recollect to have passed many evenings *with fewer objections.*'"

The Blue-Stocking Club was the name given to a society of ladies who met at Mrs. Montagu's house, which had for its object the substitution of the pleasures of rational conversation for cards and other frivolities. The name, as Mr. Forbes tells us, in his "Life of Beattie," originated in this manner :—

"It is well known that Mrs. Montagu's house was at that time (1771) the chosen resort of many of those of both sexes most distinguished for rank, as well as classical taste and literary talent, in London. This society of eminent friends consisted, originally, of Mrs. Montagu, Mrs. Vesey, Miss Boscawen, and Mrs. Carter ; Lord Lyttelton, Mr. Pulteney, Horace Walpole, and Mr. Stillingfleet. To the latter gentleman, a man of great piety and worth, and author of some works in natural history, &c., this constellation of talents owed that whimsical appellation of 'Bas Bleu.' Mr. Stillingfleet being somewhat of a humorist in his habits and manners, and a little negligent in his dress, literally wore grey stockings ; from which circumstance Admiral Boscawen used, by way of pleasantry, to call them 'The Blue-Stocking Society,' as if to intimate that when these brilliant friends met, it was not for the purpose of forming a dressed assembly. A foreigner of distinction hearing the expression, translated it literally 'Bas Bleu,' by which these meetings came to be afterwards distinguished." This account is corroborated, we may here remark, by Forbes, in his "Life of Beattie," almost in the very words here used.

If we may rely on the statement of John Timbs, in his amusing sketches of "Clubs and Club Life," the earliest mention of a Blue Stocking, or *Bas Bleu, coterie* is to be found in "a Greek comedy entitled *The Banquet of Plutarch*," but which we rather imagine to be the "Symposium of Plato." He adds, "The term as applied to ladies of high literary tastes, has been traced by Mills, in his 'History of Chivalry,' to 'the Société de la Calza, formed at Venice in A.D. 1400, when consistently with the character of the Italians of marking academies and other intellectual associations by some external sign of folly, the members when they met in literary discussion were distinguished by the colour of their stockings. These colours were sometimes fantastically blended; and at other times a single colour, especially blue, prevailed.' The Société de la Calza lasted till 1590, when the foppery of Italy took some other symbol. The rejected title then crossed the Alps, and found a congenial soil in Parisian society, and particularly branded female pedantry. It then passed from France to England, and for a while marked the vanity of the small advances in literature in female *coteries.*" So far Mr. John Timbs.

Boswell, who writes, in his "Life of Johnson," under date 1781, gives a very similar account of the matter to that of Mr. Forbes, already quoted, in the following terms :—"About this time it was much the fashion for several ladies to have evening assemblies, where the fair sex might participate in conversation with literary and ingenious men animated by a desire to please. One of the most eminent members of these societies was a Mr. Stillingfleet (a grandson of the bishop), whose dress was remarkably grave; and in particular it was observed that he wore blue stockings. Such was the excellence of his conversation, and his absence was felt so great a loss, that it used to be said, 'We can do nothing without the blue stockings!' and thus by degrees the title was established." Miss Hannah More has admirably described a Blue-Stocking Club in her "Bas Bleu," a poem in which many of the persons who were most conspicuous there are mentioned; and Horace Walpole speaks of this production as a "charming poetic familiarity, called 'the Blue-Stocking Club!'"

The circle at Mrs. Montagu's used to include nearly all the persons of her time who were celebrated in art, science, or literature, including not only Boswell and Johnson—the latter of whom, in the presence of ladies, forgot his rough and rude manners—but Miss Burney, the author of "Evelina," and also Dr. Monsey, of Chelsea College, the fashionable physician, who used to send to his lady-hostess the compliment of a poem as often as her birthday returned.

After thirty-three years of married life, Edward Montagu left his distinguished wife a widow well provided for, with an income of £7,000 a year. She soon afterwards entertained thoughts of leaving Hill Street for the more northern district of Marylebone, and decided on building for herself a mansion in Portman Square. During its erection, it is related, she watched its progress with much interest. In one of her letters, Mrs. Montagu says, "I will get the better of my passion for my new house, which is almost equal to that of a lover to a mistress whom he thinks very handsome and very good, and such as will make him enjoy the dignity of life with ease;" and in another she writes, "It is an excellent house, finely situated, and just such as I have always wished, but never hoped to have."

In the year 1781, just six years after the death of her husband, the mansion was ready for her occupation, and she at once proceeded to transfer her household goods hither. Some three years previously, as we learn from one of her letters, she had "bought a large glass at the French ambassador's sale, and some other things for my new house, pretty cheap." One of the rooms in the new house was ornamented in a novel manner with "feather hangings," and Mrs. Montagu begged all sorts of birds' feathers from her friends. She tells one correspondent that "the brown tails of partridges are very useful, though not so brilliant as some others;" and another she asks for "the neck and breast feathers of the stubble goose. Things homely and vulgar are sometimes more useful than the elegant, and the feathers of a goose may be better adapted to some occasions than the plumes of the phœnix." On this unique room, where Mrs. Montagu held her court, Cowper wrote, in 1788, some lines commencing as follows :—

> "The birds put off their every hue
> To dress a room for Montagu;
> The peacock sends his heavenly dyes,
> His rainbows and his starry eyes;
> The pheasant, plumes which round infold
> His mantling neck with downy gold;
> The cock his arch'd tail's azure show;
> And, river-blanched, the swan his snow;
> All tribes beside of Indian name,
> That glossy shine or vivid flame,
> Where rises and where sets the day,
> Whate'er they boast of rich and gay,
> Contribute to the gorgeous plan,
> Proud to advance it all they can.
> This plumage neither dashing shower
> Nor blasts that shake the dripping bower,
> Shall drench again or discompose,
> But screen'd from every storm that blows,
> It boasts a splendour ever new,
> Safe with protecting Montagu."

The excitement that seems to have pervaded the mind of Mrs. Montagu during the erection of her new house, and the satisfaction which she evinced on its completion, does not appear to have worn off after she took up her residence there, notwithstanding that she was then getting well advanced in years, for we find her afterwards writing :—"I am a great deal younger, I think, since I came into my new house; from its cheerfulness, and from its admirable conveniences, less afraid of growing old. My friends and acquaintances are much pleased with it." In this last particular she was quite correct, for Walpole, who was not over-prone to praise the hobbies of others, wrote as follows to Mason:—"On Tuesday, with the Harcourts, at Mrs. Montagu's new palace, and was much surprised. Instead of vagaries, it is a noble, simple edifice. Magnificent, yet no gilding. It is grand, not tawdry, not larded, embroidered, and pomponned with shreds and remnants, and *clinquant* like the harlequinades of Adam, which never let the eye repose an instant."

Mrs. Montagu, however, used to give here, not only splendid entertainments to the Blue-Stocking Club and to a large circle of literary friends and persons of the highest distinction, but also annually, on the 1st of May, a feast on the lawn before her doors to all the chimney-sweepers in London. A writer in *Cassell's Magazine*, for May 24, 1873, remarks: "It is not generally known that this celebration took its rise in a case of kidnapping which occurred—not to one of her children, for she never had any, but to some member of her own or of her husband's family. It is said that the boy whose restoration she thus commemorated was stolen by chimney-sweeps when only three or four years old, and was brought back unintentionally to the house by some members of the sooty confraternity, when sent for to sweep the chimneys of her town mansion. If so, the only wonder is that none of our modern versifiers have seized on the incident as the subject of a poem."

The Blue-Stocking gatherings, however, did not thrive very long in the new house, for many of their chief supporters had passed away. Mrs. Montagu's breakfasts, however, were continued; but they became more sumptuous, and her rooms were often overcrowded. In 1788 Mrs. Montagu adopted giving teas, a fashion introduced from France by the Duke of Dorset. Three years before Cumberland had written an essay in the *Observer* on the assemblies at Montagu House, in which he lightly satirises the hostess as "Vanessa," and her assembly as the "Feast of Reason." Cowper afterwards more politely wrote:—

> "There genius, learning, fancy, wit,
> Their ruffled plumage calm refit."

In the year 1800 Mrs. Montagu died, when the mansion passed to her nephew, Mr. Matthew Montagu, who had taken that surname in lieu of his patronymic Robinson, on being made heir to her estate. In Sir N. W. Wraxall's "Memoirs of his

Own Times," there is an amusing anecdote relating to the confusion as to this gentleman's name, after he entered the House of Commons. There appears to have been some difficulty in distinguishing between Matthew Montagu and Montagu Matthew, until "General Matthew himself thus defined the distinction: 'I wish it to be understood,' said he, 'that there is no more likeness between Montagu Matthew and Matthew Montagu than between a chestnut-horse and a horse-chestnut.'"

After Mrs. Montagu's death the house was for some time occupied by the Turkish ambassador, who erected in the garden a "kiosk," or movable temple, where he used to sit and smoke in state, surrounded by his Eastern friends. In the year 1835 Montagu House is given as the address of the Right Hon. Henry Goulburn, M.P., Chancellor of the Exchequer under Sir Robert Peel, who married a daughter of Lord Rokeby, one of the Montagus. The mansion, however, remained in the possession of the Montagu family down to the year 1874, when the lease having expired, it has reverted into the hands of the ground-landlord, Lord Portman, whose family have made it their London residence. The pleasant memory of Mrs. Montagu, however, still survives in the Square, Place, and Street named after her.

In connection with Portman Square, a laughable anecdote is told concerning Beau Brummell, which may bear repeating. It was first related in the *New Monthly Magazine*. It appears that Brummell was once at an evening party in the square. On the removal of the cloth, the snuff-boxes made their appearance, and Brummell's was particularly admired; it was handed round, and a gentleman, finding it somewhat difficult to open, incautiously applied a dessert-knife to the lid. Poor Brummell was on thorns; at last he could not contain himself any longer, and addressing the host, said, with his characteristic quaintness, "Will you be good enough to tell your friend that my snuff-box is not an oyster?"

"The neighbourhood," writes Malcolm, in 1807, is distinguished beyond all London for its regularity, the breadth of its streets, and the respectability of the inhabitants, the majority of whom are titled persons, and those of the most ancient families."

One of the largest builders of houses in this neighbourhood was John Elwes, the well-known miser and M.P., who is said to have made a very large addition to his fortune by building speculations, especially about Portman Street, which opens into Oxford Street from the south-west corner of the square. In this street Queen Caroline took up her residence, in 1820, in the house of Lady

Anne Hamilton, one of her Ladies of the Bed-chamber.

On the east side of Portman Square, extending north and south, are Baker Street and Orchard Street. The former street, which runs into the Marylebone Road, was named after Sir Edward Baker, of Ranston, a neighbour of the Portmans, in Dorsetshire, and who seems to have lent Mr. Portman a helping hand in developing the capacities of his London estate. It consisted, at the commencement of this century, chiefly of private houses, now, however, mostly turned to business purposes. At No. 64 in this street, in the year 1800, was living Lord Camelford, who, four years later, was killed in a duel with a Mr. Best, in the grounds behind Holland House. In the year 1820 the Right Hon. Henry Grattan, the distinguished Irish orator, died at his residence in this street.

In 1826 No. 3 was in the occupation of Lord William Lennox. Mr. Thomas Spring Rice, M.P., afterwards Lord Monteagle, was at that time living in this street; and No. 69 was the residence of John Braham, the singer, already mentioned by us in our account of St. James's Theatre.*

This street has at various times been the *locale* of exhibitions of a popular character, which have come and gone, and their memory soon perished. One, however, has at all events remained, and shown that it has in it the elements of permanence, and of this we will now proceed to speak. Madame Tussaud's exhibition of wax-work figures of the celebrities of the past and present age has been established in Baker Street for a period of forty years. In our account of Fleet Street we have noticed the wax-works of Mrs. Salmon,† which have passed away, while those of Madame Tussaud seem destined to survive the present era. They were originally commenced in Paris about the year 1780, and brought, in 1802, to London, where they formed for a time the chief attraction of what is now the Lyceum, in the Strand, and after-wards at the Hanover Square Rooms. Madame Tussaud subsequently travelled with her exhibition from town to town, and in the course of twelve years succeeded in forming a goodly collection and a small sum of money. She then resolved to visit Ireland; but in the transit the vessel in which she had embarked her all was wrecked, and with great difficulty the lives of the passengers were saved; so that when she landed at Cork with her boys she found herself penniless. She then began the world anew, and this time with still greater success; and thus she was, as it were, twice the architect

of her own fortune. In 1833 she came again to London, and founded her "unrivalled" collection in Baker Street; and it has since gone on increasing, till it now includes upwards of 300 specimens, ranging from William the Conqueror down to the Duchess of Edinburgh and the impostor Arthur Orton. Of the founder of this collection, Madame Tussaud, who died in 1850, at the age of ninety, we know that she was a native of Berne, in Switzerland, and that when a child she was taught the art of modelling figures in wax by an uncle. Coming to Paris, she taught drawing and modelling to Madame Elizabeth, the daughter of Louis XVI. and of Marie Antoinette, and mixed in the best society of the French capital, where she became acquainted with Voltaire, Rousseau, La Fayette, Mirabeau, and the other heads of the party opposed to royalty. She found it convenient, however, to accept the hospitality of England, and accordingly settled here as a refugee.

The exhibition is approached through a small hall, and by a wide staircase, which leads to a saloon at its summit, richly adorned by a radiant combination of arabesques, artificial flowers, and mirrored embellishments. From the saloon the great room is at once entered. This is a gorgeous apartment—in fact, almost an "exhibition" in itself. Its walls are panelled with plate-glass, and richly decorated with draperies, and burnished gilt ornaments in the Louis Quatorze style. The principal statues and groups are placed round the four sides of the room, and the larger scenic combinations of figures in the centre of the room. The objects exhibited here are constantly varied, according to the public interest which they excite. Some, however, are shown *en permanence*, being never out of date. Of these the most noteworthy are the recumbent effigies of Wellington and Napoleon; of Henry VIII. and his six wives; Queen Victoria, the Prince Consort, and the different members of the royal family; Voltaire (taken from life a few months before his death), and a coquette of the period; Lord Nelson, the cast taken from his face; and a series of the kings and queens of England, from William the Conqueror to Queen Victoria. The apartment called the "Hall of Kings" has a ceiling painted by Thornhill; and in the richly-gilt chamber adjoining is George IV. in his coronation robes, which, with two other velvet robes, cost, it is said, £18,000; the chair is the "homage-chair" used at the coronation. The "Napoleon" room contains an interesting collection of trophies and relics connected with the first emperor, besides a fine series of portraits of the Bonaparte family. The last apartment entered, which bears the not very pleasant-sounding name of the "Chamber of Horrors," contains, as may be inferred, an array of portrait-models of some of the greatest criminals of the age, including those of the Mannings, Green-acre, and Wainwright type. Here, too, are casts of the bleeding and dying heads of Robespierre, Marat, Fouquier, and various horrible relics and mementos, even to a model of the guillotine itself. Although to view this chamber an extra charge is

in his "Curiosities of Literature," published in 1791. The author, after mentioning several attempts to produce exhibitions of wax-work in London, though not very successful ones, adds the following :— "There was a work of this kind which Menage has noticed, and which must have appeared a little miracle. In the year 1675 the Duke of Maine received a gilt cabinet, about the size of a mode-rate table. On the door was inscribed *The Chamber*

THE OLD MANOR-HOUSE, MARY-LE-BONE, IN THE TIME OF QUEEN ELIZABETH. *From an Old Print.* (*See page 429.*)

made, such is the love of the marvellous, that but few persons decline to enter it, the ladies especially liking to "have their flesh made to creep."

Ingenious as these wax-works were, they are but a proof of the old saying, that there is nothing new under the sun ; for we have already been intro-duced* to the wax-work effigies of our sovereigns, &c., in Westminster Abbey ; and we read in the first volume of the "Entertaining Correspondent," published in 1739, a long account of a group of wax-work figures to be seen in the Maze at Amsterdam, representing the scene of the Nativity of our Lord in the manger at Bethlehem ; and the proverb is further confirmed by Mr. Isaac D'Israeli,

of Wit. The inside displayed an alcove and a long gallery. In an arm-chair was seated the figure of the duke himself, composed of wax, the resemblance the most perfect imaginable. On one side stood the Duke de la Rochefoucault, to whom he presented a paper of verses for his examination. M. de Marcillac, and Bossuet, Bishop of Meaux, were standing near the arm-chair. In the alcove Madame de Thianges and Madame de la Fayette sat retired, reading a book. Boileau, the satirist, stood at the door of the gallery, hindering seven or eight bad poets from entering. Near Boileau stood Racine, who seemed to beckon to La Fontaine to come forward. All these figures were formed of wax, and this imitation must have been at once curious and interesting."

* See Vol. III., p. 446.

The basement-floor of the building is devoted to other purposes, and is known as the "Baker Street Bazaar." It was originally called the "Portman Bazaar," and had its chief entrance in King Street. It was at first established for the sale of horses; but carriages, harness, furniture, and other household goods are the only commodities now exhibited for sale. Here, in 1829, was given what the advertisements style a "magnificent exhibition of

Show, from 1839 down to 1861, when it was removed to the Agricultural Hall at Islington. The late Prince Consort was an exhibitor on several occasions, and carried off several prizes here in 1844, and again in 1850.

From Mr. Gibbs's "History of the Origin and Progress of the Smithfield Club," we learn that it was founded in 1798 by a party of noblemen and gentlemen, including the Duke of Bedford, Lords

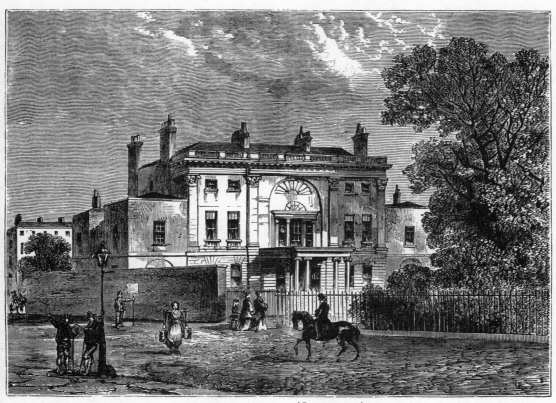

MANCHESTER HOUSE. (*See page* 424.)

musical and mechanical automata, comprising nearly twenty different subjects, including the celebrated musical lady, juvenile artist, magician, rope-dancer, and walking figure; also a magnificent classic vase, made by order of Napoleon; together with a serpent, birds, insects, and other subjects of natural history; the whole displaying, by their exact imitations of animated nature, the wonderful powers of mechanism." Here, about the year 1845, was started a field of artificial ice for skating, but it did not take with the public, and was soon given up. It is not a little singular, that the attempt to anticipate the pleasures of the skating-rinks, now so generally popular with the rising generation, should have been a failure. Here, too, the Royal Smithfield Club held its annual Cattle

Somerville and Winchilsea, and Sir Joseph Banks. Its first exhibitions were held in Smithfield, then in Barbican, and in one or two other places in that neighbourhood; and it did not move westwards hither till 1839, when the receipts taken at the doors of the bazaar amounted to only £300. Her Majesty paid a visit to the cattle show here in 1844, and the Prince Consort, who had become a member of the Smithfield Club on his marriage, carried off several prizes at the annual exhibitions held here with his cattle bred at his model farm in Windsor Park. The members of the Smithfield Club made an award of prizes, in the shape of gold and silver medals, silver cups, &c., for the successful competitors with live stock, agricultural implements, &c.

On the east side of Baker Street, at the corner of Adam Street, is Portman Chapel, a chapel of ease to Marylebone Parish Church. Like most of its neighbours, it is a dull, heavy, unecclesiastical-looking structure, and offers little or no subject for remark.

The streets which run crosswise between Gloucester Place and Baker Street, on its western side, such as George, King, Dorset, Crawford, and York Streets, if they have about them little of personal or historic interest, and are even less remarkable in an architectural point of view, at all events bear testimony to the loyalty of the House of Portman, and their attachment to their native county of Dorset. Between King Street and George Street, in a sort of mews and side passage, "gracefully retreating" from the public view, as became a chapel of Roman Catholics, when they lay under penal laws, but nestling safely under the wing of the French ambassador's house, is the Chapel of the Annunciation. This chapel was built in the reign of George III., and has always been the place whither the sovereigns of France have resorted to hear mass when in this country, and where masses are said for the repose of the souls of French royalty after death ; and though a small and poor edifice, and concealed in a back street which is little better than a mews, it has a history of its own which cannot be omitted here. It was founded by some of the *emigrés* who sought an asylum in England on the outbreak of the French Revolution in 1791, and who opened it in 1793, having previously celebrated the divine offices in a house in Paddington Street, not far off. It is said that many of the clergy, and even members of the French court, aided the workmen with their own hands in building the walls. It was solemnly blessed and dedicated on the 15th of March, 1799. Here most, if not all, of the Bourbon kings and princes who have come to England as exiles or as visitors—Louis XVIII., Charles X., Louis Philippe and Queen Amelie, the Duchesse d'Angoulême, &c. —have always heard mass ; to say nothing of the Emperor Louis Napoleon, the Empress Eugenie, and their son. Here have been preached the *oraisons funèbres* of the Abbé Edgworth, of the Duc d'Enghien, and of very many royal and distinguished personages of foreign countries, such as the King of Portugal, Queen Mary Josephine- of Savoy, Chateaubriand, Count de Montalembert, and others. In this chapel the body of the Duc de Montpensier lay in state, previous to its interment in Westminster Abbey. Here courses of sermons have been annually preached, and "Retreats" have been given, from time to time, by the most eloquent of French preachers, such as Père Ravignan, Père Gratry, and Père Lacordaire. Attached to the chapel are many religious and charitable confraternities, &c., including a branch of the Society of St. Vincent de Paul, for the benefit of the French poor of the metropolis.

York Place is the name given to the last twenty or thirty houses at the upper end of Baker Street, where it joins the Marylebone Road. The houses, which were built about the year 1800, are fine and commodious. At his residence here, in February, 1865, died his Eminence Cardinal Wiseman, at the age of sixty-two. The Cardinal removed his archiepiscopal residence hither from Golden Square, as we have stated in a previous chapter. Born at Seville, in Spain, in the year 1802, Nicholas Wiseman was the son of Irish parents, descended from the younger branch of the ancient Essex family of Sir William Wiseman, Bart. He entered the priesthood at the age of twenty-three ; in the following year he was appointed Vice-Rector of the English College at Rome, and in the year 1827 he became Professor of Oriental Literature. In 1840 he was chosen Coadjutor-Bishop to Dr. Walsh, then the Vicar-Apostolic of the Central District in England. He afterwards for some years presided over St. Mary's College, Oscott ; and on the transference of Dr. Walsh to the post of Pro-Vicar Apostolic of the London District, Dr. Wiseman was again the coadjutor. On the establishment of the Roman Catholic hierarchy in 1850, Dr. Walsh having died in the meanwhile, Dr. Wiseman was nominated Archbishop of Westminster, and at the same time elevated to the cardinalate. His eminence was acknowledged as one of the first scholars in Europe ; he was also a great Biblical scholar, a judicious critic, and a proficient in almost every branch of science. His successor in the see of Westminster, Cardinal Manning, lived in the same house from 1865 down to 1872. The house is now the " Bedford College for Ladies."

In York Place lived for some time Mr. Edward Hodges Baily, R.A., the sculptor. He executed the *bassi relievi* surrounding the throne-room at Buckingham Palace, and also designed several of the figures on the Marble Arch. Among his principal works are " Eve Listening," the group of " The Graces," and " The Fatigued Huntsman ; " and among his most recent works are statues of Mansfield and Fox, erected in St. Stephen's Hall, in the Houses of Parliament ; and a statue of " Genius," from Milton's Arcades, for the Mansion House of London. His last work was a bust of Mr. Hepworth Dixon. Mr. Baily died in 1867.

Midway between Marylebone Road and Crawford

Street, and extending from York Place westward into Seymour Place, is a broad thoroughfare called York Street; but, like the two or three small streets connecting it with Marylebone Road, its history is a blank. Seymour Place and Street took their designation from the original family name of Lord Portman's ancestor, who was not a Portman, or even a Berkeley by birth, but a Seymour, but took the name of Portman on inheriting the estate of Orchard-Portman.

Making our way back into Oxford Street, we pass through Orchard Street, which runs from the south-east corner of Portman Square, and is called after Orchard-Portman, in Somersetshire, one of the seats of Lord Portman. Here Sheridan, soon after his marriage with the beautiful Miss Linley, took his first town-house, and here he wrote *The Rivals* and *The Duenna*.

There used formerly to be some barracks between Portman Street and Orchard Street; they were removed about the year 1860, and Granville Place built on their site.

In Oxford Street, in the immediate neighbourhood of Orchard Street, was Fladong's Hotel, which in the days of the Regency acquired some celebrity. Captain Gronow, in his "Reminiscences," speaks of it as mostly frequented by "old salts," as at that time there was no club for sailors.

CHAPTER XXXIII.

OXFORD STREET.—NORTHERN TRIBUTARIES (*continued*).

"Oh! who will repair
Unto Manchester Square?"—*T. Moore.*

Duke Street—Somerset and Lower Seymour Streets—The Samaritan Hospital—Manchester Square—The Prince Regent and the Marquis of Hertford—Theodore Hook on the Ladder of Fame—Talleyrand and other Distinguished Residents in Manchester Square—Hinde Street—Thayer Street—A "Fast-Living" Earl—Spanish Place and the Roman Catholic Chapel—Manchester Street—Joanna Southcote—Death of Lady Tichborne—Dorset Street—Charles Babbage and his Calculating Machines—Paddington Street—The Cemeteries—George Canning—Historical Remarks concerning the Parish of Marylebone—Marylebone Lane—Nancy Dawson—The Old Manor House—The Parish Church—Devonshire Terrace, and Charles Dickens' Residence—Nottingham Place—Colonel Martin Leake—The Workhouse—Marylebone Road—A Batch of Charitable Institutions—The Police-court—Marylebone Gardens—Dangerous State of the Neighbourhood—Gallantry of Dick Turpin—Demolition of the Gardens—Wimpole Street—Stratford Place—Archæological Discoveries in Oxford Street—The Deaf and Dumb Association—Laurie and Marner's Coachbuilding Establishment.

As in the previous chapter we have pointed out that most of the streets and squares through which we have passed have been named with direct reference to Lord Portman, his family, and his property, so we shall find in the locality we are about to enter the same with reference to the ducal house of Portland, and to that of Harley, Earl of Oxford.

Duke Street, through which we now pass on our way northward, leads direct into Manchester Square, and was so named in honour of the Duke of Manchester, to whom the square itself owes its origin. Of Somerset Street, the first thoroughfare crossing Duke Street, there is little or nothing to record. In Lower Seymour Street, which runs from Duke Street westward into Portman Square, a valuable freehold property, consisting of two houses, was purchased in 1875, through the influence of Lady Petre, for the purposes of establishing a night home for girls and unmarried women of good character. This charity is to be combined in management with a *crèche*, or infant nursery, in Bulstrode Street, on the east side of Manchester Square. Another charitable institution in this street is the Samaritan Hospital for Women and Children, which was established in 1847, and is supported entirely by voluntary contributions. The hospital provides for "the reception of poor women afflicted with diseases peculiar to their sex, where they have home comforts and hospital treatment without publicity." Attendance is also furnished to poor married women at their own homes in peculiar cases. Close by this hospital is the Quebec Institute, or, as it is sometimes called, Seymour Hall; it is a building where miscellaneous lectures, concerts, &c., are held. In 1835 the Right Hon. Sir John Sinclair, M.P., the eminent writer on agriculture, was a resident in this street. He was President of the Board of Agriculture for Scotland. In this capacity a good story is told of him. He was vain and ambitious enough to tell Pitt that the head of such a board ought to have a peerage. Pitt affected not to understand him, but treated his remark as equivalent to a resignation, and nominated Lord Somerville to the post.

"Manchester Square," observes a writer in the *Builder*, "was erected soon after Portman Square, on a site which had been previously proposed for a square, with a church in the centre, to be called Queen Anne's Square." Her Majesty's death, however, threw a damp upon the suggestion. The ground, after lying waste for a time, was taken by the Duke of Manchester, who, in 1776, commenced the building of Manchester House (now called Hertford House), which occupies nearly all the northern side. Two years later, on the duke's death, it was bought as the residence of the Spanish ambassador. From him it passed into the hands of the second Marquis of Hertford, one of the friends of George, Prince Regent, who used daily to call at the door in his chariot or pony phaeton. To this habit Thomas Moore refers, in his " Diary of a Politician : "—

" Through Manchester Square took a canter just now,
    Met the old yellow chariot, and made a low bow."

The marchioness, of course, was the great attraction of the Prince. Moore thus refers to her elsewhere as the reigning beauty of the day :—

" Or who will repair unto Manchester Square,
    And see if the lovely Marchesa be there?
    And bid her to come, with her hair darkly flowing,
    All gentle and juvenile, crispy and gay,
    In the manner of Ackerman's dresses for May."

Some idea may be formed of the unpopularity under which royalty laboured in the interval between the commencement of the Regency and the accession of the " first gentleman in Europe " to the throne as George IV., from a facetious mock advertisement which was inserted in the *Scourge* for 1814 :—" Lost between Pall Mall and Manchester Square, his Royal Highness the Prince Regent."

Besides serving as the Spanish embassy, it is said by a writer in the *Builder* that Manchester House was at one time occupied by the French ambassador, and that Talleyrand lived in it; but we have not been able to confirm the statement. The mansion was the property of the late Marquis of Hertford, who left it to Sir Richard Wallace, who remodelled and nearly rebuilt it in 1873-4. The house is built of staring red brick, with white stone dressings, in a very heavy, unattractive style; but it contains a splendid gallery of pictures. The ground on which it stands belongs to the Portman estate.

Manchester House is famous as having been one of those social stepping-stones which helped poor Theodore Hook in his introduction to the fashionable and West-end world. Through the good offices of Sheridan and his son, the gay Tom Sheridan, favourable mention of his talents was made to the Marchioness of Hertford, then one of the lights in the brilliant firmament of the Regency. She was so pleased with his musical and metrical facility that she sang his praises in every direction, and he was called on to minister to the amuse-

ment of the Prince Regent himself at a supper in Manchester Square. He used to describe his presentation to the Prince : his awe at first was something quite terrible, but good-humoured condescension and plenty of champagne by-and-by restored him to himself ; and the young man so delighted his Royal Highness, that as he was leaving the room he laid his hand on his shoulder, and said, " Mr. Hook, I must see and hear you again." After a few more similar evenings at Lady Hertford's, and, we believe, a dinner or two elsewhere, the Regent made inquiry about his position, and finding that he was without profession or fixed income of any sort, signified his opinion that " something must be done for Hook."

In spite of his humble extraction, Hook's gaiety and brilliancy soon made him generally acceptable, especially with the ladies, and he speedily became a favourite throughout the regions of May Fair. He saw its boudoirs, too, as well as its salons, and " narrowly escaped various dangers incidental to such a career ; among the rest, at all events, a duel with General Thornton, in which transaction, from first to last, he was allowed to show equal tact and temper."

The centre of Manchester Square is formed into a circular enclosure, laid out with grass, shrubs, and a few trees, and surrounded by an iron railing. The houses forming the remaining three sides of the square possess no particular interest, with the exception, perhaps, that between the years 1828 and 1830 No. 12 was the residence of William Beckford, the author of " Vathek," and the owner of the once magnificent mansion of Fonthill, between Salisbury and Shaftesbury.

Hinde Street, which runs out of the square on the eastern side, was called after one Mr. Jacob Hinde, whose name occurs as lessee of part of " Marylebone Park " in the middle of the last century.

In Thayer Street—the thoroughfare connecting Hinde Street with Marylebone High Street—in small lodgings, almost forgotten by the world, died, in July, 1857, the fifth Earl of Mornington, better known by his former name of Mr. W. Long-Pole-Tylney-Wellesley. In the early days of the Regency he was a dandy about town, and distinguished himself by giving sumptuous dinners at Wanstead Park, in Essex, where he owned one of the finest mansions in England, in right of his wife, Miss Tylney-Long, an heiress with £50,000 a year, whom he ruined, and broke her heart. He used to ask his friends down to Wanstead to dine *after* the opera at midnight, the drive from London, through the dreary streets of Whitechapel and Stratford, being deemed by him *appétisant*. Every luxury that money could command he would place upon his table at that unusual hour of the night, and he often protracted the dessert into the next day. Having had the enjoyment of such wealth, although he was the head of the Wellesley family, he died almost a beggar; "in fact," says Captain Gronow, "he would have starved if it had not been for the charity of his cousin, the Duke of Wellington, who allowed him a pension of £300 a year." The authors of the "Rejected Addresses" wrote of him, in 1820—

"And long may Long-Pole-Tylney-Wellesley live."

They had their prayer granted; for his lordship enjoyed for nearly forty years more the lease of life.

The whole of the west side of Spanish Place, which bounds Manchester Square on the east, is formed by the somewhat sombre-looking walls of Manchester House; and the name of Spanish Place, we need hardly say, serves to keep in remembrance the occupancy of the mansion by the Spanish ambassador in the last century. As was the case in other parts of the town, so here the Roman Catholics were glad to be allowed to practise their religion under the shelter of a foreign embassy whilst the penal laws were still in force. The chapel on the eastern side was built from the designs of Bonomi, an Italian architect, in 1796; it is dedicated to St. James, the patron saint of Spain. It was enlarged in 1846, and further beautified and adorned internally under Cardinal Wiseman. The building is disproportionately broad for its length, and is Italian rather than ecclesiastical in its character.

In the north-west corner of the square—crossing George and Blandford Streets, and terminating in Dorset Street—is Manchester Street. Here, in 1814, died the arch-impostor, Joanna Southcote, who deluded hundreds and thousands of credulous persons in London and elsewhere that she was destined to become the mother of the future "Shiloh," and that he was soon to be born of her. Her imposture occupied the public attention for several months, and even well-informed and sensible medical men were victims of her assertions. She was buried at St. John's Wood Chapel, and we shall have more to say about her when we reach that place. Manchester Street is almost wholly occupied by private hotels or houses let out in furnished lodgings. At Howlett's Hotel, No. 36 in this street, died suddenly, in 1868, Lady Tichborne, the mother of Roger Tichborne, who was lost at sea in 1854, and whose title and estates were claimed by the impostor, Arthur Orton, who pretended to be her long-lost son.

Dorset Street, into which we now pass, was so named, as we have already shown, after the county in which is situated a large portion of the estates of Lord Portman, whose property extends thus far eastwards. At No. 1 in this street, now a branch establishment of the Samaritan Free Hospital for Women and Children, noticed above, formerly lived the celebrated Mr. Charles Babbage, the inventor of the machine for calculating and printing mathematical tables. From the "Percy Anecdotes" we learn that Mr. Babbage constructed several of these machines. One is capable of computing any table by the aid of differences, whether they are positive or negative, or of both kinds. One remarkable property of this machine is, that the greater the number of differences, the more the engine will outstrip the most rapid calculator. By the application of other parts of no great degree of complexity, this may be converted into a machine for extracting the roots of equations, and consequently the roots of numbers. Mr. Babbage likewise constructed another machine, which he says "will calculate tables governed by laws which have not been hitherto shown to be explicitly determinable, and it will solve equations for which analytical methods of solution have not yet been continued. Supposing," continues Mr. Babbage, "these engines executed, there would yet be wanting other means to ensure the accuracy of the printed tables to be produced by them. The errors of the persons employed to copy the figures presented by the engines would first interfere with their correctness. To remedy this evil, I have contrived measures by which the machines themselves shall take from several boxes containing type, the numbers which they calculate, and place them side by side, thus becoming, at the same time, a substitute for the compositor and the computer, by which means all error in copying, as well as printing, is removed." Mr. Babbage died here in 1871.

On the north side of Dorset Street, a thoroughfare called East Street will take us at once into Paddington Street, so called because it led in the direction of the then distant rural village of Paddington, and which forms the connecting link between Crawford Street and High Street, Marylebone. A great part of Paddington Street is taken up on either side with cemeteries for the use of the parish. They are not quite so tastily laid out as that of Père la Chaise, at Paris, nor is the list of their occupants a very interesting or illustrious one. In the cemetery on the south side of the street it is computed that near 100,000 persons have been interred. An inscription here records the deaths of several infants, children of J. F. Smyth Stuart, "great-grandson of Charles II." Among those who lie buried here are Baretti, the friend of Johnson, and the author of the "Italian Dictionary," already mentioned in our account of the father of the Premier; and William Guthrie, the historian. The southern cemetery was consecrated in the reign of George I., the northern early in that of George III.

In "Marylebone, near London," on the 11th of April, 1770, was born George Canning, the future

MARYLEBONE CHURCH IN THE SIXTEENTH CENTURY AND IN 1750. (*See page* 430.)

Haymarket. For many years he lived at the hospitable table of the Thrales at Streatham, but eventually—like Dr. Johnson—he quarrelled with Mrs. Thrale, afterwards Mrs. Piozzi. An account of the quarrel between these irritable and touchy votaries of the Muses may be seen in the *European Magazine.* Baretti was foreign secretary to the Royal Academy, and some members of that learned body attended his funeral here.

Here, too, lie buried Mr. George Canning, the

Premier of England. His father, mentioned above, was a young gentleman of good family, whose father had cast him off for making a poor marriage; and while Canning was an infant, his father died of a broken heart, his mother being glad to support herself and her bairn by keeping a small school. Sent by an uncle to Eton, the boy so distinguished himself that he was entered at Christ Church, Oxford, where he showed himself one of the best scholars of his age, and soon afterwards

MARYLEBONE GARDENS. *From a Print of* 1780. (*See page* 431.)

entered upon that political career which led him ultimately to the premiership.

In Dorset Mews East, Paddington Street, a house served as the home of the French *emigré* clergy, in 1791-3, and here they said mass and celebrated the divine offices, till they could open their chapel in King Street.

Before proceeding with our perambulation of the streets and thoroughfares lying to the east and south-east of Paddington Street, and crossing the boundary-line which separates the property of Lord Portman from that of the Duke of Portland, we may be pardoned for introducing a few historical remarks concerning the parish of Marylebone. The name is said to be a corruption or an abridgment of "St. Mary-le-Bourne," or "St. Mary on the Brook," so called from a small chapel dedicated to the Blessed Virgin which stood on the banks of a small brook, or bourne, or burn, which still runs down from the slopes of Hampstead, passing under Allsop Buildings, where, of course, it is arched over. This is the derivation of the name as given by most writers, who compare with it the termination of Ty*burn*. Some writers have asserted that the parish was itself originally called Tybourne, or Tyburn, from the brook (bourne) of which we have just spoken, a name which gradually was exchanged for Marylebourne or Marylebone. If, however, we might hazard an opinion, we would suggest that it is possibly a corruption of "St. Mary la Bonne."

But whatever may be its derivation, two centuries ago it was still a rural spot, and Macaulay reminds us that at the end of the reign of Charles II. "cattle fed and sportsmen wandered with dogs and guns over the site of the borough of Marylebone." It was, in fact, nothing more than a small country village, separated from London by green fields. In one of the fields in the neighbourhood, as late as the year 1773, was fought a duel between Lord Townshend and Lord Bellamont, in which the latter was dangerously wounded, being shot through the groin.

Almost at the beginning of the last century, writes Lambert, in his "History of London," published in 1806, "Marylebone was a small village, almost a mile distant from the nearest part of the metropolis; indeed, it was formerly so distinct and separate from London, as not to be included in most histories and topographical works devoted to the metropolis. Its increase began between 1716 and 1720, by the erection of Cavendish Square." Maitland, in his "History of London," in 1739, gives the number of houses in "Marybone" as 577, and the persons who kept coaches—that is,

carriages—as thirty-five. At the beginning of the nineteenth century, the houses had risen to 9,000, and the number of "coaches" is estimated at about 530. But even this is a sorry total in comparison of the Marylebone of to-day, which at the last census had a population of upwards of 477,000 souls, and no less than 32,000 electors, having increased no less than 11,000 since its erection into a Parliamentary borough in 1832. According to Malcolm, in 1807, there were over 7,000 houses, with a population of 27,000 males and 37,000 females.

The parish of Marylebone is now the largest in the metropolis, being more than twice the size of the actual City proper, and having also a larger population; indeed, its population is larger than that of London and Westminster combined, in the reign of Elizabeth. According to the last census returns, the population of this parish numbered 477,532, or nearly double what it was only a quarter of a century ago. Its present population (1876) is estimated at about 600,000.

The manor of Marylebone was granted by King James I. to Edward Forset, in 1611, and afterwards passed into the family of Austen, by the marriage of Arabella Forset to Thomas Austen. In 1710 John Holles, Duke of Newcastle, purchased the manor of John Austen, afterwards Sir John Austen; and his only daughter and heir, Lady Henrietta Cavendish Holles, marrying Edward Harley, second Earl of Oxford and Mortimer, it passed into that family. The only daughter and heir of the Earl and Countess of Oxford, Lady Margaret Cavendish Harley, marrying William, second Duke of Portland, took the property into the Portland family, with whom it still remains, the present duke being lord of the manor. The various names of these noble families are all represented in the streets of the neighbourhood. Lady Henrietta Cavendish Holles gave her names to Henrietta Street, Cavendish Square, and Holles Street; her husband to Harley Street, Oxford Street, and Mortimer Street; and their daughter, Lady Margaret, to Margaret Street. Bentinck, Duke, and Duchess Streets, as well as Portland Place, all take their names from the Duke and Duchess of Portland. One of the titles of the Earl of Oxford was Lord Harley of Wigmore, after which place Wigmore Street was named. Welbeck Abbey, an estate of the Duke of Portland, and Bulstrode, a former seat of the family, are represented by Welbeck and Bulstrode Streets.

In Marylebone was one of the many chapels or churches which the Huguenot refugees established on settling in London after the revocation of the Edict of Nantes, whose number is estimated by

Mr. Smiles at thirty-five, and by Mr. Burn at forty. It was founded about the year 1656.

In a map published in 1742 we see the small village church of Marylebone, or "St. Mary-at-the-Bourne," standing quite alone in the fields. It is approached by two narrow zigzag lanes, one winding up from about the bottom of the east side of Stratford Place—then the western boundary of all continuous houses—following the line of what is still called Marylebone Lane; the other lane crosses the fields diagonally from Tottenham Court Road. This lane, the northern end of which is now called Marylebone High Street, was in olden times a footway through the fields from Brook Field, the site of which is now covered by Brook Street, to Marylebone Manor House. The lane exhibits proofs of its antiquity, by its winding and its narrowness. No doubt it was an old rural lane, along which the farm-horses went to the great city to market from the farmers of the outlying districts. It now terminates on the north side of Oxford Street; but it would seem to have formerly continued in a winding manner by Shug Lane and Marylebone Street to the east end of Piccadilly and the Haymarket, much in the same way that Drury Lane led from St. Giles's-in-the-Fields to St. Clement's Danes, and Tyburn Lane (now Park Lane) from Tyburn to Hyde Park Corner. The Marylebone Street above mentioned was built about the year 1680, and was so called because it led from "Hedge Lane" to Marylebone. It is described in the "New View of London," in 1708, as a "pretty straight street, between Glasshouse Street and Shug Lane, near Pickadilly."

Mr. Smith, in his "Book for a Rainy Day," tells us how that "at this time (1744) houses in High Street, Marylebone, particularly on the western side, continued to be inhabited by families who kept their coaches, and who considered themselves as living in the country, and perhaps their family affairs were as well known as they could have been had they resided at Kilburn. In Marylebone great and wealthy people of former days could hardly stir an inch without being noticed; indeed, so lately as the year 1728, *The Daily Journal* assured the public that 'many persons arrived in London from their country houses in Marylebone.'"

The "Rose of Normandy," a public-house in High Street, is said to be the oldest house in the parish. It is described in the *Gentleman's Magazine*, vol. lxxxiii., p. 524, as having had, in the year before the Restoration, "outside a square brick wall, set with fruit-trees, gravel walks 204 paces long, 7 broad; the circular wall 485 paces long, 6 broad; the centre square a bowling-green, 112 paces one way, 88 another; all, except the first, double set with quickset hedges, full-grown, and kept in excellent order, and indented like town walls." "The street having been raised," writes Mr. Larwood, "the entrance to the house is now (1866) some steps below the roadway. The original form of the exterior has been preserved, but the garden and large bowling-green have dwindled down into a miserable skittle-ground." It is currently reported that the celebrated Nancy Dawson, as a young girl, was employed in setting up the skittles at a bowling-alley in High Street, probably in these identical grounds.

The old Manor House, of which we have given a view on page 420, stood on the south side of what is now called the Marylebone Road, and its site is now occupied by Devonshire Mews. The house, as Mr. Smith tells us, in the work above quoted, consisted of a large body and two wings, a projecting porch in the front, and an enormously deep dormer roof, supported by numerous cantalivers, in the centre of which there was, within a very bold pediment, a shield surmounted by foliage, with labels below it. The back, or garden front, of the house had a flat face with a bay window at each end, glazed in quarries, and the wall of the back front terminated with five gables. The mansion was wholly of brick, and surmounted by a large turret containing a clock and bell. From the style of decorations of the interior, Mr. Smith considers it was probably of the Inigo Jones period: the hand-rails of the grand staircase were supported with richly-carved perforated foliage. The house was turned into a school, kept by a certain clergyman named Fountayne, who had here among his pupils the eccentric and wayward George Hanger, afterwards Lord Coleraine.

In connection with this old manor house, or rather with reference to Mr. Fountayne's academy, Mr. J. T. Smith tells us, that one Sunday morning his mother allowed him, before they entered the "little church in High Street, Marylebone, to stand to see the young gentlemen of Mr. Fountayne's boarding-school cross the road. I remember well," he adds, "a summer's sun shone with full refulgence at the time, and my youthful eyes were dazzled with the various colours of the dresses of the youths, who walked two and two, some in pea-green, others sky-blue, and several in the brightest scarlet; many of them wore gold-laced hats, while the flowing locks of others, at that time allowed to remain uncut at schools, fell over their shoulders. To the best of my recollection, the scholars amounted to about one hundred."

During the time that it was vested in the Crown,

the manor house was occasionally used as a temporary royal residence, particularly by Queen Elizabeth, who appears by many accounts to have used her various palaces in rapid succession. The park attached to the manor stretched away northward, and its site is now the Regent's Park, of which we shall speak in a future chapter.

There was an old church in Marylebone which had come down from the times before the Reformation, but having fallen out of repair, it was pulled down in 1741, to make room for another structure, which served as the parish church, until the erection of a third structure in the New Road, some eighty years later, reduced it to the rank of a mere chapel of ease. Lambert, in his "History of London," places the old village of Tyburn on the site of the north-west part of Oxford Street, and supposes, from the number of bones dug up there,* that the old Marylebone Court House covered the site of the old church and churchyard of that village. "This church," he writes, "was dedicated to St. John the Evangelist, and being left alone by the highway side, in consequence of the decay of the village, was robbed of its books, vestments, bells, images, and other decorations;" therefore the parishioners petitioned the Bishop of London for leave to build a new church on another site, and this being dedicated to St. Mary, and standing near the bourne, came to be called "St. Mary of the Bourne." This village of Tyborne appears in "Domesday Book" to have belonged to the abbess and sisters of Barking in Essex. The first church was the one selected by Hogarth for the plate in his "Harlot's Progress," where he has introduced his "Rake at the Altar with an Old Maid." As the print was published in 1735, the scene could not have taken place within the little dingy building now standing in the High Street: a part of the inscription in the picture, nevertheless, still remains to be seen in one of the pews in the gallery. In Smith's "History of Marylebone," it is stated that "the first two lines of this inscription are the originals; the last two were restored in 1816, at the expense of the Rev. Mr. Chapman, the minister."

Among those baptised in this ugly little structure were the poet Byron, in the year 1788; and "Horatia," the daughter of Lord Nelson, by Emma Lady Hamilton, in 1803. The list of those who are buried here is rather long, including John Wesley's brother Charles; Gibbs, the architect of St. Martin's-in-the-Fields; Hoyle, the author of "Whist" and a work on "Games;" Caroline Watson, the engraver; Bower, author of a "History

of the Popes;" Allan Ramsay and Vanderbank, the portrait-painters; John Dominic Serres, the marine-painter; Rysbrack, the sculptor; Ferguson, the astronomer; and James Figg, the celebrated prize-fighter, whose portrait figures in one of the engravings of Hogarth, in the "Rake's Progress."

The present parish church is situated in the New (or, as it is now styled, the Marylebone) Road, opposite York Gate. It was originally intended to be only a chapel of ease; but it was so much admired, both externally and internally, that it was subsequently converted, under an Act of Parliament, to parochial uses. It was erected, under an Act of Parliament, in 1813–17, at a cost of about £60,000, its architect being Mr. Thomas Hardwick, a pupil of Sir William Chambers, and one of a family of architects, his son Philip being the designer of Lincoln's Inn Hall and Library; and his grandson, Mr. Philip C. Hardwick, of the new buildings of the Charter House, on the Surrey Hills. A double gallery forms a feature of its interior; and a peculiarity in its construction is that the portico faces the north, an arrangement necessitated by the nature of the ground whereon it is erected. The altar-piece, by Benjamin West, President of the Royal Academy, was a present from that celebrated painter to the church: it represents the Nativity of our Lord.

Here lie buried James Northcote, R.A., the pupil and biographer of Sir Joshua Reynolds, and also another Royal Academician, Richard Cosway, who died in 1821, at his residence in Edgware Road.

In the Marylebone Road, near the east end of the parish church, and close by the High Street, is Devonshire Terrace. Here, in 1839, Charles Dickens took up his abode, when newly married, and in the first flush of his fame as the author of "Pickwick," "Nicholas Nickleby," and "Oliver Twist." His residence is described by Mr. J. Forster as "a handsome house, with a garden of considerable size, shut out from the New Road by a high brick wall, facing the York Gate into the Regent's Park." Here he used to gather round his friends, Macready, Stanfield, Landseer, Harrison Ainsworth, Talfourd, and Bulwer; and here he composed the principal portion of "Master Humphrey's Clock," the "Old Curiosity Shop," and "David Copperfield." How fond Dickens was of his residence here may be gathered from his remark, later on in life, "I seem as if I had plucked myself out of my proper soil when I left Devonshire Terrace, and could take root no more until I return to it." A sketch of the house, by Maclise, will be found in Mr. Forster's "Life of Dickens."

* Several skeletons were dug up here in March, 1876.

Nottingham Place is the name given to the thoroughfare at the west end of the church, running from the Marylebone Road into Paddington Street. Its designation is probably derived from the county in which the chief landed property of the Duke of Portland is situated. Here, at No. 26, lived for many years Colonel William Martin Leake, the accomplished traveller, and author of so many topographical and antiquarian works on Ancient Greece and Asia Minor, &c. Nottingham Place is crossed by a short street bearing the same name.

Marylebone Road, owing to its great breadth, and the houses standing so far back from the road, has always been a favourite place for hospitals, charitable institutions, &c. Within a short distance of the church is the parish workhouse, which stands partly on the Portman estate, and partly on that of the Duke of Portland. It was originally built in 1775, but was greatly altered and enlarged in 1875. The house is conveniently fitted up with workshops, washhouse, laundry, wards, kitchen, bakehouse, chapel, infirmary, and officers' rooms, all of which are well adapted to their different purposes. Close to the workhouse, at the corner of Northumberland Street, is the Home for Crippled Girls, which was established in 1851, and was formerly in Hill Street, Dorset Square. The building, which is known as Northumberland House, was built about the year 1800; no reason can be found for the name. The poor afflicted inmates of this institution occupy their time, so far as their ability serves them, in the manufacture of fancy articles in straw and other material suitable for presents; and there is also a public laundry in connection with the Home.

The New Hospital for Women, at No. 222, was founded in 1866, for the purpose of affording to poor women and children medical and surgical treatment from legally qualified women. This institution was originally established in Seymour Street, but was removed hither in 1875.

In 1830 was established in this road the Western General Dispensary, for the relief of the sick poor in the north-west parts of Marylebone and the parish of Paddington. The number of patients relieved during the year amounts, on an average, to about 15,000. Between York Place and Gloucester Place are the offices of the Marylebone Association for Improving the Dwellings of the Industrious Classes. Judging from the description of some wretched tenements in this parish, as given by the Medical Officer of Health, it would almost seem that there is still work to be done by the above association in this neighbourhood. The dwellings referred to are described as consisting of twenty cottages placed in four parallel rows, which are reached by an avenue twenty-five feet wide, with a narrow, wretchedly-paved footway. "In some of the forecourts of these cottages," says Dr. Whitmore, "there is an attempt to cultivate the soil, while in others rubbish is strewn about, and puddles of filthy stagnant water lie there long after a fall of rain. None of the cottages have rooms above the ground floor; the front rooms have an average of 850 feet of cubic space each, while the backs have only 750 feet. The ceilings are seven feet from the floor, but the flooring is six feet below the level of the forecourt; consequently the eaves of the roof are but little above the level of the ground." An inhabitant of one of these hovels, nevertheless, declared that if she were forced to leave she would soon die.

At the corner of Marylebone Road and Seymour Place are the police-court buildings of the parish. The building, which was erected in 1874-5—the old police-court in the High Street having become unsuited for its purposes—consists of a large and commodious court-room, private rooms for the magistrates, and the requisite offices for other officials. The basement of the edifice is of rusticated Portland stone, and the upper part is built of white Suffolk brick with stone dressings; and the central portion of the front elevation is surmounted by a pediment enclosing a sculptured representation of the royal arms.

A little northward of Manchester and Cavendish Squares, and on the east side of Marylebone Lane, towards the close of the last century, was the place of fashionable amusements so well known to fame as "Marylebone Gardens." These gardens were formed towards the end of the seventeenth century, by throwing together the place of public resort called "The Rose" and an adjoining bowling-green, mentioned above. The chief entrance was in the High Street; and there was also an entrance at the back, from the fields, through a narrow passage, flanked with a small enclosure, known as "The French Gardens," from their having been cultivated by refugees who had settled in London after the passing of the Edict of Nantes. At first, and for many years, the gardens were entered *gratis* by all ranks of the people; but the company resorting to them becoming more respectable, a shilling was charged as entrance-money; for which the party paying was to receive an equivalent in viands. They afterwards met with such success as to induce the proprietor to form them into a regular place of musical and scenic entertainment; and Charles Bannister, Dibdin (who both made their first public appearance here when youths), and other eminent vocalists, contributed to enliven them with their talents. Chatterton wrote a burlesque burletta, after the fashion of Midas, called the *Revenge*, which was performed here in 1770. Splendid *fêtes*, balls, and concerts, during the run of the season, were given here, as at Vauxhall; and their details are to be found advertised in the papers of the day. In one of these *fêtes*, given on the King's birthday, June 4, 1772, after the usual concert and

covered by Beaumont Street and Devonshire Street." It is mentioned by Pepys, two years after the great " fire of London," in his own quaint manner, in these words: "Then we abroad to Marrowbone, and there walked in the garden; the first time I ever was there, and a pretty place it is." Its bowling-alleys were famous in the days of Pope and Gay, and the latter writer alludes to this place more than once in the *Beggar's Opera*, as a

THE "FARTHING PIE HOUSE." *From a Drawing,* 1820. (*See page* 433.)

songs, was shown a representation of Mount Etna, with the Cyclops at work, and a grand firework, consisting of vertical wheels, suns, stars, globes, &c., which was afterwards copied at Ranelagh. On another occasion a great part of the garden was laid out in imitation of the Boulevards at Paris, with numerous shops and other attractions.

In the old time London was surrounded with places of amusement—its Vauxhall, Ranelagh, &c.; but none were more popular than these gardens, the very name of which seems now to have almost passed away. Chambers writes, in his " Book of Days:" " Of these places of amusement in the north-west suburbs, the most important was that known as Marylebone Gardens. It was situated opposite the old parish church, on ground now

rendezvous for the dissipated, putting it on a level with one of bad repute already mentioned. In one of his "Fables" he thus alludes to the dog-fights allowed here:—

> " Both Hockley-hole and Marybone
> The combats of my dog have known."

The gardens and the adjoining bowling-green seem to have been frequented by the rank and fashion of the town. Lady Mary Wortley Montagu alludes to the fondness of Sheffield, Duke of Buckingham, for this place of amusement; she writes—

> " Some dukes at Marybone bowl time away."

Here, at the end of each season, as the actor Quin told the antiquary Pennant, the Duke of Buckingham used to give a dinner to the guests who frequented the place, when he always proposed as a particular standing toast, "May as many of us rogues as remain ' *unhanged* ' next spring meet here again!" An anecdote book, in recording this toast, amusingly prints the word in italics " *unchanged*."

Smith was a lad, commanded a view of the fields, over hillocks of ground, now occupied by Norfolk Street; and the north and east outer sides of Middlesex Hospital garden wall were entirely exposed. Mr. John Timbs, in his "Romance of London," completes the picture by telling us that

STRATFORD PLACE.   (*See page* 437.)

Although the memory of Marylebone Gardens has perished to a very great extent, we fortunately have, in Mr. J. T. Smith's "Book for a Rainy Day," a quantity of curious information respecting them and the pleasant sights and sounds which there amused the ladies of the western suburbs, whilst the City dames were showing off their finery at such places of amusement as Bagnigge Wells, and the Mulberry Garden in Clerkenwell. The houses of the north end of Newman Street, at the time Mr.

at that time a cottage with a garden and a rope-walk were here; and that "under two magnificent rows of elms Richard Wilson, the landscape painter, and Baretti might often be seen walking." To the right of the rope-walk was a pathway on a bank, which extended northward to the "Farthing Pie House," now the sign of the "Green Man;" it was kept by Price, the famous player on the salt-box, of whom there is an excellent mezzotinto portrait. It commanded fine views of the distant heights of Highgate, Hampstead, Primrose Hill, and Harrow; and Mr. Smith tells us that, as a boy of eight years old, he frequently played at trap-bat beneath the elms. The south and east ends of Queen Anne and Marylebone Streets were then unbuilt: the space consisted of fields to the west corner of Tottenham Court Road, thence to the extreme end of High Street, Marylebone Gardens, Marylebone Basin, and another pond then called "Cockney Ladle," which were the terror of many a mother. Upon the site of the "Ladle" now stands Portland Chapel.

In the *London Gazette*, January 11, 1691, mention is made of "Long's Bowling-green, at the 'Rose,' at Marylebone, half a mile distant from London." The distance here mentioned doubtless refers to the utmost limits of bricks and mortar in the neighbourhood of Oxford Street.

The *Daily Courant*, for Thursday, May 29, 1718, contains the following announcement:—"This is to give notice to all persons of quality, ladies and gentlemen, that there having been illuminations in Marylebone Bowling-green on his Majesty's birthday every year since his happy accession to the throne, the same is (for this time) put off till Monday next, and will be performed with a *consort* (*sic*) of musick in the middle green, by reason there is a ball in the gardens at Kensington with illuminations, and at Richmond also."

The gardens, as we have observed, were at first opened gratuitously; but in 1738–9 they were enlarged, and an orchestra built. Silver tickets were at first issued, at 12s. each for the season, each ticket admitting two persons. From every one without a ticket 6d. was demanded for the evening; but afterwards, as the season advanced, the admission was 1s. for a lady and gentleman.

About this time, when these gardens were in a flourishing state, selections from Handel's music were often played here, under the direction of Dr. Arne. Concerning one of these performances, Mr. Smith tells an amusing anecdote, which will bear repeating. "One evening," he says, "as my grandfather and Handel were walking together and alone, a new piece was struck up by the band. 'Come, Mr. Fountayne,' said Handel, 'let us sit down and listen to this piece; I want to know your opinion of it.' Down they sat, and after some time Mr. Fountayne, the old parson, turning to his companion, said, 'It is not worth listening to; it is very poor stuff.' 'You are right, Mr. Fountayne,' said Handel, 'it is very poor stuff; I thought so myself, when I had finished it.' The old gentleman, being taken by surprise, was beginning to apologise, but Handel assured him there was no

necessity; that the music was really bad, having been composed hastily, and his time for the production being limited; and that the opinion was as correct as it was honest."

In 1741 a "grand martial composition of music" was performed here by Mr. Lampe, in honour of Admiral Vernon, for taking Carthagena.

The proprietor of the Mulberry Garden, Clerkenwell, apparently stirred up by feelings of envy or jealousy at the success of his brother caterers in the same line of business, indulged in some sarcastic remarks upon five places of similar amusement, in which he described this suburban retreat as "Mary le Bon Gardens down on their marrowbones."

About the year 1746 robberies accompanied by violence were of so frequent occurrence in this neighbourhood that "the proprietor of the gardens was obliged to have a guard of soldiers to protect the company to and from London."

In 1753 the *Public Advertiser* announced that the gardens had been "made much more extensive by taking in the bowling-green, and considerably improved by several additional walks; that lights had been erected in the coach-way from Oxford Road, and also on the footpath from Cavendish Square to the entrance to the gardens; and that the fireworks were splendid beyond conception." A large sun was exhibited at the top of a picture; a cascade, and shower of fire, and grand air-balloons were also most magnificently displayed; and likewise "red fire was introduced." This has been considered as probably the first occasion of air-balloons and "red fire" being exhibited in England.

Towards the end of the reign of George II. the gardens appear to have risen somewhat in popularity, and to have had rather more of the aristocratic element in its visitors; for we learn that in 1758 "no persons were admitted to the ball-rooms without five-shilling tickets, and only twenty-six tickets were delivered for each night." In the following year we are told that the gardens were opened for breakfasting; nor is it forgotten to be added that "Miss Trusler made the cakes." The father of this young lady was the proprietor of the gardens, and being a cook, gave dinners and breakfasts. In the following year the gardens, having been greatly improved, were opened in May "with the usual musical entertainments." They were opened also every Sunday evening, when "genteel company were admitted to walk gratis, and were accommodated with coffee, tea, cakes, &c." Miss Trusler, it would seem, was an adept in the art of cake-making, for in the *Daily Advertiser* of May

6, 1759, appears the following announcement :— "Mr. Trusler's daughter begs leave to inform the nobility and gentry, that she intends to make fruit-tarts during the fruit season; and hopes to give equal satisfaction as with the rich cakes and almond cheesecakes. The fruit will always be fresh gathered, having great quantities in the garden; and none but loaf sugar used, and the finest Epping butter. Tarts of a twelvepenny size will be made every day from one to three o'clock. New and rich seed and plum cakes," too, we are reminded, "are sent to any part of the town."

In 1761 there was published an engraving, after a drawing made by J. Donowell, representing these gardens, probably in their fullest splendour. "The centre of this view exhibits the longest walk, with regular rows of young trees on either side, the stems of which received the irons for the lamps at about the height of seven feet from the ground. On either side of this walk were latticed alcoves; on the right hand of the walk, according to this view, stood the bow-fronted orchestra, with balustrades supported by columns. The roof was extended considerably over the erection, to keep the musicians and singers free from rain. On the left hand of the walk was a room, possibly for balls and suppers. The figures in this view are well drawn and characteristic of the period."

In 1762 the gardens were visited by the Cherokee Kings; and in the following year the celebrated Tommy Lowe became the proprietor. Among the singers here at that time was Nan Cattley.

Notwithstanding the patronage bestowed upon these gardens by many of the nobility, the place seems in the end to have fallen into bad repute; for in Dodsley's "London and its Environs" we find mention of it as "the noted gaming-house at Marylebone, the place of assemblage of all the infamous sharpers of the time." The security of the outlying districts, too, does not seem to have improved, for we are told that in 1764 Mr. Lowe, the then proprietor, offered "a reward of ten guineas for the apprehension of any highwayman found on the road to the gardens." An attempt, nevertheless, seems to have been made by the Sabbatarian party to render this place of amusement less attractive for visitors on the people's only holy day; for we read that in "this year a stop was put to tea-drinking in the gardens on Sunday evenings."

Well may Sir John Fielding console the public by writing as follows, just a century ago :—"Robberies on the highway in the neighbourhood of London are not very uncommon; these are usually committed early in the morning, or in the dusk of the evening, and as the times are known, the danger may be for the most part avoided. But the highwaymen here are civil, as compared with other countries; do not often use you with ill-manners; have been frequently known to return papers and curiosities with much politeness; and never commit murder, unless they are hotly pursued and find it difficult to escape." That highway robberies here, in Sir John Fielding's time, were no new thing, may be learnt from the *Evening Post* of March 16, 1715–16 :—"On Wednesday last four gentlemen were robbed and stripped in the fields between London and Marylebone."

Amongst other distinguished personages whose names are connected by tradition with this place is Dick Turpin, the prince of highwaymen. He was a gay and gallant fellow, and very polite to the ladies. A celebrated beauty of her day, the wife or sister-in-law of a dean of the Established Church, Mrs. Fountayne, was one day "taking the air" in the gardens, when she was saluted by Dick Turpin, who boldly kissed her before the company and all "the quality." The lady started back in surprise and offended. "Be not alarmed, madam," said the highwayman; "you can now boast that you have been kissed by Dick Turpin. Good morning!" and the hero of the road walked off unmolested. Turpin was hanged at York in 1739.

In 1768 Mr. Lowe gave up the gardens, at the same time declaring that his loss in the concern had been considerable. He conveyed his property in the gardens to trustees for the benefit of his creditors; and in the deed of conveyance, Mr. John Timbs tells us, it is recorded that the premises of Rysbrack the sculptor were formerly part of the gardens. The grounds, however, were not finally closed; for in 1770 there was a concert of vocal and instrumental music, in which James Hook, the father of Theodore Hook, is announced as having taken part; and in that same year various alterations were made in the grounds for the better accommodation of the visitors. Two years later, as Mr. Smith informs us, "for the convenience of the visitors, coaches were allowed to stand in the field before the back entrance. Mr. Arnold was indicted at Bow Street for the fireworks. Torre, the fire-worker, divided the receipts at the door with the proprietor."

In 1773, proposals "were issued for a subscription evening to be held every Thursday during the summer, for which tickets were delivered to admit two persons. The gardens were now opened for general admission on three evenings in the week only. On Thursday, May 27th, *Acis and Galatea* was performed, in which Mr. Bannister, Mr. Reinholdt, Mr. Phillips, and Miss Wilde were singers. Signor Torre, the fire-worker, was assisted by Monsieur Caillot, of Ranelagh Gardens. On Friday, September 15th, Dr. Arne here conducted his celebrated catches and glees."

In the following year (1774) the gardens were again opened for promenading, sixpence being charged for admission; and Dr. Kenrick delivered a series of lectures on Shakespeare in the gardens in this year.

The newspaper advertisements of these gardens in 1775 are curious. As a specimen, we quote one which appeared in the *Morning Chronicle and London Advertiser* of May 29th :—

AT MARYBONE GARDENS,

To-morrow, the 30th instant, will be presented
THE MODERN MAGIC LANTERN.

In three Parts, being an attempt at a sketch of the Times in a variety of Caricatures, accompanied with a whimsical and satirical Dissertation on each Character.

By R. BADDELEY, Comedian.

BILL OF FARE.

EXORDIUM.

PART THE FIRST.

A Serjeant at Law.	A Modern Patriot.
Andrew Marvel, Lady Fribble.	A Duelling Apothecary, and
A Modern Widow.	A Foreign Quack.

PART THE SECOND.

A Man of Consequence.	Lady Tit for Tat.
A Hackney Parson.	An Italian Tooth-drawer.
A Macaroni Parson.	High Life in St. Giles's.
A Hair-dresser.	A Jockey, and
A Robin Hood Orator.	A Jew's Catechism.

And Part the Third will consist of a short Magic Sketch called

PUNCH'S ELECTION.

Admittance 2s. 6d. each, Coffee or Tea included. The doors to be opened at seven, and the Exordium to be spoken at eight o'clock.

Vivant Rex et Regina.

At the foot of Mr. Baddeley's subsequent bills the gardens are announced as being still open on a Sunday evening for company to walk in. Some of the papers of this year declare, under Mr. Baddeley's advertisements, that "no person going into the gardens with subscription tickets will be entitled to tea or coffee."

Subsequently, George Saville Carey here gave his Lecture on Mimicry. In 1776 the gardens opened in May, "by authority," when the "Forge of Vulcan" was represented, followed a few days later by some feats of sleight of hand, &c.

After existing for upwards of a century, and undergoing many vicissitudes, the gardens were closed about the year 1778, and the site soon afterwards turned to building purposes. The grounds were, however, opened again for a short time in 1794, as a sort of last expiring flicker. Some of the trees under which the company promenaded and listened to the sweet strains of music are still standing behind the houses in Upper Wimpole Street.

A Prussian writer, D'Archenholz, at the end of the last century, remarks with great truth of the English people, and especially of the Londoners, that "they take a great delight in public gardens near the metropolis, where they assemble and drink tea together in the open air. The number of these gardens," the writer continues, "in the neighbourhood of the capital is amazing, and the order, regularity, neatness, and even elegance of them is truly admirable. They are, however, rarely frequented by people of fashion; but the middle and lower classes go there often, and seem much delighted with the music of an organ which is usually played in an adjoining building." When he wrote thus it is difficult to persuade oneself that the foreign author had any other place more entirely before his mind's eye than Marylebone Gardens.

These gardens were commemorated by the great London magistrate, Sir John Fielding, in his judgment on Mrs. Cornelys, when he condemned her operas in Soho as "illegal and unnecessary," on the ground that, besides other places such as the three patent theatres, "there was Ranelagh with its music and fireworks, and Marylebone Gardens with music, wine, and plum-cake."

Northouck calls the gardens "small," and contrasts them with those of Vauxhall, with a note of admiration which indicates a sneer. "Marylebone," he says, "may now (1772) be esteemed a part of this vast town (though it is not yet included in the bills of mortality), as the connection by new buildings is forming very fast."

The entire parish of Marylebone, in the last century, appears to have been devoted to the Muses; for Dr. Arne, and Samuel and Charles Wesley, then stars of the first magnitude in the musical firmament, lived in the neighbourhood; and since that time Marylebone has given a home to many painters and sculptors.

The principal thoroughfares now occupying the site of Marylebone Gardens as well as the adjoining bowling-greens, are Devonshire Place, Upper Harley, Weymouth, Upper Wimpole, Marylebone, and Devonshire Streets.

Wimpole Street, down which we now proceed on our return to Oxford Street, was so named after Wimpole, on the borders of Hertfordshire and Cambridgeshire, formerly the country seat of the Harleys, Earls of Oxford, and subsequently that of Lord Chancellor Hardwicke, whose family became possessed of it by purchase in the last century. The street was, at all events, begun before the complete demolition of the gardens, for we find that Edmund Burke took up his residence here in 1757, soon after his marriage with the daughter of an Irish physician at Bath, a Dr. Nugent. He was happy in his wife and his home, and his house became a centre of attraction to his friends. The expenses of housekeeping on a larger scale than that to which he had been accustomed, spurred him on to increased exertions in the field of literature, and the author of the "Essay on the Sublime and Beautiful" here wrote some of those other political and philosophical works which speedily raised him to a high post as an author, including the early volumes of the "Annual Register."

At No. 21 was living, in 1826, Mrs. Cipriani, the widow of the eminent painter, and friend of Wedgwood. At her father's house (No. 50) in this street, lived for some time between 1840 and 1845, Miss Elizabeth Barrett, then known as the author of a volume of poems, and who afterwards was better known to fame as Mrs. E. Browning. Most of her married life was spent, on account of delicate health, at Florence, where she died in 1861. In this street, too, lived the Duchess of Wellington during the Peninsular War.

From the year 1826 to 1841, and probably longer, No. 67 was the residence of Henry Hallam, the historian; here he wrote his "History of the Middle Ages" and his "Constitutional History of England." He died in 1858. In 1841 No. 10 was in the occupation of the fashionable portrait-painter of his time, Mr. Alfred E. Chalon, and of his brother, John James Chalon, both Royal Academicians. These two brothers appear to have been inseparable, for a few years previously they were living together in Great Marlborough Street. At No. 12 in this street lived for some time the gallant Admiral Lord Hood. No 17 was for many years the home of the late Mr. Joseph Parkes, and of his daughter, Miss Bessie R. Parkes.

Of Weymouth Street we have nothing to record beyond the fact that it forms a connecting link between High Street, Marylebone, and Harley Street and Portland Place; that in it Bryan W. Procter ("Barry Cornwall") lived and died; and that it was so called after Lord Weymouth, a son-in-law of the second Duke of Portland.

Great Marylebone Street, as we have said, crosses Wimpole Street about midway, connecting High Street on the west with Harley Street on the east. In this street was lodging Prince Leopold, afterwards King of the Belgians, when he came to England in 1814, at the time of the Peace Re-joicings, as aide-de-camp to one of the Allied Sovereigns, as we have already stated in our chapter on Hyde Park.

In Edward Street—as that part of Wigmore Street lying between Marylebone Lane and Duke Street was formerly called—at No. 21, the remains of General Sir Thomas Picton lay in state, on their arrival here after the battle of Waterloo, prior to their first interment in the burial-ground in the Uxbridge Road, Bayswater.

In Marylebone Lane, near the Oxford Street end, was for many years the Court-house for the parish. It was erected in 1825, adjoining an older court-house and watch-house, on ground on which was formerly situated a pound. The building, however, having become unsuited for its present requirements, a new court-house has been erected at the corner of Marylebone Road and Seymour Place, as we have already stated.

On the west side of Marylebone Lane, and abutting upon Oxford Street, is Stratford Place. This group of buildings comprises two rows of mansions facing each other, with a square court-yard at the northern end, forming a *cul de sac*. On each side of the entrance is a small house for a watchman, on the top of which is the figure of a lion carved in stone. The buildings were erected about the year 1775 by Edward Stratford, second Lord Aldborough, on land which had been leased from the Corporation of London. The place was formerly decorated with a column supporting a statue of George III., commemorative of the naval victories of Great Britain. It was erected by General Strode, and taken down in 1805, in consequence of the foundation giving way. The house in the centre of the northern side, and facing Oxford Street, is that in which Lord Aldborough himself lived for many years. The house has been occupied at various periods by the Duke of St. Albans, Prince Esterhazy, and other persons of distinction. One of these mansions at the commencement of this century was the residence of Richard Cosway, R.A. Shortly before his death, he disposed of a great part of his collection of ancient pictures and other property, and removed to a house in the Edgware Road, where he died in 1821. Two other Royal Academicians have likewise occupied houses here—namely, Sir Robert Smirke, who was living here in 1826, and Mr. H. W. Pickersgill, who died here in 1875, aged upwards of ninety.

The house at the south-east corner, fronting Oxford Street, has been for many years the home of the Portland Club, which is understood to be one of the leading clubs where high play at cards prevails, but is honourably and honestly conducted.

A code of rules for the game of whist is extant, the preparation of which was the work of a committee of gentlemen from many of the West-end clubs, among whom the Portland was largely represented. Of the inner life and history of the Portland Club little is known, and few anecdotes about it are published.

As we have already stated, here in former times stood a building known as the Lord Mayor's

which then spanned the River Fleet and up Ludgate Hill to the conduit at the west end of Cheapside. The head of water in the reservoirs was about thirty feet above the conduit mouth. The King used his influence with the owner of the lands whence the springs issued to grant the water to the Corporation; and certain merchants of Ghent, Bruges, and Antwerp provided the lead pipe, or gave the money to purchase it, in con-

WIGMORE STREET IN 1850. (*From a Drawing by Shepherd in the Crace Collection.*)

Banqueting-house, from the fact that the chief magistrate and Corporation of London used to dine here annually for many generations, after officially visiting the springs and reservoirs in this neighbourhood whence the great conduit in Cheapside was supplied with water. The supply came from the gravelly subsoil of Marylebone, where no less than nine springs oozed out of the ground at various places, and trickled down the grassy slopes into the watercourse called the *Tye-bourne*, of which we have spoken above. As far back as the year 1216 the Mayor and Corporation of London collected these springs into some reservoirs, which they constructed near Stratford Place, and laid a six-inch lead pipe from thence to Charing Cross, along the Strand and Fleet Street, over the bridge

sideration of the goods they imported into London being exempt from river dues or tolls for a term of years. For the King's service in the matter the Corporation permitted him to lay a pipe "of the size of a goose-quill" from the main pipe into his stables, which were situated where the north-east part of Trafalgar Square now stands. On the occasion of the Mayor's official visits to these springs, the company used to hunt a hare or a fox in the neighbourhood, and afterwards they dined together with much ceremony near the reservoirs. In course of time the reservoirs were arched over, and a large banqueting-house was erected upon the arches.

In August, 1875, while making some repairs or alterations in the roadway of Oxford Street at the

MARYLEBONE, FROM THE SITE OF THE PRESENT WIGMORE STREET. (*From a Print of* 1750.)

point, the workmen came upon these reservoirs and arches, which had remained in a fair state of preservation. Shortly afterwards, another interesting archæological discovery was made a short distance westward, at the corner of North Audley Street. Here, close to the curb, two much-worn iron flaps were discovered. The workmen's curiosity being aroused as to where the opening might lead, they applied their pickaxes, and after some difficulty, succeeded in raising the flaps, when they discovered a flight of brick steps, sixteen in number, leading to a subterranean chamber. On descending, they entered a room of considerable size, measuring about 11 feet long by 9 feet wide, and nearly 9 feet high. The roof, which is arched, is of stone, and, with a few exceptions, is in fair repair. The walls to the height of about five feet are built of small red brick, such as was used by the Romans, in which are eight chamfered Gothic arches, with stone panels, as though originally used as windows for obtaining light. The upper part of the wall is of more recent date. In the four corners of the chamber there is a recess with an arched roof, extending with a bend as far as the arm can reach. In the middle of the chamber is a sort of pool or bath, built of stone, measuring about five feet by seven feet. It is about six feet deep, and was about half filled with water, tolerably clear and fresh. A spring of water could be seen bubbling up, and provision was made for an overflow in the sides of the bath. From all appearances the place was originally a baptistery.

In the beginning of the reign of George III. there was only a dreary and monotonous waste between the then new region of Cavendish Square and the village of Marylebone, sometimes called Harley Fields; and even as lately as 1772, the now thickly-peopled district between Duke Street and Marylebone Lane was unbuilt. Within the last century Oxford Road, as it was then called, had houses only on one (the southern) side between the top of New Bond Street and Tyburn Turnpike; the lower parts of many of these, too, were occupied by dustmen, chimney-sweepers, and "purveyors of asses' milk." At the end of South Molton Street there projected into the road a garden, at one corner of which was a wretched mud hovel, rather a contrast to the fine buildings lately erected not far from that very spot by the Duke of Westminster. Even for some years after it was built and inhabited, "Oxford Road" remained a kind of private street, and the few shops which it contained made but little show. It was a solitude indeed compared with its present activity, its silence being principally broken by the tinkling

of the bells of long lines of packhorses proceeding to and returning from the country westwards every day at stated hours. Along this western road, we need hardly remark, the Oxford scholars and the agents of the Bristol merchants travelled, first on packhorses, and then in the long stage-wagons, which in their turn gave place to the stage-coaches of the eighteenth century.

Even down to a very late period of the seventeenth century, or possibly to the beginning of the eighteenth, the high roads in the neighbourhood of London were sadly neglected, and very frequently were in a state almost impassable for vehicles of any and every description. Anthony à Wood, in his "Diary," first mentions a stage-coach under the year 1661; and six years afterwards he informs us that he travelled from London to Oxford by such a conveyance. How much would we give to see him start along the Oxford Road, and nearing Tyburn turnpike in spite of the ruts! The journey occupied, as he tells us, two days. An improved conveyance called the "Flying Coach" was afterwards instituted; it completed the whole distance, about sixty miles, in thirteen hours, and the event was regarded as a wonder; but it was found necessary to abandon the effort during the winter months. It has been well remarked that the days of slow coaches were the Augustan era of highwaymen. Many of the last generation well remember the time when gentlemen desiring to return to town late in the evening would stop for other companions to collect on the road for mutual protection, while the more timid would stay the night at an inn at Acton or Bayswater.

Oxford Street is now the longest thoroughfare in London, being upwards of 2,300 yards in length. Towards the western extremity of the street, on the southern side, the dull monotony of its houses and shops has in some instances been relieved by the erection of spacious edifices of a more ornate character. An instance of this is afforded in the group of buildings erected in connection with the Association in Aid of the Deaf and Dumb, between Queen Street and Duke Street, nearly opposite the thoroughfare leading into Manchester Square. The buildings, which are of red brick with stone dressings, stand on ground leased from the Duke of Westminster, and were erected in 1870 from the designs of Mr. A. Blomfield, son of the late Bishop of London, and the first stone was laid by the Prince of Wales. The chief feature of this block of buildings is the Deaf and Dumb Chapel, dedicated to St. Saviour, which is subordinate to the parent church of St. Mark in North Audley Street. Although the site is somewhat limited, it has been admirably utilised. The lower floor is devoted to a lecture-hall, the upper floor being the church. The ground-plan and the upper floor exhibit nearly the form of a Maltese cross; but in the chapel an apse containing the communion-table is corbelled out over the projecting arm of the cross towards Oxford Street. About twenty feet from the floor-level the angles of the square are cut off with arches and buttressed by the walls of the projecting arms, and the square becomes an octagon. The cruciform projections are arched off, and the simple octagon is left. This has a groined ceiling, pierced with a circular opening in the centre, where there is a sunlight. The four sides of the octagon above the angles of the square are pierced with large three-light windows, and the apse is lighted with five lancets, and groined with stone ribs and brick filling-in. Externally, the main building is covered with a high-pitched octagonal roof, with a circle of small lucarnes or dormer windows near the apex. The other roofs are of a high pitch, and abut on the main building at various levels. The style of the building is Early Pointed, but it is rather French than English in the character of its details. The church affords accommodation for 250 worshippers, and is so planned that, while meeting the requirements of the deaf and dumb, it is equally available for a " hearing " congregation.

A little to the east of this part of Oxford Street, nearly opposite to Cavendish Square, is the carriage manufactory of Messrs. Laurie and Marner, at No. 313, between the top of New Bond Street and the gates of Hanover Square. It stands on a site which formerly was the garden of the town-house of Lord Carnarvon in Tenterden Street (now the Royal Academy of Music), and it still belongs to the Herberts. The garden was bounded on the north by a wall, with a terrace and summer-house inside, where George III. and his family would come and sit under shady trees and look down upon the carriers' wagons and newly-invented "fly coaches" as they made their way along the Tyburn Road. The garden extended nearly as far eastward as Hanover Gates. The premises now used as a carriage manufactory occupy nearly an acre and a half in extent, having a side entrance in Shepherd Street; underneath are vaults which once held Lord Carnarvon's store of port wine. The business of Messrs. Laurie was first established, some 300 or 400 yards further west in Oxford Street, about the year 1820; its founder was the late amiable and eccentric alderman, Sir Peter Laurie, who in 1832-3 occupied the civic chair. The carriage manufactory of Messrs. Laurie and Marner grew gradually into its present large dimensions out of a humble saddle-maker's business.

CHAPTER XXXIV.

OXFORD STREET, AND ITS NORTHERN TRIBUTARIES (continued).

"And business compelled them to go by the way
Which led them through Cavendish Square."—Old Song.

Progress of Building in Last Century—Number of Houses and Population of Marylebone—Harley Fields—The Harleys, Earls of Oxford—Vere Street—Rysbrack, the Sculptor—St. Peter's Chapel—Henrietta Street—The Old Countess of Mornington—Welbeck, Bentinck, and Wigmore Streets—Cavendish Square—The "Princely" Duke of Chandos, and his proposed Palace—Mr. George Watson-Taylor, M.P.—The Statue of the Duke of Cumberland—Harcourt House—Holles Street—The Birthplace of Lord Byron—Queen Anne Street—Turner's "Den".—Mansfield Street—Duchess Street—The Residence of Mr. Thomas Hope—Harley Street, and its Distinguished Residents—Park Crescent—Portland Place—The Langham Hotel—Langham Place—The Portland Bazaar, or German Gallery—A Skating Rink—The Royal Polytechnic Institution—Cavendish Club—Civil and United Service Club.

AT the beginning of the last century, if we may believe contemporary accounts, Marylebone was a small village, "nearly a mile distant from any part of the metropolis." In the year 1715 the plan for building Cavendish Square and several new streets on the north side of Oxford Street, then, as we have already shown, called indiscriminately by that name and Tyburn Road, was first suggested. About two years afterwards the ground was laid out, and the circular plantation in the centre enclosed, planted, and surrounded by a parapet wall and wooden railings. The buildings, however, seem to have been proceeded with very slowly; for several years

elapsed before either the square or the surrounding streets were actually completed. It was the building of this square that originally gave an impetus to the increase of Marylebone, and Maitland, in his "History of London," published in 1739, gives the number of houses in Marylebone as 577, and the persons who kept coaches (carriages) as thirty-five. "At present," writes Lambert in the year 1806, "the number of houses is near upon 9,000, and the number of coaches must have increased in a proportionate if not even a greater ratio." The present population (1876) is estimated at about 600,000 souls.

The South Sea Bubble, in the year 1720, put a stop for a time to the building of the square, which for many years later remained in an unfinished state. In the view of Hanover Square by Sutton Nicholls, which bears the date of 1754, this square is shown as standing almost alone to the north of Oxford Road, and surrounded by fields, with an uninterrupted view of Hampstead and Highgate. At this particular time Harley Street extended very little way to the north, and Harley Fields were resorted to by thousands who went to hear George Whitefield preach there.

The site of Cavendish Square is said to have been intersected by a shady lane called "Lover's Walk," leading from Margaret Street to where now stands Cavendish Square.

Cavendish Square and the adjoining streets were named after the various relatives of Robert Harley, first Earl of Oxford, K.G., and of his son, Lord Harley, afterwards second Earl. The family titles as they stood in the pages of Lodge and Burke till the extinction of the peerage, were "Earl of Oxford and Mortimer, and Baron Harley of Wigmore Castle." The second earl married the Lady Henrietta Cavendish Holles, only daughter and heiress of John, Duke of Newcastle, who carried all this property by marriage into the family of the Duke of Portland. It is necessary to state these facts in order to account for the names of Cavendish Square, Portland Place, and Henrietta, Harley, Wigmore, Mortimer, and Holles Streets, in the immediate neighbourhood.

The approaches to Cavendish Square from Oxford Street are by Old Cavendish, Holles, and Princes Streets. Another short thoroughfare, called Vere Street, leads into Henrietta Street, which opens into the south-western corner of the square. By Vere Street we now again proceed to make our way northward. The street was so called after the De Veres, who for many centuries previous to the Harleys had held the Earldom of Oxford. In this street resided Rysbrack, the sculptor, and here he died in 1770. Gibbs, the architect, in a letter to Pope, says : " Mr. Rysbrack's house is in the further end of Bond Street, and up across Tyburne Rode (sic), in Lord Oxford's grownd, upon the right hand going to his chaple." The chapel here spoken of stands at the corner of Vere Street and Henrietta Street. It is dedicated to St. Peter, and is a non-descript edifice of the reign of George I., built from the designs of Gibbs about the year 1724, and is said in the prints of the day to have been erected at Lord Harley's cost, "to accommodate the inhabitants of his manor." It may cause a smile to add that once it was thought one of the most

beautiful structures of its kind in London. In his " Guide to the London Churches " Mr. C. Mackeson thus remarks : " This is a Government church : the Government collects and reserves the pew-rents, and pays £450 to the incumbent." It has no district assigned to it ; consequently it is not burdened with any poor, and cannot require any free seats. The chief interest of the chapel lies in the fact that the late Rev. F. D. Maurice was its minister for nine years before his death in 1870. This chapel was called, down to a date within the present century, " Oxford Chapel," and is described by Lambert, in 1806, as surmounted by a steeple springing from the centre of the roof, and consisting of three stages. Here, on the 11th of July, 1734, William, second Duke of Portland, was married to the Lady Margaret Harley, the heiress of Lord Oxford, the same lady whom Prior has celebrated as "my noble, lovely, little Peggy."

Henrietta Street, which we now cross, runs from Marylebone Lane into the south-west corner of Cavendish Square. At No. 3 in this street resided for some time the venerable Countess of Morning-ton, mother of the Duke of Wellington, who, after living to witness the multiplied honours of her children, died in 1831, at the age of ninety. In this street is the studio of Mr. William Theed, the sculptor, to whose chisel we owe the group of " Asia," on the Albert Memorial at Kensington. Mr. Theed numbered among his pupils Count Gleichen, formerly known as Prince Victor of Hohenlohe, and maternally a cousin of Queen Victoria.

Extending from the western end of Henrietta Street to Marylebone Street is Welbeck Street, so named after Welbeck Abbey, near Ollerton, Nottinghamshire, the seat of the Duke of Portland. Here, at No. 59, lived the Right Hon. Henry Ellis, the diplomatist. He died in 1855. At No. 30, in 1826, lived Count Woronzow, of Russia, some time ambassador, and father-in-law of the eleventh Earl of Pembroke. Edmund Hoyle, of whist celebrity, who died here at the age of ninety-seven ; Mrs. Piozzi, and Martha Blount, were also residents in this street at various dates. This street, says Mr. J. P. Malcolm, "will long be famous in the annals of our time as the residence of that mad and honourable (?) imitator of the Wat Tylers and Jack Straws of old times, Lord George Gordon." In this street, too, resided for a short time before his death, the eccentric John Elwes.

Bentinck Street, between Welbeck Street and Manchester Square, was so named after the family surname of the Duke of Portland. In this street Charles Dickens lived for some time with his father, whilst acting as a newspaper reporter at Doctors' Commons, and in the "gallery" of the House of Commons, spending his spare time amongst the books in the library of the British Museum. Here, too, Gibbon, the historian, lived for some time at No. 7, while member for Liskeard, and here he wrote a large portion of his "Decline and Fall of the Roman Empire," and the whole of his "Defence." In a letter to Lord Sheffield, dated 17th January, 1783, Gibbon writes : "For my own part, my late journey has only convinced me in the opinion that No. 7, Bentinck Street is the best house in the world."

Wigmore Street, which extends from Duke Street, Manchester Square, to the north-west corner of Cavendish Square, derives its name from Wigmore, in Herefordshire, whence Robert Harley took his title as Earl of Oxford, Earl Mortimer, and Lord Harley of Wigmore Castle. All these names are perpetuated in the streets in this immediate neighbourhood. In Wigmore Street at one time lived the friend of Alfieri, Ugo Foscolo ; and here, at his humble lodgings, he used to entertain at breakfast Samuel Rogers, Tom Campbell, Roscoe the historian, Cyrus Redding, and other celebrities. Whilst residing here he showed in his studies that ardour which marks the man of genius. "I once found him there," writes Cyrus Redding, "at noonday in summer, with his room still shut up, and studying by candlelight, forgetful that it was day. He had prolonged his sitting from the previous night, whilst composing an article for the forthcoming *Quarterly*." We shall have more to say about his eccentric and wayward career when we come to stand by what was once his grave in Chiswick Churchyard.

From Wigmore Street we pass into Cavendish Square, at its north-western corner. In the reign of George II. the building of this square had been commenced, but had not been carried through, and the site lay desolate and incomplete. The writer of the "New Critical Review of the Public Buildings of London," in 1736, is uncertain whether he ought to call it "Oxford" or "Cavendish" Square ; but whichever name we choose, he says, "here we shall see the folly of attempting great things before we are sure that we can accomplish little ones. Here it is the modern plague of building was first stayed ; and I think the rude, unfinished figure of this project should deter others from a like infatuation. . . . . I am morally assured that more people are displeased at seeing this square lie in its present neglected condition than are entertained with what was meant for elegance or ornament in it. . . . . It is said the imperfect side (the north) of this

square was laid out for a certain nobleman's palace, which was to have extended its whole length, and that the two detached houses which now stand at each end of the line were to have been the wings. I am apt, however, to believe that this is a vulgar mistake ; for these structures, though exactly alike, could have been in no way of a piece with any regular or stately building ; and it is to be presumed this nobleman would have as little attempted any other, as he would have left any attempt unfinished." The "certain nobleman" to whom allusion is here made, is none other than the "princely" Duke of Chandos, who had succeeded in amassing a splendid fortune as paymaster to the army in Queen Anne's reign. It is said that he proposed building here a palatial residence, and to have purchased all the property between Cavendish Square and his palace of Canons at Edgware, "so that he might ride from town to the country *through his own estate.*"

Dodsley writes, in his "Environs of London," 1761 : "In the centre of the north side is a space left for a house intended to be erected by the late Duke of Chandos, the wings only being built ; there is, however, a handsome wall and gates before this space, which serve to preserve the uniformity of the square." An elevation of the grand house or palace which the duke intended to erect may be seen in the Royal Collection of Maps and Drawings in the British Museum. It bears the inscription, "Designed by John Price, architect, 1720." It is obvious to remark that the connection of the "princely" duke with this square is still commemorated by Chandos Street, which joins its north-eastern corner with the east end of Queen Anne Street.

We shall have more to say about "princely Canons," the duke's seat near Edgware, when we come to treat of the suburban districts. Meanwhile, we may be pardoned for reminding the reader that this duke is the person who figures in Pope's "Epistles" as Timon, the man who builds on a magnificent scale, but with false taste, and the downfall of whose projects the poet prophesied, and had he lived but three years longer, would actually have seen. It is to his palace at Edgware, and not to that in Marylebone, that Pope alludes when he writes—

" Another age shall see the golden ear
  Imbrow the slope and nod on the parterre ;
  Deep harvest bury all his pride has planned,
  And laughing Ceres re-assume the land."

At all events, it is not the fair goddess of corn, but the demon of bricks and mortar, who has "re-assumed" the lordship of the vicinity of Cavendish

Square. Of the duke's magnificent conceptions in building here, the satirist says that—

"Greatness with Timon dwells in such a draught
　As brings all Brobdingnag before your thought;
　To compass this his building is a town,
　His pond an ocean, his parterre a down."

The duke's scheme, we need hardly say, was never carried out, for he died of a broken heart, caused by the death of his infant heir while being

articles of *virtu*, he was quite ruined within ten or twelve years. It was of him that Sir Robert Peel said, that "no man ever bought ridicule at so high price."

The other wing of the duke's plan is the corresponding mansion at the corner of Chandos Street. It has been for many years the town residence of the Earls of Gainsborough. The central part is now principally occupied by two splendid mansions,

LANGHAM HOUSE IN 1820. *From a Print in the Crace Collection.* (*See page* 452.)

christened in the midst of the greatest pomp and magnificence. Of the two wings of the duke's mansion, which we have mentioned above, one is the large house standing at the corner of Harley Street, which has numbered among its distinguished occupants, at different periods, the Princess Amelia, aunt to George III.; the Earl of Hopetoun, and the Hopes of Amsterdam; and also the late Mr. George Watson-Taylor, M.P., who, as John Timbs informs us, "assembled here a very valuable collection of paintings." Mr. Watson-Taylor, in 1832, was declared a bankrupt. At the outset of life he had a private income of £1,500 a year, on which he lived comfortably. At forty-five he came into an income of £60,000 a year, and by extravagant living, and by squandering sums of money on

the fronts of which are ornamented with Corinthian columns, said to have been designed by James, of Greenwich, who was architect to the duke at Canons.

It was at first intended to place a statue of Queen Anne in the centre of the enclosure, and in the plan above referred to the statue is marked; the idea, however, was never realised, and the site remained vacant till 1770, when Lieutenant-General William Strode erected an equestrian statue of William, Duke of Cumberland, "the butcher of Culloden," as the inscription sets forth, "in gratitude for private kindness, and in honour of public worth." The statue, which was of lead, gilt, represented the "hero" in the full military costume of his day; it has recently been removed. On the south side, facing Holles Street, is a colossal standing bronze statue of Lord George Bentinck, some time leader of the Conservative party in the House of Commons; this was set up soon after his death, in 1848. The heavy wooden railings which originally surmounted the dwarf brick wall forming

belonging to "the quality." These extinguishers sometimes formed a part of the ornamental iron scroll-work with which the front entrances of town mansions were adorned. A good specimen of them is given on page 331 of this volume, in our account of Berkeley Square.

CAVENDISH SQUARE, 1820.

the enclosure were allowed to fall into a sad state of decay, so that in 1761 we are told that they made "but an indifferent appearance;" but the unsightly rails have long since given way to substantial iron railings. In this square, as also in Manchester Square and in Queen Anne Street, there remain, or remained till only a few years since, some good specimens of the flambeaux-extinguisher which a century ago formed an almost necessary adjunct to the front door of a house

The large and heavy mansion called Harcourt House, which occupies the centre of the west side of the square, and which was long the town residence of the Dukes of Portland, was built by Lord Bingley, in 1722-3. It was purchased after his death by the Earl of Harcourt, who had previously built a house on the east side of the square. This mansion is mentioned by the author of the "New Critical Review," already quoted, as "one of the most singular pieces of architecture about the town," and "rather like a convent than the residence of a man of quality; in fact," he adds, "it seems more like a copy of one of Poussin's landscape ornaments than a design to imitate any of the genuine beauties of building." After an interval of a century and a half, the verdict of any man of architectural taste who sees it will be very much the same. It is a dull, heavy, drowsy-looking house, and it has about it an air of seclusion and privacy almost monastic. Its seclusion of late has been increased by three high walls, which have been raised behind the house, the chief object of which appears to be to screen the stables from the vulgar gaze.

This square was the scene of one of the mad freaks of Lord Camelford, who fell in a duel fought near Holland House, at Kensington. On one occasion he and a boon companion, Captain Barry, returning home at a very late, or, more probably, very early hour, found the "Charlies" asleep at their post, and woke them up and thrashed them, an offence for which the assailants were brought up next morning at the Marlborough Street police station, and fined.

Among the celebrated inhabitants of Cavendish Square may be mentioned Lady Mary Wortley Montagu, who was living here, at all events, from 1723 to 1730, during which period she was satirised with great grossness by Pope.

At No. 24 lived for some time George Romney, the painter. He produced such exquisite portraits as to become a dangerous rival to Sir Joshua Reynolds, and by whom Romney was always referred to as "the man of Cavendish Square." Romney forsook his lawful wife, and became entangled with Emma, Lady Hamilton, whom he admitted as a model to his studio, and whom he portrayed in no less than fourteen of his most beautiful paintings; all of them are, however, more or less of the type of the Phrynes and Lesbias of Horace and Catullus. The house had been previously inhabited by Mr. F. Cotes, R.A., another distinguished portrait painter, who built it; it has been a home of arts and artists in its day, for it was subsequently tenanted by Sir Martin Archer Shee, R.A., afterwards President of the Royal Academy, who died in 1850.

The mansion No. 15 was for many years the scene of the fashionable "receptions" of the Dowager Countess of Charleville, the chief rival of Lady Blessington in her day, as a "queen of society." At No. 16 resided Field-Marshal Viscount Beresford, one of the "great Duke's" chief companions-in-arms.

In this square lived, and here died in August, 1769, aged ninety-seven, Edmund Hoyle, registrar of the Prerogative Court, but better known to the world at large as the author of "Hoyle's Games." Here, too, lived Mr. Thomas Hope, F.R.S., F.S.A., the accomplished author of "Anastasius;" and also Matthew Baillie, the fashionable physician. At No. 5, behind the premises of the Polytechnic, was played, in 1851, the great "International Chess Tournament," players from all quarters of the world taking part in the competition. In this square, in 1747, the newly-formed Dilettanti Society purchased ground on which they intended to build a house for their accommodation, but they afterwards abandoned the idea.

As a proof of the once rural character of the neighbourhood of Cavendish Square, we may here mention that Mr. Fox told Samuel Rogers that when Dr. Sydenham was sitting at his window in Pall Mall, with his pipe and a silver tankard on the sill, a fellow made a snatch at the tankard and ran off with it, and that he was not overtaken, for his pursuers could not keep him in sight further than the bushes at the top of Bond Street, where they lost him.

In Old Cavendish Street, close by Oxford Street, was the shop of Mr. Marsh, the publisher, in 1825, of the *Star Chamber*, the paper in which appeared the first literary ventures of Mr. Benjamin Disraeli, subsequently Premier of England, and Earl of Beaconsfield; but it was a periodical of which the public took but little notice. When he published his first novel, "Vivian Grey," Mr. Cyrus Redding tells us that "Disraeli reviewed and extolled his own book in his own columns." The *Star Chamber* was strongly personal. "I have heard," adds Redding, "that the author suppressed it, but not till it had attacked most of the literary men of the day." It appears that Marsh meantime published "A Key to Vivian Grey," professing to be a complete exposition of the royal, noble, and fashionable characters who figure in that most extraordinary work.

Holles Street, which runs from the south side of the square into Oxford Street, was so named after Henrietta Holles, already mentioned as the daughter and heiress of John Holles, Duke of Newcastle. The street, which was originally composed of private houses, at present consists almost entirely of shops and private hotels. At No. 24 in this street Lord Byron was born on the 22nd of January, 1788; and a tablet has been placed on the front of the house by the Society of Arts, in order to record the fact for the benefit of posterity. Lord Byron was baptised in the old parish church of Marylebone.

In May, 1831, Queen Hortense and her son Prince (afterwards Emperor) Louis Napoleon, took up their abode in Holles Street; and "assuming their own proper name and dignity, speedily found themselves the centre of a brilliant circle of sympathising friends."

At No. 10, in Chandos Street, which runs out of the square at its north-east angle, lived, for many years, the Right Hon. Joseph Planta, M.P., Chief Librarian of the British Museum—an office, the duties of which he discharged by deputy, whilst mixing in political and official circles.

Queen Anne Street, which unites the northern end of Chandos Street with Welbeck Street, has numbered among its residents, at different periods, men famous both in literature and the fine arts. Here, in 1770, Richard Cumberland was living when he wrote his play of the *West Indian;* and at the beginning of this century, No. 58 was in the occupation of Malone, the commentator on Shakespeare.

At No. 47 was living, in the year 1836, J. M. W. Turner, the prince of modern English landscape painters; and here he kept for many years the greater part of his stores of pictures, patiently biding his time till they should be worth thousands. He was right in his calculations, as well as in the estimate which he had formed of himself. Indeed, his one hundred and more paintings in the National Gallery, not to mention his drawings on the basement-floor, and at South Kensington, show a versatility and an infinite variety, endless as Nature herself. It has been, perhaps justly, observed, that "after all allowance and deduction, Turner remains the fullest exponent of nature, the man above all others who was able to reflect the glory and the grandeur, the sunshine and the shade, the gladness and the gloom which in the outward landscape respond to the desires and the wants of the human heart."

He was just commencing to climb the hill of fame when he first settled here. As a young man he was slovenly and untidy, and now he gave way to his *penchant* for dirt and disorder. The house was "subsequently known," writes Dr. W. Russell, "as 'Turner's Den.' And truly it was a den. The windows were never cleaned, and had in them breaches patched with paper; the door was black and blistered; the iron palisades were rusty for lack of paint. If a would-be visitor knocked or rang, it was long before the summons was replied to by a wizened, meagre old man, who would unfasten the chain sufficiently to see who knocked or rang, and the almost invariable answer was, 'You can't come in.' After the old man's death,

an elderly woman, with a diseased face, supplied his place."

The same writer records a visit which Turner received at this "Den" from Mr. Gillat, a wealthy Birmingham manufacturer, who called in order to purchase one of Turner's pictures. "He was met at the door by a refusal of admission, and was obliged to make an almost forcible entry. He had hardly gained the hall when Turner, hearing a strange footstep, rushed out of his own particular compartment, and angrily confronted the intruder, 'What do you want here?' 'I have come to purchase some of your pictures.' 'I have none to sell.' 'But you won't mind exchanging them for some of these?' and he took out of his pocket a roll of bank-notes, to the amount of five thousand pounds. The Birmingham gentleman was successful, and carried off his five thousand pounds worth—now, perhaps, worth five times that sum—of the great artist's creations."

A wealthy merchant of Liverpool, at a later date, was less fortunate in his visit to the "Den." He offered a hundred thousand pounds for the art treasures rolled up in dark closets, or hanging from the damp walls, in Queen Anne Street. "Give me the key of the house, Mr. Turner," said the would-be purchaser. "No, I thank you," replied Turner; "I have refused a better offer." And so he had. He could not bear to sell a favourite painting—it was a portion of his being; to part with it was a blotting out of that part of his life which had been spent in its creation. He was always dejected and melancholy after such a transaction; and he would say, with tears in his eyes, "I have lost one of my children."

Mr. C. Redding, in his "Fifty Years' Recollections," claims Turner as a native, not of Maiden Lane, as usually supposed, but of the west country. He writes, "We were sailing on the St. German's River—Turner, Collier, and myself—when I remarked what a number of artists the West of England had produced from Reynolds to Prout. 'You may add my name to the list,' said Turner; 'I am a Devonshire man.' I asked from what part of the county, and he replied, 'From Barnstaple.' I have several times mentioned this statement to persons who insisted that Turner was a native of Maiden Lane, London, where, it is true, he appears to have resided in very early life, whither he must have come from the country. His father was a barber. When Turner had a cottage near Twickenham, the father resided with his son, and used to walk into town to open the gallery in Queen Anne Street, where I well remember seeing him, a little plain, but not ill-made old man—not reserved and austere as his son, in whom the worth lay between a coarse soil."

Some time before his death, Turner abruptly and secretly quitted his "Den" and walked to Chelsea, where he took lodgings next door to a ginger-beer shop close to Cremorne Pier; here, after some days, he was discovered by his faithful housekeeper, Miss Danby; but the hand of death was upon him. He died in December, 1851, and was buried in the crypt of St. Paul's Cathedral, near the grave of Reynolds.

Between 1788 and 1793 the house No. 72 in this street was in the occupation of Fuseli, the painter; he afterwards removed to No. 75. In 1826 No. 48 was the residence of Mr. Charles C. Pepys, while practising at the Bar; he became afterwards Lord Chancellor Cottenham. At that time No. 7 was in the occupation of Prince Nicholas Esterhazy, the Austrian Ambassador, who was still living there in 1836. The prince, it will be remembered by some, at least, of our readers, was noted for the splendour of his attire when taking part in any public state ceremonial; and he is thus commemorated by Ingoldsby in "Mr. Barney Maguire's Account of the Coronation of Queen Victoria:"—

"'Twould have made you crazy to see Esterhazy,
All jewels from jasey to his di'mond boots."

In this street Edmund Burke took up his residence in 1764-5, on his return from his first public employment at Dublin, in order to resume his literary labours. Whilst living here he used to frequent the "Turk's Head," in Greek Street, and other debating societies of the metropolis; and on spare evenings was to be seen in the Strangers' Gallery in the House of Commons, studying the art of oratory in the best school, from the lips of living orators.

Mr. Serjeant Burke tells us in his life of his kinsman, that the future statesman and orator, when he first came to London to study for the Bar, found in the Strangers' Gallery a powerful attraction, which drew him away even from the tables of his friends. "It was his favourite custom to go alone to the House of Commons, there to ensconce himself in the gallery, and to sit for hours, his attention absorbed and his mind enwrapped in the scene beneath him. 'Some of the men,' he remarked to a friend, 'talk like Demosthenes and Cicero, and I feel, when listening to them, as if I were in Athens or Rome.' Soon these nightly visits became his passion; a strange fascination drew him again to the same place. No doubt the magic of his own master spirit was upon him, and the spell was working. He might be compared to

the young eagle accustoming its eyes to the sun before it soars aloft. . . . . . The House of Commons was but his recreation; literature continued to be his chief employment." Burke was still living in Queen Anne Street when he entered Parliament, by Lord Verney's influence, as one of the members for Wendover. It may be added that if Burke really wrote the "Letters of Junius," it is most probable that those letters were composed in this street.

In Queen Anne Street, at the end of Mansfield Street, and looking directly down it, is a spacious mansion, formerly called Chandos House, but now divided into two, built by the "princely" Duke of Chandos as a town residence. The side, or rather back front, of the mansion in Queen Anne Street opens into a garden on the western side adjoining Langham House.

Mansfield Street, a continuation of Chandos Street on the north side of Queen Anne Street, was built by the brothers Adam, of the Adelphi, about the year 1770, on a plot of ground which had previously been a basin or reservoir of water. Some of the houses in this neighbourhood exhibit many good architectural details, especially in the rooms and staircases.

In this street, in 1836, were living the Princess De la Beiza and the Prince of Asturias. This street appears to have been a great rallying-point for the Roman Catholic aristocracy. At various times the families of Lord Clifford, Lord Stourton, Lord Petre, the Howards of Corby, &c., have resided here. Count Woronzow, the Russian diplomatist, died at his residence in this street, in 1832, at the age of eighty-seven.

Duchess Street is a short thoroughfare connecting Mansfield Street with Portland Place. Here was the town mansion of Mr. Thomas Hope, F.R.S., the author of "Anastasius," "The Costumes of the Ancients," &c. Mr. Hope had here formed a valuable collection of works of art altogether unrivalled, and comprising paintings, antique statues, busts, vases, and other relics of antiquity, arranged in apartments, the furniture and decorations of which were in general designed after classic models, by the ingenious possessor himself. Among the specimens of sculpture was the exquisite group representing "Venus rising from the Bath," by Canova. The whole of these valuables were open to the public, under certain restrictions, during "the season."

Mr. John Timbs says that, in the decoration of his mansion in this street, Mr. Hope "exemplified the classic principles illustrated in his large work on 'Household Furniture and Internal Decorations.' Thus, the suite of apartments included the *Egyptian, or Black Room,* with ornaments from scrolls of papyrus and mummy-cases; the furniture and ornaments were pale yellow and bluish-green, relieved by masses of black and gold. The *Blue,* or *Indian Room,* in costly Oriental style. The *Star Room:* emblems of Night below; and above, 'Aurora visiting Cephalus on Mount Ida,' by Flaxman; furniture, wreathed figures of the Hours. The *Closet,* or *Boudoir,* hung with tent-like drapery; the mantelpiece, an Egyptian portico; Egyptian, Hindoo, and Chinese idols and curiosities. *Picture Gallery,* Ionic columns, entablature and pediment from the Temple of Erectheus at Athens, car of Apollo, classic tables, pedestals, &c. The *New Gallery,* for one hundred pictures of the Flemish school, antique bronzes and vases; furniture of elegant Grecian design." Mr. Hope was one of the earliest patrons of Chantrey, Flaxman, Canova, Thorwaldsen, and George Dawe; and he died here in 1831.

Harley Street dates from the same period as Mansfield Street, with which it runs parallel on its western side. It was called after the Harleys, Earls of Oxford, to one of whom Pope pays a well-deserved compliment in his "Moral Essays," in which he writes :—

" And, showing Harley, teach the golden mean."

A happy and graceful allusion to the second earl of that line, of whose marriage with the daughter and heiress of the noble house of Holles we have already spoken. Harley died in 1741, regretted by all men of taste and letters, great numbers of whom had experienced the benefits of his munificence. He left behind him one of the most noble libraries in Europe. The collection was formed by himself and his son, and was purchased for the British Museum in 1753. His name is perpetuated in the Harleian MSS. in the Museum, and in the *Harleian Miscellany.*

In this street Lord and Lady Walsingham were accidentally burnt to death in bed in April, 1831. At No. 18 lived Sir William Beechey, the celebrated painter, during the latter years of his life. He was born at Burford, in Oxfordshire, in 1753, and in early life was articled in a solicitor's office, but at nineteen found admission as a student to the Royal Academy, where he became a pupil and close imitator of the great Sir Joshua. Having attracted public notice by his portraits of the Duke and Duchess of Cumberland, he was appointed portrait-painter to Queen Charlotte. In 1793 he was elected an Associate of the Royal Academy, and attained the full honours of R.A. four years

later. He died at Hampstead in January, 1839, in his eighty-sixth year. The house No. 45 was built and occupied by Mr. John Stuart, the author of "Athenian Antiquities," published under the auspices of the Dilettanti Society; it was afterwards the town-house of Admiral Viscount Keith.

At No. 73 lived for many years Sir Charles Lyell, the eminent geologist. Born at Kinnordy, in Fifeshire, in 1797, he graduated at Exeter College, Oxford, and received the honorary degree of D.C.L. from his University in 1855. He was twice President of the Royal Geological Society, and was the author of a volume of "Travels in North America," "The Antiquity of Man," of treatises on the Elements and Principles of Geology, and of many papers in scientific journals. He was created a baronet late in life, and died here at the beginning of 1875. His house, in 1876, became the residence of Mr. W. E. Gladstone. In this street, too, lived Sir John Herschel, the son of Sir William Herschel, the astronomer. The father, who was of Hanoverian extraction, coming to England in the reign of George II., held for some time the post of organist at Halifax, and also at Bath. Whilst at the latter place he turned his attention to astronomy. He began to contribute to the "Philosophical Transactions" in 1780, and in the following year announced to the world his discovery of a supposed comet, which soon turned out to be the new planet now called Uranus. This announcement drew him immediately into the "full blaze of fame," and he was at once appointed astronomer to King George III. It was the discovery of this planet which gave the impetus to further additions to the solar system by others in more recent times. In the stellar field Herschel also achieved great results. Late in life he was elected President of the Royal Astronomical Society, and he died at Slough, near Windsor, in 1822. Sir John Herschel, who was little inferior to his father, either as an astronomer or as a mathematician, received the honour of a baronetcy at the Queen's coronation, and was for some time Master of the Mint. He died in 1871.

Allan Ramsay, the painter, who lived at No. 67, was appointed "principal painter to George III.," and died in 1784. "Allan Ramsay's house," says Mr. Peter Cunningham, "was in 1800 the residence of Colonel John Ramsay, his son." In 1826 No. 49 was in the occupation of Mr. William Horne, afterwards Sir William Horne, Solicitor-General in 1832-4, and M.P. for Marylebone. In this street, too, lived Viscount Strangford, the diplomatist and poet; and also Lady Nelson, the relict of the hero of the Nile and Trafalgar.

Dean Swift appears to have been at one time a resident here; at all events, he dates from Harley Street one of his letters to "Stella," in which he alludes with feelings of disgust to the nightly outrages then being perpetrated in London by the "Mohawks," whose street outrages we have already mentioned.* This street is now principally inhabited by physicians and surgeons. On the west side, between Queen Anne Street and Great Mary-

with it, is Portland Place, a thoroughfare remarkable for its width, being upwards of 100 feet wide, in respect of which it contrasts most agreeably with the narrow thoroughfares which prevail in most quarters of London, reminding us of the broad boulevards of Paris and other foreign cities, though falling short of them in beauty because it has no trees. In 1875, however, it was resolved by the parochial and municipal authorities that

FOLEY HOUSE, IN 1800.   (*See page* 452.)

lebone Street, are the Queen's College for Ladies and the Governesses' Benevolent Institution. The former was incorporated by Royal Charter in 1853, for the general education of ladies, and for granting certificates of knowledge. Individual instruction is given here in vocal and instrumental music, and there is a Cambridge Scholarship, open to the daughters or granddaughters of a graduate of Cambridge.

The readers of Charles Dickens will hardly need to be reminded that it was in this street that "Mr. Merdle," the gigantic swindler in "Little Dorrit," resided.

Eastward of Harley Street and running parallel

trees should be planted on either side, but as yet the suggestion has not been carried into effect. The two rows of stately houses which form Portland Place were constructed from the designs of Mr. Robert Adam in 1778, and named after the ground landlord. The north end was originally intended to have been terminated by a circus, but only one half was built; and that, now designated Park Crescent, was called, in 1816, by Nash, the architect, "the key to Marylebone Park." Had this design been carried out, it would have been the largest circle of buildings in Europe. The foundations of the western quadrant of it were even laid, and the arches for the coal-cellars turned. For some reasons, however, this plan was abandoned, and the entire chord of the semicircle left

* See Vol. III., p. 243.

J. M. W. TURNER, R.A. (*See page* 447.)

open to the Park, instead of being closed in by the intended half circus. This alteration is a manifest improvement of the entire design, and is productive of great benefit to the houses in the crescent and in Portland Place. Of Park Square, which was erected in its stead, we shall have to speak in a future chapter. In Park Crescent, facing Portland Place, is a bronze statue of the Duke of Kent, the father of Queen Victoria; it was designed and cast by Gahagan.

Among the residents in Park Crescent have been Mr. Ralph Bernal, who lived at No. 11, before settling in Eaton Square; Joseph Buonaparte; the late Sir John Taylor Coleridge and his son Sir

John Duke (afterwards Lord Chief Justice) Coleridge ; and also Sir Charles Wheatstone, the inventor of the electric telegraph, and the man who, in conjunction with Sir William Fothergill Cooke, placed that discovery at the service of the nation, and, in fact, of the world. He died at Paris in 1875, but his remains were brought over to England, and buried at Kensal Green.

Although less fashionably inhabited than when first built, Portland Place still numbers among its occupants several members of "the upper ten thousand," including peers, baronets, judges, and ambassadors. In the year 1836 No. 38 was the residence of Lord Denman, Chief Justice of the Court of Queen's Bench ; No. 58 was that of Count Batthyani ; and at No. 61 lived Sir William Curtis, the eccentric alderman, the advocate of "the three R's"—reading, 'riting, and 'rithmetic. No. 24 at that time was occupied by Mr. J. B. Sawrey Morritt, of Rokeby, the friend and correspondent of Sir Walter Scott. Lord Selborne has lived in Portland Place for over twenty years.

Here, in 1819, was the Spanish Embassy; and here the ambassador gave a splendid entertainment on the 16th of December in that year in honour of the marriage of his master, the King of Spain ; the Prince Regent, all the royal dukes, and members of the Cabinet, the Duke of Wellington, &c., were present ; the house was brilliantly illuminated, and a squadron of the Royal Horse Guards was on duty in the street in case of any disturbance arising.

In the year 1772, according to a plan and detailed account given in Northouck's "History of London," a new square was intended on the site of Portland Place, to be called Queen Square ; it was to be bounded by Foley House and gardens on the south ; by houses abutting on Portland Street on the east ; by Harley Street on the west ; and by an island of mansions on the north ; with two grand streets, one on the east, called Highgate Place ; and the other, on the west, designated Hampstead Place. Westward, towards the south, is Great Queen Anne Street, and opposite to it, on the east, Little Queen Anne Street. This design, however, was abandoned, and Portland Place built as above described.

It was part of Nash's design, in building Regent Street, that the great thoroughfare should lead through and beyond Portland Place to a magnificent palace to be built for George IV. in the centre of the Regent's Park. This design, also, was abandoned.

Foley House, at the southern end of Portland Place, was the town residence of Lord Foley ; it was a large mansion, and with its surrounding grounds occupied a considerable amount of space, stretching away to the north-east corner of Cavendish Square. The house was of the same width as Portland Place, and had a somewhat dwarfed elevation ; and the garden in front was separated from Portland Place by a brick wall. The building was pulled down about the year 1820, for the formation of Langham Place, so called after the adjoining mansion, belonging to Sir James Langham. Foley House is still kept in remembrance by the name being given to one of the mansions (No. 6) on the east side of Portland Place, and also by Foley Street, which is immediately contiguous. In Foley Place (now called Langham Street), which also occupied part of the grounds surrounding Foley House, lived John Hayter, the artist. Close by old Foley House, on part of the site now occupied by the Langham Hotel, stood till about 1860 Mansfield House, the town mansion of the Earl of Mansfield. The first Lord Mansfield, it is said, owed his first steps in professional success to the kindness of his friend and neighbour, Lord Foley, who allowed him £200 a year out of his own not very large income, to "keep up appearances " till he could achieve an income for himself.

Lord Mansfield in his early life was a great friend of Pope, who addresses him in his " Moral Essays" as " Dear Murray ; " and, in his later days, of Dr. Johnson, who, however, stoutly refused to give Scotland any very great share of the credit arising from his lordship's career, as he was educated in England. " Much may be done with a Scotchman," the prejudiced old doctor would say goodhumouredly, " if he is only caught young ! "

Close to Foley House stood also the mansion of Sir James Langham, after whom the adjoining Place was named. On its site, about the year 1862, was erected a monster hotel called the " Langham," one of the most spacious and complete establishments of the kind in London. Here families can live, being boarded by contract, escaping all the domestic worries of servants, and petty household expenses.

English inns have not lost their reputation for comfort and the attention paid to guests ; but the almost entire alteration in the methods of travelling by the introduction of railways has left them considerably behind the requirements of the age. Except in the smaller towns and villages, they have been superseded by hotels—houses of a more pretentious kind, which contain suites of apartments for families or individuals who choose to be alone, also a larger apartment for travellers generally. About the year 1861 projects were set on foot for the purpose of building several hotels in London worthy of the place, and corresponding to the vastness of modern demands, and the "Langham" was not only one of the first erected, but has ever since remained one of the most important.

The Langham Hotel was originally designed by a company about the year 1858, but the project proved abortive. The design, however, was subsequently taken in hand by another set of shareholders, who employed Messrs. Giles and Murray as the architects, and the foundations were laid in 1863. The hotel, which cost upwards of £300,000, is one of the largest buildings in London, and comprises no less than six hundred apartments. It measures upwards of 200 feet in the façade looking up Portland Place, and is upwards of 120 feet in height, the rooms rising to a sixth storey, and overtops by some forty or fifty feet all the mansions in Portland Place and Cavendish Square. The style of architecture would be called Italian; it is, however, plain, simple, and substantial, and singularly free from meretricious ornament. It includes large drawing-rooms, a dining-room, or coffee-room, 100 feet in length, smoking-rooms, billiard-rooms, post-office, telegraph-office, parcels-office, &c., thus uniting all the comforts of a club with those of a private home, each set of apartments forming a "flat" complete in itself. Below are spacious kitchen, laundry, &c., and water is laid over all the house, being raised by an engine in the basement. Some idea of the extensive nature of this establishment may be formed when we add that its staff of servants numbers about two hundred and fifty persons, from the head steward and matron down to the junior kitchenmaid and smallest "tiger." The "Langham," on an emergency, can make up as many as 400 beds. The floors are connected with each other by means of a "lift" which goes up and down at intervals. It is as nearly fire-proof as art can render it.

The hotel, which may be called, not a monster, but a leviathan of its kind, was opened in June, 1865, with a luncheon at which the Prince of Wales was present; and not long after its opening a dinner was given here, as an experiment towards utilising horse-flesh by the "hippophagists" of this country and of Paris. These monster hotels are no novelties in America; indeed, the Langham is far outstripped in size by the Palace Hotel at St. Francisco; but as this is the first experiment of the kind which has been made in London, it may be as well to add that it has paid a dividend of 20 per cent. upon the outlay.

Langham Place has had, at different times, some noted men among its residents. At No. 15 lived, and here also died, May 30th, 1832, the accomplished lawyer, philosopher, and historian, Sir James Mackintosh. His death was occasioned by a small bone of a fowl which accidentally lodged in his throat. He was buried in the churchyard at Hampstead. No. 6 was formerly the house of Sir Anthony Carlisle, the fashionable surgeon; and during the parliamentary season of 1836, No. 10 was the town residence of Daniel O'Connell, the well-known member for Dublin.

In the north-east corner of Langham Place, at the point where the road sweeps boldly round to enter Portland Place, stands All Souls' Church. It was built from the designs of Nash, in 1824, and forms a pleasing termination of the view from the junction of Regent Street and Oxford Street. It has a circular tower surrounded with Ionic columns, and Corinthian peristyle above; the "extinguisher" spire is circular and tapering. The interior arrangement is after the Italian style, being divided into a nave and aisles by colonnades. The altar-piece is a painting of "Christ crowned with Thorns," by Westall. Among the previous incumbents of this church have been Dr. Thomson, Archbishop of York, and Dr. Baring, late Bishop of Durham.

On the east side of Langham Place, about half way between the church and the north end of Upper Regent Street, is St. George's Hall. The building contains a spacious room which is occasionally used for balls, concerts, and other entertainments; and likewise for public meetings and lectures both on week days and Sundays. Here are the offices of the London Academy of Music, which was established in 1861. The academy is open to amateur as well as to professional students, and the instruction in the various branches of musical education is given by some of the first professors of the day.

The Portland Bazaar in Langham Place, better known as the "German Fair," was erected as far back as the year 1835, and was opened as a bazaar in 1839. Fourteen years afterwards it was burnt down and rebuilt with great improvements. The management of this establishment was in one respect unlike that of rival undertakings, as every young person employed had a direct interest in the profits, and was not in any way responsible for stall rents, or the purchase of stock; consequently there was no fear of her losing her little all. From November to the end of January the German Fair was literally crammed with customers, the whole stock being imported direct from Germany, France, and other foreign countries. When the bazaar was rebuilt after the fire above mentioned, the southern portion of the premises, up to that time used as a furniture warehouse, was converted into the large building known as St. George's Hall, of which we have spoken above. In the winter of 1875–6 the premises were taken for the purpose of forming a large first-class "skating-rink," and the necessary alterations were at once effected in the building. The project was started by a company, and the rink was called the "Langham." It included the conveniences of a club, a restaurant, &c., on the grandest possible scale. The rink comprised a hall fitted up for musical performances, fancy-dress fêtes, &c., and was surrounded by galleries which could be used as promenades. The project nevertheless failed, and the building has since been used by "Archdeacon" Dunbar as a ritualist chapel.

The upper part of Regent Street was made by demolishing two narrow and ill-built thoroughfares, called Edward and Bolsover Streets, which formed a continuous line from the east side of Foley House into Oxford Street, nearly opposite to Great Swallow Street, which, as we have shown in a previous chapter, was amplified into Regent Street. On the west side of Upper Regent Street was an institution perhaps as well known to country visitors to London as to Londoners themselves—the Royal Polytechnic. It was founded in 1838, for the exhibition of novelties in "the Arts and Practical Science, especially in connection with Agriculture, Manufactures, and other branches of Industry." The buildings were enlarged in 1848. The premises of this institution were capacious and well-appointed, and extend from the east entrance in Regent Street 320 feet in depth, including the mansion, No. 5, Cavendish Square. The exhibition consisted, for the most part, of mechanical and other models, distributed through various apartments; a hall devoted to manufacturing processes; a theatre, or lecture-room; a very spacious hall; and other apartments.

The "Great Hall," lighted from the roof, contained models and designs. The floor of the hall was for many years principally occupied by two canals, containing a surface of 700 feet of water; attached to which were the appurtenances of a dockyard, locks, water-wheels, steam-boat models, &c. At the west end was a reservoir, or tank, fourteen feet deep; this, with the canals, held nearly 5,000 gallons of water, and could, if requisite, be emptied in less than one minute. Beneath the west-end gallery hung the diving-bell, which had, from the commencement, been the chief and standing attraction of the Poly-

technic, especially with the young folks and country cousins.

Courses of lectures were delivered on the principal topics of the day, and indeed upon almost every subject connected with human interest, accompanied with dioramic illustrations, and various optical illusions; not the least interesting of these was the so-called "Ghost" illusion, which is associated with the name of Professor Pepper, and has obtained great popularity in all the various shapes, dramatic and other, which it has assumed from season to season. The manufacture of spun-glass was carried on in the large room almost from the commencement with great success.

The Royal Polytechnic Institution, we may add, was under the management of a council. Besides the rooms mentioned above, there was an excellent laboratory, where chemical experiments were carried out. Public classes were likewise held, in which instruction was given in the various branches of science, in music, history, geography, in Latin, and also in French, German, and other modern languages. These classes were open to ladies as well as to gentlemen, and they rendered the institution a most valuable assistant to the cause of adult education. These classes were given up after a fire in 1881, and the building was subsequently sold. It is now used as a lecture-hall and class-rooms by the Young Men's Christian Institute.

In the house over the entrance of the Poly-technic Institution was opened, in January, 1855, the Cavendish Club; its founder and proprietor was Mr. Lionel Booth. The club died a natural death at the end of 1872; it was, however, revived at the beginning of 1874, under new management, and with increased resources, especially in the culinary department, but has been again given up.

On the opposite side of the street is another house which has been at different times the home of divers clubs, some of which have had but a transient existence. At one time it was the "Corinthian," and opened professedly with the view of affording the luxury and comforts of a club to the north-west of London; but this proved a failure. In 1873 it was opened as the "Civil and Military," a title which was subsequently altered to the "Civil and United Service." It afterwards became the "Russell," admitted ladies as members, and, under the chairmanship of "Archdeacon" Dunbar, deservedly came to grief, having existed for a year or two as the "Lotus."

CHAPTER XXXV.

OXFORD STREET EAST.—NORTHERN TRIBUTARIES.

"*Miratur portas strepitumque, et strata viarum.*"—*Virgil,* "*Æn.*" i.

Condition of Oxford Street in the Beginning of the Last Century—The "Adam and Eve" Tavern—Figg, the Prize-Fighter—Selwyn and the Earl of March stopped by a Highwayman—The London Crystal Palace—Mark Lemon's Birthplace—Great Portland Street—"Homes" and Charitable Institutions—St. Paul's Church—The Central Jewish Synagogue—Sir George Smart and Von Weber—David Wilkie and Dr. Waagen—The Woodbury Permanent Photographic Printing Company—The "Girls' Home," Charlotte Street—George Jones, R.A.— Unitarian Chapel, Little Portland Street, and Charles Dickens—Riding House Street—Mortimer Street—Nollekens, the Sculptor—St. Elizabeth's Home for Incurable Women—Margaret Street—David Williams, Founder of the Royal Literary Fund—"Tom" Campbell and Belzoni—Sir Walter Scott—All Saints' Church—All Saints' Sisterhood—Great Titchfield Street—Castle Street—Oxford Market—The Princess's Theatre—Charles Kean's Shakespearian Revivals—Blenheim Street—A Strange Occurrence—Poland Street—The "North Pole" Tavern—Wells Street—St. Andrew's Church—Berners Street—The Hoax played by Theodore Hook—A Batch of Medical Societies—The Middlesex Hospital—Nassau Street—Cleveland Street—Newman Street—A Modern Worker of Miracles—Mr. Heatherley's School of Art —An Eccentric Vow.

THE region upon which we are about to enter dates its existence from the earlier years of the reign of Queen Anne. John Timbs writes thus in his "Curiosities of London:"—"In a map of 1707, on the south side, King Street, near Golden Square, is perfect to Oxford Road, between which and Berwick Street are fields; thence to St. Giles's is covered with buildings, but westward not a house is to be seen; the northern side of Oxford Road contains a few scattered buildings, but no semblance of streets westward of Tottenham Court Road." This would appear to have been literally the case, for a plan of 1708, which he also mentions, shows the "Adam and Eve" as "a detached road-side public-house." It stood, according to this plan, in the "Dung-field," near the present Adam and Eve Court, almost opposite Poland Street; in an adjoining field is represented "the boarded house of Figg, the prize-fighter," standing quite isolated from other buildings. Figg appears to have been a noted character in his time. Hogarth has preserved his face in one of his engravings; and local gossips still quote the lines, by an unknown author—

"Long live the great Figg, by the prize-fighting swains
    Sole monarch acknowledged of Marybone plains."

It appears that the amusements at "Figg's" were more varied than select, for we find that even women here could have "sets-to" in a manner marvellous to behold. One advertisement of the time announces that "Mrs. Stokes, the City Championess, is ready to meet the Hibernian Heroine at Figg's." Other advertisements of a more disgusting character we omit to quote, in mercy to our female readers.

That the street in its early days must have been anything but a pleasant or safe thoroughfare for travellers is pretty clear from Pennant's remark that he remembered it "a deep hollow road, and full of sloughs, with here and there a ragged house, the lurking-place of cut-throats; insomuch," he adds, "that I never was taken that way by night

in my hackney-coach to a worthy uncle's, who gave me lodgings in his house in George Street, but I went in dread the whole way." It was this part of Oxford Street that was probably the scene of a highway robbery, recorded in *Lloyd's Evening Post*, about the year 1760:—"Jan. 30.—Saturday last, about ten in the evening, as a post-chaise was coming to town, between the turnpike and Tottenham Court Road, ... with the Earl of March and George Augustus Selwyn, Esq., a highwayman stopped the postilion, and swore he would blow his brains out if he did not stop; on which the Earl of March jumped out of the chaise and fired a pistol, and the highwayman immediately rode off."

But we are now concerned mainly with the northern tributaries of Oxford Street which lie between Regent Street and Tottenham Court Road. We will begin, therefore, with the Circus, and work our way gradually eastwards, very leisurely, for we shall have a good deal to say before we find ourselves at Bloomsbury again.

Near the Regent Circus is the chief entrance to the London Crystal Palace, one of the most elegant bazaars in the metropolis. This building, which has also an entrance in Great Portland Street, was erected in 1858, from the designs of Mr. Owen Jones, the plan of the structure being somewhat similar to that of the Floral Hall, in Covent Garden. It is constructed chiefly of iron and glass, after the manner of its great prototype at Sydenham. The roof, which is of coloured glass, of mosaic appearance, is supported by iron columns. The nave of the building, from the Great Portland Street entrance to the western extremity, is 180 feet in length; from it there is a transept extending southwards to the Oxford Street entrance, which internally has a length of 90 feet, giving, with the entrance-hall on that side, a total length, from north to south, of about 140 feet. On the ground floor is a spacious hall, divided by iron columns on each side into a nave and aisles, the floor being occupied by counters for the exhibition and sale of fancy goods of all descriptions; there is on each side a gallery above, and in and under these galleries there are also convenient and well-lighted stalls. The building was advertised for sale while this sheet was in the printer's hands. In a house on this site was born, in November, 1809, Mark Lemon, the genial editor of *Punch* during the first quarter of a century of its existence.

Great Portland Street is a broad and respectable

land Street, is a building called the Langham Hall, which is used for concerts and other entertainments of a similar character. It is also occasionally used for religious services. It was formerly known as the Lyric Hall.

On the same side of the way, about half-way up, stands St. Paul's Church, for many years known as Portland Chapel. It was erected in 1775–6, and stands on a site which formed part of a basin of the Marylebone Waterworks. John Timbs tells us

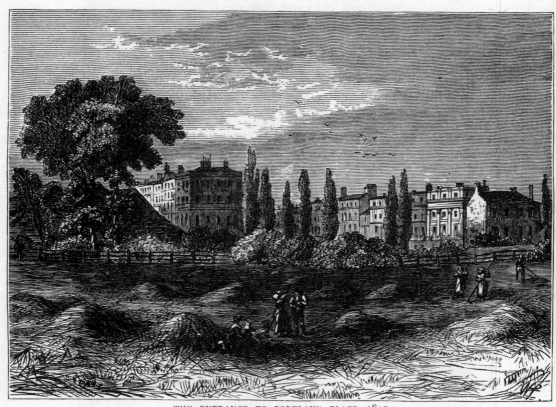

THE ENTRANCE TO PORTLAND PLACE, 1815.

thoroughfare, at present almost entirely consisting of shops, largely occupied by picture-dealers and music-sellers, &c. It extends, in a direct line from Oxford Street to the Marylebone Road, close by the eastern end of Park Crescent. The houses on each side, towards the northern end, stood back from the roadway, with gardens in front; but of late years shops have been thrown out on both sides of the way.

At this end of the street are various charitable institutions, or "homes." Amongst others are the National Dental Hospital, the Western Dispensary for Skin Diseases, and Miss Gladstone's Female Servants' Home.

On the west side of the street, near Little Port-

that there is a view, by Chatelain, of this basin, which was the scene of several fatal accidents and suicides. The chapel was first consecrated in 1831, when it was dedicated to St. Paul.

Near the above church is another religious edifice, which forms a conspicuous architectural feature in the street. It is the central Jewish Synagogue, which was completed and opened in 1870. The building is a fine specimen of Moorish design, its thoroughly Oriental style being especially exemplified in the interior, with its tiers of columns decorated with Saracenic capitals, supporting the gallery, clerestory, and lofty vaulted roof. The ark, in which are placed the sacred scrolls of the law, is situated at the south-east end of the building, looking towards Jerusalem, and is covered by a heavy curtain, embroidered with gold. Immediately over it are the two tables of stone inscribed with the ten Commandments; and above them, through a small circular window, shines the "per-

At No. 204 was originally the West London School of Art, now removed to 155, Great Titchfield Street. This institution has classes in architectural drawing, in drawing from life and the antique, and in design, as applied to mural, textile,

INTERIOR OF THE JEWISH SYNAGOGUE, GREAT PORTLAND STREET.

petual light" which is never extinguished. The ark rests on a platform of white marble, raised several steps above the floor. The *almemar*, a large raised pew, where the readers, choristers, and harmonium are placed, stands conspicuously in the centre of the synagogue, and is richly ornamented with gilt stanchions.

The Rothschild family showed much interest in, and subscribed largely to, the building fund of this new tabernacle.

and other decorations. It is in connection with the Government Department of Science and Art.

Among the eminent residents in this street mentioned by Mr. Peter Cunningham, were William Seward, author of the "Anecdotes" which bear his name; Dr. William Guthrie, author of a well-known grammar; James Boswell, Dr. Johnson's biographer; and Carl Maria von Weber. The two last-mentioned persons died here; the latter very suddenly, on the 5th of June, 1826, at No. 91, for many years the house of the late eminent composer, Sir George Smart. Sir George, we may here remark, is thus celebrated by "Ingoldsby," in "Mr. Barney Maguire's Account of the Coronation of Her Majesty:"—

> "That same Sir George Smart, O !
> Who played the consarto,
> With his four-and-twenty fiddlers all of a row."

Weber was buried at the Roman Catholic Church of St. Mary's, Moorfields, whence his body was afterwards taken to Germany. On his death Mr. J. R. Planché, who knew him well, penned the following exquisite lines, which were set to music, and sung by Braham :—

> "Weep, for the word is spoken !
> Mourn, for the knell hath tolled !
> The master-chord is broken,
> And the master-hand is cold.
> Romance hath lost her minstrel ;
> No more his magic strain
> Shall throw a sweeter spell around
> The legends of Almaine.
>
> "His fame had flown before him
> To many a foreign land ;
> His lays were sung by every tongue,
> And harped by every hand.
> He came to seek fresh laurels,
> But Fate was in their breath,
> And turned his march of triumph
> Into a dirge of death."

In this street, in a hackney-coach, which was conveying her home from the Seven Dials, his mother, in 1766, gave birth to Mr. J. T. Smith, afterwards the superintendent of the print-room at the British Museum, and the author of "Nollekens and his Times," and of "A Book for a Rainy Day," from which we have quoted very largely in these pages.

In this street lodged Wilkie in the early part of his career in London, as we learn from Cyrus Redding's "Fifty Years' Recollections." In 1835 he was in the very height of his fame and popularity. Dr. Waagen tells us that on one occasion he met Callcott, Eastlake, and Etty the painter at dinner. "Wilkie," he adds, "is now unhappily so overwhelmed with orders for portraits that he has hardly a moment for his good-natured humorous subjects." At No. 157 are the offices of the Woodbury Permanent Photographic Printing Company.

Charlotte Street, between Great Portland Street and Portland Place, and running parallel to both, at one time bore a very bad character for its residents. A clearance, however, was made by the parochial authorities about the year 1860, and now it is largely occupied by public institutions, among which may be mentioned the "Girls' Home," which

was instituted in 1867 for the purpose of lodging, clothing, and educating destitute girls, who may not have been convicted of crime—a sister institution to the "Boys' Home" in Regent's Park Road, which we shall describe hereafter. Here also are the offices of the Central Synagogue and of the United Synagogue.

At No. 10, New Cavendish Street, George Jones, R.A., was living in 1806. He was a well-known painter of battle-pieces, and some time Librarian and afterwards Keeper of the Royal Academy. He died in 1869.

In Little Portland Street is the leading West-end Chapel of the Unitarian body. Its minister was for many years Mr. James Martineau, a brother of Harriet Martineau. In this chapel Mr. Charles Dickens for a time held sittings, though in later years he frequented a parish church. Mr. Forster tells us that he was led to frequent the Unitarian worship on account of his "impatience of differences with the clergymen of the Established Church on the subject of creeds and formularies."

The neighbourhood of Great Portland Street, towards the upper end, is largely the home of artists and sculptors' studios; and on the southern side of the Euston Road the marble-yards are not unlike the Piccadilly of a century ago. Clipstone Street and Carburton Street, in this neighbourhood, are both named after villages belonging to the ducal estate ; the former in Nottinghamshire, and the latter in Northamptonshire.

Facing the New Road, in the garden of the top house on the east side of what was formerly known as Norton Street, but is now styled Bolsover Street, a few yards east of the top of Great Portland Street, were two fine elm-trees, standing as lately as the year 1853. It was said by the late Mr. Robert Cole, to whom the house then belonged, that Lord Byron had once spent an evening under their shade.

Riding House Street, which connects the top of Regent Street with Great Portland Street, bears witness in its name to an establishment long since forgotten, one of the Riding Academies so popular in the days of our great-grandfathers.

At No. 30, Foley Place (now called Langham Street), Campbell was living in 1822, and here he wrote some of his shorter poems.

Mortimer Street, which crosses Great Portland Street, extending from the north-east corner of Cavendish Square to Charles Street, was so called after the earldom of Mortimer, which was borne by the Harleys, conjointly with that of Oxford. At No. 9 in this street was the studio of the sculptor Nollekens, almost as remarkable for his parsimony as for the artistic power of his chisel. Here Dr. Johnson came to sit to him for his bust, and Mr. J. T. Smith, who was then a boy working at art under Nollekens, was busy drawing in the studio at the time. He thus describes Dr. Johnson to the life:—"The doctor, after looking at my drawing, then at the bust I was copying, put his hand heavily upon my head, pronouncing 'Very well, very well.' Here I frequently saw him, and recollect his figure and dress with tolerable correctness. He was tall, and must have been, when young, a powerful man : he stooped, with his head inclined to the right shoulder : heavy brows, sleepy eyes, nose very narrow between the eye-brows, but broad at the bottom; lips enormously thick ; chin wide and double. He wore a stock and wristbands; his wig was what is called a *Busby*, but often wanted powder. His hat, a three-cornered one ; coats, one a dark mulberry, the other brown, inclining to the colour of Scotch snuff; large brass or gilt buttons ; black waistcoat, and small clothes —sometimes the latter were corduroy; black stockings; large easy shoes, with buckles ; latterly he used a *hooked* walking-stick ; his gait was wide and awkwardly sprawling." The late Mr. C. Towneley, the collector of the Towneley Marbles in the British Museum, was also a frequenter of Nollekens' studio, and on one visit he tipped or "pouched" young Smith half-a-guinea to buy a store of paper and chalk. Though an exquisite sculptor, Nollekens was utterly uneducated, and could not even spell his own language. His wife, a daughter of Mr. Justice Welch, was as niggardly as himself. It is said that he attended the Royal Academy Club dinners, at the cost of a guinea a year, because he could carry off in his pockets enough nutmegs to make that difference in his housekeeping. He died in April, 1823, very rich; and eccentric to the last, left a very long drawn will, with no less than fourteen codicils to it.

At No. 67 in this street is a charitable institution in connection with All Saints' Home, in Margaret Street. It is called St. Elizabeth's Home, and its object is to relieve women whom the present London hospitals reject as incurable. The persons received here are chiefly those who have "seen better days," and are unable to support themselves without assistance. In each case it is required that the applicant should be able herself, or through her friends, to guarantee a small annual payment.

Running parallel with Mortimer Street, and extending from the south-east corner of Cavendish Square to Wells Street, is Margaret Street, which keeps in remembrance the name of Lady Margaret Cavendish, the daughter and heiress of the second and last Duke of Newcastle of that line, and wife of John Holles, Marquis of Clare and Duke of Newcastle. The duke died without male issue, and his daughter married Edward Harley, second Earl of Oxford and Mortimer, whose daughter and heiress became, in her turn, as we have already seen, the wife of the second Duke of Portland. The name of the duke's second title, Marquis of Titchfield, is given to the street running parallel with Great Portland Street, on its eastern side, and reaching from Oxford Street to the Marylebone Road ; whilst Bolsover Street, close by, is named after the duke's estate in Derbyshire.

In Margaret Street was the chapel of the Rev. David Williams, the founder of the Royal Literary Fund. For the facts contained in the following account of him we are indebted to Dr. Robert Chambers' "Book of Days :"—Born in a humble sphere of life, near Cardigan, in 1738, he was originally a minister of the Unitarian body, and settled at Highgate. He next set up a very liberal form of worship in Margaret Street, where he preached mainly on social subjects, such as the bad effects of gaming. We next catch a glimpse of him at Chelsea, where he kept a school, and had Benjamin Franklin for a guest at the time when the American philosopher was subjected to the abuse of Wedderburn before the Privy Council. He wrote works on education, politics, public worship, economy, &c., in all of which he showed a spirit of philanthropy ; but soon after the outbreak of the French Revolution we find him joining the Girondists, whom he helped to frame a constitution. When, however, the rabble at Paris began to thirst for blood, he returned to England, and set to work on the more sensible task of founding a society for the aid of men of letters. In this he succeeded, after many years of persevering labour, in which he collected £6,000. He had the satisfaction of seeing the society regularly constituted and founded in May, 1790. The society distributes between £1,000 and £2,000 a year regularly in aiding poor authors in their struggles. David Williams died in 1816, and was buried in St. Anne's Church, Soho.

In Margaret Street Campbell occupied chambers during the day, whilst editing the *New Monthly Magazine*, though he lived at Sydenham, and went home every night by the stage-coach. Mr. Cyrus Redding writes thus of him in his "Fifty Years' Recollections :"—"When Belzoni returned from Egypt I went to see his exhibition of the Egyptian tombs. He appeared little altered, and as I was going to take coffee with Campbell, I asked him if he would like to be acquainted with the poet,

Campbell being curious about everything relating to the East. He said he should like to go at that moment, and I took him. The king, the queen, and Bergami then occupied the attention of the public. Belzoni and I passing through Bond Street, his remarkable stature and foreign appearance attracted attention. Somebody gave out that it was Bergami. People stopped to stare at us, and a crowd rapidly collected. Belzoni proposed we should get out of the larger thoroughfares, which we did, he moving his Herculean form rapidly onwards. We crossed into Hanover Square, still followed by some of the mob; then crossing Oxford Street, we were soon in Margaret Street, and ensconced in the poet's lodgings. When Belzoni stood by Campbell, I thought of 'Ajax the Less and Ajax the son of Telamon.' I never saw Belzoni but once after this, before he started on the African expedition in which he died. He was an unassuming, quiet man, on whose merit I am convinced there were wrongful attempts made to cast a cloud. His knowledge was strictly practical; indeed, he pretended to nothing more."

On another occasion Cyrus Redding paid a visit to the poet in his apartments here, which he thus records :—"Walter Scott was in town soon after the *New Monthly Magazine* commenced. He was too much engaged, and too 'anti-Whig' to be enrolled at any price in our pages. One day Scott called in Margaret Street; he was going away as I went in. When he was gone, Campbell tried at an impromptu. 'Don't speak for a moment,' said the poet, 'I have it.'

"Quoth the South to the North, 'In your comfortless sky
    Not a nightingale sings.' 'True,' the North made reply;
'But your nightingale's warblings, I envy them not,
    When I think of the strains of my Burns and my Scott !'"

Cyrus Redding, like a "Fidus Achates," took the lines down on a letter-cover at the moment, and so saved them from perishing. Let us be grateful for the boon.

In this street, between Great Portland and Regent Streets, was formerly the West London Jewish Synagogue. It was built in 1850, from the designs of Mr. Mocatta, and consisted of a square building, surrounded on three sides with Ionic columns supporting the ladies' gallery, whence rose other columns, receiving semi-circular arches, crowned by a bold cornice and lantern light. The ark, which completed the fourth side, was surmounted by a decorated entablature, above which were placed the tablets of the Ten Commandments. This edifice has been superseded by the new building in Great Portland Street, above described.

In Margaret Street stands All Saints' Church, a handsome modern building of red brick, in the simplest and severest style externally, though its interior is more richly decorated than any other church of the Anglican communion in London. Until about 1850 there stood here a poor, meagre, and gloomy little structure, built in the year 1788, and known as "Margaret Street Chapel." It had been originally a meeting-house belonging to Lady Huntingdon's connection. On the publication of the "Tracts for the Times," this chapel, then under the Rev. W. Dodsworth, became a focus of extreme Tractarian views, and its incumbent and his colleague, the Rev. F. Oakeley, both became Roman Catholics. The new church, of which the architect was Mr. W. Butterfield, was built in 1850–9. The first stone was laid by Dr. Pusey, its first minister being the late Rev. W. Upton Richards. The spire rises to the height of 230 feet. The interior is richly decorated with carving, and with frescoes of the Birth and Crucifixion of our Lord, and the Court of Heaven, showing the saints with our Lord in the centre, by Mr. W. Dyce, R.A. The painted windows are by O'Connor. At the entrance of the church is a baptistery, and adjoining it is a residence for its clergy, who are mostly celibates. The music of this church is of a very ornate and elaborate character; and its ritualistic services attract large congregations, especially of the upper classes, the majority being ladies. There are separate seats provided for the male and female worshippers.

The following *jeu d'esprit*, said to be from the pen of a clerical wit of our day, in all probability contains an allusion to this sacred edifice :—

"In a church that is furnished with mullion and gable,
    With altar and reredos, with gurgoyle and groin,
The penitents' dresses are seal-skin and sable,
    The odour of sanctity 's Eau de Cologne.

"But if only could Lucifer flying from Hades
    Gaze down on this crowd with its panniers and paints,
He could say, as he looked at the lords and the ladies,
    Oh ! where is 'All Sinners,' if this is 'All Saints ?'"

At the corner of Margaret and Wells Street, opposite the church, and more or less dependent on it and its clergy, are various religious houses and homes, in which the work of Christian charity is conducted by ladies, who style themselves the "All Saints' Sisterhood;" they work under the sanction of the Bishop of London. The works in which they are engaged are various. They teach in the night-school of the district, and visit and nurse the poor and sick at their own houses; and they take charge of orphan girls, and receive aged and infirm women, incurable sick women, and young serving girls into the Home. These latter, as well as the orphans are trained up for service, and are instructed in the various kinds of household work ; and if any show an aptitude for teaching, they are trained to be schoolmistresses. The Sisters have also an industrial school, in which all kinds of plain needlework are done. The building once used as the temporary church in Margaret Street has been fitted up as an orphanage. Attached to the Home is a pharmacy, where medicines are dispensed by the Sisters to the sick and needy, under the supervision of able and experienced physicians, who regularly visit the institution, and give their services gratuitously. The buildings are of red brick, in the severest style of Gothic architecture, and serve the double purpose of a home and national schools.

Great Titchfield Street has had in its time, among its residents, a few men of note in the world of art. Mr. Cunningham mentions the names of Richard Wilson, the landscape painter, who, in 1779, lived at No. 85. Again, Loutherbourg, the landscape painter, resided for some years at No. 45 ; and No. 76 was the residence of Mr. Bonomi, R.A.

In this street was formerly a place of worship for the " Independents ;" it was known as " Providence Chapel," and was under the ministry of the eccentric preacher, William Huntington.* The fabric was burnt down in 1810, and on the minister being spoken to respecting its rebuilding, he is said to have observed that " Providence having allowed the chapel to be destroyed, Providence might rebuild it, for he would not," and in consequence the site was afterwards occupied as a timber-yard.

Cirencester Place, the former name of the north end of Great Titchfield Street, recorded one of the inferior titles of the Duke of Portland, who is also Baron of Cirencester. Like Norton Street, it was formerly tenanted by an unsatisfactory population ; but these were cleared out a few years ago ; and, the houses being numbered as part of Titchfield Street, the name disappeared.

Castle Street, a thoroughfare extending from Upper Regent Street to Wells Street, and passing across the north of Oxford Market, is probably named after an inn which bore that sign, and it has a history of its own. At No. 36, James Barry, the Royal Academician, resided in 1773, when in the height of his professional reputation and engagements. Here Edmund Burke gave him sittings for a portrait painted at the request of their mutual friend, Dr. Brocklesby. The painter here entertained Burke at a homely dinner, cooking the beefsteak on the fire in his parlour, and availing himself of the great orator's aid in the operation. Barry

died in 1806, at the house of his friend and neighbour, Mr. Bonomi.

At No. 6, Dr. Johnson and his wife were living, as we learn from Boswell, in 1738, on his second visit to London ; and it was in this street, at the house of some Miss Cotterells, his opposite neighbours, that the great lexicographer first met and was introduced to Sir Joshua Reynolds. It was also whilst living here that he made the acquaintance of Edmund Cave, to whom he addressed several letters, and dated from this house.

Oxford Market was so called either from the Oxford Road, to which it was adjacent, or, more probably, after Harley, Earl of Oxford, the original ground landlord. It was erected in 1721, as shown by the date in the brass vane which surmounted its centre. The vane bore upon it the initials " H. E. H.," which are probably those of Edward Lord Harley and his wife, Henrietta (the heiress of the house of Holles, Duke of Newcastle), who gave the site. It is called by the painter Barry "the most classic of London markets ;" but it is certainly difficult to see in what its "classic" nature consists. It was originally a plain hexagonal structure, mostly of wood ; this was pulled down, either entirely or to a great extent, about the year 1815, when it was rebuilt, small dwelling-rooms above being added to the shops below. It was the only daughter of the above-named Lord Harley who carried this and other adjoining property by marriage into the family of the Duke of Portland. In 1876, the site of the market was disposed of for £27,500 ; the market was removed in 1880–82, and the Oxford Mansions, a block of buildings in the Queen Anne style, erected in its place.

The Princess's Theatre stands on the north side of Oxford Street, about four hundred yards east of the Circus ; it stretches backwards as far as Castle Street. It occupies the site of a building formerly known as the Queen's Bazaar, which had existed for some years, but never gained popularity. It was destroyed by fire in 1829, but rebuilt. In 1833 were exhibited here Mr. Roberts's great picture of the " Departure of the Israelites out of Egypt," and also the " Physiorama," comprising twelve views arranged in a gallery 200 feet long. The edifice, like its successor, had a back entrance in Castle Street.

The building of the original theatre was a costly and unsuccessful speculation, and it nearly ruined Hamlet, the silversmith of Leicester Square. In 1841 it was entirely remodelled from the designs of Nelson, and decorated by Mr. Crace ; and it was opened in the September of that year with a series of promenade concerts. It was a chaste, elegant,

* See Vol. II., p 284.

and commodious house, having three tiers of boxes, besides another row just below the ceiling.

The history of the old theatre is chiefly remarkable for its having been the scene of Mr. Charles Kean's Shakespearian revivals, which were commenced in 1849, and continued for ten years. In putting these plays on the stage Mr. Kean spared no expense, and shirked no amount of study and trouble; and the theatrical world and the public

manager. Shortly afterwards, in recognition of his efforts to raise the dramatic profession and elevate the English stage, Mr. Kean was presented with a handsome service of plate.

The theatre subsequently passed into the hands of Messrs. Webster and Chatterton, of the Adelphi, and Mr. Dion Boucicault for some time figured as the leading actor. In 1864 a drama entitled the *Streets of London* was performed here to overflow-

THE MIDDLESEX HOSPITAL. (*See page* 465.)

at large are largely indebted to his liberality and erudition for the admirably correct costumes and *mise en scène* which were in his time characteristic of the plays at the Princess's. In all this he was ably seconded by Mrs. Kean (formerly known as Miss Ellen Tree), who entered warmly into the spirit of his work of revival. In the first year he adapted and produced Byron's play of *Sardanapalus*, and varied his Shakesperian revivals by putting on the boards at various times Sheridan's *Pizarro, Louis XI.*, and other standard dramas. In the year 1860, on his resigning the management of the theatre, Mr. Kean was invited to a dinner in St. James's Hall, where a large company, with the Duke of Newcastle in the chair, assembled to do honour to the famous tragedian and spirited

ing houses. The play, however, like many others of a similar character which have been since produced, appears to have aimed more at "sensationalism" than to have rested on its literary merits, and, therefore, as stated in Charles Dickens's "Life," may be put down as "but an inferior style of theatrical taste." Mr. Kean died in 1868.

In 1879–80 the theatre was rebuilt on an enlarged and more elaborate scale, and has since been under the management of Mr. Wilson Barrett.

We must here cross for a few minutes to the south side of Oxford Street, in order to speak of one or two matters which escaped us in our wanderings westward. Nearly opposite the Princess's Theatre, in Blenheim Street, was at one

OXFORD MARKET, 1870.

time the residence of Ugo Foscolo, of whom we shall have more to say hereafter.

A strange occurrence is related by tradition as having happened in Blenheim Street about the time that Dr. Johnson lodged in it. A coach drew up late one evening at the door of a surgeon, Mr. Brooks, who was in the habit of buying "subjects" for dissection. A heavy sack was taken out and deposited in the hall, and the servants were about to carry it down the back stairs into the dissecting-room, when a living "subject" thrust his head and neck out of one end, and begged for his life. The servants in alarm ran to fetch pistols, but the "subject" continued to implore for mercy in such tones as to assure them that there was no ground for alarm, for he had been drunk, and did not know how he had got into the sack. Dr. Brooks coming in, ordered the fellow to have the sack tied up again loosely round his chin, and sent him off in a coach to the watch-house, where it is to be hoped that he recovered his senses.

In Poland Street, the next turning eastward on the same side of Oxford Street, was living, in 1765, Mr. Burney, the friend and correspondent of Dr. Johnson, so often mentioned by Boswell. This street has also numbered among its residents Dr. Macaulay, the husband of the authoress, Mrs. Macaulay; Dr. Burney, the author of the "History of Music;" and the old Earl of Cromartie, who was pardoned by George II. for his share in the Scottish rising of 1745.

In Oxford Street, on the same side, not far from Wardour Street, is an inn called the "North Pole," so named, no doubt, to commemorate one of those many arctic expeditions which from time to time have left our shores, and those of adjoining countries, in search of the spot "where there is no north beyond it."

Re-crossing Oxford Street, we now leave the Portland property on our left, and pass into that belonging to Lord Berners' family. Wells Street, which crosses the eastern end of Castle Street, is narrow and crooked, and therefore more ancient than its neighbours. Its name is probably a corruption of Well Street, and so called after Well, in Yorkshire, the seat of the family of Strangeways, from whom Lady Berners descends. Here Dr. Beattie, the author of "The Minstrel," and of the essay on "Truth," &c., was living during his stay in London, in 1771. He was one of the last of Dr. Johnson's contemporaries, surviving till 1803.

In this street is the handsome district church of St. Andrew's, erected in 1846 from the designs of Mr. Dankes. It is in the Early Perpendicular Gothic style, and has a tower and spire upwards of 150 feet high. At the east end is a large painted glass window, by Hardman. The services are intoned, but "plain-song and anthems are used instead of Gregorian compositions;" and the church has been always remarkable for the excellence of its choir.

Berners Street, so called after the family title of its ground-landlord, runs northward a little to the east of Wells Street. It was built about the middle of the last century, and has always been celebrated as the "home and haunt" of artists, painters, and sculptors. Among its former residents are to be reckoned Opie, Fuseli, and Sir William Chambers, the latter of whom we have already mentioned in connection with Somerset House. Opie was buried in St. Paul's Cathedral. His second wife, Amelia, the learned Quakeress, was well known by her writings, "Tales of Real Life," "Poems," "Simple Tales," &c. In this street was the bank in which Fauntleroy, the forger, was a partner.

As we saunter up Berners Street we are irresistibly reminded of one of Theodore Hook's earliest pranks, when his life was already a succession of boisterous buffooneries. This was in the year 1809; and the lady on whom it was practised, says Mr. Peter Cunningham, was a Mrs. Tottingham, living at No. 54. Hook, it appears, had laid a wager that "in one week that nice quiet dwelling should be the most famous in all London." The bet was taken; and in the course of four or five days he had written and dispatched several hundred letters, conveying orders to tradesmen of every sort "within the bills of mortality," all to be executed on one particular day, and as nearly as possible at one fixed hour. From "wagons of coal and potatoes, to books, prints, feathers, ices, jellies, and cranberry tarts," nothing in any way whatever available to any human being but was commanded from scores of rival dealers scattered all over the metropolis. At that time the Oxford Road (as it was then called) was not approachable either from Westminster or from the City otherwise than through a complicated series of lanes. It may be feebly guessed, therefore, what was the crush, and jam, and tumult of that day. We are told that "Hook had provided himself with a lodging nearly opposite the fated house; and there, with a couple of trusty allies, he watched the development of his midday melodrame. But some of the *dramatis personæ* were seldom, if ever, alluded to in later times. He had no objection to bodying forth the arrival of the Lord Mayor and his chaplain, invited to take the death-bed confession of a peculating commoncouncilman; but he would have buried in oblivion that no less liberty was taken with the Governor of the Bank, the Chairman of the East India Company, a Lord Chief Justice, a Cabinet Minister—above all, with the Archbishop of Canterbury, and his Royal Highness the Commander-in-Chief. They all obeyed the summons—every pious and patriotic feeling had been most movingly appealed to. We are not sure that they all reached Berners Street; but the Duke of York's military punctuality and crimson liveries brought him to the point of attack before the poor widow's astonishment had risen to terror and despair. Perhaps no assassination, no conspiracy, no royal demise or ministerial revolution of recent times was a greater godsend to the newspapers than this audacious piece of mischief. In Hook's own theatrical world he was instantly suspected, but no sign escaped either him or his confidants. The affair was beyond that circle a serious one. Fierce were the growlings of the doctors and surgeons, scores of whom had been cheated of valuable hours. Attorneys, teachers of all kinds, male and female, hair-dressers, tailors, popular preachers, parliamentary philanthropists, had been alike victimised, and were in their various notes alike vociferous. But the tangible material damage done was itself no joking matter. There had been an awful smashing of glass, china, harpsichords, and coach-panels. Many a horse fell, never to rise again. Beer-barrels and wine-barrels had been overturned and exhausted with impunity amidst the press of countless multitudes. It had been a fine field-day for the pickpockets. There arose a fervent hue and cry for the detection of the wholesale deceiver and destroyer."

Hook, after this escapade, found it convenient to have a severe fit of illness, and then to recruit his health by a prolonged country tour. The affair, however, having been a nine days' (or, possibly, a nine weeks') wonder, blew over, and the unknown author of the hoax re-appeared with his usual coolness in the green-room of the theatre.

Berners Street forms the head-quarters of several foreign and charitable institutions, some of which have been established ever since the last century. In 1788 was founded the Society for the Relief of Widows and Orphans of Medical Men. The Medical and Chirurgical Society was established in 1805, and incorporated in 1834, for the cultivation and promotion of medicine and surgery. The society possesses a good library, numbering some 25,000 volumes. Here, too, are the Obstetrical Society of London, instituted in 1858; and the Pathological Society, founded in 1846. The last-named society was instituted for the exhibition and examination of specimens, drawings, microscopic preparations, casts or models of morbid parts, with accompanying written or oral descriptions, illustrative of pathological science. All the above-mentioned medical societies, together with another styled the Clinical Society of London, are accommodated in the same house (No. 53).

No. 54 in this street was originally St. Peter's Hospital for Stone. This charitable institution was established in 1860, and its object is to benefit as large a number as possible of suffering poor by affording them, without a letter of recommendation, the advantages of hospital accommodation; to improve medical and surgical knowledge on the subjects specially treated of here, by bringing together a large number of patients suffering from those diseases, and thus affording opportunities for observation and classification; and, in the cases of patients suffering from stone, to investigate the best means of accomplishing its removal with the least possible danger to the life of the patient, and, whenever practicable, to substitute lithotrity for lithotomy. The hospital is now located in Henrietta Street, Covent Garden.

At No. 22 are the offices of the Ladies' Sanitary Association, and also the Society for Promoting the Employment of Women. At No. 9 was started, about 1875, the Berners Women's Club —one of the first experiments which was made in this direction—but the institution seems to have been soon broken up. The London Association for the Protection of Trade has its office at No. 16. in this street.

In Charles Street, at the top of Berners Street, the view down which it commands, is the Middlesex Hospital. The building, which is of brick, and very extensive, comprises a centre and wings; it is fitted up with baths, laboratory works, ventilating shaft, and, indeed, all the necessary appliances for comfort, &c. The hospital dates from about ten or twenty years after the splendid bequest of Thomas Guy, the penurious bookseller of Lombard Street. It was first established, in 1745, in Windmill Street, Tottenham Court Road, for sick and lame persons, and for lying-in married women. It was removed, in 1755, to its present site, when it stood among green fields and lanes. Since 1807 the midwifery patients, to the number of nearly a thousand yearly, instead of being received as inmates, are attended at their own homes by the medical officers of the hospital. The cancer wards were founded by a gift of £4,000 from Mr. Samuel Whitbread, in 1807, to which other gifts and legacies were added. A remarkable incident in the history of the hospital is that in 1793 it became a refuge for many of the French royalist emigrants driven from France by the Jacobin Reign of Terror. The buildings were enlarged by new wings constructed in 1775, and again in 1834. Lord Robert Seymour, a zealous and munificent friend of this institution, obtained for it the royal patronage of George IV., which is continued by her present Majesty. The medical school, established in 1835, enjoys a high reputation; it is furnished with a museum of valuable collections.

The hospital contains beds for upwards of three hundred patients. Of these twenty-six are devoted to the cancer establishment, instituted in the year 1791, where the patient is allowed to remain "until relieved by art or released by death;" eight are appropriated to women suffering from diseases peculiar to their sex; the remainder of the beds being set apart for general miscellaneous cases. Upwards of nine hundred lying-in married women are attended at their own habitations, and eighteen thousand out-door patients are relieved every year. The hospital is unendowed. The annual subscriptions amount to not more than £2,355, while of late years the expenditure has been increased by some necessary works of improvement.

This hospital has numbered among its surgeons and physicians men of the highest eminence in the medical profession; besides which it has been the cradle of many eminent careers in surgery.

In 1812 Sir Charles Bell was appointed surgeon to this hospital, an important step in his early professional progress. We have spoken of him somewhat later in life, in our account of the Windmill Street School of Surgery (page 236). It was he to whom is ascribed the saying that "London is a place to live in, not to die in;" and his remarks, perhaps, may explain the reason which led him, in the midst of a successful career in the metropolis, to retire to his native city of Edinburgh—a step which few Scotchmen take, if successful on the south of the Tweed.

The southern side of Charles Street, which is continued by Goodge Street into Tottenham Court Road, presents a busy appearance, especially on Friday and Saturday evenings; and as one of the few street markets remaining at the West-end, and probably destined at no long interval to disappear, may claim a short notice. To the long row of stall-keepers on its southern side, who display their stores of fish, fruit, and vegetables in hand-barrows and baskets, and on movable slabs, we may apply the words of Henry Mayhew :—" The scene in these parts has more of the character of a fair than of a market. There are hundreds of stalls, and every stall has its one or two lights; either it is illuminated by the intense white light of the new self-generating gas-lamp, or else it is brightened up by the red smoking flame of the old-fashioned grease lamps. One man shows off his yellow haddock with a candle stuck in a bundle of firewood; his neighbour makes his candlestick of a huge turnip, and the tallow gutters over its sides; while the boy shouting 'Eight a penny pears!' has rolled his dip in a thick coat of brown paper, that flares away with the candle. Some stalls are crimson with a fire shining through the holes beneath the baked chestnut stove. Others have handsome octohedral lamps; while a few have a candle shining through a sieve. These, with the sparkling ground-glass of the tea-dealers' shops, and the butchers' gas-lights streaming and fluttering in the wind like flags of flame, pour forth such a flood of light, that at a distance the atmosphere immediately above the spot is as lurid as if the street was on fire."

Nassau Street, which runs north and south, a little to the west of the Middlesex Hospital, was so named in compliment to the royal house from which King William III. was sprung.

Cleveland Street, which severs the Portland from the Southampton estate, is a good broad street, extending from Euston Road in a south-easterly direction to the corner of Charles Street, close by Middlesex Hospital, and, together with Newman Street, affords a direct communication into Oxford Street. On the eastern side of Cleveland Street is a dull, heavy building, formerly the Strand Union Workhouse, but which was taken, in 1874, as the Central London Sick Asylum Infirmary, by the joint action of the several parishes of Westminster, St. Pancras, the Strand, and St. Giles's.

Newman Street was built between the years 1750 and 1770, and was, from the first, inhabited by artists of celebrity, and its shops at the present time still having among them several devoted to art studies. Banks and Bacon, the sculptors, both lived in this street; as also did Benjamin West, the president of the Royal Academy. Cyrus Redding, in his "Fifty Years' Recollections," speaks of him as "a man of few words, grave, and I imagine," he adds, "not possessed of much acquired information beyond his art. I remember there were numerous sketches in his gallery, but that of 'Death on the Pale Horse' struck me most as a composition. It was, indeed, of a high character." West's gallery was in the year 1832 converted into a chapel by the Rev. Edward Irving, on his expulsion from the National Scottish Church in Regent Square, Gray's Inn Road.

In 1826, No. 28 was in the occupation of Thomas Stothard, R.A., the designer of the Waterloo shield at Apsley House; and four other royal academicians of lesser note figure in the Royal Blue Book of that year as residents here. In 1836, three of these five R.A.'s have disappeared ; but the name of Copley Fielding, as yet without those mystic letters appended to it, is entered as part occupant of No. 26.

At No. 73 is the Atlas Club. The National Hospital for Diseases of the Heart was for some time located in this street.

In this street is a large public room called St. Andrew's Hall, where lectures on secular and religious subjects are delivered. In 1870 some temporary celebrity was given to it by a man named Newton, who professed to be able to work miraculous cures on all who came to him with a sufficient stock of faith. Numbers of persons responded to his call, most of them being females, of course ; and in some of them faith, or mind, had so great a command over the body and the nervous system, that they went away feeling or regarding themselves as cured. But this strange " popular delusion " soon passed away, and Mr. Newton was forgotten.

At No. 79 is Mr. Heatherley's School of Art, where many, if not most, of the rising artists of the time have made their commencement in artistic practice. It was formerly kept by a Mr. Leigh, who succeeded William Etty, the Royal Academician. Though the artists are "flown to another retreat," yet their aroma still remains in Newman Street, for half the shops are devoted to the sale of articles subservient to artistic purposes.

Some of the shop-fronts on the north side of Oxford Street about this point are very fanciful and picturesque. At the corner of Berners Street, No. 54, the shop of Messrs. Battam and Co., decorators, has a *Rénaissance* or Elizabethan front, " a picturesque composition of pedestals, consoles, or semi-caryatid figures."

Amid all its bustle and business, Oxford Street has nevertheless had a touch of "the romantic," if a peculiar eccentricity, brought about by disappointment in love affairs, can be called a romance. At all events, we read how a certain Miss Mary Lucrine, a maiden of small fortune, who resided in this street, and who died in 1778, having met with a disappointment in matrimony in early life, vowed that she would "never see the light of the sun !" Accordingly the windows of her apartments were closely shut up for years, and she kept her resolution to her dying day. It would, of course, be impossible at this distant date to fix with accuracy upon the exact house in which this singular whim of turning day into night was carried out, for, as the lady was merely occupying "apartments," it is probable that her name does not appear on the parish register of ratepayers, and a further search would be profitless.

CHAPTER XXXVI.

OXFORD STREET : NORTHERN TRIBUTARIES.—TOTTENHAM COURT ROAD.

" There is a fiercer crowded misery
In garret-toil and London loneliness
Than in cruel islands in the far-off sea."—*Anon.*

Rathbone Place—Mrs. Mathew and her Literary and Artistic Friends—The " Percy Coffee House " and the " Percy Anecdotes "—Noted Inhabitants of Rathbone Place—Reminiscence of Mr. J. T. Smith—Hanway Street—Jonas Hanway and the Introduction of Umbrellas into England—A Veritable Centenarian—An Ingenious Piece of Glass-painting—The " Oxford " Music Hall—Experiments in Street-paving—Percy Street and Percy Chapel—Charlotte Street—George Morland—The Small-pox Hospital—Tottenham Street—The Prince of Wales's Theatre—St. John's Church—The Hogarth Club—Dressmakers' and Milliners' Association—Fitzroy Square—A Favourite Locality for Artists—Warren Street—Dr. Kitchiner—Whitfield Street—Tottenham Court Road—Tottenham Court Fair—Whitefield's Tabernacle—A Grim Story—An Eccentric Character—" Peg " Fryer, the Actress—The " Blue Posts " Tavern—Dickens' Fondness for Stale Buns.

WE have now fairly turned our backs on the fashionable quarter of London, for a time, at least, and in the last and present chapters find ourselves in quite a different world from that over which we have been travelling ever since we left the neighbourhood of the Strand and the purlieus of Westminster. We no longer move about under the windows of dukes and duchesses, lords and ladies, gay courtiers, or well-dressed wits ; we come back into the midst of a prosaic and work-a-day world— a world which lives in furnished and often in unfurnished lodgings, in garrets and attics, and even in cellars; a world which knows more of the interior of the pawnbroker's shop and the gin palace than of a club or a church ; and where poverty is almost hopeless. And yet the view is not all black or dark : intermixed with those low and squalid thoroughfares are some fine streets and handsome squares; there are a few public buildings or private mansions ; but the carriages that roll by, or stand at the doors of some of the residents, are perceptibly fewer ; and, generally speaking, there is about the neighbourhood an air of repose and retirement which contrasts agreeably, in the height of the season, with the bustle which pervades Regent Street, and with what the poet calls—

> " Beatæ
> Fumum et opes strepitumque Romæ."

In this locality have lived and toiled many men who, in after life, have won for themselves names that will remain imperishable in the annals of art and literature; and some of the streets through which we are about to proceed have been rendered

The above lines, evidently drawn from life, might be applied with equal truth in former times to many a poor struggling artist as to those who wield the pen; but let us hope that now-a-days, as a rule, genius, whether literary or artistic, is better housed.

Rathbone Place, the first turning to the eastward of Newman Street, perpetuates the name of its builder, a Captain Rathbone, and an inscription on one of the houses, " Rathbone Place, Oxford

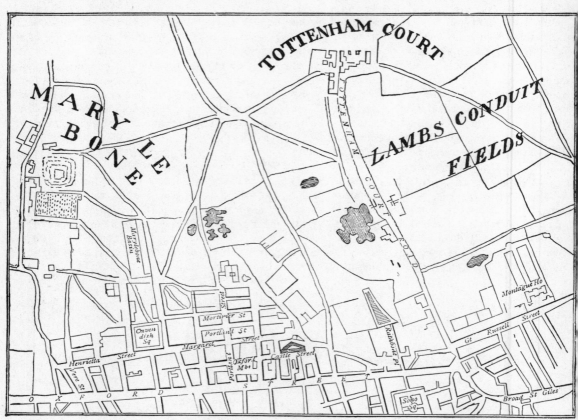

MAP OF RATHBONE PLACE AND NEIGHBOURHOOD. (*From Rocques's Map*, 1746.)

sacred by the early struggles of many an artist who has subsequently reached the highest honours of the Royal Academy.

Few who have read Goldsmith will forget his description of an author's bedchamber in this immediate neighbourhood:—

> " Where the ' Red Lion ' staring o'er the way,
> Invites the passing stranger—that can pay;
> Where Calvert's butt and Parsons' black champagne
> Regale the drabs and bloods of Drury Lane;
> There in a lowly room, from bailiffs snug,
> The Muse found Scroggins stretched beneath a rug.
> A window patched with paper lent a ray
> That dimly showed the state in which he lay,
> The sanded floor, that grits beneath the tread,
> And humid walls with paltry pictures spread."

Street, 1718," fixes the date of its erection. As the " Tyburn Road " does not appear to have been generally known as " Oxford Street " till some ten or eleven years later, though occasionally so named in legal documents,* the inscription is the more worthy of being placed on record here. In Ralph Aggas's plan of London, the commencement of this street is designated " The Waye to Uxbridge;" further on, in the same plan, the highway is called " Oxford Road." In this map cows are represented grazing in a field on the site now occupied by Rathbone Place.

---

* For instance, in the Act of Parliament, in 1678, laying down the boundaries of the new parish of St. Anne's, Soho.

In 1784, according to Mr. J. T. Smith, in his "Book for a Rainy Day," this street consisted entirely of private houses, and its inhabitants were all of high respectability. "I have heard Mrs. Mathew say," he adds, "that the three rebel lords, Lovat, Kilmarnock, and Balmerino, had at different times resided in it."

Mrs. Mathew was the wife of the Rev. Henry Mathew, for whom Percy Chapel, close by, was issued in 1782. We have already spoken of Blake's career in our account of the neighbourhood of Golden Square. In return for the friendly welcome which he always received from Mr. and Mrs. Mathew, Flaxman decorated the walls of their parlour with models of figures in classical and tasteful niches. But these have long since perished.

Rathbone Place has always borne an artistic

EXTERIOR OF THE TOTTENHAM STREET THEATRE, 1830. (*See page* 473.)

built. At their house, towards the close of the last century, used to meet a knot of literary, musical, and artistic celebrities, including Flaxman and William Blake, the long-forgotten artist and poet, who would sometimes recite his verses to the company. Of Blake Mr. Smith predicted, with great judgment, that a day would come when his drawings would be sought after with the most intense avidity, adding that, although little known to the world at large, he was regarded by Flaxman and Stothard with the highest admiration. The prophecy has of late years been fulfilled, and Blake's powers, as an artist and a poet, are now recognised at their true worth. It was through Mr. Mathew's influence, combined with that of Flaxman, that Blake's first volume of poems was reputation, and at present it is the head-quarters of artists' repositories, and of vendors of paints and drawing materials. Mr. Peter Cunningham reminds us in his "Hand-book of London" that "the well-known publication called the 'Percy Anecdotes,' edited by Sholto and Reuben Percy, derives its name from the 'Percy Coffee-house,' in Rathbone Place—now no more—where the idea of the work was first started by two friends, Mr. George Byerley and Mr. Joseph C. Robinson, who assumed the *noms de plume* of the Brothers Percy, of a certain apocryphal monastery." These brothers also wrote a "History of London," in three small volumes; one of them was also editor of the *Mechanics' Magazine* and the other editor of the *Mirror*. Mr. John Timbs, in his " Autobiography," tells us that the idea of the " Percy Anecdotes " was likewise " claimed by Sir Richard Phillips, who stoutly maintained that he suggested to Dr. Tilloch and Mr. Mayne to cut the anecdotes from the many years' files of the *Star* newspaper, of which Dr. Tilloch was then editor, and Mr. Byerley assistant editor ; and to the latter over-hearing the suggestion, Sir Richard contended, might the 'Percy Anecdotes' be traced. The *Star* was an evening paper, and well-timed anecdotes were its *spécialité*. Mr. Thomas Boys, the publisher of Ludgate Hill, realised a large sum by the sale of the 'Percy' work ; and no inconsiderable portion of its success must be referred to the publisher's taste. The portrait illustrations, mostly engraved by Fry, were admirable. The work had, moreover, this remarkable commendation of Lord Byron, who said, ' No man that has any pretensions to figure in good society can fail to make himself familiar with the 'Percy Anecdotes.'"

Rathbone Place numbered among its residents, in former times, Mr. Nathaniel Hone, R.A., the painter of the picture called the " Conjurer." He died here in 1784. In 1826, Mr. E. H. Baily, R.A., the sculptor, was living here ; as also was Mr. Peter De Wint, the water-colour painter. Here lived the learned Baron Maseres, author of the " Scriptores Logarithmici." He died in 1824, at the age of ninety-three. In 1836, all mention of the street is struck out from the " Blue Book." Such is the westward march of fashion.

The locality of Rathbone Place and Windmill Street, which lies immediately to the north of it, is thus mentioned by Mr. J. T. Smith, in " Nolle-kens and his Times : "—

" One day, in a walk with me, Nollekens stopped at the corner of Rathbone Place, and observed that when he was a little boy his mother used often to take him to the top of that street to walk by the side of a long pond near a windmill, which then stood on the site of the chapel in Charlotte Street, and that he recollected that a halfpenny was paid by every person at the hatch belonging to the miller for the privilege of walking in his grounds. He also told me that his mother took him through another 'halfpenny hatch' in the fields between Oxford Street and Grosvenor Square, the northern side of which was then in the course of building. When we got as far as the brew-house, between Rathbone Place and the end of Tottenham Court Road, he told me that he recollected thirteen large and fine walnut-trees standing on the north side of the way, between Hanover Yard and the Castle Inn, a little beyond the Star Brewery."

Passing along Oxford Street for a short distance, we arrive at Hanway Street, which was originally a zigzag country lane, leading out of the Uxbridge Road into Tottenham Court Road. It was at first, says Mr. J. T. Smith, better known by the vulgar people under the name of " Hanover Yard," and subsequently Hanway Yard, and it was for some time the resort of the highest fashions for mercery, and other articles of dress ; and it has continued to this day to be noted for its china-dealers and curiosity shops, as it was in days of yore when high-heeled shoes and stiff brocades were all the rage.

The author of " The Old City," who wrote under the assumed name of " Aleph," and was a native of St. Giles's, remembered this thoroughfare when it was still called Hanway Yard. It was narrow and dirty, and full of old china-shops, including Baldock's, " a sort of museum for Chinese horses and dragons, queer-looking green vases, and doll-sized teacups ;" and at the Oxford Street end stood a muffin and crumpet shop, which had about it an air of mystery and romance, as a suspected depository of smuggled goods. Another shop, for the sale of Dutch toys, was kept by an old woman named Patience Flint, a thin, little, shrunken old dame, who dressed in a close-fitting gingham gown, and wore a stiff muslin cap tightly drawn over her forehead. She rarely spoke, but conducted her business by signs, holding up four fingers to denote that the price of a cup or a saucer was fourpence, and scarcely eating, drinking, or sleeping at all. One winter's morning " Aleph " went to the shop, but found it closed, and that the neighbours were about to follow the old woman of Hanway Yard to the burial-ground at St. Pancras. The coffin-plate bore the inscription, " Patience Flint, aged 109 years."

In Hanway Street, in 1808, there was living a certain Mrs. Elizabeth Alexander, aged 106, under a portrait of whom, published in that year, appear the words, " Supposed to be the oldest woman in England."

How Hanway Street came to be so called, we have no definite authority for stating. It may probably have been named after one Jonas Hanway, to whom we are mainly indebted for bringing into general use in England that very necessary article of daily need—in our variable climate, at least—the umbrella. Hanway's name had already become favourably known in London, from his many schemes of benevolence. He originated both the Marine Society and the Magdalen, and, in con-junction with Captain Coram, he was active in pro-moting the foundation of the Foundling Hospital, of which we shall speak in a future chapter. In respect to his courage and perseverance in bringing umbrellas into general use, Hanway was a greater benefactor than at first might be supposed. Gay's poem of "Trivia," it is true, commemorates the earlier use of an umbrella by poor women, "tuck'd-up-sempstresses" and "walking maids;" but even with this class it was a winter privilege, and woe to the woman of a better sort, or to the man, whether rich or poor, who dared at any time so to invade the rights of coachmen and chairmen. But Hanway steadily underwent all the staring, laughing, jeering, hooting, and bullying; and having punished some insolent knaves who struck him with their whips as well as their tongues, he finally succeeded in over-coming the prejudices against it. Jonas made a less successful move when he tried to write down the use of tea.

With reference to the above subject, we quote the following from Chambers's "Book of Days:"— "The eighteenth century was half elapsed before the umbrella had even begun to be used in England by both sexes, as we now see it used. In 1752 Lieutenant-Colonel (afterwards General) Wolfe, writing from Paris, says: 'The people here use umbrellas in hot weather to defend them from the sun, and *something of the same kind to save them from the snow and rain.* I wonder a practice so useful is not introduced in England.' Just about that time a gentleman did exercise the moral courage to use an umbrella in the streets of London. He was the noted Jonas Hanway, newly returned from Persia, and in delicate health, by which, of course, his using such a convenience was justified both to himself and the considerate part of the public. 'A parapluie,' we are told, 'defended Mr. Hanway's face and wig.' For a time no others than the dainty beings called Macaronies ventured to carry an umbrella. Any one doing so was sure to be hailed by the mob as 'a mincing Frenchman.' One John MacDonald, a footman, who has favoured the public with his memoirs, found, as late as 1770, that on appearing with a fine silk umbrella which he had brought from Spain, he was saluted with the cry of 'Frenchman, why don't you get a coach?' It appears, however, as if there had previously been a kind of transition period, during which an um-brella was kept at a coffee-house, liable to be used bv gentlemen on special occasions by night, though still regarded as the resource of effeminacy. In the *Female Tatler* of December 12, 1709, there occurs the following announcement: 'The young gentle-man belonging to the Custom House, who, in the fear of rain, borrowed the umbrella at Will's Coffee-house, in Cornhill, of the mistress, is hereby adver-tised that to be dry from head to foot, he shall be welcome to the maid's pattens.' It is a rather early fact in the history of the general use of umbrellas, that in 1758, when Dr. Shebbeare was placed in the pillory, a servant stood beside him with an umbrella to protect him from the weather, physical and moral, which was raging around him. . . . About thirty years ago, there was living in Taunton a lady who recollected when there were but two umbrellas in that town; one belonging to a clergyman, who, on proceeding to his duties on Sunday, hung up the umbrella in the church porch, where it attracted the gaze and admiration of the townspeople coming to church."

We must not, however, be too severe in our censure of the folly of the public in mocking at the use of umbrellas, when we remember in our own day, even so very recently as the beginning of the Crimean War, it was regarded as almost a mark of insanity for a private gentleman to wear a beard.

At No. 15 in Oxford Street, a few doors eastward of Hanway Street, was exhibited, in 1830, a most ingenious piece of glass-painting of the "Tourna-ment of the Field of Cloth of Gold," elaborately worked out from Hall's "Chronicles," and con-taining upwards of a hundred figures and forty portraits. It cost the designer, a Mr. Wilmhurst, upwards of £3,000, and covered 432 square feet. After it had been exhibited in the metropolis for little more than a year, this painting was acci-dentally destroyed by fire.

Further eastward, and near the junction of Oxford Street with Tottenham Court Road, is the "Oxford" Music Hall, occupying the site of the old "Boar and Castle Hostelry and Posting House," which dated back to about the year 1620. The "Oxford" was one of the earliest and most popular of the metropolitan music-halls, and the present is the third building of the kind which has occupied the same site, the two previous halls having been destroyed by fire. It consists of a spacious room in the rear of the hotel, facing the street, and to which it is attached; and it has a lofty arched entrance, which, together with the hall itself, is tastefully decorated. The hall is fitted up with a stage, and around the other three sides there is a gallery or balcony. The performances given here consist of selections from popular operas, comic and senti-mental singing, glees, duets, &c., with an occasional acrobatic performance.

In 1839 the roadway of Oxford Street was made the subject of some experimental paving. The space between Tottenham Court Road and Charles Street was laid with a dozen different specimens either in wood, stone, bitumen, asphalte, or some other material; the whole, being laid in different patterns, presented a most even and beautiful roadway. The *Mirror* remarks that "the portion to which attention was more particularly directed was that of the wooden blocks, the noiseless tendency of which made the vehicles passing along appear to be rolling over a thick carpet or rug." These experiments being somewhat in advance of the age, and the public taste not being ripe for change, the roadway was suffered to remain unaltered. The subject, in fact, appears at that time to have elicited but little public interest; indeed, one magnate, Sir Peter Laurie, was as strongly resolved to oppose all wood-paving as he was to "put down suicide."

In connection with these experiments, a statement was published by the Marylebone Vestry, which will give the reader some idea of the immense traffic in the streets of London in 1839:—"On Wednesday, the 16th of January, from six in the morning until twelve at night, by the Pantheon, 347 gentlemen's two-wheel carriages, 935 four-wheel, 890 omnibuses, 621 two-wheel and 752 four-wheel hackney carriages, 91 stage-coaches, 372 wagons and drays, 1,507 light carts and sundries; total, 5,515. By Stafford Place, on Friday, the 18th of January, the total is 4,753, out of which 1,213 were omnibuses; on Tuesday, the 22nd of the same month, by Newman Street, the total was 6,992; and on Saturday, by Stafford Place, the total is stated to be 5,943." The number of vehicles passing through Oxford Street at the present time, we need hardly state, is probably double what it was forty years ago, notwithstanding the introduction of underground railways.

Passing from these dry matter-of-fact statements, we may add that this thoroughfare has witnessed some amusing scenes: for instance, the punishment of a Tom and Jerry boy of the older school, as recorded in the *Post Boy* of December 14th, 1747. The culprit, a carpenter, was whipped from the watch-house in Great Marlborough Street to the "Blue Posts" in Poland Street, for stealing the knockers from gentlemen's doors. He had two brass knockers tied round his neck.

A much pleasanter scene, however, was witnessed in Oxford Street, in the early part of 1872, on the occasion of the Prince of Wales returning thanks at St. Paul's Cathedral on his recovery from a dangerous illness. In obedience to the wishes of the inhabitants, the return journey of the Queen and the Royal Family to Buckingham Palace was made by way of Holborn and Oxford Street, and the whole line of route was beautifully decorated with flags and streamers.

At the northern end of Rathbone Place, and running eastward into Tottenham Court Road, is Percy Street, which is chiefly noticeable on account of the chapel near its western end. The fabric, which is known as Percy Chapel, was erected about 1790 by the Rev. Mr. Mathew, of whom we have spoken above. It was for some years the scene of the pastoral labours of the Rev. Robert Montgomery, the author of "Satan," "Luther," "Oxford," "The Christian Life," "The Omnipresence of the Deity," and other poems, who died in 1855. The article on his poems in "Macaulay's Essays" is probably one of the severest pieces of criticism ever published.

In this street lived the parents of Henry West Betty, "the youthful Roscius," at the time when the child made his first appearance at Covent Garden Theatre, and took the town by storm. We shall have occasion to speak of him further, when we come to Camden Town.

Charlotte Street, the thoroughfare leading from Rathbone Place to Fitzroy Square, was named either after Charlotte, Duchess of Grafton, or after the Queen of George III. Here, in the house formerly occupied by Sir Thomas Apreece, George Morland, the celebrated painter, was living in 1796. Mr. J. T. Smith thus records a visit which he paid him in that year, in company with a generous patron of art and artists, Mr. Wigston:—"He received us in the drawing-room, which was filled with easels, canvases, stretching-frames, gallipots of colour, and oilstones; a stool, chair, and a three-legged table were the only articles of furniture of which this once splendid apartment could then boast. Mr. Wigston immediately bespoke a picture, for which he gave him a draft for forty pounds, that sum being exactly the money he then wanted; but this gentleman had, like most of that artist's employers, to ply him close for his picture."

On the east side of Charlotte Street is Windmill Street. Here, in the early part of the reign of George III., the Small Pox Hospital was first established; it was afterwards removed to King's Cross, and thence to Highgate Rise.

Goodge Street was so called after the speculating builder who erected the houses in it. In 1772, the date of the map in Northouck's "History of London," it appears to have been called Crabtree Street.

Further northward, running parallel with Goodge Street, and crossing Charlotte Street, is Tottenham Street. Here was one of the most fashionable of the London theatres, the Prince of Wales's. The building was originally the concert-room of Signor F. Pasquali, and was purchased and enlarged by the directors of the Concerts of Ancient Music, who built a superb box for George III. and Queen Charlotte. Early in the present century it was fitted up by Colonel Greville for a body of amateur dramatists, called the "Picnics," "whose celebrity," writes Mr. J. Timbs, "rendered them objects of alarm to the professional actors of the day, and exposed them to the attacks of the caricaturist, Gilray." In 1807, or the following year, like the Olympic, it was converted into a sort of circus for equestrian performances, but it never in this respect rivalled Astley's. In 1820 it passed into the hands of Mr. Brunton, whose daughter, Mrs. Yates, was one of its greater stars. The ring had, in due course of time, given place to a pit, which is described, six years later, by Mr. J. R. Planché, as being "about as dark and dingy a den as ever sheltered the children of Thespis." Its out-of-the-way and unfashionable situation, however, did not prevent the "upper ten thousand" from patronising it occasionally.

In some of the earliest bills it is called "The New Theatre," the "King's Ancient Concert Rooms," Tottenham Street; afterwards it took the names of the "Regency," the "Theatre of Varieties," and the "West London," and after the accession of William IV., "The Queen's," out of compliment to Queen Adelaide. An attempt was made, in the year 1831, by Mr. Macfarren, to turn it into a sort of English Opera House, but it was not successful. Two years or so later it acquired a transitory celebrity under the name of "The Fitzroy," as the home of burlesque, and afterwards of French plays. In 1835 it was taken by Mrs. Nesbitt, who re-opened it under its old name of "The Queen's." It was for some time under the management of Madame Vestris; but its career seems to have been anything but flourishing until the year 1865, when it was taken by Miss Marie Wilton (afterwards Mrs. Bancroft), in the joint capacity of lessee and manager, who partly reconstructed the theatre and altered its name to the "Prince of Wales's." On Mrs. Bancroft giving up the management, it was taken in hand by Mr. Edgar Bruce, under whom the theatre continued its popularity till it was finally closed in 1882.

In Charlotte Street, on the east side, between Tottenham and North Streets, is the church of St. John the Evangelist. The edifice, which is in the Norman or Romanesque style, was built from the designs of Hugh Smith, and was consecrated in 1846. At No. 84 in this street is the "Doric Club." Originally the "Hogarth," it was founded in 1870, and limited to artists, architects, and sculptors. Here *conversazioni* are held during the season, and the pictures and drawings of members are shown

previous to being exhibited publicly at the Royal Academy, the Dudley Gallery, or the Gallery of British Artists.

At No. 98 were the offices of the Association for the Aid and Benefit of Dressmakers and Milliners. This institution, which was founded in 1844, and is now located in Gower Street, provides a home for deserving young persons, and assists them in obtaining employment; it also affords pecuniary and medical aid to those in distress, and almhouses for the aged and decayed.

The erection of Fitzroy Square, which we now enter, was begun about the year 1790. According to Mr. Cunningham, it commemorates the name of Charles Fitzroy, the second Duke of Grafton (whose father, the first duke, was a natural son of King Charles II., by Barbara Villiers, Duchess of Cleveland), to whom the lease of the Manor of Tottenham Court descended in right of his mother, Lady Isabella Bennet, the daughter and heiress of Henry Bennet, Earl of Arlington, one of the five statesmen who composed the "Cabal" Ministry of the above-named king.

In consequence of the stagnation to trade generally, caused by the wars at the close of the last and the beginning of the present centuries, this square remained a long time unfinished, the south and east sides alone being built. In the "Beauties of England and Wales," published in 1815, it is described as "not yet completed. The houses," continues the writer, "are faced with stone, and have a greater portion of architectural embellishment than most others in the metropolis." They were designed by the brothers Adam, already familiar to our readers in connection with the Adelphi and Portland Place.

Between Fitzroy Square and Tottenham Court Road was Fitzroy Market. It consisted of a number of small and dark tenements, and was pulled down in 1875.

The neighbourhood of Fitzroy Square has for a long time been a favourite haunt of painters, no doubt on account of the excellence of the light on the northern side, by reason of the vicinity of the Regent's Park. Indeed, from 1810 to 1830, all the neighbourhood between this square and Oxford Street appears, from an examination of the "Blue Books" and "Court Guides," to have been studded with artists, among whom figure a few R.A.'s, *rari nantes in gurgite vasto.* Among the former, living in Charlotte Street, are the names of Mr. C. L. Eastlake (afterwards President of the Royal Academy), Mr. (afterwards Sir) W. C. Ross, A.R.A., miniature painter to the Queen; in this street, too, lived John Constable, R.A., during the last fifteen years of his life. He died in 1837, and lies buried at Hampstead.

In Russell Place lived Daniel Maclise, the gifted Royal Academician, until a short time before his lamented decease, in 1870, whilst in the zenith of his fame. Maclise was a native of Cork, but settled in London in 1827, and in the following year became a student at the Royal Academy. He became an Associate of the Royal Academy in 1835,

Peacock." One of Mr. Maclise's latest works was "The Earls of Desmond and Ormond," painted in the year of his death. In 1835-6 Mr. Maclise was living in the same neighbourhood, at No. 63, Upper Charlotte Street. At this house a sketching society used often to meet, including Eastlake, Stanfield, David Roberts, Decimus Burton, and the brothers Alfred and John Chalon. They met at each other's rooms, the host of the evening giving out

WHITEFIELD'S TABERNACLE, 1820. (*See page* 478.)

and five years later attained the full honours. In 1866, on the death of Sir Charles Eastlake, the presidential chair of the Royal Academy was offered for his acceptance, but was declined. Besides his two large wall-paintings in the new Houses of Parliament—"The Meeting of Wellington and Blucher at Waterloo," and the "Death of Nelson," Maclise will be, perhaps, best remembered by his "Play Scene in *Hamlet*," in the national collection, the "Banquet Scene in *Macbeth*," and the "Vow of the Ladies and the

the subject, and an hour was the time allowed for each to work out his conception. When the artists went further a-field into the suburbs, this little coterie broke up. In the "Blue Books" of the period above mentioned there is also a sprinkling of "honourables," and baronets, and knights named as living here; but these have all disappeared when we come to the reign of Victoria.

In London Street, which runs from Cleveland Street into Tottenham Court Road, lived, in 1841, E. W. Wyon, the sculptor, and Miss Chalon, sister

THE "ADAM AND EVE" TAVERN, 1750.

THE MANOR HOUSE OF TOTEN HALL.　(*From a View published by Wilkinson,* 1813.)

to the brothers Chalon, and herself also an artist of considerable repute. Upper Fitzroy Street, in 1826, had among its residents, Mr. (afterwards Sir) Robert Smirke, R.A., the architect of the General Post Office and other public buildings.

Warren Street, on the north of Fitzroy Square, running parallel to the Euston Road, was so called, probably, after the wife of the first Lord Southampton, Anne, daughter and co-heiress of Admiral Sir Peter Warren. Some of the houses in it have a double frontage. In this street in 1817, and for several years subsequently, resided the celebrated Dr. Kitchiner, author of some works which have made his name widely known—the most celebrated being "The Cook's Oracle," which has passed through several editions. He was the son of a coal merchant residing in Beaufort Buildings, Strand, and was born in 1775. He received his education at Eton, and took his degree at Glasgow ; but as he inherited a good fortune from his father, he did not follow his profession. In Allibone's "Dictionary of English Literature" he is described as "a native of London, celebrated for writing good books and giving good dinners." His hours of rising, eating, and retiring to rest were all regulated by system. His lunches, to which only the favoured few had the privilege of *entrée*, were superb. They consisted of potted meats of various kinds, fried fish, savoury *pâtes*, rich *liqueurs*, &c., in great variety and abundance. His dinners, unless when he had parties, were comparatively plain and simple, served in an orderly manner, cooked according to his own maxims, and placed upon the table invariably within five minutes of the time announced. His public dinners were things of more pomp, ceremony, and etiquette : they were announced by notes of preparation, of which the following will serve as a specimen :—

"Dear Sir,—The honour of your company is requested to dine with the Committee of Taste, on Wednesday next, the 10th inst. The specimens will be placed upon the table at five o'clock precisely, when the business of the day will immediately commence. I have the honour to be your most obedient servant, W. KITCHINER, Secretary.

"At the last general meeting it was unanimously resolved that—1st. An invitation to *Eta, Beta, Pi* must be answered in writing as soon as possible after it is received, within twenty-four hours at latest, reckoning from that on which it is dated, otherwise the secretary will have the profound regret to feel that the invitation has been definitely declined. 2nd. The secretary having represented that the perfection of several of the preparations is so exquisitely evanescent, that the delay of one

minute after their arrival at the meridian of concoction will render them no longer worthy of men of taste : therefore, to ensure the punctual attendance of those illustrious gastrophilists who on grand occasions are invited to join this high tribunal of taste for their own pleasure and the benefit of their country, it is irrevocably resolved, 'That the janitor be ordered not to admit any visitor, of whatever eminence of appetite, after the hour which the secretary shall have announced that the specimens are ready.' By order of the Committee, WILLIAM KITCHINER, Secretary."

Dr. Kitchiner possessed an extensive library, for in the introduction to the "Cook's Oracle" he gives a list of the titles of about 217 different books treating of the subject of cookery, all of which, he tells us, he consulted in the preparation of the book above named. Another of his books was entitled, "The Art of Invigorating and Prolonging Life by Food, Clothes, Air, Exercise, Wine, Sleep, &c., and Peptic Precepts," to which is added "The Pleasure of Making a Will." He was likewise a connoisseur in telescopes, and in his "Economy of the Eyes"—a book abounding with many curious facts of great interest to amateur astronomers—he gives a description of fifty-one telescopes, reflecting and achromatic, which he purchased or had made for him during his thirty years' experience as an astronomical amateur, at an expense of more than £2,000. Among other eccentric habits of Dr. Kitchiner which are on record, is one to the effect that it was his practice always to take his own wine with him when he went out to dinner. His will was remarkable for its eccentricity, and it is said that another, making serious alterations in the disposal of his property, was intended for signature on the day following his death, which happened suddenly, on the 26th of February, 1827.

The Euston Road ; Cleveland Street, which runs thence southwards, towards Newman Street ; Grafton Street, which leads from the south-east corner of Fitzroy Square into Tottenham Court Road ; and Southampton Street, which skirts the west side of the square, are all so called after the various family connections of the ducal house of Grafton, and of Lord Southampton.

On the east side of Fitzroy and Charlotte Streets, and running parallel with Tottenham Court Road, is Whitfield Street, so named after the Rev. George Whitfield, or Whitefield, of whom we shall speak on reaching the "Tabernacle" in Tottenham Court Road. Here are two cross streets, bearing the names of Pitt and Lord North respectively, and thereby declaring the date of their erection ; but they are quite barren of incident and history.

Passing through Grafton Street, we enter Tottenham Court Road. This name, like that of Covent Garden, is a popular corruption, sinning, however, rather strangely, by way of elongation instead of abridgment. The country road which, three or four centuries ago, ran northwards from St. Giles's Pound, between green hedges and open fields, was so called from Totten, or Totham, or Totting Hall, the manor-house of which stood at the north-west corner of four cross-ways, on the site of what now is the "Adam and Eve," celebrated in Hogarth's picture in the last century, and of which we shall have to speak in a future chapter. This manor-house, it appears, belonged to one William de Tottenhall, as far back as the reign of Henry III. It is described in "Domesday Book" as belonging to the Dean and Chapter of St. Paul's. After changing hands several times, the manor was leased for ninety-nine years to Queen Elizabeth, when it came popularly to be called Tottenham Court. In the next century it appears to have become the property of the Fitzroys, who erected Fitzroy Square, upon a part of the manor estate, towards the end of the last century; and the property still belongs to the Fitzroys, Lord Southampton. In the map in Northouck's "History of London" (1772), a turnpike-gate is marked at the top of Tottenham Court Road, but this has long since disappeared.

In 1748 Tottenham Court Fair was kept for fourteen days without interruption, but "it does not appear," says Mr. Frost, in his "Old Showmen," "to have been attended by any of the shows which contributed so much to the attractiveness of the fairs of Smithfield and Southwark Green." In fact, although the notices of the fair make mention of a great theatrical booth, it seems to have been devoted rather to wrestling and singlestick than to purely Thespian purposes. These booths were occasionally used for the settlement of "affairs of honour" by means of pugilistic encounters. The challenges were duly announced in the newspapers of the day, in the form of advertisements. Here is one which appeared in 1772:—"Challenge.—I, Elizabeth Wilkinson, of Clerkenwell, having had some words with Hannah Hyfield, and require satisfaction, do invite her to meet me upon the stage, and box me for three guineas; each woman holding half-a-crown in each hand, and the first woman that drops the money to lose the battle." "Answer.—I Hannah Hyfield, of Newgate Market, hearing of the resoluteness of Elizabeth Wilkinson, will not fail, God willing, to give her more blows than words, desiring home blows, and from her no favour; she may expect a good thumping!" The

half-crowns were an ingenious device to prevent scratching. Cock-fighting, bull-baiting, and other "sporting" advertisements, accompany these lady-like diversions.

Mr. J. T. Smith thus writes in his "Book for a Rainy Day:"—"Notwithstanding that Tottenham Court Road was for the most part frequented by persons of the lowest order, who kept in it what they styled a 'Gooseberry Fair,' it was famous at certain seasons, and particularly in the summer, for its booths of regular theatrical performers, who deserted the empty benches of Drury Lane Theatre, under the management of Mr. Fleetwood, and condescended to admit the audience at sixpence a head. Mr. Yates, and other eminent performers, had their names painted on their booths." This must have been about the year 1777.

Tottenham Court Fair appears, from Mr. Frost's "Old Showmen," to have risen into sudden fame and celebrity about the end of George I. or the beginning of George II. Mr. Frost is unable to trace the origin of the fair, but contents himself with telling us that "it began on the 4th of August, and that Lee, Harper, and Petit set up a 'show' in it, behind the 'King's Head,' in the Hampstead Road. The entertainments," he adds, "were *Bateman* and the *Ridolto al fresco.*" Of the exact time when this fair was discontinued we have no authority for stating; but the truth is, that when the good people of St. James's ceased to patronise the "Old Showmen," those of Bloomsbury voted them low, and followed in the wake of their wealthier and more aristocratic neighbours.

In a previous chapter we have spoken of the insecurity of these northern districts of the metropolis in the last century, in consequence of the numerous bands of highwaymen infesting the locality; and in the *London Magazine* we read that as lately as 1773 two prisoners were sentenced to death at Newgate for robbing a gentleman and his wife near Tottenham Court turnpike.

The vicinity of Tottenham Court Road, being near to the Middlesex Hospital, appears to have enjoyed an unenviable notoriety as a depository for dead bodies. At all events, Hunter tells us, in his "History of London," that in 1776 the town was startled by the discovery of the remains of more than a hundred corpses in a shed hereabouts, which were "supposed to have been deposited there by traders to the surgeons, many of whom, especially in the Borough, were known to have made an open profession of this traffic."

On the west side of the road, between Tottenham and Howland Streets, is Tottenham Court Chapel, or, as it is generally called, "Tabernacle."

It was designed by the Rev. George Whitefield, the eloquent colleague and fellow-worker of John Wesley. The immediate cause of its erection was the opposition which he met with, as minister of a chapel in Long Acre, from the Vicar of St. Martin's-in-the-Fields, who had no sympathy with the new "Evangelical" doctrines. Hindered thus in his ministry, he obtained from the Fitzroys a lease of a plot of ground in what was then called, in maps and surveys, "The Crab and Walnut-tree Field," close to a pond known as "The Little Sea," on the road which ran from St. Giles's Church to the "Adam and Eve Tavern." In writing to his patroness, the Countess of Huntingdon, Whitefield says, "I have taken a piece of ground not far from the Foundling Hospital whereon to build a new chapel." When he built it, he desired to place it within the pale of the Established Church, and had hoped to have done so all the more easily on account of his position as chaplain to a peeress of the realm ; but in this he was disappointed. He sailed, however, as near to the model of the English Church worship as the law allowed him. The foundation-stone was laid in May, 1756, Mr. Whitefield himself preaching on the occasion. It was a large but plain double-brick building, seventy feet square, and capable of holding a large congregation ; over the door, we are told, were the arms of Mr. Whitefield. But the preacher was so popular that the edifice had soon to be enlarged ; and three or four years later an octagonal front was added, which gave it a singular appearance. Twelve alms-houses and a chapel-house soon grew up by its side, all the result of private subscriptions among the adherents of "Evangelicalism." Indeed, so celebrated was Mr. Whitefield as an orator that he numbered among his occasional hearers the Prince of Wales and several of his brothers and sisters, Lords Chesterfield, Halifax, and Bolingbroke ; also David Hume, Horace Walpole, and David Garrick. Ned Shuter, the actor, also, who was acting the *Rambler* at the time, came in one day, when Whitefield, turning to him, implored that in the course of his wanderings he might be led to "ramble" towards his Saviour. Shuter was struck at the unexpected attack on himself, and expostulated with the preacher, but in the end he became a Methodist. Whitefield died in America, in September, 1770, and his funeral sermon was preached here by John Wesley. There is in the chapel a monument to George Whitefield, and another to his wife, who was buried here. There is another to Augustus Toplady, author of the well-known hymn "Rock of ages, cleft for me." John Bacon, R.A., the sculptor, is buried under the north

gallery. The chapel was satirically called by the opponents of the new doctrines, Whitefield's "soul-trap ;" on which the latter merely said, "I pray that God may make it indeed a soul-trap to many of his wandering creatures." Whitefield was also burlesqued by Samuel Foote, on the stage of old Drury Lane, in *The Minor* and *The Hypocrite.* This, however, provoked him no further than to observe, with a smile, "I am afraid Satan is angry." There are few anecdotes told in favour of Foote's magnanimity ; but one deserves to be recorded. The epilogue to his farce of *The Minor* contained a burlesque of the style and manner of the well-known preacher, under the title of "Dr. Squintem." During the run of the farce it happened that Whitefield died. The epilogue was withdrawn. On its being loudly called for by the audience, Foote came forward, and said that he was incapable of holding up the dead to ridicule.

Following in the wake of the great preachers of the previous century—South and Barrow—and in a style which was afterwards copied by Rowland Hill at the Surrey Chapel, and by one or two preachers even in the present day, Mr. Whitefield increased his popularity by using eccentric terms and modes of expression in his sermons, and by reference to commonplace and trivial matters. In fact, his discourses often sparkled with wit and fun. Both Whitefield and Wesley contrived, as the Established Church disclaimed their acts, to disown and to defy its authority in turn, and therefore they gradually found themselves forced to take up the position of Nonconformists and Dissenters. A man of superhuman energy and power, John Wesley has been able to exercise the widest influence over the English-speaking race. Macaulay observes of him that "his genius for government and organisation was not inferior to that of Cardinal Richelieu," and others have compared him with St. Ignatius Loyola.

It is recorded in the *Gentleman's Magazine* that during a violent thunder-storm which passed over London, on Sunday, March 15, 1772, a man was killed by the lightning in this chapel. The electric fluid penetrated the roof just over the man's head, and entering a little above his breast, pierced his heart. He had two children by him at the time, neither of whom received the least hurt.

It is said that Whitefield wished to have the ground adjoining consecrated as a burial-ground, but that the Bishop of London refusing to perform the ceremony, he obtained several cart-loads of consecrated earth from a churchyard in the City, conveyed them hither, and spread them over the adjacent surface, which he thenceforth regarded as sacred. How deep the consecration went downwards was a question he did not even attempt to decide.

It would appear that the ministers of the two chapels in Tottenham Court Road and Moorfields often preached alternately in these edifices. At any rate, the eccentric Matthew Wilks, who was minister at Moorfields from 1775 to 1829, is stated to have had the oversight of the two chapels.

On the expiration of Whitefield's lease, in 1828, the chapel was closed for two years, when it was purchased by trustees, and greatly altered in its appearance, the exterior being coated with stucco. About the year 1860 the fabric was enlarged and re-fronted with stone.

There were persons living in 1832, as is clear from a letter published at that date in Hone's "Year Book," who "remembered when the last house in London was the public-house in the corner, by Whitefield's Chapel." The writer remarks that he himself remembered the destruction of a tree which once shadowed the skittle-ground and roadside of the same house. It was cut down and converted into firewood by a man who kept a coalshed hard by. Persons living at the above date could recollect Rathbone Place ending at Percy Street, and the mill still in position which gave its name to Windmill Street, and the neighbourhood of Charlotte Street being occupied by large open soil-pits. The writer above referred to tells the following grim story about this neighbourhood:—" A poor creature, a sailor, I believe, was found dead near here, and denied burial by the parish on the ground of a want of legal settlement. The body was placed in a shell and carried about the streets by persons who solicited alms for its interment. A considerable sum was collected, but the body was thrown into one of those pits, the money being spent in other ways. After a time the corpse floated, and the atrocity was discovered, but the perpetrators were not to be found. A friend of mine," he adds, " saw the fragments of the coffin floating about on the surface of the pool."

At " King John's Palace," a public-house in this street, lived an eccentric character named Shooter. He had been pot-boy at a tavern in Covent Garden, and became on such friendly terms with the rats in the cellars of the house, by giving them sops from his porter—for at that time everybody, if he liked, might have a bit of toast in his beer—that they would creep about him, and over his hands and face, without fear and without injury. He would carry them about the streets between his shirt and his waistcoat, to the surprise of every one, and even make them answer to their names. Later in

life he became a Methodist, through listening to the preaching of Wesley and Whitefield.

Tottenham Court Road in the present day is one of the busiest thoroughfares in London, and can boast of several monster commercial establishments, notably among them being those of Messrs. Moses and Son, outfitters, at the corner of the Euston Road; Messrs. Shoolbred and Co., linendrapers; and Messrs. Hewetson and Milner, upholsterers. At No. 216 are the offices of the North London Consumption Hospital, of which we shall speak on reaching Hampstead, where the hospital itself is situated.

This thoroughfare being of comparatively recent growth, there is but little to say in the way of anecdote connected with it. Here "Peg" Fryer, a wonderful old actress, who quitted the stage in the reign of Charles II., kept a public-house in her latter days. A farce called the *Half-pay Officer*, by Charles Molloy, was brought out at Drury Lane Theatre in 1720; and to Mrs. Fryer, then eighty-five years of age, was assigned the part of an old grandmother. In the bills it was mentioned:—" The part of ' Lady Richlove ' to be performed by Peg Fryer, who has not appeared on the stage these fifty years." The character in the farce was supposed to be a very old woman, and Peg exerted her utmost abilities. The farce being ended, she was brought again upon the stage to dance a jig. She came tottering in, and seemed much fatigued; but on a sudden, the music striking up the Irish trot, she danced and footed it almost as nimbly as any girl of twenty. She resided in Tottenham Court Road until her decease, which took place in 1747, at the reputed age of 117 years.

The " Blue Posts," a tavern still standing at the corner of Hanway Street and Tottenham Court Road, says Mr. J. T. Smith, in his " Book for a Rainy Day," " was once kept by a man of the name of Sturges, deep in the knowledge of chess, upon which game he published a little work, as is acknowledged on his tombstone in St. James's burial-ground, Hampstead Road."

Charles Dickens, as a boy, when living at Camden Town, and acting as a drudge at the blacking shop at Hungerford Stairs, used to frequent the second-class pastry-cooks along this route, and spend his coppers on stale buns at half-price.

At the southern extremity of the road, where it joins Oxford Street, and on the west side, are three or four isolated houses, the little foot-passage behind which is called Bozier's Court. They stand on what was waste land adjoining the old Pound. The removal of these old houses has been often threatened, but never carried into effect.

THE FIELD OF THE FORTY FOOTSTEPS. (*From an Original Sketch, taken in* 1830.)

CHAPTER XXXVII.

BLOOMSBURY.—GENERAL REMARKS.

" By thee transported, I securely stray
Where winding alleys lead the doubtful way ;
The silent court and opening square explore,
And long perplexing lanes untrod before."—*Gay's "Trivia."*

The Locality a Century ago—A Pair of Eccentric Old Maids—The Field of Forty Footsteps—A Singular Superstition—Street Brawls and Roysterers —The Game of Base—Bloomsbury deserted by the Aristocracy—Albert Smith's Remarks on this once Patrician Quarter of London— The "Rookery," or "Holy Land"—Meux's Brewery—The "Horse-shoe" Tavern, New Oxford Street—The Royal Arcade—George Street—Bainbridge and Buckeridge Streets—The "Turk's Head"—Old Dyot Street—"Rat's Castle"—The "Hare and Hounds," originally called "The Beggar's Bush"—A Dangerous Locality—Model Lodging Houses in Streatham Street—Bloomsbury and Duke Streets—Mudie's Library—Museum Street—Great Russell Street.

THE district now known under the general name of Bloomsbury lies on the north side of Holborn, stretching away as far as the Euston Road, and is bounded to the east and west respectively by Gray's Inn Road and Tottenham Court Road. It was originally called Lomsbury, or Lomesbury, and the manor and village are said to have occupied the site of Bloomsbury Square and the surrounding streets. At the time when Lomesbury was a retired village, the royal mews, an establishment for horses and also for hawks, stood here ; but on these stables being burnt down, in 1537, the hawks and steeds were removed to the stabling at Charing Cross, which was altered and enlarged for their reception. "Indeed," remarks Mr. Jesse, in his

work on London, "as late as the middle of the last century it (the mews) would seem to have been still kept up as a branch of the royal stables."

Of this neighbourhood, about the year 1685, Macaulay writes thus in his "History of England :" —" A little way north from Holborn, and on the verge of pastures and corn-fields, rose two celebrated palaces, each with an ample garden. One of them, then called Southampton House, and subsequently Bedford House, was removed early in the present century to make room for a new city which now covers, with its squares, streets, and churches, a vast area renowned in the seventeenth century for peaches and snipes. The other, known as Montagu House, celebrated for its furniture and its frescoes, was, a few months after the death of King Charles II., burned to the ground, and was speedily succeeded by a more magnificent Montagu House, which, having long been the repository of such various and precious treasures of art, science, and learning as were scarce ever before

country, the only buildings that met the eye in the interval being Whitefield's Chapel, in Tottenham Court Road, and Baltimore House, which, as we shall see presently, now forms one of the mansions in Russell Square.

Mr. Smith also remarks that when he was a boy

THE "ROOKERY," ST. GILES'S, 1850. (*See page* 484.)

assembled under a single roof, has since given place to an edifice more magnificent still." The building here referred to, we need hardly remark, is the British Museum.

Nor was Bloomsbury only an isolated village, but it was quite rural in its retirement. Mr. Smith tells us, in his "Book for a Rainy Day," that in 1777, when he went on a sketching excursion to St. Pancras Churchyard, the whole of the space between that spot and the British Museum was open

—that is, about 1774—"the ground behind the north-west end of Great Russell Street was occupied as a farm by two old maiden sisters named Capper. They wore riding-habits and men's hats; one rode an old grey mare, and it was her spiteful delight to ride with a pair of shears after the boys who were flying their kites, in order to cut their strings. The other sister's business was to seize the clothes of the lads who trespassed on their premises to bathe. From Capper's farm were several straggling houses ; but the principal part of the ground to the 'King's Head,' at the end of the road, was unbuilt upon. The 'Old King's Head,' opposite to the 'Adam and Eve,' forms a side object in Hogarth's celebrated picture of ' The March to Finchley,' which may be seen, with other fine specimens of art, in the Foundling Hospital."

The whole of the ground north of Capper's farm, so often mentioned as frequented by duellists, was in irregular patches, and many of the fields had turnstiles. The pipes of the New River Company were propped up in several parts to the height of six and eight feet, so that persons walked under them to gather watercresses, which grew in great abundance and perfection, or to visit " The Brothers' Steps," or " Field of the Forty Footsteps."

Dr. E. F. Rimbault, in *Notes and Queries*, gives the following particulars of these remarkable footprints, and of the locality in which they were situated :—" The fields behind Montagu House were, from about the year 1680, until towards the end of the last century, the scenes of robbery, murder, and every species of depravity and wickedness of which the heart can think. They appear to have been originally called the 'Long Fields,' and afterwards (about Strype's time) the 'Southampton Fields.' These fields remained waste and useless, with the exception of some nursery grounds near the New Road to the north, and a piece of ground enclosed for the Toxophilite Society, towards the north-west, near the back of Gower Street. The remainder was the resort of depraved wretches, whose amusements consisted chiefly in fighting pitched battles, and other disorderly sports, especially on Sundays. Such was their state in 1800. Tradition had given to the superstitions at that period a legendary story of the period of the Duke of Monmouth's Rebellion, of two brothers, who fought in this field so ferociously as to destroy each other ; since which their footsteps, formed from the vengeful struggle, were said to remain, with the indentations produced by their advancing and receding ; nor could any grass or vegetable ever be produced where these *forty footsteps* were thus displayed. This extraordinary area was said to be at the extreme termination of the north-east end of Upper Montagu Street. . . . . The latest account of these footsteps, previous to their being built over, with which I am acquainted, is the following, which I have extracted from one of Joseph Moser's Common-place Books :—'June 16, 1800. Went into the fields at the back of Montagu House, and there saw, for the last time, the *forty footsteps ;* the building materials are there ready to cover them from the sight of man. I counted *more than forty*, but they might be the foot-prints of the workmen.' This extract is valuable, as it establishes the period of the final obliteration of the footsteps, and also confirms the legend that *forty* was the original number."

The story is also recorded in Southey's " Common-place Book,"* where, after quoting a letter from a friend, recommending him to " take a view of those wonderful marks of the Lord's hatred to *duelling*, called *The Brothers' Steps*," the author thus records his visit to the spot :—" We sought for nearly half an hour in vain. We could find no steps at all within a quarter of a mile, no, nor half a mile of Montagu House. We were almost out of hope, when an honest man, who was at work, directed us to the next ground, adjoining to a pond. There we found what we sought, about three-quarters of a mile north of Montagu House, and 500 yards east of Tottenham Court Road. The steps are of the size of a large human foot, about three inches deep, and lie nearly from north-east to south-west. We counted only seventy-six ; but we were not exact in counting. The place where one or both the brothers are supposed to have fallen is still bare of grass. The labourer also showed us the bank where (the tradition is) the wretched woman sat to see the combat." Mr. Southey then speaks of his full confidence in the tradition of their indestructibility, even after ploughing up, and of the various conclusions to be drawn from the circumstance.

In the third edition of the " Book for a Rainy Day" appears the following note upon the above mysterious spot :—" Of these steps there are many traditionary stories ; the one generally believed is, that two brothers were in love with a lady, who would not declare a preference for either, but coolly sat upon a bank to witness the termination of a duel which proved fatal to both. The bank, it is said, on which she sat, and the footmarks of the brothers when pacing the ground, never produced grass again. The fact is," adds the writer, " that these steps were so often trodden that it was impossible for the grass to grow. I have frequently passed over them ; they were in a field on the site of Mr. Martin's Chapel, or very nearly so, and not on the spot as communicated to Miss Porter, who has written an entertaining novel on the subject." It may be added here that at Tottenham Street Theatre (afterwards the Prince of Wales's), about the year 1830, was produced an effective melodrama, by the Brothers Mayhew, founded upon the same incident, entitled the *Field of Forty Footsteps*.

Apart from the air of superstition which seems to have settled round the remarkable footprints spoken of above, the Long Fields had, from a much earlier period, been associated with superstitious notions, for Aubrey tells us, that on the eve of St. John Baptist's (Midsummer) Day, in 1694, he saw, at midnight, twenty-three young women in "the parterre behind Montagu House, looking for a coal, under the root of a plantain, to put under their heads that night, and they should dream who would be their future husbands." The superstition, we may here remark, is a very ancient one, and not confined to London or even to England, and is probably connected with the fire and serpent worship, which came at an early date into Europe from the East. But this is a matter foreign to the subject in hand.

The street brawls which disgraced the times of our later Stuart sovereigns frequently ended in a duel on this spot. In the days of Charles II., when there was next to no pavement, and when among the population of London there were so many strange characters that the peaceful way-farer was obliged to pick his steps with circumspection, and be ready for conflict at the turning of every alley, each passer-by endeavoured to take the wall, and this gave rise to numerous quarrels. Indeed, as Macaulay tells us, "if two roysterers met, they cocked their hats in each other's faces, and pushed each other about till the weaker was shoved into the kennel. If he was a mere bully he sneaked off, muttering that he should find a time. If he was pugnacious, the encounter probably ended in a duel behind Montagu House. The mild and timid gave the wall; the bold and athletic took it."

Occasionally, however, this neighbourhood witnessed encounters of a less sanguinary nature. "About the year 1770," writes Strutt, in his "Sports and Pastimes," "I saw a grand match at base (Prisoner's Base) played in the fields behind Montagu House and the British Museum, by twelve gentlemen of Cheshire against twelve of Derbyshire, for a considerable sum of money, which afforded much entertainment to the spectators." The game, we may add, is described in detail by Strutt in the chapter from which we make our quotation.

At the above period the grounds at the back of Montagu House were open to the fields extending to Lisson Grove and Paddington; north, to Primrose Hill, Chalk Farm, Hampstead, and Highgate; and east, to Battle Bridge, Islington, St. Pancras, &c. The north side of Queen Square was left open that it might not impede the prospect. Dr. Stukeley, many years Rector of St. George's Church, describes (in his MS. diary, 1749) the then sylvan character of Queen Square and its neighbourhood. On the side of Montagu Gardens, next Bedford Square, was a fine grove of lime-trees; and the gardens of Bedford House, which occupied the north side of the present Bloomsbury Square, reached those of Montagu House. "We can, therefore," adds Dr. Rimbault, "understand how, a century and a half since, coachmen were regaled with the 'perfume of the flower-beds of the gardens belonging to the houses in Great Russell Street,' which then enjoyed 'wholesome and pleasant air.' Russell Square was not built until the year 1804, although Baltimore House was erected in 1763; the latter appears to have been the only erection made in this neighbourhood from the publication of Strype's 'Survey' down to this period, with the exception of a chimney-sweeper's cottage, still further north, and part of which is still to be seen in Rhodes's Mews, Little Guildford Street. In 1800 Bedford House was demolished entirely, with its offices and gardens; this house had been the home where the noble family of the Southamptons and the illustrious Russells had resided during more than 200 years."[*] About the middle of the last century, when the gardens of Gray's Inn became deserted by the beaux and belles of that period, those at the back of Montagu House became for a time fashionable as a lounge and promenade.

Where Euston Square is now, in the year 1820 was a large nursery garden, in which the children of privileged neighbours were glad to be allowed to take their morning walk and to play. There is extant a small print, by Corbould, published in the first decade of this century, showing the distant and quite rustic view of Primrose Hill, and Hampstead with its spire beyond, taken from the top of Woburn Place. In the foreground is a rustic wooden bridge, and a little further off, as nearly as possible where is now the terminus of the London and North-Western Railway, stands a small group of farm-buildings quite isolated.

No doubt the district at present under notice cannot be regarded as fashionable; it is too near to St. Giles's to have much in common with the courtly region of St. James's. It nevertheless includes within its area as great a number of commodious dwellings around open spaces as can be met with in any other spot of similar dimensions within the scope of the Registrar-General's functions. When we remember that this was, until no

---

* Quoted from John Timbs's "Romance of London."

very distant date, an aristocratic part of London, it is not surprising that the associations which cluster around it, from the memory of great and eminent men, are as abundant and interesting as its claims to be still considered one of the most convenient and sanitary divisions of the modern Babel are well founded. This particular quarter, more especially about Bedford and Russell Squares, appears to have been a highly favoured one with "gentlemen of the long robe;" indeed, those two squares have had more than a fair share of judicial occupants. Like those parts of the metropolis lying eastward of Temple Bar, this neighbourhood, when once deserted by the wealthier classes, came to be looked upon by them—or some, at least—with a sort of reproachful feeling; indeed, as a witty writer has observed, the very absence of knowledge of its locality "was accounted a mark of high breeding," and this notion was once forcibly illustrated by Mr. Croker's inquiry in the House of Commons, "But where *is* Russell Square?" *Apropos* of this joke, another may be told, how that a nobleman once commissioned his son to go into the City for him to transact some business, and rung for his carriage to convey the young gentleman. "The City? the City? my lord?" he said, inquiringly; "I've been told that is a dreadful way off; where shall I change horses?"

"It is very curious," writes Albert Smith, "to speculate as to what part of England will ultimately be the West-end of London—no less than to watch the gradual progress that the apparent desire of the fashionable world to get still nearer the sunset has made in that direction for many years. Keeping within the recollection of old inhabitants still extant, we find that the anomalous neighbourhood between the Foundling Hospital and Red Lion Square, north and south, and Gray's Inn Lane and Bloomsbury, east and west, was once the patrician quarter of London. The houses, even in their decay of quality, have a respectable look. Their style of architecture is *passé*, it is true; but they evidently make a great struggle to keep up appearances. If chance leads you into them, you will find that they are all similarly appointed, even to their inhabitants. All the furniture is rubbed up to the last degree of friction polish, and the carpets are brushed cleanly threadbare. The window-curtains, blanched in the sun of thirty or forty summers, until their once crimson hue has paled to a doubtful buff; the large semi-circular fireplace, with its brass-handled poker and latticed fender; the secretary and large flap-table, on which is the knife-case with its forlorn single leaf, or shell, in *marqueterie* on the cover—all remain as they

were. Even the ancient landladies have given the same conservative care to their flaxen fronts and remarkable caps. They are grave and dignified in their demeanours, for they believe Great Ormond Street still to be the focus of the West-end. It is long since they have been out to learn to the contrary: left stationary, whilst time has flown by them, like an object in the tranquil side-water of a stream, whilst similar ones are hurried past with the torrent, they still regard Russell and Bedford Squares as their *Belgravia*—for at every epoch all fashionable parts of town had an ultra-aristocratic neighbourhood. So, when the superior classes still moved on towards the west, colonising Percy and Newman Streets and the old thoroughfares about Soho, then Fitzroy and Golden Squares were in turn looked up to with respect."

Of that part of Bloomsbury which lies between New Oxford Street and High Street and Broad Street we have already spoken in our account of St. Giles's.* The parish of St. George's is co-extensive with what used to be called the Bloomsbury side of St. Giles's-in-the-Fields; in other words, with that part of the parish which lay to the north of the old line of Holborn. What is now called "Broad Street, Bloomsbury," still forms part of St. Giles's parish, and of old was called by its proper name of "Broad Street, St. Giles's." Even at the commencement of the present century, the scene which the said "High Street" presented was not very inviting. On both sides of the way were rows of chandlers' shops, low public-houses, cook-shops —or rather cellars—for the accommodation of the poorer Irish, who even then formed a colony here before what was called "the ruins" of St. Giles's were cleared away, and the site devoted to broad and spacious streets. This "colony" was generally known as "The Rookery," but it was also called the "Holy Land" and "Little Dublin," on account of the number of Irish who resided there. It is true, although the place bore anything but a reputable name, some of its residents were honestly employed, even in the humblest walks of industry. Of the inhabitants of the "Holy Land" there was, at least, a floating population of 1,000 persons who had no fixed residence, and who hired their beds for the night in houses fitted up for the purpose. Some of these houses had each fifty beds, if such a term can be applied to the wretched materials on which their occupants reposed; the usual price was sixpence for a whole bed, or fourpence for half a one; and behind some of the houses there were cribs littered with straw, where the wretched might

---

* See Vol. III., p. 206, &c.

sleep for threepence. In one of the houses seventeen persons have been found sleeping in the same room, and these consisting of men and their wives, single men, single women, and children. Several houses frequently belonged to one person, and more than one lodging-house-keeper amassed a handsome fortune by the mendicants of St. Giles's and Bloomsbury. The furniture of the houses was of the most wretched description, and no persons but those sunk in vice, or draining the cup of misery to its very dregs, could frequent them. In some of the lodging-houses breakfast was supplied to the lodgers, and such was the avarice of the keeper, that the very loaves were made of a diminutive size in order to increase his profits. Yet amidst so much wretchedness, there was much of wanton extravagance; and those who might have traversed the purlieus of the "Holy Land" on a Saturday night, must have felt convinced that the money squandered away in dissipation would have procured much daily comfort both in bed and board. But the extravagance of beggars is proverbial; and an anecdote is related of old Alderman Calvert going in disguise to one of their suppers, and being much alarmed at hearing some of them ordering an "alderman in chains," until he learnt from the landlord that it was but another name for a turkey and sausages.

At the angle of Tottenham Court Road and New Oxford Street stands the celebrated brewery of Messrs. Meux and Company, one of the largest in London. It was founded early in the reign of George III., by Messrs. Blackburn and Bywell, whose name it bore until Mr. Henry Meux, at that time a partner in the brewery of Messrs. Meux, in Liquorpond Street, joined the firm. He was a cousin of Lord Brougham, and was created a baronet by William IV., in 1831.

The brewery covers nearly four acres, and its interior arrangements are well worth a visit. The stranger is shown over several ranges of buildings, each devoted to some one process or other, by which ale, porter, and stout are manufactured. These we shall not attempt to describe, but will simply state that the brewery contains seven or eight huge vats, one of which holds 1,500 barrels of liquid, and others hold 1,000 or 900. It is said that the firm employ some 150 hands and fifty horses, and that they turn out of their manufactory not very much less than half a million of barrels yearly. The demand for ales, it may be interesting to learn, is steadily on the increase, while that for the dark-coloured liquids shows a slight tendency to diminish.

It may not be out of place here to state the circumstances under which London "porter" came to be so called. Prior to the year 1722 the malt liquors in general use were ale, beer, and "twopenny," and it was customary for the drinkers of malt liquors to call for a pint or tankard of half and half—i.e., half of ale and half of beer, half of beer and half of twopenny. In course of time it also became the practice to call for a pint or tankard of three-threads, meaning a third of ale, beer, and twopenny, and thus the publican had the trouble to go to three casks and turn three cocks for a pint of liquor. To avoid this trouble and waste, a brewer of the name of Harwood conceived the idea of making a liquor which should partake of the united flavours of ale, beer, and twopenny. He did so, and succeeded, calling it "entire," or entire butt beer, meaning that it was drawn entirely from one cask or butt; and being a hearty, nourishing liquor, it was very suitable for porters and other working people. Hence it obtained its name of "porter."

In 1816 this brewery was attacked by a London mob, who were anxious to wreak upon it—why or wherefore is not clear—their dislike of Lord Liverpool and Lord Sidmouth, and the rest of the Tory ministers.

Adjoining the entrance to Messrs. Meux and Co.'s Brewery is the "Horse-shoe Tavern," so called from the shape of its original dining-room—a shape doubtless assumed for a reason which will presently appear. By absorbing the adjoining premises, and erecting large additions, the modest tavern has lately grown into a monster hotel, where the *table d'hôte* system has been introduced, on a plan similar to that which we have mentioned in our account of the "Langham."

The sign of the "Horse-shoe," though common in combination with other subjects, as Mr. Larwood tells us, in his "History of Sign-boards," is rarely found by itself. Its adoption here is due, doubtless, to the large horse-shoes nailed up at the entrance of Meux's Brewery, and conspicuous both on the trappings of the dray-horses of that establishment, and also as the trade-mark of the firm. There was formerly, and perhaps may be still, a "Horse-shoe Tavern" on Tower Hill, and another in Drury Lane, because it is mentioned in connection with Lord Mohun's attempt on Mrs. Bracegirdle,* as the place where he and his comrades drank a bottle of sack while they lay in wait for that lady. It is also mentioned by Aubrey, in his "Anecdotes and Traditions," as the scene of a bloody duel. The horse-shoe, from its pronged shape, was regarded

MESSRS. MEUX'S BREWERY, 1830. (See page 485.)

in the Middle Ages as a potent charm against witchcraft. Thus Robert Herrick writes :—

> " Hang up hooks and speres to scare
> Hence the hag that rides the mare ! "

There is, or was till lately, a " Horse and Horse-shoe Tavern " in Great Titchfield Street.

New Oxford Street, which we now enter, extends from the corner of Tottenham Court Road to Bury Place, where it forms a junction with High Holborn.

George Street, crossing New Oxford Street, and leading from Great Russell Street to Broad Street, was formerly known as Dyot Street, being so called after one Richard Dyot, a parishioner of St. Giles's, in the reign of Charles II., and possibly a man of considerable importance at that time. Bainbridge and Buckeridge Streets were built prior to 1672, and were named after their respective owners ; of these streets the latter disap-

ENCAMPMENT IN THE GARDENS OF MONTAGU HOUSE, 1780. (*See page* 493.)

It runs through what once was the thickest part of St. Giles's " Rookery," and was opened in 1847. Many of the houses, particularly on the north side, have a pleasing appearance, built as they are of red brick and stone dressings, in the domestic Tudor and Louis XIV. style of architecture, whilst some of the house-fronts are of Ionic and Corinthian character. In about the centre is what is called the Royal Arcade, a glass-roofed arcade of shops extending along the rear of four or five of the houses, and having an entrance from the street at each end. The shops here are mostly confined to the sale of drapery and haberdashery. This arcade was opened about 1852, with great expectations, but it never " took " with the public, and is almost unknown and unnoticed.

peared in the general clearance which was effected in the formation of New Oxford Street. In old Dyot Street was a public-house called the " Turk's Head," where Haggarty and Holloway, in November, 1802, planned the murder of Mr. Steele, on Hounslow Heath, and to which they returned after the murder. It may be here mentioned that at the execution of the murderers at the Old Bailey twenty-eight people were crushed to death. " Rat's Castle " was another rendezvous in Dyot Street for some of the vilest denizens and outcasts of the " Rookery." The Rev. T. Beames, in his " Rookeries of London," in speaking of this famous thieves' public-house, says : " In the ground floor was a large room, appropriated to the general entertainment of all comers ; in the first floor, a free-and-easy, where dancing and singing went on during the greater part of the night, suppers were laid, and the luxuries which tempt to intoxication freely displayed.   The frequenters of this place were bound together by a common tie, and they spoke openly of incidents which they had long since ceased to blush at, but which hardened habits of crime alone could teach them to avow."   In our account of the beggars of St. Giles's we have already mentioned one curious character, " Old Simon," who used to take up his quarters in this den of infamy,* appearing in the street near the church in the daytime.

During the improvements which were effected about the year 1844-5, when the greater part of the " Rookery," or the " Holy Land," was swept away, one at least of the houses which disappeared had a history of its own.   This was a public-house called the " Hare and Hounds."   It stood nearly in the centre of what is now New Oxford Street, and, says Mr. Jacob Larwood, in his " History of Sign-boards," " it was one of those places associated with ' the good old customs of our ancestors.' "   " The ' Hare and Hounds,' " writes Mr. Richardson in his " Recollections of the Last Half Century," " was to be reached by those going from the West-end towards the City, by going up a turning on the left hand, nearly opposite St. Giles's Churchyard.   The entrance to this turning or lane was obstructed or defended by posts with cross bars, which being passed, the lane itself was entered.   It extended some twenty or thirty yards towards the north, through two rows of the most filthy, dilapidated, and execrable build-ings that could be imagined ; and at the top or end of it stood the citadel, of which ' Stunning Joe' was the corpulent castellan.   I need not say that it required some determination and some address to gain this strange place of rendezvous.   Those who had the honour of an introduction to the great man were considered safe, wherever his authority extended, and in this locality it was certainly very extensive.   He occasionally condescended to act as a pilot through the navigation of the alley to persons of aristocratic or wealthy pretensions, whom curiosity, or some other motive best known to themselves, led to his abode.   Those who were not under his safe-conduct frequently found it very unsafe to wander in the intricacies of this region. In the *salon* of this temple of low debauchery were assembled groups of all ' unutterable things,' all that class distinguished in those days, and, I be-lieve, in these, by the generic term ' cadgers.'

* See *ante*, Vol. III., p. 207.

' Hail cadgers, who, in rags array'd,
    Disport and play fantastic pranks,
Each Wednesday night in full parade,
    Within the domicile of Banks'.'

A ' lady ' presided over the revels, collected largess in a platter, and at intervals amused the company with specimens of her vocal talent.   Dancing was ' kept up till a late hour,' with more vigour than elegance, and many Terpsichorean passages, which partook rather of the animation of the ' Nautch ' than the dignity of the minuet, increased the in-terest of the performance.   It may be supposed that those who assembled were not the sort of people who would have patronised Father Mathew, had he visited St. Giles's in those times.   There was, indeed, an almost incessant complaint of drought, which seemed to be increased by the very remedies applied for its cure ; and had it not been for the despotic authority with which the dispenser of the good things of the establishment exercised his rule, his liberality in the dispensation would certainly have led to very vigorous developments of the reprobation of man and of woman also.   In the lower tier, or cellars, or crypt, of the edifice, beds or berths were provided for the company, who, packed in bins, after the ' fitful fever' of the evening, slept well."   This notorious house was a favourite resort of Londoners in the sixteenth and seventeenth centuries.   It was known by the sign of the " Beggars' Bush " previous to the reign of Charles II., when the name became altered to the " Hare and Hounds," in consequence of a hare having been hunted and caught on the premises, where it was afterwards cooked and eaten.   The *Beggars' Bush* formed the title of a play brought out in the seventeenth century.   In Pepys' " Diary," under date November 20, 1660, is this entry :— " To the new play-house, near Lincoln's Inn Fields (which was formerly Gibbons's Tennis-court), where the play of the *Beggars' Bush* was newly begun ; and so we went in and saw it well acted."

In one part of what was the " Rookery "—now Streatham Street, at the rear of Meux's Brewery— stands a block of model lodging-houses, with per-fect ventilation and drainage, and rents probably lower than the average paid for the miserable dens that once existed here.   These houses were erected by the Society for Improving the Condition of the Working Classes, on ground leased on easy terms from the Duke of Bedford.

Resuming our walk along New Oxford Street, we pass Bloomsbury Street and Duke Street.   The first of these streets is formed by a junction of two, named Charlotte Street and Plumtree Street re-spectively.   They were altered into one street and the name changed in 1845. Museum Street, the next thoroughfare eastward, leads from the top of Drury Lane as far as the British Museum. It was originally called Peter Street, but its name was altered soon after the establishment of the Museum. The southern end was called Bow Street, and the northern end Queen Street. At the corner of New Oxford Street and Museum Street is Mudie's Circulating Library. In describing this establishment we cannot do better than quote the words of a writer in *Once a Week*, in 1861 :—" At the present moment the establishment owns no less than 800,000 volumes. If all these were to come home to roost at one time, it would require a library almost as big as the British Museum to hold them. As it is, the house is one mass of books. Up-stairs are contained the main reserves, from which supplies are drafted for the grand saloon down-stairs. This room is itself a sight. It is not a mere store-room, but a hall, decorated with Ionic columns, and such as would be considered a handsome assembly-room in any provincial town. The walls require no ceramic decorations, for they are lined with books, which themselves glow with colour. . . . Light iron galleries give access to the upper shelves, and an iron staircase leads to other books deposited in the well-lit, well-warmed vaults below. We were curious to inquire if volumes ever became exhausted in Mr. Mudie's hard service. Broken backs and torn leaves are treated in an infirmary, and volumes of standard value come out afresh in stouter and more brilliant binding than ever. There is, however, such a thing as a charnel-house in this establishment, where literature is, as it were, reduced to its old bones. Thousands of volumes thus read to death are pitched together in one heap. But would they not do for the butter-man? was our natural query. Too dirty for that. Nor for old trunks? Much too greasy for that. What were they good for, then? For manure! Thus, when worn out as food for the mind, they are put to the service of producing food for our bodies! . . . The great majority of the works circulated by Mr. Mudie consists of books of travel, adventure, biography, history, scientific works, and all the books of *genre*, as they say in painting, which are sought for by the public. . . . Taken altogether, no less than 10,000 volumes are circulating diurnally through this establishment."

The amount of reading which the above figures represent is enormous; and it cannot be denied that, as an educating power, this great Circulating Library holds no mean position among the better classes of society. Its value to authors, moreover,

cannot be lightly estimated, inasmuch as its machinery enables a bountiful supply of their works to be distributed to the remotest parts of the island, thereby increasing the demand for their works, and therefore also their reputation in an ever-widening circle.

Passing through Museum Street, we enter Great Russell Street, which runs from Tottenham Court Road to the north-west corner of Bloomsbury Square. It was built in the year 1670, and was named after the Russells, Earls and Dukes of Bedford. It is now a street of shops, but was formerly, as Strype tells us (circa 1700), " a very handsome, large, and well-built street, graced with the best buildings in all Bloomsbury, and the best inhabited by the nobility and gentry, especially the north side, as having gardens behind the houses, and a prospect of the pleasant fields up to Hampstead and Highgate."

In this street John Le Neve, the antiquary, was born in 1679. Here, at one period, lived Sir Godfrey Kneller; and here the Speaker of the House of Commons, Arthur Onslow, died in 1768. Here, too, lived Admiral Sir Sidney Smith, in 1828 ; and also the great actor, John Philip Kemble, in a house on the north side, afterwards occupied by Sir Henry Ellis, as principal librarian of the British Museum, but pulled down about the year 1848, to make room for extensions. Here, too, in Queen Anne's reign, stood Montagu House and Thanet House. The first of these mansions occupied the site of the British Museum, which will be best dealt with in a separate chapter.

We learn from Horace Walpole, under date January, 1750, that in this street the Lady Albemarle was "robbed in the evening by nine men." Her loss, however, was made up by the king presenting her with a new gold watch and chain the next day.

In this street died, in 1858, Monsieur Louis Augustin Prevost, a celebrated linguist. The son of a French functionary of the town of Arcy, he was born in 1796, and as a boy was an eye-witness of the famous battle fought near that town. He afterwards went to Paris, and studied at a college at Versailles. In 1823 he entered as a tutor into the family of Mr. Ottley, afterwards Keeper of the Prints in the British Museum, and for some years gave lessons in French and other European languages. In 1843 he was appointed by the Trustees of the Museum to the superintendence of the Catalogue of Chinese Books, which he accomplished after mastering almost incredible difficulties. The remains of Monsieur Prevost were interred at Highgate Cemetery.

CHAPTER XXXVIII.

THE BRITISH MUSEUM.

"Ædes Musis et Apolline dignæ."—*Juvenal.*

Origin of the Museum—Purchase of Montagu House by the Government—Evelyn's Description of the First Montagu House—Destruction of the Mansion by Fire—Description of the Second Building—Ralph, First Duke of Montagu—The Gardens of Montagu House—The Troops stationed there at the Time of the Gordon Riots—Singular Anecdote of John, Second Duke of Montagu—Sir Hans Sloane and his Public Benefactions—A Skit on the Formation of Sir Hans Sloane's Collection—Appointment of Governors and Trustees of the British Museum—Lord Macaulay's Opinion of the Board of Governors—Original Regulations for the Admission of the Public, and Mr. Hutton's Opinion thereon—More Liberal Arrangements made for Admission—Gradual Extension of the Old Building—The Elgin Marbles—The Royal Library of George III.—The King's Library—The Towneley and Payne-Knight Collections—The Old Museum described—Regulations for Admission—The Old Reading-room.

THIS institution, which occupies the northern side of the eastern portion of Great Russell Street, is far removed from all the other departments under the control of the Government, and is by far the most interesting of all to the people at large, though it can boast of no very great antiquity.

It owes its origin to Sir Hans Sloane, a man of high scientific attainments, who, during a long period of practice as a physician, had accumulated at his house at Chelsea, in addition to a considerable library of books and manuscripts, a vast collection of objects of natural history and works of art. These treasures he directed to be offered to the nation at a certain price after his death, which took place in the year 1753. The offer was accepted, and an Act was passed directing the purchase, not only of Sir Hans Sloane's collection, but also of the Harleian Library of Manuscripts, which we have already mentioned in a previous chapter; and at the same time enacting that the Cottonian Library, which had been presented to the nation by Sir John Cotton, during the reign of William III., and was deposited in Ashburnham House, Dean's Yard, Westminster, should, with those, form one general collection. To these George III. added a large library, collected by the preceding sovereigns since Henry VII. To accommodate the national property thus accumulated, the Government raised, by lottery, the sum of £100,000, of which £20,000 was devoted to the purchase of the above collections; and in 1754 Montagu House, in Great Russell Street, was bought from the two heiresses of the Montagu family, as a repository for the then infant establishment. This mansion, however, was not the first that stood upon the same site. Before proceeding with our description of the Museum it would be well to speak of these two houses.

The first and short-lived Montagu House, erected in 1678 by Robert Hooke, is thus described by John Evelyn, under date November 5, 1679:—"To see Mr. Montagu's new palace, near Bloomsberry, built by our (*i.e.*, the Royal Society's) curator, Mr. Hooke, somewhat after the French

[style]; it is most nobly furnished, and a fine but too much exposed garden." He also records, in his "Diary," a second visit which he paid to the house, October 10, 1683:—"Visited the Duchess of Grafton, not yet brought to bed, and dining with my Lord Chamberlain (her father); went with them to see Montagu House, a palace lately built by Lord Montagu, who had married the most beautiful Countess of Northumberland. It is a stately and ample palace. Signor Verrio's fresco paintings, especially the funeral pile of Dido, on the staircase, the 'Labours of Hercules,' 'Fight with the Centaurs,' his effeminacy with Dejanira, and 'Apotheosis,' or reception among the gods, on the walls and roof of the great room above, I think exceeds anything he has yet done, both for design, colouring, and exuberance of invention, comparable to the greatest of the old masters, or what they so celebrate at Rome. In the rest of the chambers are some excellent paintings of Holbein and other masters. The garden is large, and in good air, but the fronts of the house not answerable to the inside. The court at entry and wings for offices seem too near the street, and that so very narrow and meanly built, that the corridor is not in proportion to the rest, to hide the court from being overlooked by neighbours, all which might have been prevented had they placed the house further into the ground, of which there was enough to spare. But on the whole it is a fine palace, built after the French pavilion way."

But the mansion was not destined to live long. "This night," thus writes Evelyn, in his "Diary," under date January 19, 1686, "was burnt to the ground, my Lord Montagu's Palace, in Bloomsbury, than which for paintings and furniture there was nothing more glorious in England. This happened by the negligence of a servant in airing, as they call it, some of the goods by the fire." It seems the house was at this time occupied by the Earl of Devonshire as a tenant, as we learn from Ellis's "Letters:"—"Whitehall, the 21st January, 1685-6—"On Wednesday, at one in the morning, a sad fire happened at Montagu House, in Bloomsbury, occasioned by the steward airing some hangings, &c., in expectation of my Lord Montagu's return home, and sending afterwards a woman to see that the fire-pans with charcoal were removed, which she told him she had done, though she never came there. The loss that my Lord Montagu has sustained by this accident is estimated at £40,000, besides £6,000 in plate ; and my Lord Devonshire's loss in pictures, hangings, and other furniture is very considerable." The fire is described by Lady Rachel Russell, who was living close by, at Southampton House, in a letter dated the following day to Dr. Fitzwilliam :—" It burnt with so great violence that the whole house was consumed by five o'clock. The wind blew strong this way, so that we lay under fire a great part of the time, the sparks and flames continually covering the house and filling the court." She adds, with a womanly attention to details, that her little boy was almost stifled by the smoke, but would get up to see the fire, and that Lady Devonshire and her youngest child were glad to take refuge for the night with her, the child being carried by his nurse, wrapped up in a blanket.

If the first Montagu House was "somewhat after the French," the second, with its high roofs and dormer windows, was scarcely less foreign in its general design. Nor is that to be wondered at, for it is said to have been designed by a French architect, M. Pougey (or Puget), of Marseilles, eminent as a sculptor, painter, and both civil and naval architect, and that he was sent from Paris expressly to superintend it ; but in the " English Encyclopædia " it is stated that the building bore no trace of the peculiar style which induced some to call him the " French Michael Angelo ; " and, moreover, in the " Biographie Universelle " no mention is made of his having come to England.

There is a good view of the house in the heyday of its prime in Wilkinson's " Londinia Illustrata," another in Strype's " Survey of London " for 1754, and another curious bird's-eye view may be seen in Stowe's " Survey."

This mansion is described in the " New View of London," in 1708, as " an extraordinary, noble, and beautiful palace, in the occupation of the Duke of Montagu. It (*i.e.*, the shell) was erected in 1677. The building constitutes three sides of a quadrangle, and," the writer quaintly adds, " is composed of fine Brick and Stone Rustick-work, the Roof covered with Slate, and there is an Acroterio (*sic*) of four Figures in the Front, being the four Cardinal Virtues. From the House the Gardens lie northwards, where is a Fountain, a noble Tarrass (*sic*), a Gladiator, and several other statues.

The Inside is richly furnished and beautifully finished ; the Floors of most Rooms finnier'd (*sic*) ; there are great variety of noble paintings, the Staircase and the Cup-lo Room particularly curious, being architecture done in Perspective, &c.; and there are many other notable things too numerous to insert here. On the South side of the Court, opposite to the Mansion House is a spacious Piazza, adorned with columns of the Ionic Order, as is the Portal in the middle of a regular and large Frontispiece toward the Street."

" Montagu House," writes the author of the " New Critical Review of the Public Buildings of London," in 1736, " has been long, though ridiculously, esteemed one of the most beautiful buildings about the town. I must own it is grand and expensive, will admit of very noble ranges of apartments within, and fully answers all the dignity of a British nobleman of the first rank ; but after I have allowed this, I must add that the entrance into the court-yard is mean and Gothic (!), more like the portal of a monastery than the gate of a palace. . . . I am ready to confess the area (to be) spacious and grand, and the colonnade to the wings graceful and harmonious ; but the wings themselves are no way equal to it, and the body of the house has no other recommendation than merely its bulk and the quantity of space that it fills." And then he proceeds to discuss in detail its roofs, " garrets," windows, and the cupola with which it was surmounted, as all open to adverse criticism.

The building was erected on the plan of a firstclass French hotel, of red brick, with stone dressings, a lofty domed centre, and pavilion-like wings. In front of the house was a spacious court-yard, enclosed with a high wall, within which was an Ionic colonnade, extending the whole length of the building. The principal entrance, in Great Russell Street, was known as the " Montagu Great Gate ; " over it rose an octangular lantern, with clock and cupola ; and at each extremity of the wall was a square turret. On each side of the quadrangle were the lodgings of the different officers, by which the colonnade was connected with the main building.

From the pages of the *Gentleman's Magazine* (May, 1814) we condense the following particulars of the second Montagu House :—" It was erected by Ralph, first Duke of Montagu, who was a great favourite of Charles II., under whom he was twice Ambassador at the Court of Louis XIV. Though constantly in disgrace with James II., he was honoured by William and Anne. It appears that he expended the greater part of his income in erecting this pile after the French taste ; on its erection and embellishments a variety of French architects, painters, &c., were engaged to design and embellish it. We are told," adds the writer, "that 'the architecture was conducted by Mons. Pouget, in 1678,' but nothing occurs as to the period when it was brought to a conclusion; yet gardens in the rear. In the former, on the ground-floor, were the hall, grand staircase, and two state-rooms; and in the latter, a grand central saloon, and three state-rooms, right and left. The upper floor was laid out in a similar manner, excepting that the portion over the hall served as a vestibule.

MONTAGU HOUSE, GRAND STAIRCASE. 1830.

from the various combination of features pervading the whole mass, we are induced to fix its main point of execution towards the close of James's reign." The plan of the entire premises was nearly a square, upwards of 200 feet each way. On either side of the principal entrance were porters' lodges, and at each end of the colonnade were entrances to the offices in the wings of the building. The principal or state apartments were divided into two lines, facing both the court-yard and the

The principal doorway in the south front was richly carved with scrolls, &c., and had an elaborate frieze, the centre consisting of a wreath of flowers and fruit, inclosing the initial letter "M," after the quaint fashion of the time, richly ornamented. The roof was lofty, with a high pitch; the centre portion dome-fashion, with rustic quoins and pedimented, dormer windows. On the breaks at the springing of the roof to the centre portion were originally statues, and urns on the apex of the dome.

A full description of the decoration of the interior of the mansion is likewise given in the *Gentleman's Magazine* of the above year; but it will be sufficient for our purpose to state that the principal rooms, one and all, were alike enriched with painted walls and ceilings; the subjects generally were the pagan gods and goddesses, including several of the stories in Ovid's "Metamorphoses," landscapes, fruit and flowers, the execution of which was entrusted to

and shaded by numbers of trees and shrubs. This communicated with a lawn on the north side. On the west side of the lawn was a double avenue of lime-trees; but the garden on this side of the mansion was tasteless and formal. They are stated to have been laid out "after the French manner;" and John Timbs tells us, though we know not on what authority, that the gardens of the houses in its front in Great Russell Street were noted for

FRONT OF MONTAGU HOUSE, GREAT RUSSELL STREET, 1830. (*See page* 491.)

La Fosse, Rousseau, and Jean Baptiste Monnoyer. The stately hall, together with the grand staircase, were the most striking features of the interior architecture, a representation of which is given in Ackermann's "Microcosm of London." There were in all twelve show-rooms on the ground-floor and as many on the first-floor, and these were in general stately and well lighted. On coming into the possession of the nation, prior to the establishment of the Museum, Montagu House underwent some trifling alterations in a few of its details; but, on the whole, it remained much in its original condition down to the time when it was demolished, between the years 1845 and 1849.

On the west side of the house was a flower-garden and a terrace, disposed with much taste,

their fragrance. Strype and Stow add that "the place is esteemed the most healthful in London."

Montagu House and gardens occupied in all about seven acres of ground. In the gardens were encamped, in the year 1780, the troops stationed to quell the Gordon Riots, one of the centres of which was in Bloomsbury. A print of the period, by Paul Sandby, shows the ground in the rear of the mansion laid out with grass, terraces, flower-borders, lawns, and gravel-walks, where the gay world resorted on summer evenings. In the print here referred to, the white tents of the troops are shown, and in front is a grave-looking old gentleman, walking alone with an air of consequence along a path in the direction where now stands Montagu Place, with his wig, and a sword-cane on his shoulders—probably intended for the king. In the foreground is a soldier, conversing with a well-dressed woman, who is seated by his side.

Ralph, Duke of Montagu, mentioned above, married the proud heiress of Henry, Duke of Newcastle, to whom we have before alluded in our account of Clerkenwell.* The duke, who died in the year 1709, was succeeded by his only surviving son by his first marriage, John Montagu, second duke. His grace officiated as Lord High Constable of England at the coronation of George I., and during that reign filled several public situations of the highest importance. At the accession of George II. he was continued in favour, and at his coronation he carried the sceptre with the cross. He died in 1749, when all his honours became extinct. If we may judge from the following anecdote, his grace would seem to have been of a somewhat eccentric turn of mind, for he appears to have made two codicils to his will, one in favour of his servants, and the other of his dogs, cats, &c. Whilst writing the latter one of his cats jumped on his knee. "What!" says he, "have you a mind to be a witness, too? You can't, for you are a party concerned and interested."

A few years after the death of this nobleman—namely, in 1754, as stated above—an Act was passed for vesting Montagu House in trustees, and for enabling them to convey it to the Trustees of the British Museum for a general repository. We have already stated that this national institution originated in the purchase by Government of Sir Hans Sloane's accumulation of objects of natural history, &c. This splendid collection—at which, by the way, Pope sneered at as mere "butterflies" —was fortunately preserved entire after Sloane's death. He generously bequeathed to the public his books, manuscripts, medals, and "butterflies," on certain conditions. The terms were accepted. The valuable manuscripts of Harley, Earl of Oxford —known as the Harleian Library—were added to it; and these two collections, afterwards increased by the Cottonian manuscripts, together formed, as we have said, the nucleus of our great national Museum.

It may not be out of place here to say a few words about Sir Hans Sloane, and of his public benefactions. He was a native of Ireland, but of Scotch extraction, the son of a gentleman who had settled in Ireland in the reign of James I. He was a governor of almost every hospital about London; to each he gave a hundred pounds in his lifetime, and at his death a sum more consider-

able. He formed the plan of a dispensatory, where the poor might be furnished with proper medicines at prime cost; which, with the assistance of the College of Physicians, was afterwards carried into execution. For a quarter of a century he was President of the College of Physicians, as well as physician to the king, and succeeded Sir Isaac Newton as President of the Royal Society. He gave the Company of Apothecaries the entire freehold of their botanical garden at Chelsea; in the centre of which is erected a marble statue of him, admirably executed, by Rysbrack. He helped largely in founding the colony in Georgia, 1732, and also the Foundling Hospital, in 1739, and formed the plan for bringing up the children of the latter. He was the first in England who introduced into general practice the use of bark, not only in fevers, but in a variety of other cases, particularly in nervous disorders, in mortifications, and in violent hæmorrhages. His cabinet of curiosities, which he had taken so much pains to collect, he bequeathed to the public, as above stated, on condition that the sum of £20,000 should be paid to his family; which sum, though large, was not the original cost, and scarce more than the intrinsic value of the gold and silver medals, the ores and precious stones, that were found in it. Besides these, there was his library, consisting of more than 50,000 volumes, many of which were illustrated with cuts, finely engraven, and coloured from nature; 3,500 manuscripts; and an infinite number of rare and curious books. Thus Sir Hans Sloane became the founder of one of the noblest collections in the world. But the wits, who never spare a character, however eminently great and useful, more than once took occasion to ridicule this good man for a taste, the utility of which they did not comprehend, but which was honoured with the unanimous approbation of the British Legislature. Thus Young, in his "Love of Fame:"—

'But what address can be more sublime
Than Sloane—the foremost *toyman* of his time?
His nice ambition lies in curious fancies,
His daughter's portion a rich *shell* enhances,
And Ashmole's baby-house is, in his view,
Britannia's golden mine—a rich Peru!
How his eyes languish! how his thoughts adore
That painted coat which Joseph *never* wore!
He shows, on holidays, a sacred pin,
That touch'd the ruff that touch'd Queen Bess's chin."

Then again, in "Hone's Year Book," there is a skit on the formation of Sir Hans Sloane's collection, which we here quote. It is from a printed tract entitled "An Epistolary Letter from T—— H—— to Sir H—— S——, who saved his life

---

* See Vol. II., pp. 331–2.

and desired him to send over all the curiosities he could find in his travels :—

> " Since you, dear doctor, saved my life,
>   To bless by turns and plague my wife,
> In conscience I'm obliged to do
>   Whatever is enjoined by you.
> According then, to your command,
>   That I should search the western land,
> For curious things of every kind,
>   And send you all that I could find,
> I've ravaged air, earth, seas, and caverns,
>   Men, women, children, towns, and taverns,
> And greater rarities can show
>   Than Gresham's children ever knew ;
> Which carrier Dick shall bring you down
>   Next time his wagon comes to town.
> I've got three drops of the same shower
>   Which Jove in Danaë's lap did pour ;
> From Carthage brought, the sword I'll send
>   Which brought Queen Dido to her end ;
> The stone whereby Goliath died,
>   Which cures the headache when applied ;
> A whetstone, worn exceeding small,
>   Time used to whet his scythe withal ;
> St. Dunstan's tongs, which story shows,
>   Did pinch the Devil by the nose ;
> The very shaft, as all may see,
>   Which Cupid shot at Anthony ;
> And what above the rest I prize
>   A glance from Cleopatra's eyes.
> I've got a ray of Phœbus' shine,
>   Found in the bottom of a mine ;
> A lawyer's conscience, large and fair,
>   Fit for a judge himself to wear ;
> In a thumb-vial you shall see,
>   Close cork'd, some drops of honesty,
> Which, after searching kingdoms round,
>   At last were in a cottage found ;
> An antidote, if such there be,
>   Against the charms of flattery.
> I ha'nt collected any Care,
>   Of that there's plenty everywhere ;
> But, after wond'rous labour spent,
>   I've got one grain of rich content.
> It is my wish, it is my glory,
>   To furnish your Nicknackatory ;
> I only wish, whene'er you show 'em,
>   You'll tell your friends to whom you owe 'em ;
> Which may your other patients teach
> To do as has done yours,   "T. H."

But to proceed. On the completion of the purchase of the various collections above mentioned, Governors and Trustees, consisting of the most eminent persons in the kingdom, were at once appointed ; among them were the Archbishop of Canterbury, Lord Chancellor, and Secretaries of State, who were declared Trustees for the public. To these were added Lord Cadogan and Mr. Hans Stanley, who had married Sir Hans Sloane's daughters. After their decease, others were to be chosen in their stead, either by themselves, or by the family of Sir Hans Sloane, from time to time, as their perpetual representatives in the trust.

On the purchase of the Cottonian Library it was settled that Mr. Samuel Burrows and Mr. Thomas Hart, the then trustees, and their successors, should be nominated by the Cotton family, as perpetual representatives, in the same manner as those of Sir Hans Sloane. The same arrangement was entered into with respect to the trusteeship of the Harleian collection of manuscripts ; and the Earl of Oxford, the Duke of Portland, and their successors, to be chosen by themselves, or by the Harley family, were made perpetual trustees for the same. These trustees were made a body corporate, by the name of the " Trustees of the British Museum," with power to make statutes, rules, and ordinances ; to choose librarians, officers, and servants, and to appoint their several salaries ; upon this special trust and confidence, " that a free access to the said general repository, and to the collections therein contained, shall be given to all studious and curious persons, at such times and in such manner, and under such regulations, for inspecting and consulting the said collections, as by the said trustees, or the major part of them, in any general meeting assembled, shall be limited for that purpose."

The trustees at the present time are fifty in number. Of these, one is nominated by the Sovereign ; twenty-five are official, among whom the Archbishop of Canterbury, the Lord Chancellor, and the Speaker of the House of Commons are always included ; nine are " family " trustees—the Sloane, Cotton, and Harley families being represented by two each, and the Towneley, Elgin, and Knight families by one each ; whilst the remaining fifteen are chosen by the former thirty-five. Of the Towneley, Elgin, and Knight collections we shall speak in due course.

Lord Macaulay was one of the trustees, and was anxious to improve the administration, but found it apparently a hopeless task. He writes, in his diary, Nov. 25, 1848 :—" After breakfast I went to the Museum. I was in the chair. It was a stupid, useless way of doing business. All boards are bad, and this is the worst of boards. If I live, I will see whether I cannot work a reform here."

The nomination of the subordinate officers rests with the trustees, the candidates being subjected to a test examination before the Civil Service Commissioners. There are two grades, in each of which promotion is supposed to go by seniority ; occasionally, however, an officer is promoted from the lower to the higher grade, but only in a case of singular merit.

After coming into possession of Montagu House, the trustees immediately laid out between twenty and thirty thousand pounds on necessary repairs and alterations.

The Museum was opened to the public for the first time on January 15th, 1759. The establishment then consisted of three departments only, devoted respectively to printed books, manuscripts, and natural history. That the Museum was highly appreciated, even in the earliest stages of its existence, may be easily imagined when we say that Northouck (1772), describing it when first founded, styles it "the wonder of all that beheld it, and confessed, all things considered, to be superior to any other Museum in the world !!"

The regulations for the admission of the public at first bore some resemblance to those which are still observed at the Soane Museum, in Lincoln's Inn Fields*—namely, it was provided that "admission" to such "studious and curious persons" as are desirous to see the Museum should be obtained by means of printed tickets, to be delivered by the porter, upon their application in writing, which writing shall contain their names, condition, and places of abode, also the day and hour at which they desire to be admitted. This list was to be submitted every night to the principal Librarian, or in his absence, to another officer of the Museum, who, if he considered the parties admissible, was to "direct the porter to deliver tickets to them according to their said request, on their applying a second time for the said tickets," observing, however, that not more than ten tickets were delivered for each time of admission." The parties who produced these tickets were to be allowed three hours for their inspection of the Museum, spending one hour in each department, and being taken in charge by a different officer for each. How these regulations operated in some instances may be learned from the account of a visit which was paid to the Museum by Mr. William Hutton, the historian of Birmingham, on the 7th of December, 1784, which he described in his "Journey from Birmingham to London," published in the following year. He says, "The British Museum justly stands in the first class of rarities. I was unwilling to quit London without seeing what I had many years wished to see, but how to accomplish it was the question. I had not one relation in that vast metropolis to direct me, and only one acquaintance; but assistance was not with him. I was given to understand that the door, contrary to other doors, would not open with a silver key;

that interest must be made some time before, and admission granted by a ticket, on a future day. This mode seemed totally to exclude me. As I did not know a right way, I determined to pursue a wrong, which probably might lead me into a right. Assiduity will accomplish weighty matters, or how could Obadiah Roberts count the grains in a bushel of wheat? By good fortune I stumbled upon a person possessed of a ticket for the next day, which he valued at less than two shillings; we struck a bargain in a moment, and were both pleased. And now I feasted upon my future felicity. I was not likely to forget 'Tuesday at eleven, December 7, 1784.' We assembled on the spot, about ten in number, all strangers to me, perhaps to each other. We began to move pretty fast, when I asked with some surprise, whether there were none to inform us what the curiosities were as we went on? A tall, genteel young man in person, who seemed to be our conductor, replied with some warmth, 'What! would you have me tell you everything in the Museum? How is it possible? Besides, are not the names written upon many of them?' I was too much humbled by this reply to utter another word. The company seemed influenced; they made haste, and were silent. No voice was heard but in whispers. The history and the object must go together; if one is wanting, the other is of little value. I considered myself in the midst of a rich entertainment, consisting of ten thousand rarities, but, like Tantalus, I could not taste one. It grieved me to think how much I lost for want of a little information. In about thirty minutes we finished our silent journey through this princely mansion, which would well have taken thirty days. I went out much about as wise as I went in, but with this severe reflection, that for fear of losing my chance, I had that morning abruptly torn myself from three gentlemen, with whom I was engaged in an interesting conversation, had lost my breakfast, got wet to the skin, spent half-a-crown in coach hire, paid two shillings for a ticket, been hackneyed through the rooms with violence, had lost the little share of good humour I brought in, and came away quite disappointed. Hope is the most active of all the human passions. It is also the most delusive. I had laid more stress on the British Museum than on anything I should see in London. It was the only sight that disgusted me."

The system which Hutton has thus described continued for many years longer, probably till 1803, when several alterations in the management were effected. In 1808, when the first "Synopsis," or official guide, was printed, the regulations stated that "on the first four days of the week, 120 persons may be admitted to view the Museum, in eight companies of fifteen each ;" but no mention is made of the necessity of their previously obtaining tickets. Two years later a greater advance appears to have been made, for we then find that "the Museum is open for public inspection on the Monday, Wednesday, and Friday in every week (the usual vacations excepted), from ten till four o'clock ; and all persons of decent appearance who apply between the hours of ten and two are immediately admitted, and may tarry in the apartments or the Gallery of Antiquities without any limitation of time, except the shutting of the house at four o'clock." From that time the regulations have been constantly growing more liberal, and the corresponding increase in the number of persons admitted, as years have rolled along, has been very striking.

In the year 1850 the numbers were just above a million ; and in the following, or "Exhibition year," when multitudes flocked to London from all quarters of the globe, the astonishing total of 2,527,216 visitors was registered—a number at that time surpassing the entire population of the metropolis.

With the commencement of the present century the character of the Museum began to improve, and, gradually, from a stationary, it became an eminently progressive institution. A more liberal system of admission to its treasures, as we have shown, was adopted. The Government annual vote for purchases was increased considerably towards the close of the reign of George IV., and again after the passing of the first Reform Bill.

The acquisition of sundry Egyptian antiquities, for the most part discovered by Belzoni, led to the establishment of a separate Department of Antiquities in the Museum ; and in order to provide suitable rooms for their accommodation, a new edifice was erected in the gardens and completed in 1807. This building, which communicated by means of a passage with old Montagu House, was of an entirely different architectural character from it, and comprised a series of thirteen classical saloons. The subsequent addition of the Elgin marbles, for which a grant of £35,000 had been made by Government, and which were for some years exhibited in a wooden shed, rendered necessary a further extension of the building ; and lastly, the presentation of the library of George III., in 1821, to the nation, made it imperative to provide a suitable room for its reception, which was one of the conditions of the gift.

Lord Elgin commenced the work of collecting the "marbles" which bear his name during his mission to the Ottoman Porte in the year 1802 ; but his right to carry them off as spoils, and also his judgment in selecting these particular specimens, was much discussed at the time. When the question of voting a sum of money for them was brought forward in Parliament, the opinions of eminent artists as to his spoils from the Temple of Minerva were sought and collected. It is curious to compare the manner in which each artist expresses his admiration of them. Benjamin West, the then President of the Royal Academy, declared that if he had seen these emanations of genius in his youth, the feeling which he entertained of their perfection would have animated all his labours, and would have led him to infuse more character, expression, and life into his historical compositions. His successor in the President's chair, Sir Thomas Lawrence, expressed his opinion that the statues brought to England by Lord Elgin were superior even to the well-known "Apollo Belvidere," because they united beauty of composition and grandeur of form with a more perfect and correct imitation of nature than is to be found in the "Apollo." He particularly admired in the Elgin Marbles the correct representation of the harmonious variety produced in the human form by the alternate motion and repose of the muscles. Canova declared that Lord Elgin deserved to have altars erected to him as the saviour of the arts, and considered himself fortunate in having visited London, were it only for the opportunity of seeing those masterpieces. In the opinion of Nollekens, the "Theseus" is equalled only by the "Apollo." Flaxman and Chantrey were not quite so decided as to the object of their preference ; while Rossi and Westmacott declared that they knew of nothing superior to these "admirable fragments of antiquity."

The gift of the Royal Library to the British Museum by George IV. was certainly a munificent present ; but when it is described as a gift "greater than has been bestowed by any sovereign on any nation since the library of the Ptolemies was founded at Alexandria," one cannot help smiling at the loyal exaggeration. The following is the text of the letter by which the gift was accompanied, addressed by the King to Lord Liverpool, then Prime Minister :—

"Pavilion, Brighton, Jan. 15, 1823.

"DEAR LORD LIVERPOOL,—The King, my late revered and excellent father, having formed, during a long series of years, a most valuable and extensive library, consisting of about 120,000 volumes, I have resolved to present this collection to the British nation.

"Whilst I have the satisfaction by this means of advancing the literature of my country, I also feel that I am paying a just tribute to the memory of a parent whose life was adorned with every public and private virtue.

a separate building to be erected to receive the treasure.

In a lecture entitled "Brief Personal Reminiscences of Forty Years in the National Library," delivered in 1875 by Mr. Robert Cowtan, author

SIR HANS SLOANE. *From a Print published in* 1793. (*See page* 490.)

"I desire to add, that I have great pleasure, my lord, in making this communication through you. Believe me, with great regard, your sincere friend,
　　　　　　　　　　　　　　　"G. R.

"To the Earl of Liverpool, K.G., &c."

This letter was communicated to the Houses of Parliament in the following month, and the cheering with which it was received in the House of Commons showed that the people appreciated the king's generosity. The royal library was handed over to the trustees of the Museum, who ordered

of "Memories of the British Museum," &c., the fact of the King's Library being a *gift* to the nation is somewhat negatived. Mr. Cowtan observes that "The books in the 'King's Library,' a kingly room for a kingly collection, were all purchased at the private expense of George III., at the instigation of Dr. Samuel Johnson, who was consulted by Sir Francis Barnard, the king's librarian. These books, which were all large paper copies, included a Bible, which was the first book printed with movable type. There were inscriptions over the door of

THE KING'S LIBRARY.

this room, one in English and one in Latin, stating that the collection was presented to the nation by George IV.; but it was said in the *Quarterly Review* that George IV., not caring much about books (he found books in ladies' faces), was about to sell this collection to a foreign purchaser, when, on the fact becoming known, they were *bought* of him out of some Admiralty funds, and so secured for the nation. So the inscription was like that other 'bully,' which, as Pope said, 'lifted up its head and lied.'"

The design for the King's Library, which was prepared on that occasion by Sir Robert Smirke, the architect of the Museum, formed part of a general plan for rebuilding the whole institution, involving the demolition not only of Montagu House, but of the saloons erected, as we have already mentioned, for the department of antiquities. Sir Robert's proposals were adopted by the trustees, and in the course of twenty-five years were gradually carried into execution.

On the donation, or, at all events, the acquisition of this library, the Government ordered drawings to be prepared for the erection of an entirely new Museum, a portion of one wing of which was to be occupied by the recently-acquired library. This wing, on the eastern side of the Museum garden, was finished in 1828; the northern, southern, and western sides of the quadrangle have since been progressively added.

It may be observed here that in 1827 Charles Lamb, speaking of "poor condemned Montagu House," anticipates the speedy erecting of another and handsomer building in its place; but, as we have just seen, the work of rebuilding had then already commenced. The author of the "Essays of Elia" speaks, however, with great satisfaction of the excellent collection of old plays bequeathed to the Museum by David Garrick.

The Towneley collection of antiquities, comprising a quantity of marble sculptures bought at Rome, Naples, &c., were purchased by the nation at the commencement of the present century. They were collected by Charles Towneley, Esq., who died in 1805, as we have stated in a previous chapter, at his house in Park Street, Westminster. His collection of bronzes, coins, and gems were added to the Museum in 1814. Mr. Richard Payne Knight, the classical scholar, whom we have already mentioned as residing in Soho Square, bequeathed to the Museum his matchless collection of drawings, bronzes, and medals, worth at least £30,000. The collection includes a single volume of drawings by the inimitable Claude, which was purchased by Mr. Knight for £1,600

from a private individual, who a short time before had bought it for £3.

The Museum, as a building, is described in a work published in 1830, as "a large and imposing, rather than a grand or graceful edifice; entered by a simple, if not mean, portal, which opens into a quadrangle, formed on three sides by a long and lofty front and wings, and on the fourth side by a dilapidated Ionic colonnade, never handsome, with the gate in the centre."

The hall, which was approached from the courtyard by a broad flight of steps, was of the Ionic order, and decorated with pilasters, in pairs, with the entablature supporting a horizontal and plain ceiling. Over the great door was a coarse painting of Vesuvius in eruption. From the hall the vestibule was entered through two tall arches, filled with fanciful iron-work and gates. A passage from the vestibule led to the western apartments. The ante-room was comparatively small, with nothing remarkable in its architecture, but the ceiling was richly ornamented with paintings by Rousseau and La Fosse, the subjects by the latter being the "Apotheosis of Iris" and the "Assembly of the Gods."

The staircase was painted with representations of Cæsar and his military retinue; the feasts and sacrifices of Bacchus, and gigantic figures, emblematical of the Nile and the Tiber, with various views of landscapes and pieces of architecture.

The room adjoining the ante-room northward was, till the winter of 1803, the reading-room; but, "having only two windows, which were insufficient to illuminate the most remote parts of the table," another room, both larger and better lighted, was substituted. This apartment had a vaulted ceiling; it was surrounded by shelves of books, and above the cases hung several portraits on the walls. There was a large marble chimney-piece, and the room was lighted by three windows on the north side and one on the west. All the rooms on the north side of the house partook of the same character with the reading-room; they were very spacious, and each was entirely filled with shelves of printed books.

In the Act of Parliament already referred to, it is particularly set forth, that "the collections and libraries are to be reposited, and remain in the Museum, *for the public use;*" and further, "that free access shall be given to this repository *to all studious and curious persons*, at such time, and in such manner, and under such regulations for inspecting and consulting the collections, as the trustees shall think fit." We have already seen in what manner and number the *curious* portion of the public was admitted in obedience to the above law; and it will doubtless be equally interesting to know what facilities were afforded, at that early period, to the *studious* and the *man of letters.*

In the "Statutes and Rules relating to the inspection and use of the British Museum," published in 1757, it is ordered, "That no one be admitted to make use of the Museum for study, but by leave of the trustees, in a general meeting, or the standing committee; and that the said leave be not granted for a longer term than half a year, without a fresh application." It is further ordered, "That a particular room be allotted for the persons so admitted, in which they may sit, and read, or write, without interruption, during the time the Museum is kept open; that a proper officer do constantly attend in the said room, so long as any such person or persons shall be there; and for the greater ease and convenience of the said persons, as well as security of the collection, it is expected *that notice be given in writing the day before, by each person, to the said officer, what book or manuscript he will be desirous of perusing the following day;* which book or manuscript on such request will be lodged in some convenient place in the said room, and will thence be delivered to him by the officer of the said room," &c.

Since the above period many alterations have been made in the mode of admission, which, at the same time that they have increased the facility of access, have in no wise lessened the precautions so necessary for the safety of the collection.

In Weale's " London and its Vicinity Exhibited " (1851), it is stated that the library contained about 500,000 volumes, and that it was visited by about 70,000 readers during each year, and that every accommodation was afforded in the pursuit of their studies. With regard to the application for admission as a reader being backed " by a proper recommendation," the editor of the above work considers it so very indefinite, as to require, in behalf of the public, some revision on the part of the trustees. " It is left too much to the will of the librarian," he adds, " as to whom he may, in his temper, think a proper person to recommend. My own case may not be singular. In the course of my career as publisher I have contributed to the Museum books not far from a thousand pounds in value; yet this public servant negatived my recommendation of Mr. Robert Armstrong, an engineer, who, as a scientific man, was desirous of a reading-ticket; remarking to that gentleman, 'We don't like the recommendations of booksellers.'"

The first apartment specially appropriated for the use of a reading-room was opened towards the close of the year 1757. It was situated in the basement of the old mansion, at the west corner of the building, and here the readers apparently continued to assemble until the year 1810, when they were transferred to a larger and much more commodious apartment, upon the second storey, at that time forming part of the manuscript department. This state of things continued for nearly twenty years, when another transfer took place, two rooms situated at the southern extremity of the east wing of the new building being *temporarily* devoted to the service of the then rapidly increasing body of readers. In 1838 the erection of the north front of the present structure was brought to a completion, when another change in the situation of the "reading-room" was effected. The rooms then brought into use were two in number, at the north-east corner of the building, adjoining to Russell Square. Passing, or slinking in almost surreptitiously, through an iron gate near the lower end of Montagu Place, the "readers" were directed by a porter, seated in a kind of sentry-box, to a narrow door in the lower part of the building. Here a short flight of stone steps, ending in a glass door, led to the rooms placed at their disposal, which were narrow and quite inadequate. The tables, twenty-six in number, were arranged in such a manner as to leave a free passage down the centre and round the sides of the room; chairs were placed for the accommodation of eight readers at each table, and, as is the case at the present time, book-stands, pens, ink, and blotting-paper were gratuitously furnished.

For a long time the library and reading-room were used by a very few individuals—scholars, historians, antiquaries of the Dryasdust class, and collectors of literary curiosities. The attendants at the reading-room enjoyed quite a sinecure in those "good old days," when perhaps they had not half-a-dozen individuals daily to supply with books. In fact, there was no provision made for a large number of visitors. Indeed, in the rooms of which we are now speaking, accommodation was provided for only 170 persons. The presses round the rooms were filled with books of reference, encyclopædias, dictionaries, lexicons, topographical and geographical works, &c. The rooms themselves, which still form part of the library, have little architectural decoration, beyond what they derive from their ceilings, in each compartment or panel of which there is a rose or flower, which serves as a ventilator, as well as for ornament. The floors are of oak, and have a slip of marble along the centre, and underneath the book-cases; and the rooms are warmed by hot-water apparatus.

CHAPTER XXXIX.

THE BRITISH MUSEUM (*continued*).

"*Scripta Palatinus quæcunque recepit Apollo.*"—*Horace.*

Commencement of the New Buildings—The Edifice described—The New Reading-room—Rules and Regulations for "Readers"—The Catalogue —Presses and Press-marks—The Chief Books of Reference—A Classic Picture of the Reading-room—Offences for which Readers are expelled—The Printed Book Department—The Grenville Library—Specimens of Early Printed Books—Autographs—Magna Charta, and other Historical Documents—Manuscripts—Newspapers—Acquisition of Books by the Museum under the Copyright Act—The Department of Prints and Drawings—Principal Librarians of the Museum—Mr. J. T. Smith—Celebrated Frequenters of the Reading-room.

THE difference of the appearance of Montagu House from that of the Museum of the present day is very striking, not only with regard to the building in itself, but also as to its situation, relatively to the country and the town. The old house, as we have shown, remained down almost to the close of the last century quite open on the north side, and commanded views of the surrounding fields; whilst the present edifice, although occupying the same site, and indeed covering a much larger space of ground, is almost completely shut in on three sides by streets and squares which are built up close to its walls, so that the only view of the edifice that can be obtained is that of the principal, or southern, front in Great Russell Street.

The new buildings, which were commenced by Sir Robert Smirke, were continued in 1846 by his brother, Mr. Sydney Smirke; the walls of old Montagu House being removed piecemeal as the new edifice progressed; the last portion of it disappeared in 1845. In place of the dull brick wall which separated the old house from Great Russell Street, there was erected a handsome iron railing, partly gilt. Through this the magnificently enriched front of the new building can be surveyed by the passer-by in all its entire length; it presents a recessed portico and two projecting wings; and as the edifice fronts the south, the play of light and shade caused by the forest of Ionic columns with which the whole is faced, is such as no other portico in London possesses. At either extremity of the court-yard is a range of houses for the resident officials of the Museum. In the centre of the iron railing—which is raised upon a granite curb, and is formed of spears painted of a dark copper-colour, with the heads gilt, and an ornamental band—is the principal carriage-gate and foot entrance, strengthened by fluted columns with composite capitals, richly gilt, and surmounted by vases.

The style of architecture adopted throughout the exterior of the new building is the Grecian-Ionic. The southern façade consists of the great entrance portico, eight columns in width, and two inter-columniations in projection. This is approached by a broad flight of steps. On either side is an advancing wing, giving to the entire front an extent of 370 feet; the whole surrounded by a colonnade of forty-four columns, raised upon a stylobate five feet and a half high. The columns are five feet at their lower diameter, and forty-five feet high; the height from the pavement of the front court-yard to the top of the entablature of the colonnade, upwards of sixty-six feet. Professor Cockerell, in a lecture delivered in 1850, remarked that "since the days of Trajan or Hadrian, no such stones have been used as those recently employed at the British Museum, the front of which is formed by 800 stones, each from five to nine tons weight. Even St. Paul's contains no approach to these magnitudes." In the tympanum of the pediment there is a group of allegorical figures, representing the "Progress of Civilisation," which has been thus described by Sir Richard Westmacott, R.A. :— "Commencing at the western end or angle of the pediment, man is represented as emerging from a rude savage state through the influence of religion. He is next personified as a hunter and tiller of the earth, and labouring for his subsistence. Patriarchal simplicity then becomes invaded, and the worship of the true God defiled. Next, Paganism prevails, and becomes diffused by means of the Arts. The worship of the heavenly bodies, and their supposed influence, led the Egyptians, the Chaldeans, and other nations to study astronomy, typified by the central statue, the key-stone to the composition. Civilisation is now presumed to have made considerable progress. Descending towards the eastern angle of the pediment is the genius of Mathematics, in allusion to science being now pursued on known sound principles. The Drama, Poetry, and Music balance the group of Fine Arts on the western side; the whole composition terminating with Natural History, in which such objects or specimens only are represented as could be made most effective in sculpture."

The building erected by Sir Robert Smirke consists of four ranges of apartments—east, west, north, and south; and these formerly enclosed a hollow square, forming a large open quadrangle. The eastern range, which was completed in 1828, was in use some years previous to the gradual erection of the others. It contains the apartments appropriated to the manuscript collection, and also the Royal Library, of which we have spoken above; a magnificent series of corridors 300 feet in length, and forty wide, with inlaid floors and coffered ceilings. The ground-floor of the northern range of apartments is allotted to the general library, and is less ornate in appearance than the eastern range; but it nevertheless contains one or two rooms of a striking character. The western range was erected partly on the site of the old Gallery of Antiquities, which was opened in 1807, and presents one large apartment, corresponding in length with the Royal Library; this is appropriated to Egyptian and other sculpture. The southern range, the last completed, occupies the exact site of old Montagu House. This range contains the great hall and staircase; on the east of which is a room containing the Grenville library, and on the west a saloon containing sculptured antiquities. The increasing collections of the Museum had rendered it necessary to make various additions to the original design of Sir Robert Smirke, some of them even before that design had been carried out. Of these may be mentioned a gallery or saloon for the Elgin marbles, which was erected on the western side of the western range. The most extensive addition, however, is that erected in the inner quadrangle, under the superintendence of Mr. Sydney Smirke, who had some time previously succeeded his brother, Sir Robert, as architect to the Museum. This new building contains the reading-room and the accommodation prospectively necessary for the annual increase of the collection of printed books. It is one of the principal architectural features of the Museum, and the only one that is visible at a distance, the dome that crowns it forming part of the view of London as seen from Hampstead Heath, and from the Norwood and Sydenham hills near the Crystal Palace. The approach to the room is by a long passage, which is adorned with a bust of Sir Anthony Panizzi, who was some time principal librarian, and at whose suggestion the new reading-room was built. The subject had indeed been under consideration many years previously, and some discussion has arisen as to the real author of the original suggestion. Mr. Hawkins, an architect, who published a pamphlet of " Observations on the Reading-room," in 1858, assigns the earliest notion of building in the above-mentioned quadrangle to Mr. Edward Hawkins, in 1842; but the idea seems to have been ventilated even as early as the years 1836 and 1837, when it was introduced in a series of letters on the Museum, published at that time anonymously in the *Mechanics' Magazine*, but which were subsequently acknowledged by Mr. Watts, one

of the officers of the Printed Book Department. " The space thus unfortunately wasted," says Mr. Watts, speaking of the quadrangle, " would have provided accommodation for the whole library. A reading-room of ample dimensions might have stood in the centre, and have been surrounded on all four sides by galleries for the books, communicating with each other, and lighted from the top."

On crossing the threshold of the reading-room, the visitor finds himself in a large circular apartment crowned with a dome of the most magnificent dimensions, 140 feet in diameter, and 106 feet high. It is the largest dome in the world, with one exception, the Pantheon at Rome. The cylinder or drum which sustains the dome, presents a continuous circular wall of books, which are accessible from the floor, or from low galleries running round the apartment; it comprises in the part open to the " readers " about 20,000 volumes of books of reference and standard works, and in the part round the galleries more than 50,000 volumes of the principal sets of periodical publications, old and new, and in various languages.

" In the decoration of the interior dome "—we use the words of the authorised " Guide to the Museum"—" light colours and the purest gilding have been used. The great room, therefore, has an illuminated and elegant aspect. The decorative work may be shortly described. The inner surface of the dome is divided into twenty compartments by moulded ribs, which are gilded with leaf prepared from unalloyed gold, the soffites being in ornamental patterns, and the edges touching the adjoining margins fringed with a leaf-pattern scalloped edge. Each compartment contains a large circular-headed window, with three panels above, the central one being medallion-shaped, the whole bordered with gilt mouldings and lines, and the field of the panels finished in encaustic azure blue, the surrounding margins being of a warm creamcolour. The details of the windows are treated in like manner—the spandril panels being blue; the enriched column and pilaster caps, the central flowers, the border moulding and lines being all gilded; the margins cream-colour throughout. The moulded rim of the lantern light, which is painted and gilded to correspond, is forty feet diameter. The sash is formed of gilt moulded ribs radiating from a central medallion, in which the royal monogram is alternated with the imperial crown. The cornice, from which the dome springs, is massive and almost wholly gilded, the frieze being formed into panels bounded by lines terminating at the ends with a gilt fret ornament."

The floor of the room is occupied with nineteen

large and sixteen smaller tables, fitted up with ample accommodation for more than 300 readers ; two of these are reserved for the exclusive use of ladies, who have been admitted as "readers" since about the year 1854; ladies, however, are always at liberty to take a seat at any other table which they prefer. By the simple expedient of raising the partition down the middle of each of the larger tables so high that a reader cannot see his opposite neigh-

are familiar now," says a writer in the "English Encyclopædia," " to all the readers of Europe and America, and will be familiar, in all probability, centuries hence, from the very labours in which they are aided by the Museum reading-room. . . From the nature of the library around them, not only such men as Carlyle and Thackeray, Kossuth and Montalembert, but the humblest labourer in the literary vineyard, from the most distant corners of

THE READING-ROOM OF THE BRITISH MUSEUM.

bour, privacy is secured to the literary working-bees, and on entering the room when it is quite full, a stranger might at first suppose that it was nearly empty. The tables are all arranged so as to converge towards the centre of the room, near which are two circular ranges of stands for the gigantic Catalogue, the entries of which—mostly printed—fill upwards of 3,000 volumes, and a portion of which is thus, if not at the reader's fingers' ends, yet actually at the end of every table. In the centre is the "quarter-deck" of the chief superintendent, whose position commands a general view of all the tables and their occupants, often between 200 and 300 in number, and comprising among them some of the best known names in the world of literature and learning—"names that

the world, may be certain that on the walls around them there exists some record of his labours, or the copy of some lines traced by his hand."

What a difference exists between the reading-room of to-day and that of a century ago! Not only is its whole aspect changed with regard to the building, the accommodation provided, and the regulations respecting its management and rules for admission, but the increase in the number of its "readers" has kept equal pace with the increase in the thousands who visit the other parts of the Museum. The regulations for its management at the outset, in 1759, were, as we have shown in the previous chapter, of the same cautious and restrictive character with those for the general establishment. Gray, the poet, was one of the first to avail himself of the opening of the room; and some mention of it will be found in two or three of his letters. Thus, in one, dated August, 1759, he writes, "I often pass four hours in the day in the stillness and solitude of the reading-room;" and in another letter he describes the company, which at that time consisted of only four other readers, two of whom were Prussians, while Dr. Stukeley, the antiquary, and a copyist made up the number.

volumes, one of the best and largest general collections in Europe. Their seats are furnished with every accommodation for writing and reading, and they are met on all sides with attention and civility; indeed, a nobleman in his private library may often miss facilities to be found in the reading-room of the Museum. The following are the most important directions respecting it, taken from a printed paper which is given to every reader:—

THE BOOK-CASES AT THE BRITISH MUSEUM.

In like manner, Mr. D'Israeli tells us that when his late father, the author of "Curiosities of Literature," &c., first frequented the reading-room, at the end of the last century, his companions never numbered half a dozen. In 1836, after the removal of the readers' quarters to more spacious rooms, the numbers rose to nearly 200 daily; and on the opening of the present reading-room the number was instantaneously doubled, the daily average in the year 1858 being 424. Those who obtain admission have at their command, arranged on the walls around them, a library of 20,000 volumes, comprising books of reference of all kinds. They may at pleasure, by merely writing for what they want, obtain as many volumes as they please of a printed and manuscript library of about 1,550,000

"The reading-room of the Museum is open every day, except Sundays, Good Friday, Christmas Day, and any Fast or Thanksgiving days appointed by authority; except also the first four week-days of March and October.

"The Hours throughout the year are from nine in the morning till eight in the evening from September to April; and till seven during the other months.

"Persons desiring to be admitted to the Reading-room must apply in writing to the Principal Librarian, specifying their profession or business, their place of abode, and, if required, the purpose for which they seek admission.

"Every such application must be made two days at least before admission is required, and must be accompanied by a written recommendation from a householder (whose address can be identified from the ordinary sources of reference), or a person of recognised position, with full signature and address, stated to be given on personal knowledge of the applicant, and certifying that he or she will make proper use of the Reading-room.

"The tickets of admission are renewable at the discretion of the Principal Librarian.

"The tickets of admission given to readers are not transferable, *and each person must, if required, produce his ticket.*

"Persons under twenty-one years of age are not admissible, except under a special order from the trustees.

"Readers, before leaving the room, are to return the books, manuscripts, or maps which they have received to an attendant, and are to obtain the corresponding ticket; *the reader being responsible for such books, manuscripts, or maps so long as the ticket remains uncancelled.*

"It may be sufficient merely to suggest, that *silence* is absolutely requisite in a place dedicated to the purposes of study."

During the winter evenings, the Reading-room is lighted by electricity.

There are various printed catalogues of portions of the collection, such as the King's Library, the Grenville Library, &c., and subsidiary catalogues to the magazines, newspapers, and serial publications, as well as to the Bibles and works illustrative of the Holy Scriptures. But the *magnum opus* is the General Catalogue, to which reference has been already made. The entries were formerly all made in manuscript by an army of scribes, whose daily work was to add to it the names of all the new books which reach the Museum. Since about 1880, however, the additional entries have been printed. These are entered under their author's name, or, where published anonymously, according to the subjects of which they treat. To the title of each book is affixed a "press-mark," which, by certain figures and letters familiar to the practised eyes of the officials, gives a clue to its whereabouts on the shelves of the Collection. Every reader who wants a book must give in writing its full title and "press-mark," in order to enable the attendants to bring it to him when seated at his table. It is to be much wished that there were another *classified* catalogue as well, in order to help the literary explorer when he knows the subject of a book, but is at a loss for the name of the author.

A New General Catalogue, embodying the Old and the Supplemental Catalogues, was compiled between the years 1849 and 1880, and comprised many hundred volumes; and a special catalogue of the printed books from the time of Caxton down to 1640 is now (1883) in course of publication.

The "English Encyclopædia" gives the following curious information concerning the compilation of the Catalogue :—

"The catalogue of the British Museum has been a subject of frequent discussion in the public press, since the committee of the House of Commons in 1835. Before that time, in 1824, the Rev. Thomas Hartwell Horne had been appointed to superintend the preparation of a classed catalogue; but in 1834, his labours, and those of his colleagues, had been suspended, and the Rev. Mr. Baber had been directed to draw up plans for an alphabetical catalogue. A long correspondence on the subject will be found in the Appendices to the Reports of the Commons' Committee, and of the Royal Commission. When, after Mr. Panizzi's appointment to the keepership, the library had been removed from the old to the new building, the question of cataloguing and of printing the catalogue again came up, and a small committee of the Printed Book Department, presided over by Mr. Panizzi, drew up, in 1839, a series of rules for that purpose, which amounted, when they finally received the sanction of the trustees, who re-discussed them, to the number of ninety-one. Objection has been made to their number; but it must be remembered that it was requisite to provide beforehand for all the contingencies to be foreseen in operating on a large library for several hands; and experience shows that the variety in the notions of catalogues is wonderful. In the King's Library Catalogue, for instance, though it is professedly alphabetical, all the novels and tales by anonymous authors, from Amadis de Gaul to Waverley, are entered in a mass, under the singular heading of 'Fabulæ Romanenses.' In such a title as the 'Second Report of the Auxiliary Trinitarian Bible Society, of St. James's, Clerkenwell,' there is hardly a word, except the particles, which has not been selected by some cataloguers as a heading, many taking even the word 'Second'; though it is evident that, on that principle, a set of twenty of these reports would figure in twenty different parts of the same list. It is evident that difficulties of this kind do not diminish when foreign languages are to be treated, which, in the case of the Museum Library, are not few in number. A commencement was made of printing the catalogue compiled on the new principles, and in 1841 the first volume, containing the letter A, appeared under the superintendence of Mr. Panizzi;

but immediately afterwards the printing was suspended, and one of the objects of the Royal Commission of 1847 was to inquire into the cause of this suspension. The commission approved of the step which had been taken, for the reasons assigned by Mr. Panizzi, that it was evidently unadvisable to print any portion of an alphabetical catalogue before the whole was ready for the press. Since this decision has been arrived at, the revision of the old catalogues has continued in manuscript, while all the fresh books added have been dealt with on the same principles ; but, as has already been stated, the number of volumes in the Museum before the year 1839 was about 235,000, while the number since added exceeds 335,000, so that the bulk of the supplements, had the catalogue been printed, would in 1859 have already exceeded that of the principal. The immense labour expended on this gigantic work would, perhaps, have been more highly appreciated by the public, had some of its results been embodied in print. The knowledge and care required in settling the items of an extensive catalogue might often win a reputation if exerted in some other direction, but apparently will never in England win a reputation in this.

"When a new book has been catalogued, the next step to be taken with it is to place it on one of the shelves in a press, or book-case, that it may receive its appropriate 'press-mark,' that is, the indication of its locality. At the Museum each press or book-case has a certain number, and the different shelves are indicated by the letters of the alphabet. Thus the press-mark ' 1,340 *a*' indicates that the book is placed on the ' *a*,' or topmost shelf of press or book-case 1,340. Nothing can be more simple, yet this simplicity is rare. In another library in London, for instance, the system is exactly reversed : the presses are marked with the letters of the alphabet, and the shelves with numbers ; the consequence is, that as the letters of the alphabet are soon exhausted, the librarians have to commence a second series by repeating them thus, AA, BB, &c. ; then a third and a fourth on some other principle, and long before they have arrived at as high a number as 1,340, the system will be found involved in inextricable entanglement. As the shelves in any book-case never amount to the number of the letters of the alphabet, no difficulty of the kind can occur with them. Yet the system of numbering the presses appears to have been slow in suggesting itself to librarians in general. Sir Robert Cotton named his book-cases after the Twelve Cæsars, and in order to find a book it was necessary to remember the succession of Otho, Vitellius, and Vespasian. When his book-

cases outgrew the number of twelve, he abandoned even this system for a worse, and instead of proceeding in succession with the ' five good Emperors,' arbitrarily introduced Cleopatra and Faustina. At the Advocates' Library in Scotland, the presses were patriotically named after the succession of the Scottish kings, then the additional presses after the signs of the zodiac, &c., till necessity drove them to the adoption of numbers, lest they should be compelled to make every new attendant go through a course of the sciences before he could find a book. The great problem in the arrangement of a library, which is increasing, is so to place every book as it comes in, that it may receive a press-mark which will never have to be altered, and yet to provide that the classes of books shall be kept together ; that a new book of travels in Australia, for instance, shall stand with other books of travels in Australia, and not with Spanish plays or Acts of Parliament. A system of this kind would seem to be peculiarly difficult to establish in a library which is increasing at the rate of 20,000 volumes a year, and yet at the Museum a plan of extreme simplicity has been adopted, which is found to answer its purpose. Let us suppose that a room has been built which contains 100 book-cases, each capable of containing 150 volumes, and therefore that the room will contain 15,000 volumes in all, but that the possessor has 1,000 volumes only to place in it at the outset, intending to purchase for the next fourteen years 1,000 volumes a year. It is evident that if he numbers his presses from 1 to 100, and proceeds to place his several books, the very first few volumes that he marks with a press-mark hamper him in a certain degree as to the places of all the others. If he assumes that his purchases of books in English history will finally occupy a single press, and therefore places an edition of Hume in press 77, and occupies press 76 on one side of it with ancient history, and press 78 with the history of France ; he may find a year after that his purchases in English history have filled press 77, and in French history press 78, and that he requires more room for both, but that the only space he has left is in press 2, among the Bibles, or in press 99, which is entirely vacant, but stands next to the works of Shakespeare. The order which he has endeavoured to preserve is therefore spoiled : he must either fill up the vacant spaces with incongruous books, or shift the position of a number of them and alter the press-marks. The problem will be certain to recur over and over again before the room is filled, and each time the remedy will be more hard to effect and more wearisome. One simple change of feature in the arrangements adopted at the outset will obviate all the difficulty. We have supposed that he has marked his presses with fixed consecutive numbers from 1 to 100; let us suppose that he marks them instead with movable numbers not consecutive, leaving gaps between, and the whole trouble is got over. Assume, for instance, that he places his Hume just in the same position, but marks the press 283, and places the French history still in the next press, but marks that press 315. When, in the course of a year or two, he finds that he wants additional room for English history, and that the last press but one in the room is vacant, he removes the contents of the last press but two into the last press but one, removing the number with it, and by repeating the process obtains a vacant press immediately after his press of English history, which is exactly what is required. Each new press between 283 and 315 he marks with some intermediate number. The process can be repeated as often as requisite, and the gain is obvious; the press-marks remain the same, and, though not consecutive, they stand in sequence, and serve as a ready and easy guide. The books are movable, and yet the press-marks are permanent. The processes we have supposed are precisely those which have actually occurred at the British Museum. When, in 1838, the old library was moved from Montagu House to the new apartments in the northern range, the press-mark of every book, and of every tract in a book (and there are sometimes more than a hundred tracts in a volume), was altered. The task of arranging the library in its new position was entrusted to Mr. Watts, who, in the course of that and the eighteen following years, during which every book that entered the Museum passed through his hands, must have examined and classed upwards of 400,000 volumes. The rapid augmentation of the collection, and the system of marking the presses with consecutive numbers, made it necessary that the accumulations should be arranged in three successive sets or series. The idea of the plan of *in*consecutive numbers occurred to Mr. Watts long before it could be carried into effect, as, in order to carry it out practically, it was required that all, or nearly all, the presses should be of similar height and size, and the presses in the new building often varied considerably. The new scheme, on receiving the sanction of Mr. Panizzi, was finally commenced in the long room by the side of the King's Library. The presses in that room amounted to about 600, but in the numbering a range of numbers was assumed from 3,000 to 12,000. The numbers from the beginning of 3,000 to the end of 4,000 were assigned to Theology; from 5,000 to

6,000, to Jurisprudence; from 7,000 to 8,000, to Philosophy, Science, and Art; from 9,000 to 10,000, to History; from 11,000 to 12,000, to Literature. A particular sub-division was assigned to each century of numbers; it was assumed, for instance, that dramatic literature would occupy a hundred presses, from 11,700 to 11,799, and thus every drama which has been placed on the new system bears in its press-mark 117 for the first three figures of the five. This system, which is known by the name of the elastic system, appears to promise several advantages besides those which have been already derived from it. It is evident, for instance, that if one copy of the title-slips of the books thus placed and marked were arranged in the order of the press-marks instead of that of the author's names, it would *ipso facto* produce a rough classed catalogue; and thus a problem, which has been thought insoluble, would be solved in the simplest manner.

" When the title-slip of a new book has received the press-mark of its locality, it is ready to be entered in the manuscript catalogue, and passes therefore into the hands of the 'Transcribers.' The present catalogues of the Museum are as novel as many other of its arrangements. Formerly, the titles were simply written into an interleaved copy of the printed catalogue, a copy of which was kept in the reading-room. As it could not be calculated beforehand what the insertions were to be, the same difficulty was perpetually recurring with the alphabetical order of the entries as with the classified arrangement of the books, and the only remedy in use was to cancel a sheet whenever required, and re-write the entries over a larger space. The system was not found adequate to the requirements of the Museum, when the augmentations rose to the rate of 20,000 volumes a year. The present system is that of using prepared paper and a kind of stylus, so that four copies of each entry are produced at once. These copies, which are necessarily on thin paper, are mounted on thicker paper by the book-binder, so as to be equal to considerable wear and tear, and are then fastened on the pages in the volumes of the catalogue, in such a way that, if required, they can be readily taken up again and removed to another page. By this means the exact alphabetical arrangement of the catalogue is continually kept up, to the great advantage of the readers who consult it."

The chief books of reference in the reading-room, as we have already shown, are arranged on shelves round the floor of the building, and are available for readers without the necessity of writing an order for them. They are divided into Theology;

Law ; Philosophy ; Fine Arts ; Biography ; Belles Lettres ; Poets ; Bibliography ; Ancient Classics ; Geography ; Voyages and Travels ; Topography ; History ; Literary Journals and Libraries ; Encyclopædias ; Dictionaries of Languages ; and lastly, Peerages and Genealogical works. To each of these subjects a separate department of the shelves is assigned ; and there hangs up on every table in the room a " ground-plan" which will show their order and distribution, so as to save the searcher's time.

Of the scene to be daily witnessed in the reading-room, a classic picture is presented to us by a writer in the " Comprehensive History of England," which we here take the liberty of quoting :—

"So immense an accumulation in every language, of every period, and upon every department of human study, is adequately furnished for the purpose it was designed to serve, and the accommodation of those who use it. An ample reading-room, properly lighted and heated, well served by a numerous staff of attendants, and provided with all the apparatus for reading and writing, leaves the student no cause to regret that by the rules of the institution he can only use the books within the premises, instead of carrying them to his own home. Equally liberal, also, are the terms of admission, so that with a simple recommendation from some literary person or even known respectable householder, an applicant is at once admitted to the full use and range of the collection, let his rank, station, or country be what it may. Here, then, the chief amount of British authorship is daily, weekly, and yearly to be found collected, the veritable living men and women whose names only are known in the provinces, and regarded with veneration and wonderment ; and here those works are elaborated which swarm from the press with an abundance and facility at which our ancestors would have been astonished. As intellect also is of no sex, here may be found among the hundreds who regularly assemble within that crystal dome, ladies mingled with gentlemen, but each pursuing his or her separate task apparently unconscious of the presence of another. One is extracting notes from a pile of volumes, or carrying on a hunt of hours or days after a stray fact, date, or name. Another is transcribing from an old smoke-dried or half-burned MS., which none can read but himself. Another is dashing on with pen in full career, and against time, in the lighter departments of literature, where imagination is half the game, and where the work of research is confined to an occasional glance at two or three volumes lying before him. What strange varieties of country, of station, of physiognomy, of intellectual occupation meet daily within these walls ; and what results are there produced, from the ponderous folio to the fugitive essay or tale ! No conversation the while—no whispering—nothing is heard but the slight rustle of the pen upon paper, or the occasional roll of the truck-wheels along the oaken floor, conveying volumes too heavy to be carried, while foreigners, astonished at such silence among so great a multitude, cannot comprehend how mind can possibly live in such an atmosphere. But it is a true British characteristic ; and, like the awful silence of a British battle-charge, it is the expression of confirmed and concentrated resolve."

It may be as well to add here a list of a few of the offences against the code of rules and regulations for which "readers" have at various times been excluded from the reading-room. Writing (or making marks) in pencil as well as ink, in Museum books, manuscripts, &c., even corrections of the press and the author ; damaging book-bindings, &c. ; tracing and colouring without permission ; leaving the library-books on the tables, instead of returning them, and obtaining the vouchers, or book-tickets ; transferring reading-tickets to other persons for their use ; taking books out of the reading-room ; annoying lady-readers ; insulting the officials ; disturbing students ; carrying lighted cigars into the room ; uncleanly habits ; conveying away the property of the trustees (for which offence, we need hardly say, a term of imprisonment has followed the exclusion) ; and also for employing fictitious names and initials in order to gain admission, or for passing under fictitious names and titles after admission gained. For this offence a " reader" of some standing, a foreigner, who had fraudulently assumed a sham title of nobility, in 1874, had his reading-ticket stopped.

Passing from the reading-room to the "printed book department," we will proceed to note down a few of the many interesting works that are here preserved. At the time when the British Museum was first opened, towards the close of the reign of George II., the library of printed books, as we have shown above, had already received a donation which emphatically marked it as the national library of England. This was the royal library, which had been presented to it by the king. The collection, although not large, being estimated only at about 10,500 volumes, was nevertheless rich in interest, from its numerous memorials of the Tudors and the Stuarts. The volumes brought together by Henry VII. comprised a remarkable series of illuminated books on vellum, from the press of the early French printer, Anthony

Verard. One of them, a French Boëthius, has a dedication addressed to the King of England, while in another copy in the library, the dedication is to the King of France; but on examination it will be found that, in the King of England's copy, the word "Engleterre" has been inserted with a pen. A splendid vellum copy of the Bible ot 1540 is interesting, as containing in the title-page, said to be from a design by Holbein, a figure of Henry giving the Bible to his subjects. It is something to know that "bluff King Hal" possessed a Bible; but the sacred work does not, it is true, bear marks of having been much used by its royal owner. We will not pretend to say that this is the identical copy of the Bible which was placed upon the floor by a companion of the youthful and pious

Edward VI., in order that, by standing upon it, he might reach something from a shelf in the room in which they were amusing themselves. At all events, such an anecdote is told; and it is added that the young offender was warmly reproved by his royal playmate for his want of reverence for the Scriptures. In the same press is a copy of the New Testament which belonged to Anne Boleyn. There is also King Henry's copy of his "Assertion of the Seven Sacraments," the book which procured for him, from Pope Leo X., the title of "Defender of the Faith," ever since borne by the British sovereigns. Of the three children of Henry who successively came to the throne, there are likewise interesting memorials to be found here—in the Greek Grammar of Edward VI.; in Queen Mary's

THE TOWNELEY GALLERY. (*See page* 533.)

COURT-YARD OF MONTAGU HOUSE, 1830.

copy of Bandello's novels, which, it is asserted, supplied many of the plots for Shakespeare's plays; and in the volume of the "Lives of the Archbishops of Canterbury," the first book privately printed in England; the last-named work is handsomely bound in embroidered velvet, and was presented to Queen Elizabeth by its author, Archbishop Parker. Another volume, which must once have belonged to the royal collection, but which came to the Museum through the bequest of a private gentleman, is Queen Elizabeth's copy of the first book printed in Anglo-Saxon, the edition of the Gospels superintended by John Fox, who, as a memorandum in the title-page assures us, personally presented it to the queen. There are numerous memorials of James I., in books offered to him by the universities, the synod of Dort, &c.; and of his unfortunate successor, Charles I., there are the volumes of almanacks in which he scribbled his name when Prince of Wales; then there is Bacon's "Advancement of Learning," printed at Oxford in 1640, which contains twenty-three apophthegms inserted by King Charles with his own hand. Here, too, are some beautifully-bound volumes of the Protestant nuns of Huntingdonshire, the illustrated "Harmony of the Evangelists;" this work was brought to the king by Nicholas Ferrar, 1635, and a minute account of the delightful reception of it by his Majesty will be found in the "Life of Ferrar." Among the books which belonged to Charles II. is a fine copy of the second edition of the "Pilgrim's Progress." The collection of pamphlets and publications bearing on the state of public affairs during the time of the Civil War, is one of great interest. It was commenced in 1641, at the very outbreak of the rupture between the King and the Parliament, by George Thomason, a bookseller of St. Paul's Churchyard, who, observing the direction which public affairs were taking, and the extraordinary activity of the press, conceived the idea of collecting all the pamphlets and publications on either side, from folios to broadsides, as they made their appearance. "For the twenty years following," says the author of the article in the "Encyclopædia" already quoted, "though we are told it was a heavy burden to himself and his servants, and though at one time it was thought advisable to effect a colourable sale of the collection to the University of Oxford to save it from the Commonwealth, the design appears to have been never relinquished for a day. On one occasion, the king himself sent to borrow a pamphlet, and chancing to drop it in the dirt, sent a courteous apology to Mr. Thomason, who made a memorandum of the circumstance in the volume (one which contains Shawe's 'Broken Heart') on which the dirt remains to this day to attest the fact. The whole collection at last amounted to about 30,000 pamphlets, bound up in chronological order, in 2,220 volumes. Ill, indeed, was the collector requited. In a statement bound up with his catalogue, and written apparently by his son, we are told that in his lifetime, which lasted till 1666, he refused £4,000 for the collection, supposing that sum not sufficient to reimburse him. His heirs offered it to Charles II. for purchase, and he appears to have directed the royal stationer, Mearne, to buy it on his account, it is not known for what sum, and afterwards to have granted as a favour permission to re-sell it, which the heirs of the Mearne family did not succeed in doing till they disposed of it in 1762 to George III., for £300. The collection, when presented to the Museum, was known there by the name of the 'King's Pamphlets,' the name and merits of the collector who had displayed such sagacity, energy, and perseverance, having sunk into total oblivion."

That portion of the library which passed to the national repository from George III. was originally collected in Buckingham House. There, as we have shown in a previous chapter,* Dr. Johnson frequently consulted its books. "It is curious," writes Mr. John Timbs, in his "Autobiography," "that the royal collector (George III.) and his venerable librarian (Mr. Barnard) should have survived almost sixty years after commencing the formation of this, the most complete private library in Europe, steadily appropriating £2,000 per annum towards this object, and adhering with scrupulous attention to the instructions of Dr. Johnson, contained in the admirable letter (see *Quarterly Review*, June, 1826), printed by order of the House of Commons."

As to the formation of the King's Library, Sir Henry Ellis informs us in his "evidence" on the subject of the Museum collections, that it was commenced in the year 1765, by the purchase of the library of an "eminent character" at Venice, and subsequently enriched by the spoils of the libraries of the Jesuits, consequent on the suppression of that Order on the Continent, when many fine and rare books were to be bought at low prices. It is worthy of remark that the King's Books are kept separate from the rest, and that there is also, as we have already stated, a separate catalogue. In the centre of the King's Library are several upright glazed show-cases, in which are displayed for a time such prints and engravings as may be bequeathed to the Museum, before their final consign-

---

* See *ante*, p. 64.

ment to the room set apart to the Department of Prints, &c.

Of smaller collections which have found their way, either by bequest or by purchase, on to the shelves of the Museum, may be mentioned a large and choice collection of Bibles belonging to Dr. Charles Combe, bought in 1817 as a nucleus; a large group of books on the topography of Italy, presented by Sir Richard Colt Hoare, in 1825, four batches of tracts on the French Revolution, acquired by purchase, which form a sort of pendant to the Thomason collection spoken of above, and also the Didôt collection, lately purchased in Paris. In 1846 a most valuable addition was made to the library by a bequest of the Right Hon. Thomas Grenville. Mr. Grenville, who had signed the treaty of American Independence in 1783, died in the full possession of his faculties in the last named year, upwards of ninety years of age. In a codicil to his will, dated in October, 1845, he thus expresses himself:—" A great part of my library has been purchased from the profits of a sinecure office given me by the public, and I feel it to be a debt and a duty that I should acknowledge this obligation by giving that library, so acquired, to the British Museum, for the use of the public." It is devoutly to be wished that other holders of sinecures had been equally conscientious. The collection comprised upwards of 20,000 volumes, and is said to have cost more than £54,000. This library is kept in a room entirely set apart for it, on the east side of the entrance-hall. In both the Royal Library and the Grenville Library are a number of tables with show-cases, in which some of the choicest literary treasures are displayed. In the case devoted to the earliest production of the printing-press of Germany, there is a copy of the Latin Bible, known as the " Mazarine Bible," because the copy which first attracted notice in modern times was discovered in the library of Cardinal Mazarine. It is supposed to have been issued from the press of Guttenburg about the year 1455. This book, according to general belief the earliest that was ever printed, is here in company with the Latin Psalter of 1457, printed by Faust and Scheffer; this is said to be the earliest book bearing a date, and it is renowned for the splendour of its initial letter, printed in colours.

Of the specimens of the earliest productions of the printing-press in England, which are here preserved, are, of course, several from the press set up by Caxton in Westminster Abbey, towards the close of the fifteenth century. These include " The Game and Playe of the Chesse "—the first book printed in England—" The Book of the Tales of Cauntyrburye," and the English version of Æsop's Fables. Then there are some real treasures in the various old copies of the Scriptures that have found a safe keeping; and among them are the Elector of Saxony's copy of Martin Luther's translation of the Bible; Myles Coverdale's Bible, bearing the date of 1530, the first printed in England; and Martin Luther's own copy of the German Bible, which is dated 1542. The collection of autographs is very large and valuable, and full of interest, being limited not to those of persons who belong to modern history, but to " all time." Among them are the signatures of W. Shakspere (sic), on a copy of Montaigne's " Essays " translated by Florio, printed in 1603; of Milton, on a copy of Aratus, printed at Paris; of Ben Jonson, on the presentation copy of his "Volpone " to John Florio; of Lord Bacon, on a copy of the works of Fulgentius; of Bentley, and of Martin Luther, 1542, in the copy of the Bible mentioned above. The same copy was afterwards in the possession of Melancthon, who, in 1557, wrote a long note, still preserved, on the fly-leaf of the second volume. Handwritings and letters of Edward IV., V., and VI.; Richard III. (application to the Duke of Gloucester for the loan of a hundred pounds); Richard II. (document concerning the surrender of Brest), Henry VII., Queen Anne Boleyn, Knox, Calvin, Erasmus, Ridley, Cranmer, Latimer, Queen Mary, Bonner, Sir Thomas More, Sir Walter Raleigh, Sir Isaac Newton, Cardinal Wolsey, Galileo, Hampden, Sidney, Burghley, Tasso, Drake, Hawkins, Oliver Cromwell, Queen Elizabeth, Lady Jane Grey, Addison, Leibnitz, Dryden, Franklin, Charles I. and II., James II., Voltaire, George I., II., and III., William III., Queen Anne, Pope, Sully, Marlborough, Gustavus Adolphus, Emperor Charles V., Henry IV. of France, Francis I. of France, Peter the Great, Emperor of Russia, Frederick the Great of Prussia, Napoleon Bonaparte, Catherine de Medici, Mary Queen of Scots (part of her will in her own handwriting in French), Louis XIV. of France, pen-and-ink sketch of Battle of Aboukir by Nelson, Condé, Turenne, Washington, Wellington, Sir Walter Scott, T. B. Macaulay, and Charles Dickens. Some of the autograph stores in the Museum are exhibited under glass cases in the Manuscript Department; many of those which are not so exhibited are published in Sir Henry Ellis's "Original and Royal Letters."

Two documents, which form part and parcel of the history of England, will be found among the historical treasures of the Museum. One of these is superscribed—" Bull of Pope Innocent III., whereby he receives in fee the Kingdom of

England, given to the Roman Church by virtue of a Charter confirmed by the Golden Seal of King John, and takes it into his apostolical protection. Given at St. Peter's, 11 Kalends of May, A.D. 1214, and of the Pontificate of Pope Innocent the 17th year." The rupture between King John and the Pope, as all readers of history know, had lasted for several years. How that in the end the Pope declared that John had forfeited his crown, released his subjects from their allegiance, proclaimed a crusade against England, and commissioned the French king to execute it; and how that John eventually surrendered to the Pontiff, acknowledged his appointment to the primacy of the English Church, consented to do homage to the Pope, and finally drew up the charter cited in the Bull now before us, in which he formally "resigned England and Ireland to God, to St. Peter and St. Paul, and to Pope Innocent and his successors in the apostolical chair, agreeing to hold his dominions as feudatory of the Roman Church, by paying a thousand marks yearly"—all these things are matters of history; and fortunately the actual voucher for the transaction is here to convince the most sceptical.

The other historical deed is a time-worn and highly-valued piece of parchment, bearing the signatures (or copy of the signature) of King John and several of the Barons—the famous Magna Charta. This is enclosed within a glass frame, and has a fragment of the seal, totally defaced, depending from it. After the injury sustained by this unfortunate document, when the library in which it was formerly kept (the Cottonian) was nearly all destroyed by an accidental fire, at Ashburnham House, in 1731, it was carefully extended upon coarse canvas; but through the effects of time and other circumstances, the ink has become very pale, and the writing is now nearly illegible. Many years ago, however, an admirable fac-simile of the deed, in its original state, was made by permission of the trustees; this is surrounded by the arms of the twenty-five barons who witnessed the king's act, and is placed side by side with the original.

Mr. John Timbs, in his "Curiosities of London," says that this copy of Magna Charta is "traditionally stated to have been bought for fourpence, by Sir Robert Cotton, of a tailor, who was about to cut up the parchment into measures! But this anecdote, if true, may refer to another copy of the charter, also preserved at the British Museum in a portfolio of royal and ecclesiastical instruments, marked 'Augustus II., art. 106;' for the original charter is believed to have been presented to Sir Robert Cotton by Sir Edward Dering,

Lieutenant-Governor of Dover Castle; and to be that referred to in a letter dated as far back as May 10, 1630, still extant in the Museum Library, in a volume of correspondence. But it would appear that the original Magna Charta is still a matter of dispute."

Mr. Richard Thomson, the author of "An Historical Essay on the Magna Charta of King John," published in 1829, observes that "The Commissioners on the Public Records regarded the original of Magna Charta, preserved at Lincoln, to be of superior authority to either of those in the British Museum, on account of several words and sentences being inserted in the body of that charta, which in the latter are added at the foot, with reference-marks to the four places where they were to be added. These notes, however, possibly may prove that one of the Museum charters was really the first written, to which those important additions were made immediately previous to the sealing on Runnymede, and therefore the actual original whence the more perfect transcripts were taken."

We have space to notice only two or three other ancient charters in this part of the collection. One of these is the Bull of Pope Leo X., conferring on Henry VIII. the title of "Defender of the Faith." This document was also injured by the fire which partly destroyed the Cottonian Collection. One of the oldest English charters is the title to Battle Abbey, in Sussex, granted by William the Conqueror. This once famous ecclesiastical foundation owed its origin to the battle of Hastings, which decided the Norman conquest, in 1066. The abbey was commenced by the Conqueror the year after.

Another of the treasures of the Cottonian Collection is what antiquaries supposed to be the oldest royal letter in existence—a short note from King Henry V. to the Bishop of Durham, dated 10th of February, 1418.

The history of the Manuscript Department, of which the Harleian, Sloanean, and Cottonian manuscripts formed the nucleus, is in its general outline similar to that of the Printed Book Department, but its development has, of course, not been so immense. It was formed at the outset by the union of four great collections, the three above mentioned, to which shortly afterwards were added the manuscripts of the ancient royal library of England. Old scholastic divinity abounds in this department; but "the great ornament of the collection," says Sir Henry Ellis, "is the 'Codex Alexandrinus,' an ancient Greek copy of the Scriptures, supposed to have been executed by

Thecla, a lady of Alexandria, in the fourth or sixth century, and presented by Cyril Lucar, the Patriarch of Constantinople, to King Charles I. It is generally acknowledged by critics to be one of the two most ancient copies of the Scriptures in existence, and an elaborate edition of the New Testament portion of it was executed by Dr. Woide, and of the Old Testament portion, at the public expense, by the Rev. H. H. Baber, from 1822 to 1837 keeper of the printed books." The department contains also many volumes enriched by the finest illuminators of different countries, in a succession of periods to the sixteenth century; a numerous assemblage of the domestic music-books of Henry VIII.; and the "Basilicon Doron" of King James I., in his own handwriting. This latter work is a treatise on the art of government, addressed by the king to his promising son, Prince Henry, who died young, and "showing how much easier it is to speculate plausibly than to rule well." Among the other literary treasures of the Museum is a copy of the earliest newspaper, so-called the *English Mercurie*, which, by authority, was imprinted at London by her Highness's printer, in 1588; in fact, there are several such papers, printed while the Spanish fleet was hovering about in the English Channel in that year. "These, however," observes D'Israeli, in his "Curiosities of Literature," "were but extraordinary gazettes, and not published regularly. In this obscure origin they were skilfully directed by the policy of that great statesman, Burleigh, who, to inflame the national feeling, gives an extract from a letter from Madrid, which speaks of putting the queen to death, and of the instruments of torture on board of the Spanish fleet." The first newspaper in the collection is printed in Roman type, not in black letter, and contains the usual articles of news like the *London Gazette* of the present day. Under the date of July 26th in that year, for instance, there is a notice of the Scots' Ambassador being introduced to Sir F. Walsingham, and having an audience of her Majesty, to whom he gave a letter from the King, his master, assuring her of his firm adhesion to her interests, and those of the Protestant faith.

The *English Mercurie* came into the possession of the Museum in 1766, through a bequest of Dr. Birch; and from 1796, when George Chalmers first called attention to it, it had been looked on not merely as the first English newspaper, but the first in the world—"an honour," says Sir Henry Ellis, "which it was destined to lose in 1839, when Mr. Thomas Watts, in his letter to Antonio Panizzi, on the reputed earliest newspaper, proved beyond dispute that it was a fabrication, which was subse-quently shown to have originated, probably in a frolic, with one of the sons of Lord Hardwicke, the Chancellor, and with Dr. Birch, who was the friend of the family." Many of the genuine early newspapers were acquired by the Museum in the purchase of the library and collections of Dr. Burney; one of the oldest is dated in 1616, and it is mainly occupied with "News out of Holland." Till long after this period occasional pamphlets and tracts served the purpose of the newspaper, which did not assume anything like its present character till after the Revolution of 1688. Macaulay, in his "History of England," describes the earlier efforts of our countrymen at newspaper literature. He mentions that in 1685 nothing like the London daily paper of our time existed, or could exist, for want of capital, skill, and freedom. The political conflicts which preceded the Civil War gave rise to a number of publications, which are thus described: "None exceeded in size a single small leaf. The quantity of matter which one of them contained in a year was not more than is often found in two numbers of the *Times*." With reference to the *London Gazette*, writes Macaulay, "the contents generally were a royal proclamation, two or three Tory addresses, notices of two or three promotions, an account of a skirmish between the Imperial troops and the Janissaries on the Danube, a description of a highwayman, an announcement of a grand cock-fight between two persons of honour, and an advertisement offering a reward for a stray dog. The whole made up two pages of moderate size. Whatever was communicated respecting matters of the highest moment, was communicated in the most meagre and formal style. The most important parliamentary debates, the most important state trials recorded in our history, were passed over in profound silence. In the capital the coffee-houses supplied in some measure the place of a journal. Thither the Londoners flocked, as the Athenians of old flocked to the market-place, to hear whether there was any news. There men might learn how brutally a Whig had been treated the day before in Westminster Hall, or what horrible accounts the letters from Edinburgh gave of the torturing of Covenanters." In 1690 there were nine London newspapers published weekly. In Queen Anne's reign, in 1709, they had increased to eighteen, including one daily paper. In the reign of George I. there were three daily, six weekly, and ten three times a week. The collection of newspapers in the Museum was commenced by Sir Hans Sloane. The Burney Collection was added to these in 1818, at the cost of £1,000.

From 1818 the Stamp Office was directed to supply to the Museum its copies of London newspapers after the lapse of two years, a lapse which had previously converted them into a "perquisite," and consigned them to destruction as waste paper to be sent to the mill. The English country newspapers were not regularly added to the library till about 1820; the Scotch in 1844, and the Irish not until even some years later. Numerous files of

We learn from the "English Encyclopædia" that the donation of the Royal Library to the Museum by George II., in 1757, was accompanied by that of the royal privilege of claiming from the publishers a gratuitous copy of every work printed in the English dominions. This had first been granted to the Crown by an Act of Parliament of the 14th of Charles II., and subsequently renewed after its expiry by the famous Copyright Act of the 8th of

THE NINEVEH GALLERY. (See page 531.)

Continental and American newspapers have been added at different times. On the ground floor of the library, surrounding the reading-room, large shelves of newspapers occupy the two sides of a circular passage about 600 feet in length. The newspapers here are not confined to particular languages or dialects, countries, provinces, or cities; they are in every language, and come from places situated in all parts of the world. But while there are numerous foreign and colonial series of papers complete or nearly so, those of Great Britain generally, and those of London especially, are the most extensive, and probably the most perfect.

For the augmentation of the collection of English books, reliance had been placed, in the earlier stages of the Museum, on its legal rights.

Queen Anne. This does not include privately-printed books, in which department our national collection is not so rich as it should be; neither does it extend to the printed papers of the House of Commons, one consequence of which is that in our great National Library there is no complete set of Parliamentary Blue-books to be found, and that there never is a specimen less than two or three years old. Dr. Bentley, when keeper of the Royal Library, complained of the constant evasion of the above-mentioned Act by the booksellers; and the complaints were often renewed by the librarians of the Museum, though from about the year 1818, when Mr. Barber, then keeper of the printed books, gave some curious evidence on the subject before the Copyright Committee, there was certainly a great improvement. The new Copyright Act of 1842 gave a pre-eminence to the Museum among other libraries to which the privilege was conceded, and provided that, in case of non-compliance with the Act, the negligent publisher might be taken before a magistrate and fined. In 1850, the superintendence of this part of the Museum business was transferred to Mr. Panizzi, as keeper of the Printed Book Department, and the strictness with which he

to be found in the British Museum, or apparently anywhere else.

As to whether this library or that of the Louvre in Paris has the most books, is a disputed point; probably we are below the Louvre in manuscripts, and about equal to it in the number of printed books. Owing, however, to the regulation already mentioned referring only to books published in the three kingdoms, it is not every foreign work that

THE MAMMALIA SALOON, 1882. (*See page* 520.)

enforced the Act led to a great augmentation in the number of books received. At present, all is collected that issues from the English press down to the most insignificant work on crochet, a Child's Missionary Magazine, the directory of a country town, or a circulating library novel; and everything that is collected finds its place on the shelves and in the catalogue, in the conviction that it may often be a point of importance to preserve one copy of even a worthless work in a repository where it may instantly be referred to in case of need. A different system prevailed in former days, when it does not seem to have struck a single individual that it might probably be of advantage to preserve a set of the "London Directory" or the "Navy List," and a complete collection of either is, in consequence, not

will be found here. Books published in India and the colonies ought to be sent to the British Museum, but there seems to be some difficulty in the way of enforcing this right. Also with regard to foreign books, a few are sent in order to comply with the regulations for securing the rights of international copyright; but here, too, the rule is not carried out very strictly.

The author of the "Cities and Principal Towns in the World," in 1830, thus speaks of the library: " Regarded as a source of reference, it is deficient in the selection of editions and also in extent, lamentably in arrear of foreign works, and most unmethodically arranged." As we have notified above, the statement here regarding the arrears of foreign works may perhaps hold good even at the present time ; but with reference to the general arrangement and selection of books of reference, considerable improvement has been made since the erection of the present reading-room, and the consequent increase in the space devoted to the purposes of the library. At the close of the year 1882 the entire number of volumes in the library amounted to about 1,500,000, besides which there were about 50,000 manuscripts.

Although there is a very large number of prints, drawings, and photographs kept with the collection of printed books and manuscripts, and accessible to students in the reading-room and the apartment attached to the manuscript-room, the most extensive and valuable works of these descriptions are preserved in a separate division of the Museum, called the Department of Prints and Drawings, and are open to the inspection only of persons who hold cards of admission to that department. Members of the Royal Academy are admitted to this room without any recommendation or letter of introduction ; they have merely to make a written application, addressed to the principal librarian of the Museum. Other persons are admitted upon applying by letter to the same individual—very much as in the case of readers—and forwarding a written recommendation from some person of standing, either as an artist or otherwise. Drawing and sketching are very freely allowed in this department ; and every facility is given for copying ; but as the drawings are irreplaceable, and the whole collection intended for "all time," it is scarcely necessary to add that the greatest care of the works entrusted to students is earnestly enjoined. The entrance to this department is in the western range of the building, at the north end of the main gallery of Egyptian antiquities.

For the most part, the Civil Service of the Crown is officered by natives of the United Kingdom ; but to this rule the Museum appears to form an exception, as the names of several foreigners figure among its *employés*, and out of its chief librarians, half have been of foreign extraction. None of its earlier heads are men who have left any deep marks behind them, though Mr. Joseph Planta, of Swiss extraction, who held that post in the reign of George III. and George IV., became Secretary of the Treasury, a member of Parliament, and a Privy Councillor. His successor, Sir Henry Ellis, who died in 1869, at the age of upwards of ninety, was, however, a man of deep and varied learning, and is widely known as the editor of the best complete edition of Dugdale's "Monasticon." Sir Antonio Panizzi, to whom, as already stated, is due the erection of the great central reading-room, was a native of Brescello, in Italy. He came to England as a refugee, and, obtaining the patronage of Lord Brougham, was nominated to an assistant-librarianship in the Museum ; and, on a vacancy occurring in the keepership of printed books, he received that appointment. Some twenty years later he was promoted to the principal librarianship. On his retirement, in 1866, he was succeeded by Mr. J. Winter Jones, whose knowledge of books and manuscripts was probably unrivalled in England. On his death, which happened in 1878, Mr. Winter Jones was succeeded by Mr. Edward A. Bond, who was at the time keeper of the Manuscript Department.

During the interval between the years 1838 and 1857 the arrangement of the books in the library was under the management of Mr. Thomas Watts, and when the new reading-room was opened in 1857, it was placed under his direction. He presided there until the retirement of Sir A. Panizzi, in 1866, when he became keeper of the Department of Printed Books, an office which he held down to the time of his death, in 1869, when he was succeeded by Mr. Rye, on whose retirement in 1875, Mr. Geo. Bullen was appointed to the office.

One of the former keepers of the Department of Prints and Drawings was Mr. John T. Smith, the author of the "Antiquities of London and Westminster," "Vagabondiana," and other antiquarian works of high merit. He was the son of Mr. Nathaniel Smith, a sculptor, and afterwards a well-known printseller of St. Martin's Lane, and, as we have stated in a previous chapter, was literally born in a hackney-coach in the year 1766, whilst his mother was proceeding to her residence in Great Portland Street. At an early age, young Smith commenced studying drawing at the Royal Academy, and he was for many years a drawing-master, and at one time resided at Edmonton. His name, however, has been handed down to us as the author of some useful and entertaining topographical works on the metropolis, and also of the "Book for a Rainy Day," &c. Mr. Smith died in 1833, having held his post nearly half a century. In the album of a friend, the late Mr. W. Upcott, he wrote a playful account of himself, in which he observed : "I can boast of seven events, some of which *great* men would be proud of. When a boy I received a kiss from the beautiful Mrs. Robinson, was patted on the head by Dr. Johnson, have frequently held Sir Joshua Reynolds's spectacles, partook of a pot of porter with an elephant (at Exeter Change), saved Lady Hamilton from falling when the melancholy news of Lord Nelson's death arrived, three times conversed with George III., and was shut up in a room with Mr. Kean's lion."

It may interest the curious reader to learn the names of some, at least, of the more celebrated literary men of the last two or three generations who have made the library and reading-room the frequent scene of their researches. Among them have been Sir James Mackintosh, Sir Walter Scott, Charles Lamb, Washington Irving, William Godwin, Dean Milman, Leigh Hunt, Hallam, Macaulay, Grote, Tom Campbell, Sir E. Bulwer-Lytton, Edward Jesse, Charles Dickens, Ruskin, Jerrold, Thackeray, Shirley Brooks, Mark Lemon, and Count Stuart d'Albany. Lord Macaulay, it may be added, when at work upon his "History," used to sit day after day, not in the large reading-room, but in the King's Library, where, in virtue of being a trustee, he had the right of taking down with his own hands from the shelves the numerous pamphlets which he desired to consult and search, without the attendance and aid of an assistant. We are told, in his "Life" by Mr. Trevelyan, that

the place where he used to sit was a little desk near the centre of the room, and away from the wall, in order to obtain better light.

Her Majesty the Queen and the Prince Consort on one occasion visited the library. The only object for which Her Majesty asked in the MS. department was the paper signed at the foot by the prince who afterwards became Charles II. This was the piece of paper which, when his father's life was in the balance, he sent to Cromwell with the message, "Fill it up in any way you like, but spare my father."

Among the foreigners of note who have frequented the library and reading-room, either as visitors or as "readers," may be mentioned the names of Guizot, Thiers, Louis Napoleon (who, after his escape from the fortress of Ham, was introduced to the library by Count D'Orsay and the Countess of Blessington, in order to glean materials for his book upon artillery practice), Louis Philippe, when he came to England as an exile, Count Cavour, and Garibaldi.

CHAPTER XL.

THE BRITISH MUSEUM (continued).

Rescue of a Discarded Art Treasure—Acquisition of the Natural History Collections—Dr. Gray's Report on the Collection of Mammalia—A Stroll through the Zoological Galleries—Collection of Portraits—Nests of Foreign Birds—Minerals and Fossils—A Gigantic Tortoise—A Fossil Human Skeleton—The Botanical Collection—The Department of Antiquities—Historical Relics—The Portland Vase—Queen Anne's Farthings—The Pulteney Guinea—Greek, Roman, and Etruscan Bronzes—The Slade Collection of Ancient and Modern Glass—Egyptian Mummies—Egyptian Sculptured Antiquities—The Famous Rosetta Stone—Belzoni—Mr. Layard's Assyrian Collections—The Hellenic and Elgin Rooms—Fragments of the Mausoleum at Halicarnassus—The Lycian Gallery—The Temple of Diana at Ephesus—The Græco-Roman Rooms—Mr. Towneley's Choicest Gem—Concluding Remarks.

RETURNING to the entrance-hall, we find ourselves once more at the foot of the principal staircase. Against the wall, near the foot of the stairs, is a statue, executed by Westmacott, of the Hon. Mrs. Damer, holding in her hands a small allegorical figure, sculptured by herself, representing the "Genius of the Thames." On the opposite, or eastern, side of the hall, on each side of the doorway to the Grenville Library, are two marble statues — Shakespeare, by Roubilliac, and Sir Joseph Banks, by Chantrey. In the centre of the hall is a gigantic vase, standing upon a pedestal. It was purchased by the Museum authorities about the year 1859, from a resident of Croydon, in whose garden it had been discovered, broken to fragments. It is of Italian workmanship, and is elaborately ornamented with raised figures of a classical design, illustrative of Bacchanalian subjects. At the top of the staircase commences the suite of rooms appropriated to natural history, mineralogy, zoology, and botany. The depart-

ment of antiquities occupies the whole of the western part of the ground-floor, several rooms connected therewith on the basement, and the western side of the upper floor. We do not pretend in these pages to act the part of cicerone in pointing out to our readers all the wonders of the Museum, together with the exact spot in which they are to be found : all that we can do is to ask the reader to accompany us in imagination through the various corridors whilst we endeavour to set before him a few of the most important and interesting objects that are here brought together.

Before, however, commencing our stroll through the galleries, we may simply remark that in the year 1876 extensive alterations were commenced in various parts of the building. Instead of the approach to the reading-room which we have described in the previous chapter, a lobby of half the length is substituted, entered through a new gallery of antiquities. New apartments in the basement are set apart for the display of some of those sculptures which have been for some time stored away and never yet exhibited. A new room above, which is to supersede half of the long approach to the reading-room, will serve for the exhibition of marbles. This alteration will involve the replacing of the ladies'-room in another part of the building. Another alteration will consist of an additional apartment on the upper floor of the building, intended also to be devoted to antiquities. Although the construction of these new rooms will place a large space at the disposal of the trustees, it is believed that this will soon be found insufficient, in consequence of the large additions which are constantly being made.

Sir Hans Sloane's natural history collection, which, however limited it may now appear, was doubtless considered one of the greatest importance at the time it was formed, served as the nucleus of the present extensive departments of zoology, paleontology, mineralogy, and botany. In the infancy of the Museum all miscellaneous artificial curiosities, and even antiquities and anatomical preparations, were consigned to the natural history departments; but all of these have since been separated from it. In 1769 the trustees purchased a fine collection of stuffed birds, which had been brought over from Holland, and many additions to it were afterwards made by purchase and donation. The voyages of discovery by Captain Cook and others, early in the reign of George III., brought numerous acquisitions, and in 1816 the valuable collection of British zoology, which had belonged to Colonel Montague, of Knowle, in Devonshire, and included a very large number of birds, was purchased. General Hardwicke's collection of stuffed birds was bequeathed to the Museum in 1835, since which time still larger acquisitions have been made by presents and purchase, particularly in the case of ornithology, so that the aggregate now forms a collection probably as extensive as any in Europe.

With reference to the collection of mammalia, fishes, reptiles, insects, and crustacea in the British Museum, the late Dr. J. E. Gray, in the year 1849, submitted the following statement to the Commissioners of Inquiry into the constitution and management of the British Museum:—"In 1836 Mr. Gray gave some account of the state of the Museum collections, compared with those on the Continent. Since that period he has had the opportunity of again inspecting those collections, and others in the south and eastern parts of Germany, and the south of France, which he had not then seen, and he considers the statements made at that time to require no corrections; but the comparison is now much more favourable for the British Museum, that collection having been increasing very rapidly—indeed, in a most unexampled manner—while most of the Continental collections have, for the last six or seven years, for some political reason, been nearly stationary; or, at most, increasing a single part of their collections, or receiving specimens from a single locality where they happened to have a collector staying. To enter into a few details, Mr. Gray believes that the Museum collections of mammalia, birds, shells, and lepidopterous insects are much more extensive than any other public collection, and superior to all the public collections together. This is certainly the case with the first and last mentioned groups, and he believes also with the other two. The collections of reptiles, fish, and crustacea are second only to those at Paris, if at all below them, in spite of all the assistance of Baron Cuvier. Our collection in each of these classes contains many species which the Paris collection wants, and our collection of insects, taken as a whole, is much larger and better arranged than that of Paris." Since the above period the collections have continued to increase both in number and importance. In 1880 the authorities decided to transfer the whole of the Natural History collections to a new building erected at South Kensington.

The following account of these collections was written prior to their removal:—Arrived at the top of the grand staircase, we find ourselves in the central saloon, the first of three large rooms devoted to the exhibition of specimens selected from the existing classes of animals. The collection here is extremely varied. Arranged round the walls, in glass cases, are a number of antelopes, sheep, goats, and bats; and above the cases are horns of various kinds of oxen, some of them of gigantic dimensions; whilst in the centre of the room are the towering giraffes, the morse or walrus from the Arctic regions, the rhinoceros, hippopotamus, and the Indian elephant. In two large glass cases are shown stuffed specimens and skeletons of those apes or monkeys which, on the whole, are most like man, and therefore are named "anthropoid apes;" however, it will be perceived that their similarity to man is much greater during their early youth than at an advanced age. To this group of monkeys belong the gorilla and chimpanzee, inhabitants of the forests of Western and Central Africa; and the two kinds of orangoutang from Borneo and Sumatra, brutes possessing an extraordinary strength, which they well know how to use when attacked. Here are numerous specimens of antelopes; they are generally of a sandy colour, and specially fitted to inhabit extensive plains, with tracts of desert. A few of the species live among rocks, where they are as sure-footed as the goat. They are most abundant in Africa, especially in the southern districts. A few are found in India. Among the more interesting species may be pointed out the water-buck and sable antelope; the oryx, which, when seen in profile, probably suggested the unicorn mentioned by the ancients; the sassaybe of South Africa; the large-eyed gazelle, so often referred to by Eastern poets; the springbok, so called from its springing bounds, when the white fur of its back opens out like a sheet; the gnu, which at first seems a compound of horse, buffalo, and antelope; the Indian antelope, with its curious cheek-pores; the wood antelopes, with short horns often concealed amongst a brush of hairs; and the chickara of India, with its four little horns. North America and Europe have each a single species, namely, the prong-buck of the United States, and the chamois which frequents the Alps.

Of the varieties of wild sheep from the mountains of Asia, North America, and North Africa, one of the most remarkable is the bearded sheep of Morocco, which has enormous strength in its neck and horns; it sometimes reaches a great size, one specimen exhibited measuring fifty-six inches in a straight line from tip to tip. That these wild sheep are good climbers may be inferred from the fact that one of them was discovered by the Venetian traveller, Marco Polo, in the thirteenth century, on the great Pamir Mountains, at an altitude of 16,000 feet. In three or four cases we find the various kinds of ibex and wild goats of Siberia, India, and Europe, together with some of their domestic varieties; and also the Cashmere and Angora goats, celebrated for the delicate wool growing among their hair, and manufactured into the finest shawls. Several of the larger bats, of which we here see specimens before us, are to be found in Africa, in the islands of the Indian Archipelago, the Pacific, and in Australia; they are called fox-bats, or flying foxes, have blunt, grinding teeth, and eat fruit only. Though bats in general are sombre-coloured, some of these fox-bats have brilliantly-coloured furs. The blood-sucking bats, commonly called vampires, are, we are told, confined to South America, and perhaps it is as well that it should be so, seeing that they delight in attacking animals and "sometimes even men, while sleeping, fanning the victims with their wings." These bats are of small size, have a long tongue, and a deep notch in the lower lip; and the wounds which they inflict, it is stated, often continue to flow after the animals are satiated, and do not readily heal.

In the next room are exhibited the continuation of the collection of hoofed quadrupeds, such as oxen, elands, deer, camels, llamas, horses, as well as the various species of swine. Here also are placed the species of armadillo, manis, and sloth. The four corners of this room are occupied by various specimens of the wild cattle and buffaloes of Europe, Africa, and Asia; by the eland, the largest kind of antelopes acclimatised in England and Ireland; and by the elk, the most bulky species of deer inhabiting North America and some districts of North-eastern Europe. In the centre of this gallery there is a magnificent specimen of the basking shark, captured in March, 1875, near Shanklin, in the Isle of Wight. It is about twenty-eight feet in length, and thirteen feet in its greatest circumference. This shark is an inhabitant of the northern parts of the Atlantic Ocean, and approaches annually the west coast of Ireland, rarely straying to the coasts of England and Scotland. It is of a harmless disposition, its food consisting of small fishes and other marine animals swimming in shoals. On the west coast of Ireland it is chased for the sake of the oil which is extracted from the liver, one fish yielding from a ton to a ton and a half. However, its capture, we are told, is attended with great danger, as one blow from its enormously strong tail is sufficient to stave in the sides of a large boat.

The llamas, of which there are some fine stuffed specimens here, are used as beasts of burden in the Andes of South America, one species furnishing an excellent wool. The wild species are brown, while the domesticated ones are black, white, or brown, and often variegated.

Among the animals in this gallery, classed under the heading of "oxen," may be specified the Lithuanian bison, or aurochs, which in ancient times inhabited the European forests, but is now nearly extinct, a few only having been preserved by the care of the Russian Emperors; the American bison, or "buffalo," which still wanders in gradually diminishing herds over the prairies of North America; the musk-ox, limited to Arctic America, where, with its peculiar head and feet, it manages to find food even during the long winter of those regions; and the yak of Thibet, the tail of which is used as a fly-flap by the Asiatics.

Then we have a continuation of the series of antelopes, such as the bontebok, with its inscribed sides; the fine striped strepsiceros, with spiral horns; the nylghau, often called the horned horse of India; and the anoa of the Celebes. In these cases are also contained some others of the thick-skinned beasts, as Baird's tapir of Central America; the African swine, with warts on the head, and formidable tusks; the babyrussa, with recurved horn-like tusks; the social South American peccaries, with a gland on their back emitting a fœtid odour. All these animals have muscular and callous noses, which fit them well for grubbing in the ground. The curious hyrax, one of the species of which is the "coney" of Scripture: in structure it resembles a diminutive rhinoceros. The "shielded beasts," as the manis, or scaly ant-eaters of India and Africa, with very long claws, which are turned in when they walk; the burrowing armadilloes of South America, which, if danger threatens, can roll themselves into a ball, covered with jointed mail, whence they have derived their name. The ant-eaters of South America, which are covered with hair, and have a very long worm-like tongue which they exert into ant-hills, and, when covered with ants, draw into their mouths.

The next room eastward is called the Saloon of Mammalia. Here there is a very extraordinary col-

THE PORTLAND VASE. (*See page* 526.)

lection, which includes the various species of monkeys. One of the most remarkable is the proboscis monkey of Borneo, with its singular long nose. Here also may be noticed the sacred monkey of the Hindoos, which is religiously preserved about their sacred enclosures. Other notable "specimens" in this group are the "colobi," so called from their fore-hands wanting the thumb. Of these the most handsome is the Abyssinian guereza, with long white hairs flowing over its sides, and with the white tail contrasting strongly with the deep black fur. The skin of this monkey is used to ornament the shields of the Abyssinian chiefs. In this saloon are also animals of the feline tribe, such as lions, tigers, leopards, bears, &c. The collection of corals, too, is very perfect. Suspended from the ceiling of this saloon is the skeleton of a whale from New Zealand, a species as important to commerce as the whale of the northern hemisphere. It is stated to be a young

individual, not quite half grown. Near it is the skeleton of the bottle-nosed dolphin, of which a large shoal was taken near Holyhead in 1866. Here is also the skeleton of the narwhal, one of the most singular animals of the whale tribe, distinguished by a long spirally twisted tusk, which projects from the snout in the line of the animal's body. This tusk is developed on one side of the snout only (the left), very rarely on both sides. In the adult male it reaches a length of six or eight feet, but is seldom developed in the female; hence it is probable that its use is the same as that of the antlers in the stag. The ivory of the tusk commands a high price in the market, and was still more valued in former times, when it was believed to be the horn of the unicorn. The narwhal is an inhabitant of the Arctic seas, and rarely strays to more temperate regions.

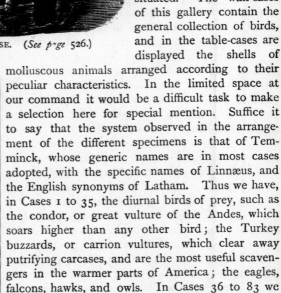

The eastern zoological gallery corresponds in length and general arrangement with the King's Library, above which it is situated. The wall-cases of this gallery contain the general collection of birds, and in the table-cases are displayed the shells of molluscous animals arranged according to their peculiar characteristics. In the limited space at our command it would be a difficult task to make a selection here for special mention. Suffice it to say that the system observed in the arrangement of the different specimens is that of Temminck, whose generic names are in most cases adopted, with the specific names of Linnæus, and the English synonyms of Latham. Thus we have, in Cases 1 to 35, the diurnal birds of prey, such as the condor, or great vulture of the Andes, which soars higher than any other bird; the Turkey buzzards, or carrion vultures, which clear away putrifying carcases, and are the most useful scavengers in the warmer parts of America; the eagles, falcons, hawks, and owls. In Cases 36 to 83 we have the perching birds, subdivided into the wide-gaped, as the goatsuckers, the swallows, kingfishers, and the like. Among the tenuirostral birds may be noticed the hoopoes and sun-birds of Africa and

FRONT OF THE BRITISH MUSEUM, 1880.

Asia. The brilliant-plumaged humming-birds come next in order; and then follow the honey-eaters, nuthatches, wrens, wood-warblers, ·thrushes, and chatterers of the American forests, &c. Further on we find cases filled with conirostral birds, including the crows and finches; the scansorial, including the parrots and cuckoos; the gallinaceous birds, as pigeons, turtles, pheasants, and partridges. Lastly, we have the wading and web-footed birds, which comprise the ostriches, trumpeters, storks, cranes, flamingoes, swans, and ducks. An extensive series of cases of eggs of birds, ranged to correspond with the cases of the birds themselves, and placed opposite them, gives completeness to the whole.

In 1874 an important addition was made to the Natural History Department by the acquisition of Mrs. J. E. Craig's collection of shells, comprising some 12,000 specimens, and representing about 4,000 different species. In the same year the collection of beetles formed by Mr. Edward Saunders, and numbering upwards of 7,000 specimens, was purchased for its use.

Above the cases which line the walls of this gallery is a series of portraits, one hundred and thirteen in number, among which are a few of particular interest, notably those of Oliver Cromwell, painted by Walker, and bequeathed to the Museum in the year 1784 by Sir Robert Rich, to whose great-grandfather, Nathaniel Rich, Esq., then serving as a Colonel of Horse in the Parliamentary Army, it was presented by the great "Lord Protector" himself; one of Mary Queen of Scots, by Jansen; and one of Queen Elizabeth, by Zucchero. Here, too, may be seen portraits of Charles II. (by Sir Peter Lely), Sir Isaac Newton, Sir Hans Sloane, and Sir Robert Cotton; Sir William Dugdale, William Camden, and John Speed, the historians; Shakespeare, Algernon Sidney, and Alexander Pope; Philip Dormer, Earl of Chesterfield, and Thomas Britton (the "Musical small-coal man"). But still the British Museum does not even claim, or pretend to contain, a National Portrait Gallery of Eminent Englishmen: we shall find such a gallery, and shall have much to say about it, when we reach South Kensington.

The first room in the northern zoological gallery contains an interesting display of the nests of birds and insects from various countries. "In one group of cases are nests of wasps and bees; some are constructed of clay, or of sand, while others are of paper, made of an admixture of the scrapings of wood and vegetable fibre. Specimens of the various insect fabricators of these structures are, in many instances, attached to the nests. In another case we find the remains of the square lintel of a door of one of the government offices in St. Helena, showing the destruction caused by a species of white ant. Then there are a series of the different stages of development, and of the products, of the Japanese silk-moths, prepared and set up in Japan. Among the more noticeable of the nests of birds are the playing avenues of the Australian bower-birds, the pendulous nests of the American orioles, and the gelatinous nests of the esculent swallow; and that of the San Geronimo swallow; which is a long pendulous tube formed entirely of the seed of a plant, secured together by the saliva of the bird; the hollow for the eggs is at the top, inside the tube; the bird has placed a false entrance on the side to deceive its enemies. Various nests of humming-birds, honey-eaters, tailor-bird, and lyre-tailed menuras are also shown. Another group of cases contains specimens illustrative of the various changes of insects, their nests and structures; the cocoon of the gigantic goliath beetle of Western Africa, the clay nests of various species of white ants, the various vegetable galls, and a series of the nests of spiders; among these the nests of the trap-door spider, and a remarkable flat web, constructed by an Australian species, are shown here. On the walls are suspended some specimens of the large gigantic land-tortoises, which once inhabited in large numbers the Galapagos and the islands of Mauritius, Rodriguez, and Aldabra. They formed a very important article of food to navigators in the seventeenth and eighteenth centuries during the protracted and tedious voyages across the Indian and Pacific Oceans, but are now almost extinct."

The succeeding rooms devoted to zoology, five in number, contain chiefly the various specimens of reptiles, such as serpents, tortoises, crocodiles, and lizards; toads, frogs, and efts; and the various species of marine products, such as star-fishes and sea-wigs. Here, too, are the spiny-rayed and anomalous fishes; insects; crustacea, including such varieties as the crab and lobster; and also sturgeons and pikes, &c.; whilst over the wall-cases, or suspended from the roof, are ranged the larger fish which could not be accommodated within, such as the famous flying sword-fish, sharks, and congers.

On the north side, running parallel with the above-mentioned rooms, is the gallery of minerals and fossils. In no department, probably, is the Museum richer than in its minerals. These occupy the table-cases of four large rooms; the fossil remains of the invertebrate animals being displayed on the floor of the fifth and sixth rooms, and in the wall-cases throughout the entire gallery. In the lobby, at the eastern end of this gallery, is a restored model of the shell of an extinct fossil tortoise, of gigantic size, from the Siwalik Hills, in India. Portions of the shell, and of other parts of the skeleton of several different individuals of this species of tortoise, are deposited in the third room of the gallery, and it is of casts from some of these portions that the restored model is, in a great measure, composed. In this gallery will be found the fossil remains of those gigantic ante-diluvian animals and reptiles, which for so many years have excited the curiosity and stimulated the energies of men learned in geological science —such as the mastodon, the megatherium, the iguanodon, and the megalosaurus ; then there are fossil plants, fishes, mammalia, insects, and shells ; and perhaps the most extraordinary of all, a fossil human skeleton. This last-named "specimen" was brought from Guadaloupe by Sir Alexander Cochrane, and presented to the Museum by the Lords of the Admiralty. It was found embedded in the solid limestone rock, and much discussion has arisen as to its antiquity ; "but," writes Sir Henry Ellis, "the most probable conjecture is that it is not more than a few centuries old." This skeleton (which is described in the "Philosophical Transactions" of the Royal Society) wants the skull, and it is a curious fact, mentioned by Sir Charles Lyell, in his "Travels in North America," that in the Museum at Charleston, South Carolina, he was shown a fossil human skull from Guada-loupe, embedded in solid limestone, "which they say belongs to the same skeleton of a female as that now preserved in the British Museum, where the skull is wanting." Dr. Moultrie, of the Medical College of that State, has described the bones, together with the entire skeleton disen-tombed from the limestone deposit at Guadaloupe, and is of opinion—taking for granted the relation of the skull at Charleston to the headless trunk in London—that the latter is not the skeleton of a Carib, as has been generally supposed, but that of one of the Peruvians, or of a tribe possessing a similar craniological development."

Before proceeding to describe the antiquities, we may say a few words about the botanical collection. This is very extensive, and is exhibited in two rooms, which are entered by a doorway on the eastern side of the central zoological saloon. The collection consists of dried plants, and other botanical specimens, and had its origin in the collection of herbaria formed from time to time by Sir Hans Sloane during his long life, or, at all events, from the year 1687, when he went out to Jamaica as physician to the Duke of Albemarle,

"his chief inducement being the opportunity that it would afford him of studying his favourite science." On his return to England, he brought with him a collection of 800 species of West India plants. These, together with various others pre-sented to or purchased by Sir Hans Sloane, are contained in about 300 volumes. To these have been added the herbarium of Baron von Moll, of Munich ; and also that of Sir Joseph Banks. The latter alone formed at one time, it is said, the most valuable assemblage of dried plants in Europe, and is still one of the most important, not only on account of its extent, but as containing the original and authentic specimens of many published species. Besides the above, we learn that additions have since been made from various other sources, which make the entire number of species amount to about 50,000—"sufficient to entitle the Museum collec-tion to rank among the finest in the world."

The department of antiquities is divided into two series : the first, consisting of sculpture, includ-ing inscriptions and architectural remains, occupies the ground-floor of the south-western and western portions of the building, besides some rooms in the basement, not originally designed for exhibition, but now supplying the only space which the exten-sive acquisitions recently made from Assyria and other countries have left available for that purpose. The second series, placed in a suite of rooms on the upper floor, comprises all the smaller remains, of whatever nation or period, such as vases, terra-cottas, bronzes, coins, and medals, and articles of personal or domestic use. To the latter division is attached the collection of ethnographical speci-mens. In the infancy of the Museum, the antiqui-ties being few in number, and of comparatively little value, were considered, with other artificial curiosities, as an appendage to the natural history ; the coins, medals, and drawings were at that time appended to the department of manuscripts ; and the prints and engravings to the library of printed books. On the purchase of Sir William Hamilton's collection of Greek and Roman antiquities, in 1772, for the sum of £8,400, the augmentations even then were not considered sufficient to require an increase of the establishment ; but on the acquisition of the Egyptian monuments at the capitulation of Alexandria, in the year 1801, and the purchase of the Towneley marbles shortly after-wards, additional accommodation was needed, and several new buildings were erected, as we have already shown. It was then that a new department was created, by the name of the Department of Antiquities ; and thus, as Sir Henry Ellis writes, "the magnificent collection of ancient sculpture was at length opened for the inspection of strangers and the improvement of artists, an advantage which the students of the Fine Arts had never before enjoyed in this country."

On leaving the rooms containing the botanical specimens, and crossing the central saloon, the visitor enters the Ethnographical room, where will be found a curious and interesting collection of antiquities, and the objects in modern use, belonging to all nations, not of European race. In one table-case are antiquities discovered during excavations in India; in another, a group of Peruvian and Mexican antiquities; whilst others contain dresses and implements in use among the Esquimaux tribes, as well as objects illustrative of the late Arctic expeditions, chiefly collected by Sir John Barrow. With reference to the contents of the wall-cases in this room, we can only remark that they comprise a very miscellaneous assortment of articles, including specimens of wearing apparel, warlike implements, idols, musical instruments, sepulchral vases, pottery, domestic utensils, &c.

The British and Mediæval room contains three collections—namely, the British, consisting of antiquities found in Great Britain and Ireland, extending from the earliest period to the Norman Conquest; the Early Christian; and the Mediæval, comprising all remains of the Middle Ages, both English and foreign. Here we have in abundance such relics of the past as urns and other funeral remains found in tumuli; flint implements of a peculiar pear-shaped form, believed to be the oldest objects of human industry hitherto discovered; stone hammers and axe-heads; implements and weapons made of bronze; also vases and lamps. Among the historical relics in the mediæval collection we may mention the casket made out of Shakespeare's mulberry-tree, at one time in the possession of David Garrick; the punchbowl of Robert Burns; and portions of the frescoes in St. Stephen's Chapel, Westminster, executed in the latter half of the fourteenth century.

Between the two rooms above mentioned is a doorway leading to a small ante-room containing the collection of gold ornaments and gems. Here we find specimens of mediæval and modern jewellery, Greek, Roman, and Etruscan ornaments of an early period. And here also are exhibited the unrivalled collection of cameos and intaglios, formed chiefly by the bequests of the Payne Knight and Cracherode collections, and by the purchase of those of Towneley, Hamilton, Blacas, and Castellani. On one of the cases in this room is placed the celebrated glass vase, placed here in 1810 by its owner, the Duke of Portland, and

thence popularly known as the Portland Vase. It was found in a marble sarcophagus in the Monte del Grano, near Rome, about the middle of the sixteenth century, and was afterwards deposited in the Barberini Palace, where it remained until 1770, when it was purchased by Byres, the antiquary, who sold it to Sir William Hamilton, of whom it was bought, for 1,800 guineas, by the Duchess of Portland, at the sale of whose property it was bought in by the family for £1,029. The ground of the vase is of dark-blue glass, and the design is cut in a layer of opaque white glass, the figures standing out in bold relief. The composition is classical; it is supposed by some to represent the meeting of Peleus and Thetis on Mount Pelion, and Thetis consenting to be the bride of Peleus, in the presence of Poseidon and Eros. On the bottom of the vase, which is detached, is a bust of Atys. This vase is considered one of the principal ornaments of the Museum, and till 1845 it was as perfect as when it was first fashioned. In that year a drunken mechanic, named William Lloyd, found his way into the Museum, and appears to have taken a dislike to the vase, a feeling which he gave vent to by deliberately hurling at it a stone which was lying close at hand; the result was that this peerless vase, as well as the glass case which contained it, was smashed to pieces. The man was at once taken before the magistrate, who sentenced him to pay the cost of damage to the case, but had no power to commit him for breaking the vase, except at the instigation of its ducal owner, who happened at the time to be out of town. In the meantime the money was paid, and the fellow was accordingly discharged. Although the vase was literally smashed into a thousand pieces, the fragments were carefully collected, and a drawing made of them, which is preserved. The fractured pieces were afterwards replaced and cemented together by Mr. Doubleday, a gentleman who had for a long time been engaged at the Museum in repairing pottery and sculpture; and the manner in which he accomplished his task was so far successful that the exquisite form and proportions of the vase have been restored in such a way that scarcely a blemish can be detected. The vase is ten inches high, and its diameter seven inches at the broadest part near the centre, and it has two handles. It diminishes gradually towards the base, and more rapidly upwards into the narrow neck, which again opens towards the lip by a graceful flower-like expansion. Copies of the vase were executed by Wedgwood, and sold at fifty guineas each; the model is said to have cost 500 guineas.

Among the miscellaneous curiosities which are preserved in this room are the gold snuff-box, set with diamonds, and ornamented with a miniature portrait of Napoleon, who, in 1815, presented it to the Hon. Mrs. Damer, the sculptress, by whom it was bequeathed to the Museum; a gold snuff-box, with a cameo lid, presented by Pope Pius VI. to Napoleon, and by him bequeathed to Lady Holland, with a card in Napoleon's handwriting; and also a cast taken from the face of Oliver Cromwell after death.

The medal-room contains a collection of coins and medals superior to almost that of any other country. Sir Hans Sloane's collection, which formed the nucleus, was worth about £7,000 as bullion. To these were added those of Sir Robert Cotton, the Hamilton and Cracherode, valued at several thousand guineas; Roberts's collection of coins from the Conquest to George III.; a series of Papal medals; a collection of Greek coins; a vast collection of foreign coins, presented by Miss Banks; and many others, both by bequest and purchase. Of Queen Anne's farthings here are seven varieties, one only of which was circulated, the others being pattern pieces. Mr. John Timbs, in his "Curiosities," remarks that "the real Queen Anne's farthing, with the figure of Britannia on the reverse, and below it, in the exergue, the date 1714, brings from 7s. to a guinea; but at Baron Bolland's sale, in 1841, a pattern piece fetched £9 9s. The idea that there is but one Queen Anne's farthing in existence, and that only three were struck, is a popular error, several hundreds having been struck. This erroneous belief has caused the British Museum authorities almost as many annoyances as the rarity of a 'tortoiseshell tom-cat.'" In this room are preserved a few coins which have acquired an interest from their former owners or from other circumstances, rather than from their own intrinsic value; and of these we may mention the "Pulteney Guinea," respecting which the following story is told:—"William Pulteney, afterwards Earl of Bath, was remarkable alike for his oratorical talents and his long and consistent opposition to the measures of Sir Robert Walpole, the great Whig minister. On the 11th of February, 1741, a time when party feeling was at its height, Walpole received an intimation in the House of Commons that it was the intention of the Opposition to impeach him. To this menace he replied with his usual composure and self-complacence, merely requesting a fair and candid hearing, and winding up his speech with the quotation—

'Nil conscire sibi, nulli pallescere culpæ.'

With his usual tact Pulteney immediately rose, and observed 'that the right honourable gentleman's logic and Latin were alike inaccurate, and that Horace, whom he had just misquoted, had written 'nullâ pallescere culpâ.' Walpole maintained that his quotation was correct, and a bet was offered. The matter was referred to Nicholas Hardinge, Clerk of the House, an excellent classical scholar, who decided against Sir Robert. The minister accordingly took a guinea from his pocket, and flung it across the house to Pulteney. The latter caught it, and holding it up, exclaimed, 'It's the only money I have received from the Treasury for many years, and it shall be the last.' This guinea having been carefully preserved, finally came into the hands of Sir John Murray, by whom it was presented, in 1828, to the British Museum. The following memorandum, in the handwriting of Pulteney, is attached to it:—'This guinea I desire may be kept as an heirloom. It was won of Sir Robert Walpole in the House of Commons; he asserting the verse in Horace to be " nulli pallescere culpæ," whereas I laid the wager of a guinea that it was "nullâ pallescere culpâ." He sent for the book, and being convinced that he had lost, gave me this guinea. I told him I could take the money without any blush on my side, but believed it was the only money he ever gave in the house where the giver and the receiver ought not equally to blush. This guinea, I hope, will prove to my posterity the use of knowing Latin, and encourage them in their learning.'"

The bronze-room, which we now enter, contains the collection of Greek, Roman, and Etruscan bronzes, with the exception of such as have been found in Great Britain, which are placed in the British and Mediæval room. It was originally composed of the Sloane, Hamilton, Towneley, and Payne Knight collections, to which have been added, in recent years, the bronzes bequeathed by Sir William Temple, and many other interesting objects acquired by purchase or donation, including figures of divinities, furniture, mirrors, lamps and vases, personal ornaments, tripods, candelabra, &c. Several of the objects here exhibited were discovered by Mr. Layard in Assyria; whilst others are from the sepulchres of ancient Etruria, and the excavations at Pompeii and Herculaneum. Here, too, are the exquisite bronzes bequeathed by Mr. R. Payne Knight and Mr. Felix Slade. Among the most recent additions to the contents of this room may be noticed John Milton's watch. This curious timepiece, made by W. Bunting, and worn and used by the poet, was bequeathed to the nation by the late Sir C. Fellows, in 1860; the rest of his collection was added by his widow in 1874.

The two vase-rooms, through which we now pass, contain a large number of Græco-Italian vases painted from the myths or popular poetry of the day; and in the next room (Egyptian room) is dis-

interest, but as furnishing a valuable preparative for the due appreciation of the first series of sculptures (the Egyptian) which we shall find on the ground-floor. The smaller antiquities of Egypt which are

A SLAB FROM THE NINEVEH GALLERY. (*See page* 531.)

played the collections of ancient and more recent glass, including the very valuable bequest made to the Museum in 1868 by Mr. Felix Slade, number-ing about 960 specimens, to which additions have been made since his death out of a fund bequeathed for the purpose, making a total of 1,750 specimens. This room and also the next in order should be carefully inspected, not merely for its own intrinsic

here exhibited comprise divinities, royal person-ages, and sacred animals; sepulchral remains; and miscellaneous objects illustrative of the domestic manners of the Egyptians. They were acquired mainly by purchase from private collections, and by donations from the Prince of Wales, the Duke of Northumberland, the late Sir Gardner Wilkinson, and other travellers in Egypt. Charles Knight, in his "London," remarks that "ancient Egypt here revives before us—Osiris and Isis are no longer mere names; we behold them face to face, as their worshippers beheld them, who are here also represented, and that so numerously, in their mummies and mummy-cases, and who look so life-like from out their portraits upon us that one is half tempted to question them, and many a knotty riddle could no doubt be solved if the humblest of them would

"The preparations for embalming the dead, and ceremonies at funerals," as we learn from Herodotus in the words of the 'Guide to the Museum,' "were looked on as matters of importance by the Egyptians, and large sums were spent upon the sepulchral rites. There were several modes of preparing the mummies, varying not only at different periods, but also with the rank and wealth of the person to be interred. The more costly process was as

THE LYCIAN GALLERY   (*See page* 532.)

but speak. Yes, here are the very people of Egypt themselves; we see the expression of their faces, the colour of their hair, the outlines of their form; we know their very names, and their professions; this, for instance, is Otaineb, no Egyptian born, but one, no doubt, by naturalisation, as the gods of the country are exhibited on the case, taking especial care of him; Thoth, the Egyptian Mercury, is there seen introducing him to the many deities to whom the different parts of his body are respectively dedicated. This, again, is Hor, or Horus, incense-bearer to the abode of Noum-ra; this, Onkhhapê, a sacred musician; this Khonsaouonkh, a sacerdotal functionary and scribe; this Kotbi, a priestess of the Theban temple of Amoun; that, Har-sont-ioft, a priest of the same building."

follows:—The brain having been extracted, and the viscera removed through an opening cut in the left side with a stone, the body was, in earlier times, prepared with salt and wax—in later times, steeped or boiled in bitumen; then wrapped round with bands of linen, sometimes 700 yards in length; various amulets being placed in different parts, and the whole covered with a linen shroud and sometimes decorated with a network of porcelain bugles. It was then enclosed in a thin case formed of canvas, thickened with a coating of stucco, on which were painted figures of divinities and emblems of various kinds, as well as the name and titles of the deceased, and portions of the ritual of the dead. The whole was then enclosed in a wooden coffin, and sometimes deposited in a stone sarcophagus."

One of the most remarkable objects in the Egyptian collection is part of the mummy-shaped coffin of King Menkara, the Mycerinus of the Greeks, builder of the Third Pyramid. This is not only the oldest coffin in the collection, but one of the earliest inscribed monuments of Egypt. Near it is part of a body, supposed to be that of the king, found in the same pyramid. There is also a small Græco-Egyptian mummy of a child from Thebes; on the external wrapper is painted a representation of the deceased.

In the Egyptian ante-room, at the top of the staircase by which we descend to the ground-floor, the walls are partly covered with casts from sculptured and coloured bas-reliefs in Egypt, painted in imitation of the originals.

Upon the walls of the staircase are placed Egyptian papyri—documents of various character, inscribed on rolls, formed of thin layers or slices of the papyrus plant. The characters presented comprise "chiefly portions or extracts from the 'Ritual of the Dead,' the small pictures in them referring to the subjects of the various chapters; others are solar litanies and magical tracts. Among them is a caricature, and a treatise on arithmetic and geometry, one on medicine, with recipes of the age of Cheops, the romantic tale of a doomed prince, songs, dirges, criminal reports, and several contracts or deeds of sale in the demotic character."

In the vestibule at the foot of the stairs are placed monuments of the first twelve dynasties of Egyptian monarchs. Though small in size, they have considerable interest, being the most ancient sculptures in the Museum. The plaster cast from the head of the colossal statue of Rameses II., at Ibsamboul, placed over the east doorway of the vestibule, seems to keep watch and ward over the assembled treasures.

By a doorway at the foot of the stairs we enter the series of galleries devoted to Egyptian monuments and sculptured antiquities. The collection embraces a wide range of antiquity, commencing as far back as 2,000 years before the Christian era, and closing with the Mohammedan invasion of Egypt, A.D. 640. "The earlier sepulchral monuments," as we learn from the report of Dr. Birch, the keeper of this department, "are chiefly from Memphis, the capital of the most important of the more ancient dynasties, and the ruins of which are on the left bank of the Nile, opposite Cairo. Other early remains are derived from the great burial-place of Abydos. The main portion of the collection, including most of the monuments belonging to the kings of the 18th, 19th, and 20th dynasties, was obtained from the ancient city of Thebes,

which became the capital of Egypt under those monarchs." In the first gallery the larger sculptures belong to the 18th dynasty. It commenced with the expulsion of the "Shepherd Kings" from Lower Egypt, and its monarchs extended their conquests into Æthiopia and Asia, and built great edifices at Thebes. In the centre of the gallery towers aloft the colossal head of King Thothmes III., discovered by Belzoni near the granite sanctuary at Karnak, and near it is the arm of the same figure. Close by is a monument sculptured on four sides, representing in bas-relief the above-named king, supported by the god Muntra and the goddess Athor. In the central recess, on the east side of the gallery, is fixed the tablet of Abydos, said to be an inscription of great value in determining the names and succession of the kings of the various dynasties. It appears originally to have commemorated an offering made by Rameses II. to his predecessors on the throne of Egypt; and it was discovered by Mr. W. Bankes in a chamber of the temple of Abydos, in 1818. Among the curious objects here brought together are several statues of the cat-headed goddess Sekhet (Bubastis), inscribed with the name of the same monarch; the head of a colossal ram, from an avenue of ram-headed sphinxes, which led to a gateway built by King Horus, at Karnak. The king himself is also represented by two statues in black marble, one of which represents him under the protection of the god Amen-ra. The central saloon, through which we now pass, is chiefly occupied by monuments of the age of King Rameses II. Between the columns on the right is a colossal fist, in red granite, from one of the statues which stood before the great temple at Memphis, and close by are three colossal heads; one of these is a cast from a statue of Rameses, at Mitraheny; the next, a head and shoulders from the building called the Memnonium, at Thebes; and the other that of a queen. The principal objects in the southern gallery are the granite sarcophagus of Hapimen, a royal scribe; the elaborately-worked sarcophagus of the Queen of Amasis II., and another of King Nectanebo I., dating some three or four centuries before the Christian era; on the exterior are representations of the sun passing through the heavens in his boat, and on the interior various divinities; then there is a finely-sculptured group, in sandstone, of a male and female figure seated; and also a statue of King Menephtah II., on a throne, with a ram's head on his knees. One of the most interesting and valuable of the objects exhibited in this department is the famous Rosetta Stone. This stone, a black basalt, is inscribed in hieroglyphics, the ancient spoken language of Egypt, and in Greek, with the services of Ptolemy V. Tradition tells us that Professor Porson used to visit the Museum in order to read and decipher this stone, whence he got from the officials the name of "Judge Black-stone."

Several of the most important relics in the Egyptian Galleries were discovered by Belzoni, and came into the possession of the Museum through the bequest of a Mr. Salt, to whom Belzoni had engaged himself. Belzoni was a native of Padua, and came to England early in the present century. He was called "the strong man," a name which he no doubt merited, seeing that he stood nearly seven feet in height, and was well formed and stout in proportion. He exhibited his feats of strength in the minor theatres in the metropolis, and at Edinburgh. It was at Cairo that he became engaged to Mr. Salt, and from that time he was regularly employed in making discoveries, all of which are fully described in Belzoni's "Narrative of the Operations and Recent Discoveries within the Pyramids, Temples, Tombs, and Excavations in Egypt and Nubia ; and of a Journey to the Coast of the Red Sea, in search of the ancient Berenice, and another to the Oasis of Jupiter Ammon ;" this great work was published shortly after his return to England. In 1823, Belzoni, accompanied by his wife, again left England, on another journey of discovery into Africa ; but he died at Benin, on his way thither, from an attack of dysentery, in the same year.

The south end of the Egyptian Galleries opens into the Assyrian transept, which, together with a long and narrow gallery connected with it, running north and south, contain the collection of sculptures excavated, chiefly by Mr. Layard, in the years 1847-50, on the site, or in the vicinity, of ancient Nineveh. To these has been added a further collection, from the same region, excavated in 1853-55 by Mr. Hormuzd Rassam and Mr. W. K. Loftus, under the direction of Sir H. C. Rawlinson, who was at that time Her Majesty's Consul-General at Bagdad. Many of the objects here brought together are covered with pictorial representations of historical events, and inscribed with cuneiform characters. In 1873-4 valuable additions were made to this collection in the shape of a large number of burnt clay tablets, excavated at Kouyunjik, by Mr. George Smith. These tablets have been in part deciphered by Mr. Smith, who has found them to contain Chaldean legends of the creation, fall, deluge, building of the Tower of Babel, &c. The tablets were presented to the Museum by the proprietors of the *Daily Telegraph*, at whose expense Mr. Smith's labours in Assyria were conducted.

Mr. Layard's discoveries, as we learn from his "Nineveh and its Remains," were, for the most part, made in extensive mounds formed by the natural accumulation of the soil over the *débris* of ruined edifices, in the three following localities :— 1. Nimroud, believed to be the ancient Calah of Scripture, on the banks of the Tigris, about twenty miles below the modern Mosul. 2. Khorsabad, a site about ten miles to the north-east of Mosul, which was excavated for the French Government by M. Botta, and from which was procured the greater part of the valuable collection now in the Louvre, though a few specimens of sculpture have also been obtained for the British Museum. 3. Kouyunjik, still indicated by local tradition as the site of Nineveh, nearly opposite Mosul, on the Tigris.

There is monumental evidence that of the various buildings which Mr. Layard excavated, that of the palace of Nimroud was older by several centuries than the edifices of Khorsabad and Kouyunjik. To this palace, the son of a founder added a second ; subsequent additions are recorded in the inscriptions, and the place at last attained the dimensions ascribed to it by Jonah. "If (says Mr. Layard) we take the four great mounds of Nimroud, Kouyunjik, Khorsabad, and Karamles, as the angle of a square, it will be found that its four sides corresponded pretty accurately with the 480 stadia, or sixty miles of the geographer, which makes the three days' journey of the prophet." Within this space there are many mounds, ruins of edifices, vestiges of streets and gardens ; and the face of the country is strewed with fragments of pottery and bricks. As to the number of inhabitants, mentioned in the book of Jonah (chap. iv. 11) to be above 120,000, a number which seems apparently incommensurate with a city of such vast dimensions, Mr. Layard remarks that cities in the East are not like those in Europe ; for such places as London or Paris would not contain above a third of the number of their inhabitants. The women have separate apartments from the men ; there is a separate house for each family ; and gardens and arable land are inclosed by the city walls. Hence it is mentioned in the book of Jonah that there was "much cattle" within the walls of the city, and, of course, there was pasture for them. The existing ruins, Mr. Layard tells us, " show that Nineveh acquired its greatest extent in the time of the kings of the second dynasty, that is, of the kings mentioned in Scripture ; it was then that Jonah visited it, and that reports of its magnificence were carried to the west, and gave rise to the traditions from which the Greek authors mainly derived the information which has been handed down to us."

The monuments obtained by Mr. Layard from Kouyunjik are stated to date from the supposed era of the destruction of Nineveh, and were procured from the remains of a very extensive Assyrian edifice, which appears, from the inscriptions remaining on many of its sculptures, to have been the palace of Sennacherib, who is presumed to have commenced his reign about B.C. 700. For the most part, these remains consist of large slabs of alabaster or limestone, covered with carved figures and inscriptions, which occupied the place of panels in the walls of the palace. One group of slabs, six in number, formed originally part of a series illustrating the architectural works of King Sennacherib, including, probably, the construction of the very edifice from which the slabs were obtained. On two of them is seen the conveyance of a colossal human-headed bull, lying sideways on a sledge, which is propelled, over wooden rollers, partly by ropes in front, partly by a lever behind. On one side is a lofty mound, which labourers are erecting with stones or earth, and which is, perhaps, designed for the platform of the future palace. The workmen are guarded by soldiers, and superintended by Sennacherib himself, in a chariot drawn by two men. A similar mound is represented on the next slab, with an adjoining stone-quarry or clay-pit, where the materials of construction are prepared; whilst on the succeeding one is a portion of a group moving some weighty object. On the next slab is another colossal bull, represented as before; and on the last is depicted the monarch, in his chariot, directing some operation sculptured on a lost portion of the series. The background of the slabs exhibits men carrying axes, saws, ropes, and other implements; and along the top are representations of the natural scenery of the country, water filled with fish, anglers floating on inflated skins, boats, banks lined with trees, and a jungle of reeds, in which are deer, and a wild sow with her young.

By a doorway on the west side of the Nimroud Central Saloon, we pass into the Hellenic Room. Among the marbles here exhibited, the first in importance is a collection discovered by Professor Cockerell, in 1812, among the ruins of the Temple of Apollo, near the ancient Phigalia, in Arcadia. This edifice was erected by Iktinos, the architect of the Parthenon, at Athens, in commemoration of the delivery of the Phigalians from the plague, B.C. 430. The chief part of these treasures consists of twenty-three sculptured slabs, originally belonging to a frieze in the interior of the *cella* of the temple. Eleven of them represent in high relief the contest between the Centaurs and Greeks, and the remaining twelve the invasion of Greece by the Amazons.

The Elgin Room, which is next entered, forms the western side of the Museum. Here are arranged the noble sculptures from the Parthenon, a portion of the frieze of the Temple of the Wingless Victory, at Athens, some architectural remains from the Erectheum, together with a number of fragments and casts, all from Athens. The sculptures from the Parthenon, and nearly all the marbles in this room, were obtained by the Earl of Elgin, when Ambassador at Constantinople, in the years 1801–3, by virtue of a firman from the Sublime Porte. We have already spoken of the purchase of the Elgin collection by the Government in a previous chapter.

A doorway at the southern end of the Elgin Room leads into the Mausoleum Room, where are arranged the fragments of the Mausoleum at Halicarnassus, erected by Artemisia, about B.C. 352, over the remains of her husband, Mausolus, Prince of Caria, and discovered by Mr. Newton, in 1857. The structure, we are told, when perfect, "consisted of a lofty basement, on which stood an oblong Ionic edifice, surrounded by columns, and surmounted by a pyramid, on the summit of which was a chariot group in white marble. The edifice which supported the pyramid was encircled by a frieze richly sculptured in high relief, and representing the battle of Greeks and Amazons. The material of the sculptures was Parian marble, and the whole structure was richly ornamented with colour. The tomb of Mausolus was of the class called by the Greeks *heröon*, and so greatly excelled all other sepulchral monuments in size, beauty of design, and richness of decoration, that it was reckoned one of the Seven Wonders of the ancient world, and the name Mausoleum came to be applied to all similar monuments."

Passing through the Greek ante-room, we enter the Lycian Gallery. The antiquities exhibited in this room comprise architectural and sculptural remains obtained from ancient cities in Lycia, one of the south-western provinces of Asia Minor. They were removed from that country in two expeditions, undertaken by Her Majesty's Government in the years 1842–6, under the direction of Sir C. Fellows, by whom the greater part of the marbles in this room were discovered. The building, of which the sculptures and various architectural members here brought together formed a part, has, by some, been considered a trophy in memory of the conquest of Lycia by the Persians, under Harpagos, B.C. 545.

In 1874, an addition was made to the collection in this gallery, in the shape of fragments of columns, bases and capitals, &c., from the Temple of Diana at Ephesus, which had been discovered by Mr. Wood, in explorations made during the two or three previous years. Among the fragments sent hither by Mr. Wood were "the lower drum of a column, nearly entire, with figures sculptured on it in relief, and large fragments of two or more drums, similarly sculptured; also the base of a pilaster, sculptured in relief, on the same scale as the drums." These sculptured drums, it is considered, "are evidently portions of the thirty-six columns of the temple, which Pliny describes as *cælatæ*, or 'sculptured in relief.'" The architectural marbles present many interesting features; some of the smaller fragments, for instance, "retain traces of red colour; while the calcined surface of other marbles, and their charcoal smears, tell the sad story of some ancient conflagration, in which, probably, perished the beautiful timber roof and the staircase, cunningly wrought in vine-wood."

A staircase in the south-west corner of the building leads into the Græco-Roman basement room, to which the basement of the Lycian Room is annexed. In this room are shown figures and reliefs of the Græco-Roman period, miscellaneous objects in marble and other material, and the collection of tessellated pavements and mosaics, which has been formed chiefly from the discoveries at Carthage and Halicarnassus in 1856–8.

The next three rooms, extending along the southern front of the building, are known as the Græco-Roman Rooms, and are appropriated to statues, busts, and bas-reliefs, of quite a mixed class, and mostly of a classic character. Here we find several statues and busts of gods and goddesses, such as Hercules, Venus, Bacchus, Pan, and the like; but we can here notice only a few of them. In an alcove in the centre room is the Towneley Venus, found at Ostia, in 1776; and in the alcove on the opposite side is the celebrated Discobolus, or Quoit-thrower, presumed to be a copy of the famous bronze statue made by the sculptor Myron. In the western room is the beautiful female bust commonly called "Clytie." The bust is represented as emerging from the petals of a flower, and it was esteemed by Mr. Towneley as the gem of his collection. It was bought at Naples, from the Lorrenzano Palace, in 1772. The following curious anecdote connected with this piece of sculpture we quote from Charles Knight's "London:"— "During the Gordon riots, Mr. Towneley, as a Catholic, was marked out by the mob, who intended to attack the house in Park Street, where all his darling

treasures were collected. He secured his cabinet of gems, and casting a long and lingering look behind at his marbles, was about to leave them to their fate, when, moved by some irrepressible impulse of affection, he took the bust in question into his arms and hurried off with it to his carriage. Fortunately the attack did not take place, and his 'wife,' as he called the lady represented, returned to her companions."

Passing on through the Roman Gallery, the last of the series of rooms devoted to the department of sculptured antiquities, we arrive once more in the entrance-hall, and so end our perambulation of this great national storehouse. There is, however, one more object which we should mention, and that is the skeleton of, we believe, the largest whale ever captured. This monster of the deep, measuring some hundred feet in length, was for many years an attraction at country fairs throughout the kingdom, a large number of caravans being used for its conveyance and exhibition; and it has at last found a resting-place in the basement of the Museum, under the Grenville Library, where it can be seen on application to the attendants.

It will be evident that the expenses of such an establishment as the British Museum must be very considerable, and that many persons must be occupied in fulfilling the duties attached to it. We have already spoken of the principal librarian as being head and chief, under the trustees, of the whole working body of the establishment. Besides this officer, there are upwards of one hundred persons engaged in the various departments, either as "keepers," or "senior assistants," or "junior assistants;" and in addition, there is a little army of assistants dispersed through the libraries and saloons, perhaps upwards of another hundred strong. Then there are a few "fumatori," or cast-makers, and a regular corps of index-makers and bookbinders, constantly employed, as well as a goodly number of household servants. It may, perhaps, be almost needless to remark here that every precaution is taken to ensure the safety of the collection. Like the Bank of England, this building has a detachment of the Guards nightly sent to keep watch and ward against intruders from without; whilst the destruction of the edifice by fire is a thing well nigh impossible, seeing that no light is allowed to be carried about whatever, either by night or by day, and that, through the same fear of fire, all night studies are forbidden.

We conclude this subject with a few general remarks. If we compare it with similar institutions abroad, such as the Bibliothèque Nationale and the Louvre, at Paris, the Royal Libraries of Munich and Berlin, and the Vatican Library at Rome, we may safely claim for our national Museum a very high place. Viewed with reference to its collection of books, both as to quality and in quantity, it stands among the first in the world, combining as it does some 1,500,000 volumes, including nearly all the rarest specimens. Its manuscripts, also, are certainly first-rate in number, being fully equal to those of the Bibliothèque Nationale, though, per-

Towneley, the Payne-Knight, the Crackerode, and the Castellani cabinets, all of which are now incorporated together, and arranged in a mythological series. As a whole the collection ranks with that of Berlin, and though inferior to that of St. Petersburg, especially in respect of gold ornaments, it can hardly acknowledge any other rivals. Then, as to antiquities of a miscellaneous character, thanks, mainly, to Belzoni, who commenced the Egyptian

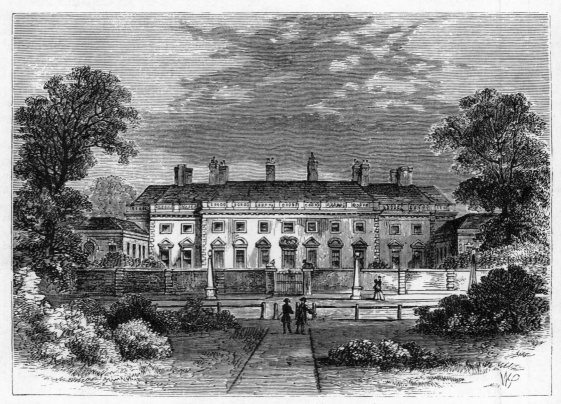

BEDFORD HOUSE, IN 1772 (*See page* 536.)

haps, in intrinsic value, they fall short of the treasures of the Vatican. Our statues from the antique, Greek and Roman, are the finest in the world, and our vases and bronzes are very good, though in modern statuary, just as in pictures, we do not pretend to make a show. Passing on to the other part of our art treasures, a very high rank may be claimed for our prints from the works of the ancient masters, though in topography, both English and foreign, the collection is poor, and our stores of portraits can be hardly said to be more than mediocre. Our coins are acknowledged to be very fine indeed; in Roman gold coins the Museum is superior even to the Bibliothèque Nationale, though inferior to it in Greek coins, and also in medallions. Our collection of gems comprises the Blacas, the

collection, we stand at the head of all; Lord Elgin robbed the Parthenon at Athens to enrich our stores of Greek statuary, as already mentioned; thanks to Mr. Layard, we are extremely rich, far richer than our rivals, in respect of treasures dug up in Assyria and at Nineveh; Sir Charles Fellows has given us a very beautiful collection of Carian and Lycian specimens; Mr. C. T. Newton has brought hither nearly all that was grand from Halicarnassus, including a large part of its celebrated Mausoleum; and more recently, as we have shown, Mr. Wood has contributed some most interesting relics from ancient Ephesus. The Crace Collection of prints of London topography, upon which we have drawn largely in this work, was added in 1881.

BLOOMSBURY SQUARE. (*See page* 536.)

CHAPTER XLI.

BLOOMSBURY SQUARE AND ITS NEIGHBOURHOOD.

——" Around what public works I see !
Lo ! stately streets. Lo ! squares that court the breeze."—*Thomson.*

Southampton (afterwards Bedford) House—The Patriot Lord Russell and his Noble-hearted Wife—An Historic Romance—Lucy, Countess of Bedford—An Episode in the Life of Anne, Wife of the Fifth Earl of Bedford—John; Fourth Duke of Bedford—Invitations to "take Tea and Walk in the Fields"—A Curious Advertisement—Richard Baxter, the Nonconformist Divine—An Anecdote about Dr. Radcliffe—Fashionable Residents—Poor Sir Richard Steele—Pope's Allusion to Bloomsbury Square—Sir Hans Sloane and his "Curiosities"—The Gordon Riots—Attack on Lord Mansfield's House—Charles Knight's Residence in this Square—Isaac D'Israeli, the Author of "Curiosities of Literature"—His Son, Benjamin Disraeli, born here—Edmund Lodge, the Eminent Biographer—Pharmaceutical Society of Great Britain—The Royal Literary Fund—The Famous Mississippi Schemer, Law—The Statue of Charles James Fox—Bloomsbury Market—Southampton Street and Row—National Benevolent Institution—Bloomsbury Place—Thomas Cadell, the Publisher—The Corporation of the Sons of the Clergy—Hart Street—St. George's Church—Archdeacon Nares—The Society of Biblical Archæology.

BLOOMSBURY SQUARE owes its origin to Thomas Wriothesley, Earl of Southampton, the son of Shakespeare's patron and friend, and also the father of Lady Rachel Russell, wife of Lord William Russell, whose tragic death we have recorded as the disgrace of Lincoln's Inn Fields.

Under date of February 9, 1665, Evelyn has the following note in his Diary, touching the building of this square :—" Dined at my Lord Treasurer's, the Earle of Southampton, in Blomesbury, where he was building a noble square or piazza, a little towne ; his owne house stands too low, some noble roomes, a pretty cedar chappell, a naked garden to the north, but good aire." It was at first called Southampton Square; and Macaulay places it among the head-quarters of the fashion of the metropolis, in the reign of Charles II. " Foreign princes," he tells us, on the authority of the " Travels of the Grand Duke of Cosmo," " were taken to see the square as one of the wonders of England, whilst Soho Square, just built, was a subject of pride, with which the present generation will hardly sympathise."

Southampton House (afterwards called Bedford House), the residence of the above-mentioned earl, stood on the northern side of the square, and a portion of the ground which it occupied is now covered by some of the outbuildings on the east side of the British Museum. The mansion was not only the scene of the childhood and early life, but also, during many of the years of her widowhood, the home of that illustrious and noble woman, Lady Rachel Russell, many of whose " Letters " are dated from within its walls.

Northouck, the topographer, writing of Bloomsbury Square, in 1772, after the house had changed its name, observes :—" The north side is entirely taken up with Bedford House, which is elegant, though low, having but one storey. It was the work of Inigo Jones. Beside the body of the house are two wings, and on each side the proper offices. The square forms a magnificent area

before it, and the grand street in front throws the prospect of it open to Holborn. Behind, it has the advantage of most agreeable gardens, commanding a full view of the rising hills of Hampstead and Highgate ; so that it is hardly possible to conceive a finer situation than that of Bedford House."

One of the wings of the house, we are told, formed a magnificent gallery, in which were copies, by Sir James Thornhill, of the cartoons of Raphael, as large as the originals ; indeed, the mansion was very rich, for that date, in works of art, both sculptures and paintings. When the house was pulled down, about 1802, its contents were sold, and Sir James Thornhill's cartoons were disposed of for a little under £500 ! They would fetch a much higher price in the present day, when high art is better appreciated.

The Wriothesleys, Earls of Southampton, were heads of a family who long enjoyed considerable influence in State affairs, and held many important public offices. As far back as the reign of Edward IV. we find John Wriothsley (as the name was then spelt) occupying the post of " Faucon Herald," and as having letters patent for the office of Garter King-at-Arms in the first year of Richard III. His two sons likewise held offices in the College of Arms, and his grandson, Thomas Wriothesley, who was esteemed "a man of learning, and a good lawyer," was elevated to the peerage as Baron Wriothesley, in 1544, and soon afterwards, on the death of the great Lord Audley, constituted Lord Chancellor of England. Three years later his lordship was advanced to the Earldom of Southampton. His son Henry, second earl, was a friend of Thomas, Duke of Norfolk, and involved himself in trouble by promoting the contemplated marriage of that nobleman with Mary, Queen of Scots, " to whom and her religion (says Dugdale) he stood not a little affected." His successor, Henry, third earl, is not only known to history as the friend of Shakespeare in his early days, when he needed friends, but also as the companion in arms of the Earl of Essex, and a participator in the treason by which that unfortunate nobleman forfeited his life in the reign of Elizabeth. Lord Southampton was also tried, condemned, and attainted ; but his life was spared. Upon the accession of James I. he was released from prison, restored in blood by Act of Parliament, and created by a new patent, in the year 1603, Earl of Southampton, " with the same rights, precedency, and privileges, that he had formerly enjoyed." His son, Thomas, who succeeded as fourth earl, was a staunch supporter of Charles I., and was the Lord Treasurer mentioned by Evelyn in his note quoted above. His lordship died at Southampton House, "near Holburne, in the suburbs of London," in May, 1667, when his honours became extinct. The mansion remained in the possession of his daughter, Lady Rachel Russell, through whose marriage it passed into the possession of the Duke of Bedford, and afterwards, as we have said, came to be called Bedford House.

Lady William Russell, as every reader of English history knows, was a woman distinguished for her ardent and tender affection, " pious, reflecting, firm, and courageous; alike exemplary in prosperity and adversity, when observed by multitudes, or hidden in retirement." Her firm and noble conduct in attending her husband's trial, for the purpose of taking notes and giving him assistance, have been themes of the highest interest and admiration alike to the historian and the artist. The bitterness of their parting is described in the most pathetic language, and a lasting grief is shown in her subsequent correspondence. Lord William Russell, as we have stated in the previous volume,* was executed in Lincoln's Inn Fields, and his widow lived here in retirement till her death, in the reign of George I., at the age of eighty-six.

Lord Russell's father was the first Duke of Bedford. His Grace came of a good old Dorsetshire family, one member of whom is said to have gained a favourable introduction to Court through one of those unexpected incidents which may be attributed solely to good fortune. Sir Bernard Burke, in his " Peerage," relates how that towards the end of the reign of Henry VII., " the Archduke Philip of Austria, only son of the Emperor Maximilian I., and husband of Joanna, daughter of Ferdinand and Isabella, King and Queen of Castile and Aragon, having encountered a violent hurricane in his passage from Flanders to Spain, was driven into Weymouth, where he landed, and was hospitably received by Sir Thomas Trenchard, knight, a gentle-

man of rank in the neighbourhood. Sir Thomas immediately apprised the Court of the circumstance, and in the interim, while waiting for instructions what course to adopt, invited his first cousin, Mr. John Russell, then recently returned from his travels, to wait upon the Prince. The Prince, fascinated by Mr. Russell's companionable qualities, desired that he should accompany him to Windsor, whither the King had invited him on a visit. On the journey the Archduke became still more pleased with his attendant's 'learned discourse and generous deportment,' and recommended him strongly to the King. Mr. Russell was, in consequence, taken immediately into royal favour, and appointed one of the Gentlemen of the Privy Chamber. Becoming subsequently a favourite of Henry VIII., and a companion of that monarch in his French wars, Mr. Russell was appointed to several high and confidential offices." He was finally elevated to the peerage in 1538-9, as Baron Russell of Cheneys, Buckinghamshire; and on the dissolution of the monasteries, in the following year, he obtained a grant of the site of the abbey of Tavistock, and of extensive possessions belonging to it. After the accession of Edward VI., Lord Russell had a grant of the monastery of Woburn, in Bedfordshire, and was created Earl of Bedford. Francis, the second earl, was a person of great eminence during the reign of Elizabeth, and three of his sons likewise greatly distinguished themselves ; he was succeeded in the earldom by his grandson Edward, son of Francis, Lord Russell.

Lucy, Countess of Bedford, to whom Ben Jonson addresses several of his best epigrams, sister and co-heir of the second Lord Warrington, and wife of Edward, the third earl, was distinguished alike by the variety of her attainments, and her liberal patronage of men of genius. Amongst those upon whom this lady specially bestowed her munificence were Ben Jonson, Drayton, Daniel, and Donne ; and they have all paid poetical homage to her merits and her bounty. " Sir Thomas Roe," says Granger, "has addressed a letter to her as one skilled in medals; and she is celebrated by Sir William Temple for projecting the most perfect figure of a garden that he ever saw." She died in 1627. Ben Jonson thus addresses her :—

" Lucy, you brightness of our sphere, who are
  Life of the Muse's day, their morning star !
  If works, not th' authors, their own grace should look,
  Whose poems would not wish to be your book?"

William, the fifth earl, to whom we now pass, was, in 1694, created Marquis of Tavistock and Duke of Bedford. He married Anne, daughter and sole heiress of Robert Carr, Earl of Somerset.

* See Vol. III., p. 45.

by his too celebrated Countess, Frances Howard, the divorced wife of Essex. " Francis, Earl of Bedford," the father of this nobleman, says Pennant, " was so adverse to the alliance, that he gave his son leave to choose a wife out of any other family but that. Opposition usually stimulates desire; the young couple's affections were only increased. At length the King interposed, and sending the Duke of Lennox to urge the Earl to consent, the match was brought about. Somerset, now reduced to poverty, acted a generous part, selling his house at Chiswick, plate, jewels, and furniture, to raise for his daughter a fortune of £12,000, which the Earl of Bedford demanded, saying, that since her affections were settled, he chose rather to undo himself than make her unhappy." It is said that the lady was ignorant of her mother's dishonour, till informed of it by a pamphlet, which she accidentally found; and it is added, that she was so struck with this detection of her parent's guilt, that she fell down in a fit, and was found senseless with the book open before her. The duke had by this admirable woman seven sons and three daughters, and the eldest surviving son was the celebrated patriot, Lord William Russell, of whom we have already spoken.

John, the fourth Duke of Bedford, to whom we now pass on, was for some time Lord Lieutenant of Ireland, and subsequently our ambassador to the Court of France, in which character he signed, at Fontainebleau, the preliminaries of peace with France and Spain. His Grace is mentioned by Lady Hervey, in her " Letters," as a " rich great person." He nevertheless had the misfortune of being very unpopular in his day, but he hardly deserved all the invectives with which Junius has " damned him to everlasting fame." In 1748 he gave at Bedford House a masqued ball, said to have been one of the most magnificent that ever had been given; the King, the Duke of Cumberland, and many of the nobility, being present in masquerade.

About this time, it is said that the Duchess of Bedford sent out cards to her guests, inviting them to " take tea and walk in the fields;" and sarcastic persons remarked, that it was expected that syllabubs would soon be milked in Berkeley Square, around the statue of his Majesty. In the same style, we are told that Lady Clermont was not more remarkable for her conversational parties than for her *al fresco* gatherings. In May, 1773, when living in St. James's Place, she issued invitations to 300 dear friends " to take tea and walk in the Park."

Having said thus much concerning Bedford House, and the families of its successive owners,

we now proceed to speak of the other parts of Bloomsbury Square. In 1642, we read, among the forts ordered by the Parliament to be raised around London, of " two batteries and a breastwork at Southampton (afterwards Bedford) House," probably in the present square.

Mr. Peter Cunningham, in his " Handbook of London," quotes one of the advertisements from the *London Gazette*, No. 946, which we take the liberty of copying here :—" Lost, from my Lady Baltinglasses (*sic*) house, in the great square of Bloomsbury, the first of this instant December (1674), a great old Indian spaniel or mongrel, as big as a mastiff; he hath curled and black hair all over, except in his fore-feet, which are a little white; he hath also cropt ears, and is bowed and limps a little in one of his fore-feet. If any can bring news thereof, they shall have twenty shillings for their pains."

In this square lived Richard Baxter, the Non-conformist divine, at the time of his persecution by Judge Jefferies; and here his wife died in 1681.

Dr. Mead, in " Richardsoniana," tells an amusing story about Dr. Radcliffe, the celebrated physician, whom we have already had occasion to mention, and who was living in this square when he gave £520 to the poor non-juring clergy. " Dr. Radcliffe," he says, " could never be brought to pay bills without much following and importunity; nor then if there appeared any chance of wearying them out. A paviour, after long and fruitless attempts, caught him just getting out of his chariot at his own door in Bloomsbury Square, and set upon him. ' Why, you rascal !' said the Doctor, ' do you pretend to be paid for such a piece of work ? Why, you have spoiled my pavement, and then covered it over with earth, to hide your bad work !' ' Doctor !' said the paviour, ' mine is not the only bad work the earth hides.' ' You dog, you !' said the Doctor, ' are you a wit ? You must be poor; come in '—and paid him."

Our readers will have already gathered from Macaulay's remark quoted above, that in Queen Anne's reign this neighbourhood could dispute for the palm of fashion with Lincoln's Inn Fields and Soho Square, and not without good reason; for at this time not only did the Russells live in Bloomsbury Square, but also Lord Paget, Lord Carleton, and the Earl of Northampton. Lord Mansfield's house was at the north-east corner. Lord Ellenborough, when Chief Justice, lived at the corner house of Bloomsbury Square and Orange Street, before he removed to St. James's Square; and Lord Chief Justice Trevor occupied a house on the west side of the square.

At his house here, in 1713, died Philip, second Earl of Chesterfield, the same who figures as a member of the Court of Charles II. and James II., in the "Memoirs" of Count Grammont. In June of the above year, too, Sir Richard Steele was living in this square, as shown by the date of a letter, re-published in *fac-simile* in Smith's "Historical and Literary Curiosities." Having already burdened himself—as we have said—with a small house near Jermyn Street, for which he was unable to pay,* Sir Richard, in 1712, could not content himself without taking a much larger, finer, and grander house in Bloomsbury Square ; and here again he got into still greater difficulties than before. It is recorded that, on giving a grand entertainment in his new mansion, he engaged half-a-dozen queer-looking individuals to wait at table on his noble and distinguished guests, to whom he coolly con-fessed that "his lacqueys were bailiffs in disguise to a man." "I fared like a distressed prince," writes the kindly prodigal, in the *Tatler*, generously complimenting Addison for his assistance — " I fared like a distressed prince who calls in to his aid a powerful neighbour. I was undone by my auxiliary ; when I had once called him in, I could not submit without dependence on him." " Poor needy Prince," writes Thackeray, tenderly ; "think of him with pity in his palace, with his allies from Chancery Lane thus ominously guarding him !" The same incident is said to have occurred a century later to another man of letters, Richard Brinsley Sheridan.†

Pope, who was at this period at the height of his fame, thus alludes to this once fashionable quarter of the town :—

"In Palace-yard, at nine, you'll find me there ;
At ten, for certain, sir, in Bloomsbury-square."

Here, in the early part of the last century, lived Dr. Akenside and Sir Hans Sloane, already mentioned as the founder of the British Museum. The house of the latter was on the south side of the square, and here Dr. Franklin came to see Sloane's "curiosities," " for which," says Franklin, " he paid me handsomely."

In the Gordon Riots of June, 1780, the neigh-bourhood of Bloomsbury gained a sad notoriety as one of the chief points of attack by the infuriated mob, which, in its zeal for the Protestant faith, very nearly laid London in ruins, being guilty, as Sir N. W. Wraxall remarks, of grosser and more senseless outrages than even the fiends of Paris in the first great Revolution. In the following account he writes with all the vividness of an eye-witness

of these fearful scenes :—" I was personally pre-sent at many of the most tremendous effects of the popular fury on the memorable 7th of June, the night on which it attained its highest point. About nine o'clock on that evening, accompanied by three other gentlemen, who, as well as myself, were alarmed at the accounts brought in every moment of the outrages committed, and of the still greater acts of violence meditated, as soon as darkness should favour and facilitate their further progress, we set out from Portland Place, in order to view the scene. Having got into a hackney-coach, we drove to Bloomsbury Square, attracted to that spot by a rumour, generally spread, that Lord Mansfield's residence, situate at the north-east, was either already burnt, or destined for destruction. Hart Street and Great Russell Street presented each to the view, as we passed, large fires composed of furniture taken from the houses of magistrates, or other obnoxious individuals. Quitting the coach, we crossed the square, and had scarcely got under the wall of Bedford House, when we heard the door of Lord Mansfield's house burst open with violence. In a few minutes, all the contents of the apartments being precipitated from the windows, were piled up and wrapt in flames. A file of foot-soldiers arriving, drew up near the blazing pile, but without either attempting to quench the fire or to impede the mob, who were, indeed, far too numerous to admit of their being dispersed, or even intimidated, by a small detach-ment of infantry. The populace remained masters, while we, after surveying the spectacle for a short time, moved on into Holborn, where Mr. Lang-dale's dwelling-house and warehouses afforded a more appalling picture of devastation. They were altogether enveloped in smoke and flame. In front had assembled an immense multitude of both sexes, many of whom were females, and not a few held infants in their arms. All appeared to be, like ourselves, attracted as spectators solely by curiosity, without taking any part in the acts of violence. The kennel of the street ran down with spirituous liquors, and numbers of the populace were already intoxicated with this beverage. So little disposi-tion, however, did they manifest to riot or pillage, that it would have been difficult to conceive who were the authors and perpetrators of such enor-mous mischief, if we had not distinctly seen, at the windows of the house, men who, while the floors and rooms were on fire, calmly tore down the furni-ture and threw it into the street, or tossed it into the flames. They experienced no kind of opposi-tion during a considerable time that we remained at this place ; but a party of the Horse Guards arriving, the terrified crowd instantly began to disperse, and we, anxious to gratify our curiosity, continued our progress on foot, along Holborn, towards Fleet Market."

Lord and Lady Mansfield, we are told, narrowly escaped falling into the hands of the lawless and infuriated mob, and only just succeeded in beating

nevertheless, the author of "Biographiana" states, without reserve or qualification, that "in these disgraceful riots the property and buildings of the metropolis were preserved by the spirited behaviour of the Sovereign." Yet it is difficult to see that the King had any claim to spirited conduct except negatively; at all events, Dr. Johnson wrote at the

ISAAC D'ISRAELI. (*See page* 542.)

a retreat by a back door. His lordship's valuable library was destroyed; indeed, "even the civilisation of the eighteenth century," writes Mr. D'Israeli, in his "Curiosities of Literature," "could not preserve from the savage and destructive fury of a disorderly mob, in the most polished city of Europe, the valuable papers of the Earl of Mansfield, which were madly consigned to the flames."

Whilst all these riots were proceeding, we are told, George III. was at the Queen's Palace;

time to Mrs. Thrale thus:—"The King said in Council that the magistrates had not done their duty, but that he would do his own; and a proclamation was accordingly published, directing us to keep our servants within doors, as the peace was now to be preserved by force. The soldiers were sent out to different parts, and the town is now quiet." Readers of "Barnaby Rudge" will not have forgotten Charles Dickens' description of the Gordon Riots.

Lord Mansfield was one of Pope's executors, and Lady Lepel Hervey in her "Letters" makes allusions to his " *artful* eloquence "—meaning, elaborate and artificial; for we may be sure that he did not forget the words of Pope to himself—

" Plain truth, dear Murray, needs no flowers of speech."

age than could have been expected, and died in the zenith of his fame; and his memory has been embalmed by the testimonies of some of the wisest and best of his contemporaries. Pope had celebrated him in a well-known distich, and other poets, *haud passibus æquis*, had followed in the

ST. GEORGE'S CHURCH, BLOOMSBURY.   (*See page* 544.)

" His lordship's night of life," writes Cradock, "was disturbed by many difficulties; yet he had undoubtedly many blessings to counterbalance them. Though his house was burnt down in Bloomsbury Square, he still possessed an elegant seat and extensive domain in the neighbourhood of London; and his nephew and heir, Lord Stormont, was appointed as the representative of Majesty at the Court of France. He lived to much greater

train. Lord Chesterfield in glowing terms had freely spoken of the rising talents both of Mr. Pitt and Mr. Murray, in a letter to his son : 'No man,' says he, 'can make a figure in this country but by Parliament. Your fate depends on your success as a speaker, and, take my word for it, that success turns much more upon manner than matter. Mr. Pitt, and Mr. Murray, the Solicitor General, are, beyond compare, the best speakers.'"

190

It has been thought strange that Lord Mansfield's will should be written only by himself on half a sheet of paper, and that the contents there enumerated, in neglect of all the forms of legal practice, should have proved valid for the disposal of half a million of property.

Of other residents of Bloomsbury Square in more recent times, may be mentioned Charles Knight, who, in 1826, lived at No. 29, when helping to lay the foundation of the Society for the Diffusion of Useful Knowledge ; and Isaac D'Israeli, the author of the " Curiosities of Literature," who a little earlier occupied the house No. 6, which, strange to say, appears to have since reverted to Jewish associations, as its late occupant was a Mr. Tabernacle. D'Israeli lived here for many years before he settled down as a country gentleman in Buckinghamshire ; and here his gifted son spent much of his childhood. "In London," says that son, " my father's only amusement was to ramble about among the bookseller's shops ; and if he ever went into a club, it was only to go into the library." With regard to the younger D'Israeli—the future Premier of England—it may be stated that as a child he used to toddle and run about the enclosure of the square with his nursemaid ; and at a fit age was sent to a small school, first at Islington, and afterwards at Walthamstow, at a seminary kept by a clergyman of Unitarian opinions, where he used to keep his schoolfellows awake at night by telling them ghost-stories. In the register of the Portuguese Synagogue for 1805, the name of Benjamin D'Israeli occurs in the January of that year, as having been initiated into the Jewish Church when only eight days old. When about fourteen years of age he exchanged Judaism for Christianity, being baptised at the Church of St. Andrew's, Holborn. He next spent a year or two as a clerk in a solicitor's office in the City, in the neighbourhood of Old Jewry and the present Moorgate Street ; and then, before he was twenty-one, had astonished the world by editing a journal of Radical sentiments, and publishing the novel of " Vivian Grey." Mr. Disraeli, in the course of one of his speeches at Taunton, made an uncomplimentary reference to Daniel O'Connell, then in the zenith of his fame. The agitator, a few days after, returned his invective with interest, and declared, alluding to Disraeli's Hebrew origin, that " he made no doubt that, if his genealogy could be traced, he would be found to be the true heir-at-law of the impenitent thief on the cross." The reply to this outrage was a challenge, not to the speaker, who was known uniformly to decline duelling, but to his son. No duel, however, took

place ; but the correspondence was published in the newspapers. A published letter, written to O'Connell by Disraeli, concluded with the magniloquent boast, " We shall meet at Philippi." This prophecy was fulfilled, in 1837, by the return of Disraeli for Maidstone. Of his subsequent Parliamentary career we have already spoken.*

At his house in this square, in January, 1839, died, at an advanced age, Edmund Lodge, Clarenceux King of Arms, the author of the " Peerage" which bears his name. This eminent biographer became a cornet in the King's Own regiment of Dragoons, in 1772 ; but having a pure taste for antiquities and literature, he left the army, and obtained the situation of Blue Mantle Pursuivant-at-Arms. He was subsequently promoted to the offices of Lancaster Herald, Norroy, and Clarenceux, and was created a Knight of the Hanoverian Guelphic Order. Among his other literary productions may be mentioned, "Illustrations of British History ; " " The Life of Sir Julius Cæsar ; " " Memoirs of Illustrious Personages of Great Britain ; " and many other works of the greatest merit, learning, and research.

The house at the north-west corner of the square forms the head-quarters of the Pharmaceutical Society of Great Britain, which was instituted " for the purposes of uniting the chemists and druggists into one ostensible, recognised, and independent body for protecting their general interests, and for the advancement of pharmacy, by furnishing such a uniform system of education as shall secure to the profession and to the public the safest and most efficient administration of medicine." A royal charter of incorporation was granted in 1843, in which, in addition to the above, the objects of the society were declared to include the providing a fund for the relief of distressed members and associates, and of their widows and orphans. The society has an excellent library and museum, and a laboratory. The museum claims to be very extensive, comprising rare specimens of the animal, vegetable, and mineral kingdoms, and substances and products used in medicine and pharmacy. It contains also groups and series of authenticated specimens, valuable for identifying, comparing, and tracing the origin and natural history of products. The museum includes the valuable collections of Cinchona barks made by eminent foreign naturalists, and formerly belonging to the late Dr. Jonathan Pereira.

In the above house, down to about 1862, was for many years carried on the work of the Royal

* See Vol. III., p. 533.

Literary Fund. The object of this society, which is now located at No. 7, Adelphi Terrace, is to administer assistance to authors of genius and learning, who may be reduced to distress by unavoidable calamities, or deprived by enfeebled faculties or declining life of the power of literary exertion. This assistance is extended at the death of an author to his widow and children. In the application of this liberality the utmost caution is used, both as to the reality of the distress and the merits of the individual. No writer can come within the views of the society who has not published a work of intelligence and public value, or been an important contributor to periodical literature; and every author, without exception, is excluded whose writings are offensive to morals or religion, and whose personal character is not proved by satisfactory testimony to be beyond suspicion. The business of the society is transacted by a committee; the most anxious consideration is given to the feelings of individuals; all names, and all circumstances which might lead to names, are carefully suppressed, and every precaution taken to avoid distressing publicity. The bounty of this institution is bestowed without regard to national or political distinctions. Here the Council of the Fund showed a small collection of curiosities and treasures, among which were the two daggers employed by Colonel Blood and his accomplice Parrot in their attempts to seize upon the crown and the other regalia in the Tower, in the reign of Charles II.

This square has not been known merely by the names of Southampton and Bloomsbury, but its different sides have been separately named: for instance, at one time the east side was called Seymour Row; the west was known as Allington, or Arlington, Row; and the south side was called Vernon Street. The latter name is still retained in Vernon Place, at the south-east corner of the square. On account of its remoteness from houses, the site now covered by this square, like the fields at the back of old Montagu House, was in former times—particularly in the reign of William III.—often chosen by the "gallants" and "bloods" of the period as a place for the settlement of "affairs of honour" with pistols and swords. Here the financial adventurer named Law, subsequently so famous as the Mississippi schemer, having picked up a quarrel with his antagonist, killed the "magnificent and mysterious Beau Wilson" in a duel.

The centre of the square is laid out in grass plats, planted with plane-trees and shrubs. On the north side of the enclosure, facing Bedford Place, is a fine bronze statue of Charles James Fox, by Sir Richard Westmacott, set up in 1816. This statue, which rests upon a granite pedestal, is considered to be one of Westmacott's best productions. Dignity and repose appear to have been the leading objects of the artist's ideas. "The English sculptors," writes the French author of a "Tour in England" in 1825, "have generally disguised their statues of historical personages by certain anachronisms in costume. Thus we see the Charleses and the Jameses clothed in the Roman toga, the royal periwigs being disregarded, an omission very creditable to the taste of the artist, though in our (French) busts and statues of Louis XIV. a wig usually encircles the brow of *Le Grand Monarque*." There is nothing offensive, however, in the figure of Charles James Fox, represented as he is in a consular robe, for there was a certain degree of Roman eloquence in the Parliamentary speeches of that great leader. He is represented as seated, with his right arm extended, and supporting Magna Charta. His name forms the only inscription on the pedestal, but that name alone is sufficient to enshrine his memory. The countenance is said to present a striking resemblance to the original. The attitude is dignified, and the statue, as a whole, reflects great credit on the genius of Westmacott.

At the south-west corner of the square was Bloomsbury Market, built by one of the Russell family for the accommodation of that part of the town. Although the market has long been discontinued, it is still kept in remembrance by one of the streets on the site being called Market Street.

Southampton Street, which connects this square with Holborn, witnessed the birth of Colley Cibber, in November, 1671. At the south-west corner of this street, with its principal entrance in Holborn, is the Chief Post and Telegraph Office of the Western Central District. At a short distance eastward is Southampton Row, a broad and well-built thoroughfare extending from High Holborn to Russell Square. It was formerly known as King Street, and is described in the "New View of London," published in 1708, as a "spacious and pleasant street between High Holborne and the fields to the north." At No. 65, on the west side, are the offices of the National Benevolent Institution. This institution was founded by the late Peter Hervé, and established in 1812, with the view of affording relief, by annual pensions, to distressed and aged gentry, merchants, tutors, and governesses, and persons who have been engaged in professional pursuits, or in the higher departments of trade. The unfortunate Dr. Dodd was at one time a resident in this row.

Connecting Southampton Row with the north-east corner of Bloomsbury Square is Bloomsbury Place. At his residence here, in 1802, died Mr. Thomas Cadell, the eminent publisher of the Strand. He was the publisher of the first edition, and of many consecutive editions, of Gibbon's "Decline and Fall of the Roman Empire." At No. 2, in Bloomsbury Place, are the offices of the Corporation of the Sons of the Clergy. This institution was established in 1655, and incorporated by Royal Charter in 1678, for the purpose of "relieving necessitous clergymen, pensioning their widows and aged single daughters, and educating, apprenticing, and providing outfits for their children." The pensions and donations are granted by the Court of Assistants, after investigation of the merits of each case; and it may be interesting to learn that the number benefited by this institution in the course of a year amounts to upwards of one thousand. The Festival of the Sons of the Clergy, which has been already mentioned in our account of St. Paul's Cathedral,* commenced in 1655, and was virtually the basis of the above-mentioned corporation. The proceeds of these festivals are placed at the disposal of the corporation for the apprenticing of the sons and daughters of necessitous clergymen in situations of credit and respectability, and other analogous purposes which the committee may approve. The stewards of the festival contribute a sum of not less than thirty guineas towards the expenses of the festival, and are subsequently elected governors of the corporation.

Hart Street—a fine and broad thoroughfare running from New Oxford Street into the south-west corner of Bloomsbury Square—together with Vernon Place, Theobald's Road, and other streets through the parish of Clerkenwell, now forms a continuous line of route through Northern London to Shoreditch and Hackney. Hart Street was probably so named—like Hart Street, Covent Garden—from an inn bearing the sign of the "White Hart," which may have stood there. On the north side of this street stands the Church of St. George. To use the words of the "Pocket Guide to London," this church "enjoys the privilege of being at once the most pretentious and the ugliest ecclesiastical edifice in the metropolis. All the absurdities of the classic style are here apparent. It was designed by Hawkesmoor, the pupil of Sir C. Wren, and was completed in 1731. The architect chose for his model the description given by Pliny of the tomb of Mausolus, in Caria; but

if the original possessed all the faults of the copy, we can scarcely understand its having been considered one of the seven wonders of the world, unless viewed in the light of a monstrosity. This church has a tower and steeple at the side of the main edifice: upon the former, at the four sides, is a range of Corinthian pillars, placed there apparently for no earthly use. The steeple consists of a series of steps, with the royal arms, guarded by excessively fierce-looking lions and unicorns, and on the summit is a statue of King George I. in a Roman costume." The statue of the king is said to have been the gift of a loyal brewer, Mr. William Hucks, sometime M.P. for Abingdon and Wallingford. On the statue being placed in its exalted situation a wag wrote the following epigram on it:—

"The King of Great Britain was reckoned before
  The 'Head of the Church' by all good Christian people;
But his brewer has added still one title more
  To the rest, and has made him the 'Head of the Steeple!'"

Horace Walpole, who speaks of this steeple as "a master-stroke of absurdity, consisting of an obelisk, crowned with the statue of King George I., and hugged by the royal supporters," treats us with the following version of the same epigram:—

"When Harry the Eighth left the Pope in the lurch,
  The people of England made him 'Head of the Church;'
But George's good subjects, the Bloomsbury people,
  Instead of the Church made him 'Head of the Steeple.'"

The steeple as applied to a building on the Grecian or Roman plan is always absurd, and even Sir C. Wren could not always rescue it from deserved and contemptuous criticism; but Hawkesmoor appears to have been the only architect who ventured to place this part of the structure at the side instead of making it rise out of the building.

The front of the church, facing Hart Street, has a grand portico, elevated on a flight of steps, which support six Corinthian columns. The church is singular from its standing north and south; hence, contrary to the established custom, the altar stands at the north end; so that, in this case at least, the "eastward position" is not rigidly carried out. The fabric is of too recent erection to contain many monuments or objects of interest; there is, however, in it a tablet to the memory of the great Lord Mansfield.

At his residence in Hart Street, in 1829, died Archdeacon Robert Nares, librarian of the MSS. in the British Museum, and the learned editor of part of the "Catalogue of the Harleian Miscellany," and for many years joint editor of the *British Critic*. He was the son of Dr. James Nares,

---

* See Vol. I., p. 262.

many years organist and composer to George II. and George III. He was a busy and voluminous writer, an acute critic, and a Fellow of the Royal and other learned societies.

At No. 11, in this street, are the offices of the Society of Biblical Archæology. This society, which holds its meetings monthly, at No. 9, Conduit Street, Regent Street, was established for the study of such archæological matters as will help to throw additional light on the Holy Scriptures.

CHAPTER XLII.

RED LION SQUARE, AND ITS NEIGHBOURHOOD.

"Where the 'Red Lion' frowns upon the way."—*Crabbe.*

Red Lion Square in the Last Century—The Old "Red Lyon" Inn—A Quack Doctor's "Puff"—The Fate of the Regicides: Cromwell, Ireton, and Bradshaw—An "Old Lady of Quality"—Lord Raymond, Jonas Hanway, and Sharon Turner, Residents in this Square—An Antiquated Law Court—London Infirmary for Diseases of the Legs—A Batch of Charitable and Provident Institutions—Milton a Resident in this Neighbourhood—Eagle Street—Martin Van Butchell, the Eccentric Quack Doctor—Fisher and Kingsgate Streets—A Royal Misadventure—Messrs. Day and Martin's Blacking Manufactory—The Holborn Amphitheatre—Red Lion Street—Theobald's Road—Lamb's Conduit Street—Lamb's Conduit rebuilt—Its Removal—Lamb's Conduit Fields—Harpur Street—Milman Street—The Chevalier D'Eon—Doughty Street—Charles Dickens a Resident here—John Street Baptist Chapel—St. John's Episcopal Chapel the Head-quarters of Fashionable Evangelicalism—The Gray's Inn Cock-pit—Bedford Row—The Entomological Society—Bedford Street—Featherstone Buildings—Hand Court—Brownlow Street—The Duke's Theatre—Warwick Court.

To the south-east of Bloomsbury Square, surrounded by a nest of narrow alleys between it and Holborn, is Red Lion Square, described by Northouck as a "neat, small square, much longer than it is broad," and having "convenient" streets entering it on three sides, with foot-passages at the corners. It had at that time (1786) not only in the centre a plain obelisk, but a stone watch-house at each corner, all of which have long been swept away. Although respectable, the square has a very dull appearance, which is thus whimsically portrayed by the author of "Critical Observations on the Buildings, &c., of London," published about the middle of the last century :—"I never go into it without thinking of my latter end. The rough sod that 'heaves with many a mouldering heap,' the dreary length of its sides, with the four watch-houses like so many family vaults at the corners, and the naked obelisk that springs from amid the rank grass, like the sad monument of a disconsolate widow for the loss of her first husband, all form together a *memento mori*, more powerful to me than a death's head and cross marrow-bones ; and were but a parson's bull to be seen bellowing at the gate, the idea of a country churchyard, in my mind, would be complete."

Hatton, in 1708, describes it as "a pleasant square of good buildings, between High Holborn south and the fields north ; " and Pennant, writing in 1790, says that in the centre was "a clumsy obelisk, lately vanished."

The "Red Lyon" Inn was in olden times the most important hostelry in Holborn, and accordingly had the honour of giving its name to Red Lion Street and to the adjoining square. If we may draw an inference from the entries in the register of St. Andrew's, Holborn, the inn had behind it a fine row of trees, for we find notices of foundlings being exposed under the "Red Lion Elmes in Holborn." The "Red Lyon" is mentioned in the following "puff" of a quack doctor, at the beginning of the last century :—" Cornelius Tilbury, sworn Chirurgeon in ordinary to K. Charles II., to his late Sovereign K. William, as also to her present Majesty Queen Anne," gives his address as " at the Blue Flower Pot, in Great Lincoln's Inn Fields, at Holbourn Row (where you see at night a light over the door). . . . And for the convenience of those that desire privacy, they may come through the Red Lyon Inn, in Holbourn, between the two Turnstiles, which is directly against my back door, where you will see the sign of the Blue Ball hang over the door. I dispose of my famous Orvietan, either liquid or in powder, what quantity or price you please. . . . This is that Orvietan that expelled that vast quantity of poyson I took before K. Charles II., for which his Majesty presented me with a gold medal and chain."

The story that some of the regicides were buried in Red Lion Square has been extensively believed ; it is told by Mr. Peter Cunningham, with a little variety, as follows :—" The bodies of Oliver Cromwell, Ireton, and Bradshaw were carried from Westminster Abbey to the Red Lion Inn, in Holborn, and the next day dragged on sledges thence to Tyburn." In support of this story he quotes Wood's "Athenæ Oxonienses," and the additional MSS. in the British Museum, where those who are curious in such matters will find the narrative.

On the fate of Cromwell's head we have already quoted at some length in the preceding volume.* It is the opinion of a writer in the *Times*, that if the body of Cromwell was removed from the Abbey and buried in Red Lion Square, it is not probable that another embalmed body could have been procured for the purpose of being sent as its substitute to Tyburn, as has been suggested.

those of Ireton and Bradshaw, whose remains were disinterred at the same time from Westminster Abbey, and exposed on the same gallows. He strengthens this supposition by observing that the contemporary accounts of the last resting-place of these remarkable men simply inform us, that on the anniversary of the death of Charles I. their bodies were borne on sledges to *Tyburn*, and after

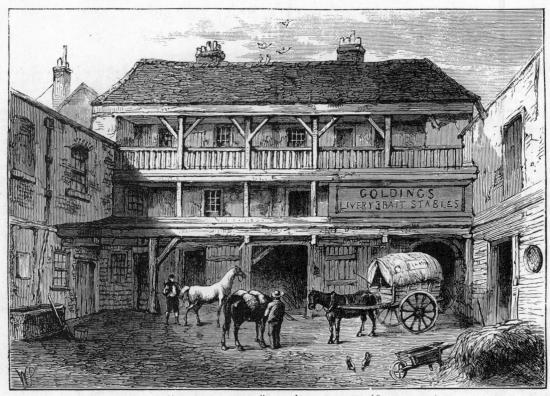

THL OLD "BLACK BULL INN," GRAY'S INN LANE. (*See page* 551.)

Pennant, as we have observed, speaks of the "clumsy obelisk" in Red Lion Square, and mentions that it was inscribed with the following lines :—"Obtusum Obtusioris Ingenii Monumentum. Quid me respicis, viator? Vade." "Could this quaint inscription," asks Mr. Jesse, in his "London," "have any hidden reference to the bones of Cromwell lying beneath it? We think not; but they are meant to mystify; and what, therefore, *do* they mean?" Mr. Jesse is inclined, however, in spite of his scepticism as to the inscription, to agree with those who believe in the tradition that the body of Cromwell was buried beneath this obelisk, and that upon this spot not improbably moulder, not only the bones of the great Protector, but also

hanging till sunset they were cut down and beheaded; that their bodies were then flung into a hole at the foot of the gallows, and their heads fixed upon poles on the roof of Westminster Hall. "From the word *Tyburn* being so distinctly laid down," Mr. Jesse adds, "it has usually been taken for granted that it was intended to designate the well-known place for executing criminals, nearly at the north end of Park Lane, or, as it was anciently styled, Tyburn Lane. However, when we read of a criminal in old times having been executed at *Tyburn*, we are not necessarily to presume that it was at this particular spot, the gallows having unquestionably been shifted at times from place to place, and the word *Tyburn* having been given indiscriminately, for the time being, to each spot. For instance, sixty years before the death of Crom-

* See Vol. III., p. 539.

RED LION SQUARE IN 1780.

well the gallows were frequently erected at the extremity of St. Giles's parish, near the end of the present Tottenham Court Road; while for nearly two centuries the Holborn end of Fetter Lane, within a short distance of Red Lion Square, was no less frequently the place of execution. Indeed, in 1643, only a few years before the exhumation and gibbeting of Cromwell, we find Nathaniel Tomkins executed at this spot for his share in Waller's plot to surprise the City. In addition, however, to these surmises is the curious fact of the bodies of Cromwell and Ireton having been brought in carts, on the night previous to their exposure on the gibbet, to the *Red Lion Inn*, Holborn, from which Red Lion Square derives its name, where they rested during the night. In taking this step, it is surely not unreasonable to presume that the Government had in view the selection of a house in the immediate vicinity of the scaffold, in order that the bodies might be in readiness for the disgusting exhibition of the following morning. Supposing this to have been the case, the place of their exposure and interment could scarcely have been the end of Tyburn Lane, inasmuch as the distance thither from Westminster is actually shorter than the distance from Westminster to Red Lion Square. The object of the Government could hardly have been to create a sensation by parading the bodies along a populous thoroughfare, inasmuch as the ground between St. Giles's Pound and Tyburn, a distance of a mile and a half, was at this period almost entirely open country."

This story of the disposal of Cromwell's body, if true, negatives the well-known lines of Dryden :—

" His ashes in a peaceful urn shall rest."

In Rede's " Anecdotes and Biography," published just before the close of the last century, it is stated that the obelisk was thought to be a memorial erected to Cromwell by an apothecary who was attached to his principles, and had so much influence in the building of the square as to manage the marking out of the ground, thus further contriving to pay this tribute to his favourite. Curiously enough, it has been discovered that an apothecary named Ebenezer Heathcote, who had married the daughter of one of Ireton's sub-commissaries, was living at the King's-gate, Holborn, soon after the Restoration.

Leigh Hunt has left a curious reminiscence of an " old lady of quality," who lived in this square, " a quarter in different esteem once from what it is now." She astounded him one day by letting her false teeth slip out, and clapping them in again.

It was at her house, he adds, that his father one evening met John Wilkes. Not knowing him by sight, and happening to fall into conversation with him, while the latter sat looking down, he said something in Wilkes's disparagement, on which the jovial demagogue looked up in his face, and burst out laughing. In this square lived, in the last century, Lord Raymond, the Chief Justice of the Court of King's Bench. At No. 23, writes Peter Cunningham, lived, and here, in 1786, died the benevolent Mr. Jonas Hanway, the eccentric traveller, remarkable as " the first person who ventured to walk in the streets of London with an umbrella over his head." We have already spoken at some length of this celebrity in dealing with Hanway Street.* The principal rooms in Hanway's house were decorated with paintings and emblematical devices, " in a style," says his biographer, " peculiar to himself. I found," he used to say, when speaking of these ornaments, " that my countrymen and women were not *au fait* in the art of conversation; and that instead of recurring to their cards when the discourse began to flag, the minutes between the time of assembling and the placing of the card-tables are spent in an irksome suspense. To relieve this vacuum in social intercourse, and prevent cards from engrossing the whole of my visitors' minds, I have presented them with objects the most attractive I could imagine; and when that fails there are the cards." At No. 32 in this square, the house at the corner of North Street, lived, for many years in the present century, Sharon Turner, the author of " The Sacred History of the World." He was a solicitor in practice, as well as an historian; he died here in 1847. Besides his " Sacred History," he was the author of the " History of England from the Earliest Period to the Death of Elizabeth," consisting of several works, each published separately and independently—namely, the "History of the Anglo-Saxons," " History of England in the Middle Ages," " History of the Reign of Henry VIII.," and " History of the Reigns of Edward VI., Mary, and Elizabeth." At No. 2 lived Judge Blackstone.

Besides the ordinary Superior Courts, so well known by name to every reader, there is in existence in Red Lion Square, at the house at the north-east corner, an ancient Baronial Court, held under the authority of the Sheriffs of Middlesex. " It is held monthly " (says the *Gentleman's Magazine* in 1829) " before the Sheriff or his deputy. Its power in judgment is as great as that of any of the present Courts of Law. It is more expeditious and less

* See p. 470, *ante.*

expensive; persons seeking to recover debts may do so to any amount at the trifling expense of only six or seven pounds. Nor is it confined to actions of account; it extends to detenue, trover, scandal, &c., and personal service of process is unnecessary. This Court was instituted," adds the writer, " by King Alfred on dividing the kingdom into shires, and subsequently continued and sanctioned by Canute the Dane, by William the Conqueror, and various statutes, including Magna Charta; and is treated upon by several eminent legal authorities, as Judge Hale, Judge Lambert, and many others."

The author of " A Tour through Great Britain" says, " This present year, 1737, an Act was passed for beautifying Red Lyon Square, which had run much to decay." Though the square has at this time a decayed aspect, there is a picturesqueness and a touch of sentiment about it not to be found in squares of a higher grade through which we have passed. The variety of the houses, dilapidated and disfigured as some of them are, is more interesting than the even respectability of continuous brick walls and unbroken roofs. Besides the old Sheriff's Court, mentioned above, several other houses in this square are, or have been, devoted to public and charitable purposes. Here, for instance, at No. 27, are the offices of the Indigent Blind Visiting Society and the British Asylum for Deaf and Dumb Females. The former, which was established in 1834, has for its object the visiting and relieving of the destitute blind at their own homes, and affording elementary education in day classes. It is the only society in London which combines the visitation, relief, and education of the blind. The number of persons benefited annually by this Society is about 700. The British Asylum for Deaf and Dumb Females, which is located at Lower Clapton, was founded in 1851.

The whole of the square, having long since been deserted by the families who used to inhabit it, has become quite a warren, so to speak, of charitable societies, which we have no room to enumerate in detail.

Milton at two different periods of his life was a resident in this immediate neighbourhood, and on both occasions he occupied houses looking upon the green fields. The first time that he resided here was in 1647, when his house " opened backwards into Lincoln's Inn Fields," where it was that he principally employed himself in writing his virulent tirades against monarchy and Charles I. The second occasion of his residing here was after the Restoration, when we are told the front of his humble dwelling looked into Red Lion Fields, the site of the present Red Lion Square.

To the south of Red Lion Square, and parallel to it, half way between the square and Holborn, and separating Dean and Leigh Streets, is Eagle Street. Here was born Martin Van Butchell, the eccentric quack doctor and dentist, of whom we have already spoken in our account of Mount Street, Grosvenor Square.*

At the south-west corner of the square, parallel with the large red-brick church of St. John the Evangelist, is Fisher Street, leading into Kingsgate Street, which opens into Holborn. Hatton, in 1708, says that Kingsgate Street was " so called because the king used to go this way to New Market." This street would seem to have witnessed one royal misadventure at the least; for under date 8th of March, 1668–9, Pepys writes in " Diary : "—" To Whitehall, from whence the King and the Duke of York went by three in the morning, and had the misfortune to be overset with the Duke of York, the Duke of Monmouth, and the Prince [Rupert], at the King's Gate, in Holborne ; and the king all dirt, but no hurt. How it came to pass I know not, but only it was dark, and the torches did not, they say, light the coach as they should."

Between Kingsgate and Dean Streets, extending back into Eagle Street, and with their principal entrance facing Holborn, are the extensive premises of Messrs. Day and Martin, the well-known blacking manufacturers. Mr. Charles Day, the founder of this establishment, died in 1836, having made a huge fortune. He had for many years before his death been totally blind, and—apparently touched by that " fellow-feeling" which " makes us wondrous kind"—in his will he directed that £100,000 should be devoted to the establishment of a charity, to be called the " Poor Blind Man's Friend." This institution, as we have already seen, has its offices in Savile Row.

A short distance eastward, between Dean Street and Red Lion Street, is a building which has undergone a variety of uses and vicissitudes. It was erected about the year 1862 as a horse and carriage repository, but the speculation was anything but successful, and in a short time collapsed. The building, which covers a large space of ground, and has an entrance in Holborn, was afterwards converted into a theatre—called first the National, and afterwards the Holborn Amphitheatre—with stage for dramatic representations, and a circus for equestrian performances. It was turned into a skating-rink, and finally re-converted into a theatre, called the Alcazar; but for some reason a licence

_____

* See page 335, *ante.*

has been withheld up to the present time (May, 1883), and it has remained closed.

Red Lion Street, like the Square—as already stated—was so called after the "Red Lion Inn." On the wall of the building at the south-west corner, a public-house called the "Red Lion," is a block of wood let in, with the date "1611." This street—and, indeed, the whole neighbourhood of Red Lion Square, if we may judge by stray allusions in the "London Spy"—would appear to have borne no very high reputation for morality in the reigns of the first and second Georges. Nor does it appear to have been very safe for pedestrians. For instance, in 1760 an apothecary was attacked in Red Lion Street by two ruffians with firearms, who carried him off by force to "Black Mary's Hole."

We gather from King's "Anecdotes of his own Times," that this street was formerly noted for its modellers and dealers in plaster casts, many of whom still linger in the neighbourhood of Gray's Inn Lane and Hatton Garden. Speaking of the Pretender's visit to London, the author says, "He came one evening to my lodgings and drank tea with me; my servant, after he was gone, said to me that he thought my new visitor very like Prince Charles. 'Why,' said I, 'have you ever seen Prince Charles?' 'No, sir,' replied the fellow; 'but this gentleman, whoever he may be, exactly resembles the busts which are sold in Red Lion Street, and are said to be the busts of Prince Charles.' The truth is, these busts were taken in plaster of Paris from his face."

Theobald's Road, which runs parallel with the north side of Red Lion Square, and separates Red Lion Street from Lamb's Conduit Street, was so named, says Mr. Peter Cunningham, "because it led to Theobalds, in Hertfordshire, the favourite hunting-seat of King James I. The king," he adds, "on leaving Whitehall, went through the Strand, up Drury Lane, and so on into Holborn, Kingsgate Street, and Theobald's Road." John Le Neve, author of "Monumenta Anglicana," lived in this road at the time of the publication of that work (1717–19), and here he advertised that his book might be bought.

A conduit, founded by one William Lamb, a gentleman of the Chapel Royal under Henry VIII., gave its name to Lamb's Conduit Street. Lamb, it is stated, here caused several springs to be so connected as to form a head of water, which was conveyed by a leaden pipe, about 2,000 yards in length, to Snow Hill, where he rebuilt a conduit, which had long been in a ruinous state and disused. He is said to have expended a very large sum of money upon these structures, and thus, by his benevolent exertions, conferred an important advantage upon a very populous neighbourhood. "Moreover," as we learn from Stow's "Summary," "he gave to poor women, such as were willing to take pains, 120 pails therewith to carry and serve water." His benefactions for other purposes were also numerous. He was buried in St. Faith's Church, and upon his tomb was inscribed an epitaph in the quaint punning language of the time.

Lamb's Conduit was rebuilt in 1667 from a design by Sir Christopher Wren, and at the expense of Sir Thomas Daws. It was taken down in 1746. Most of the City conduits, it has been remarked, were destroyed by the Great Fire in 1666, and the rest, it is darkly hinted, were swept quietly away in order to force the citizens to have the water of the New River laid on to their houses.

The fields around Lamb's Conduit, a century ago, formed a favourite promenade for the inhabitants of St. Andrew's, Holborn, and St. Giles's. An old English "Herbal," speaking of winter rocket, or cresses, says: "It groweth of its own accord in gardens and fields, by the way-side in divers places, and particularly in *the next pasture to the Conduit Head*, behind Gray's Inn, that brings water to Mr. Lamb's Conduit, in *Holborn*."

A correspondent in *Notes and Queries* (April, 1857) says: "About sixty years since I was travelling from the West of England in one of the old stage-coaches of that day, and my fellow-travellers were an octogenarian clergyman and his daughter. In speaking of the then increasing size of London, the old gentleman said that, when he was a boy, and recovering from an attack of small-pox, he was sent into the country to a row of houses standing on the west side of the upper part of the present Lamb's Conduit Street; that all the space before him was open fields; that a streamlet of water ran under his window; and he saw a man snipe-shooting, who sprang a snipe near to the house, and shot it. . . . I have myself seen a pump reputed to be erected on the Conduit Head, and standing against the corner house of a small turning out of Lamb's Conduit Street, on the right-hand side as you go towards the Foundling, and nearly at the upper end of the street." In this same small turning, now known as Long Yard, may be seen carved on the gable of the first house on the left, the inscription, "Lamb's Conduit, the property of the City of London. This pump is erected for the benefit of the public." The date is obliterated.

On the west side of Lamb's Conduit Street are two or three short streets, which, from the substantial appearance of the houses, would seem to have been formerly the abode of some of the higher classes of society. One of these is Harpur Street, which runs in a line with Theobald's Road, on the north side of Red Lion Square. It was so named after Sir William Harpur, who was Lord Mayor of London in 1562.

Lamb's Conduit Street is crossed by Ormond Street, and terminated at its northern end by Guilford Street. On the east side of the street, and running parallel between it and Gray's Inn Road, are Milman, Doughty, Great James, and John Streets, together with two or three others of little or no importance. In Milman Street, at the house of a friend, on the 21st of May, 1810, died the Chevalier D'Eon, some time equerry to Louis XV., and also Ambassador at the Court of St. James's. During his residence in England, doubts arose respecting his sex, and wagers to a large amount were laid thereon, one of which terminated in a trial before Lord Mansfield. There the witnesses declared that the Chevalier was a woman concealed in man's clothes; and no attempt being made to contradict their evidence, a verdict was given for the plaintiff for the recovery of the wager. After the trial, D'Eon put on female attire, which he continued to wear till his decease, when all doubts regarding his sex were at once set at rest, an examination of the body being made in the presence of several distinguished personages. From the notice of his death in the *Gentleman's Magazine* we learn that in private life the Chevalier was always understood to have been extremely amiable; his natural abilities were great, and his acquirements most numerous. The story which mixed up the name of the Chevalier D'Eon in an intrigue with Queen Charlotte in the early part of her married life, is shown by Mr. W. J. Thoms to be a pure invention of a French scandal-monger, M. Gaillardet.

In Milman Street Bellingham was lodging when, in 1812, he assassinated Mr. Perceval in the lobby of the House of Commons.

In Doughty Street lived Charles Dickens in the earlier days of his first achieved popularity, when as yet he was only "Boz" to the public. Whilst here he wrote, in a letter to a friend, "I always pay my taxes when they 'won't' wait any longer, in order to get a bad name in the parish, and so to escape all 'honours.'" Here was a touch of character; though Mr. Forster tells us that in after life, respectability following in the wake of success, he followed quite a different course, and paid his taxes not only regularly but punctually.

Extending from Doughty Street to Theobald's Road, which forms the northern side of Gray's Inn, is a broad and well-built thoroughfare, called John Street. On the west side of the street is the Baptist chapel where the Hon. and Rev. Baptist Noel preached to crowded congregations, after his secession from the Established Church in 1848. He had previously been for several years the minister of the Episcopal Chapel of St. John, which stood in Chapel Street, Great James Street, at the north end of Bedford Row. The old chapel, which was pulled down soon after Mr. Noel left it, was a plain square brick building, and may be described as having been for half a century the head-quarters of fashionable Evangelicalism, for the string of carriages waiting at its doors about one o'clock on Sundays sometimes extended the entire length of the street. In the early part of the present century the minister of St. John's Chapel was the Rev. Daniel Wilson, afterwards vicar of Islington, and eventually Bishop of Calcutta.

In the rear of Gray's Inn, as we learn from John Timbs, there was formerly a cockpit, which, doubtless, was frequented by the young law-students. The place is still kept in remembrance by Little Cockpit Yard, in the King's Road, close by Great James Street.

The old "Black Bull," in Gray's Inn Lane, of which we give a view on page 546, was a good specimen of the old-fashioned galleried yard.

Bedford Row, which lies between Red Lion Street and Gray's Inn, is a fine specimen of a broad thoroughfare of the early part of the eighteenth century, and must have been a pleasant residence when all to the north was open country as far as Hampstead and Highgate. It does not derive its name, as might be imagined, from the Russell family, but from the town of Bedford, to which— his native place—Sir William Harpur, Lord Mayor of London in 1562, bequeathed the land on which it stands for the foundation of a school and other local charities.

The houses in Bedford Row are now nearly all cut up into chambers and occupied by solicitors. No. 12 was for many years the head-quarters of the Entomological Society. This society was organised in 1833, and the first general meeting of its members was held in the following year, with the Rev. W. Kirby, the "father of British entomology," as its president. Periodical meetings were at first held, at which memoirs were received and read, experiments for the destruction of noxious insects suggested, communications made, and objects exhibited. A collection of insects was also formed, together with a library of books of reference. The valuable collections of Mr. Kirby were presented to the society at its commencement. In 1875, they removed to Chandos Street, Cavendish Square.

At the south end of Bedford Row is Bedford Street, which runs westward into Red Lion Street,

former days was not only a favourite public-house sign, but also one of the usual signs of the marriage-mongers in Fleet Street; and it now figures as the name of one of the London Fire Insurance Offices. Brownlow Street was named after Sir John Brown-

OLD HOUSES IN HOLBORN.

and is connected with High Holborn by three or four narrow streets and courts. One of these, Featherstone Buildings, Mr. Cunningham tells us, was so called from Cuthbert Featherstone, Gentleman Usher and Crier of the King's Bench, who died in 1615. A stone let into the wall is inscribed with the name of the passage, and the date is 1724. The next, Hand Court, is so called from the "Hand-in-Hand" Tavern, which stands at the corner in Holborn. The "Hand-in-Hand" in

low, a parishioner of St. Giles's * in the reign of Charles II. Eastward of this street stood the Duke's Theatre, which occupied a plot of ground abutting on the western boundary of Gray's Inn, formerly used as a yard for mail-carts and post-office omnibuses. It was at first opened about 1866, as the Holborn Theatre, by Mr. Sefton Parry, but subsequently underwent many changes in

---

* See Vol. III., p. 207.

style and management. Its name later on was altered to "The Mirror," which in turn was changed to the "Duke's." The theatre was eventually burnt down, and the site has been covered by a monster hotel.

Warwick Court, close by the above hotel, was pro-

bably so named after the old Earls of Warwick, whose mansion, Warwick House, mentioned in our account of the neighbourhood of Holborn,* stood at a short distance eastward of Gray's Inn Lane. Passing up this court, we find ourselves at the back gate of Gray's Inn, where we stop our journeyings eastward.

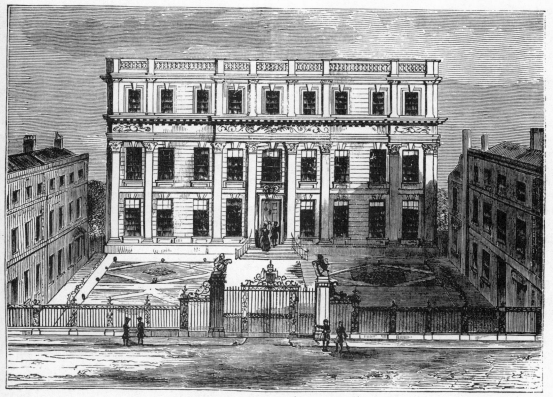

POWIS HOUSE, 1714. (*See page* 556.)

CHAPTER XLIII.

QUEEN SQUARE, GREAT ORMOND STREET, &c.

A "Colony" of French Refugees—Attack on Dr. Challoner's House during the Gordon Riots—Queen Square—The Church of St. George the Martyr—The Parish Burial-ground—Inadequate Accommodation for the Poor—Jonathan Richardson, the Artist—Dr. John Campbell and Dr. Johnson—The Poet Churchill—Dr. Stukeley, the Antiquary—The Alexandra Institution for the Blind—Hospital for Hip Diseases in Childhood—The Ladies' Charity School—National Hospital for the Paralysed and Epileptic—The College for Men and Women—The Aged Poor Society—The Society of St. Vincent de Paul—College of Preceptors—Government District School of Art for Ladies—Great Ormond Street—Noted Residents—Powis House—The Residence of Lord Chancellor Thurlow, and Anecdotes of his Lordship—The Working Men's College—The Hospital of St. John and St. Elizabeth—Provident Surgical Appliance Society—The Residence of Dr. Mead, afterwards the Hospital for Sick Children—The Home for Friendless Girls—The Homœopathic Hospital—The Residence of Zachary Macaulay—The United Kingdom Benefit Society—The Workhouse Visiting Society—Guilford Street—Brunswick and Mecklenburgh Squares.

THE district between Southampton Row and Lamb's Conduit Street was largely inhabited towards the middle and close of the last century by French refugees, who supported themselves by industrial pursuits of a somewhat higher kind than

those of Clerkenwell and Soho. Among these were many Roman Catholics, who frequented the only chapel which up to that time existed in

* See Vol. II., p. 549.

Central London, that of the Sardinian Embassy in Lincoln's Inn Fields, which we have already described briefly.* The saintly and learned bishop, Dr. Challoner, was living amongst his people, first in Gloucester Street, Queen Square, and subsequently in Lamb's Conduit Street, at the time of the Gordon Riots. His abode being known, his rooms were invaded by the mob; but the good old man was safe in a retreat a few miles from town, and he escaped with the loss of some of his books and papers.

"Queen Square," writes the fastidious author of a "New Critical Review of the Public Buildings, &c," "is an area of a particular kind, being left open on one side for the sake of the beautiful landscape, which is formed by the hills of Hampstead and Highgate, together with the adjacent fields"—an arrangement which the writer highly approves, on account alike of the inhabitants and of the square as well. "The square," observes the writer of the "Beauties of England and Wales," "forms a parallelogram, and the houses on three of the sides were erected at the commencement of the last century. It was named Queen Square out of compliment to Queen Anne, in whose reign it was built, and whose statue is placed in the midst of the garden at the north side."

At the south-west angle of the square stands the church of St. George the Martyr, erected in 1706 by private subscriptions, as a chapel of ease to the parish of St. Andrew's, Holborn. Northouck tells us that "the persons who built it intended to reimburse themselves by the sale of the pews; but the commissioners for erecting fifty new churches, resolving to make this one of the number, purchased it, assigned to it a district, and had it consecrated in 1723. It was dedicated to St. George in compliment to one of its founders, Sir Streynsham Master, who had been Governor of Fort St. George;" and it is called St. George the Martyr to distinguish it from the other church of the same name in Hart Street.

The parish burial-ground is in the rear of the Foundling Hospital. Speaking of this particular churchyard, Mr. John Timbs, in his "Curiosities," observes—"A strong prejudice formerly existed against new churchyards, and no person was interred here till the ground was broken for Robert Nelson, author of "Fasts and Festivals," whose character for piety reconciled others to the spot: people liked to be buried in company, and in good company." Nancy Dawson, the celebrated hornpipe dancer of Covent Garden and Drury Lane

Theatres, lies here. Here also are buried the good judge, Sir John Richardson, and Zachary Macaulay.

Even in the parish of St. George the Martyr, if a judgment may be formed from Dr. Stallard's work on "London Pauperism," the accommodation in the dwellings of some of the poor is most disgracefully inadequate. It is to be hoped that our children, or, at all events, our grandchildren, will refuse to believe that in the year of grace 1874 a pauper widow, her sister, and six young children were existing—we purposely do not write "living"—in a room seven feet by eight, and eight feet high, a space not more than sufficient for one person.

Queen Square, like the rest of the once fashionable neighbourhood, has had its quota of celebrities among its residents. Here, for instance, lived the worthy Jonathan Richardson, the artist, and friend of Pope, who painted Pope's mother and Lord Bolingbroke. More than one of Pope's letters are addressed to him here. He rests in the burial-ground mentioned above. Sir Godfrey Kneller would often come across from his lodgings in Great Queen Street to spend a quiet evening at Richardson's house.

In Hawkins' "Life of Johnson" we read that Dr. John Campbell's residence for some years before his death was the large new-built house situated at the north-west corner of the square; "whither," adds the author, "particularly on a Sunday evening, great numbers of persons of the first eminence for science and literature were accustomed to resort for the enjoyment of conversation." Boswell has this note on these assemblies:—"*Johnson:* I used to go pretty often to Campbell's on a Sunday evening, till I began to consider that the shoals of Scotchmen who flocked about him might probably say, when anything of mine was well done, 'Ay, ay, he has learnt this of *Cawmell.*'" Dr. Campbell was a celebrated biographical and political writer, a friend of Dr. Johnson, and the author of "Hermippus Redivivus," and of other curious works. He was also editor of the "Biographia Britannica." He was, in fact, a voluminous writer, and made a considerable fortune by his pen.

It was in this square that the poet, Charles Churchill, was employed in teaching the *belles lettres* in a lady's school whilst holding the curacy of St. John's, Westminster, and

"Passing rich on forty pounds a year."

In Queen Square, in March, 1765, died the celebrated antiquary, Dr. William Stukeley, whose labours in British archæology obtained for him the name of "the arch-druid." Returning from his house at Kentish Town, he complained that he felt a stroke of palsy, and died a week afterwards. He was buried at East Ham, in Essex. Dr. Stukely was for many years rector of the parish of St. George the Martyr.

Here were shops of sundry booksellers and print-sellers; for at the "Golden Head" in this square, in 1712, the portrait of Cunneshote, one of the Cherokee chiefs then on a visit to this country, was on sale; it was engraved after a painting by Francis Parsons.

Queen Square, as well as Great Ormond Street, into which we shall shortly pass, seems to be a favourite centre of charitable institutions. At the corner of Brunswick Row is the Hospital for Hip Diseases in Childhood, which was founded in 1867. At No. 22 was for many years located the oldest of Ladies' Charity Schools. This institution — for, although called a school, it is in reality one of our oldest charitable institutions—was established in 1702, for "educating, clothing, and maintaining the daughters of respectable parents in reduced and necessitous circumstances." The Ladies' Charity School was removed in 1883 to new quarters at Notting Hill; and the site of the building here is being utilised in an extension of the National Hospital for the Paralysed and Epileptic, which adjoined it. This hospital was instituted in the year 1859. The number of persons annually benefited here amount to about 3,000, of whom a large number of the incurable patients have pensions awarded to them ranging from £10 to £22 each. In 1875-6 a new wing was added to the hospital, founded in memory of the late Johanna Chandler, for the reception of gentlewomen of limited means, governesses, the wives and children of business men, clerks, and other persons of the middle class of society, sufferers from paralysis and other diseases of the nervous system, who are unable to pay the ordinary expenses of medical treatment in their own homes, but are able and willing to pay a portion of their maintenance while in the hospital. In this "memorial wing" hospital life is divested as far as possible of its wearisome monotony by the provision of cheerfully-furnished day-rooms, regulated occupation, and such home comforts as the exigencies of the mode of life permits.

At No. 29 is the "College for Men and Women," with which is incorporated the "Working Women's College," both being offshoots of the "Working Men's College," of which we shall speak presently. It was established in 1874, with the object "of supplying to men and women occupied during the day a higher education than had been hitherto within their reach. The classes are taught, for the most part, gratuitously, and the design is that mutual help and fellowship may be promoted between all members of the college, teachers and students, by the educational work in the classes and the social life in the coffee-room." The classes, which are held every evening (except Saturday), comprise teaching in the following subjects :— Arithmetic, book-keeping, English grammar and language, history, literature, geography, physiology, Latin, French, German, drawing, singing, &c., and the fees range from 2s. to 4s. per class per term. These colleges for the joint education of men and women, though new in England, have long been carried on with much success in America, and the combination of the two sexes in the work of self-culture works well. The house is used by day as a High School for Girls.

No. 31 formed the head-quarters of some Roman Catholic charitable institutions, among which are the Aged Poor Society, and the Society of St. Vincent de Paul, for visiting and relieving distress among the labouring classes. This society is widely spread over all the large cities of the Continent both in Catholic and in Protestant countries.

A large double house on the south side of the square is the College of Preceptors, founded in 1846, and enjoying a royal charter. Its object is to afford to commercial and other public and private schools those tests of results which were afforded to other schools by the university local examinations. In 1870 and 1881 the number of persons examined by the college were respectively 2,412 and 16,000, showing an increase of several thousands, and at the same time affording conclusive evidence of the practical use of the examinations, many of the persons who submit to these tests of fitness being teachers themselves. In the adjoining house is another educational institution— the Government District School of Art for Ladies, under the patronage of Her Majesty. Another establishment is the School of Ecclesiastical Embroidery at No. 32. At the commencement of the present reign the square was inhabited almost entirely by private families of the upper classes; but gradually these mansions have been turned into hospitals and other institutions, for which the quiet of the place fits it admirably. The building now occupied as the College of Preceptors was originally part of Queen Anne's nursery; and Gloucester Street, close by, was named after her little short-lived son. It may be mentioned here that Sir John Karslake, the late Attorney-General, was born and brought up in this square, of which his father was an old and respected inhabitant.

Great Ormond Street, which we now enter, and which runs from Queen Square eastward into Lamb's Conduit Street, dates its erection from the commencement of the last century. Hatton, in 1708, speaks of it as "a street of fine new buildings;" and it is described by the author of a "New Critical Review of the Public Buildings, &c.," in the reign of George II., as a "place of pleasure;" he adds that "the side of it next the fields is, beyond question, one of the finest situations about town." Many of the large red-brick-built houses have in their time been the residences of some of the great men of the age. Dr. Hickes, the author of the "Thesaurus," at one time lived here; as also did Robert Nelson, the author of "Fasts and Festivals."

Dr. Stukeley, the antiquary, whom we have already mentioned, lived at one time "next door to the Duke of Powis;" his "Itinerarium Curiosum" (1724) is dated from thence. In 1773 Dr. Hawkesworth was living in this street. The celebrated writer, politician, poet, and convert from infidelity, Soame Jenyns, many years M.P. for Cambridge, was a native of this street.

In this street, as Cradock tells us, in his "Miscellaneous Memoirs," lived Mr. Bankes, the great conveyancer, of Lincoln's Inn, and friend of Lord Mansfield. He was Chancellor of York, and a Commissioner of Customs, and had a country house at Mortlake, where he kept a pack of hounds. He "gave up the law for hunting, and was more convivial than studious." He laid the foundations of the fortune of the Bankeses of Dorsetshire, which was cemented by an alliance, in the next generation, with Lord Eldon.

Powis House stood near the north-west end of the street, on the site now occupied by Powis Place. Mr. Peter Cunningham tells us that it was built in the latter part of the reign of William III., by William Herbert, Marquis of Powis, son of the first marquis, who was outlawed for his adherence to James II. It was mysteriously burnt down in January, 1714, while the Duc d'Aumont, its then tenant, was entertaining the ambassador of Venice and the envoys of Sweden and Tuscany at dinner, about three o'clock in the afternoon. The alarm of fire was raised in one of the upper rooms, and in less than two hours the whole place was burnt to the ground, the plate and a few of the most valuable pictures alone being saved. "How the fire began," writes Northouck, "was then and still is a mystery. Many reports were circulated on the

occasion, one of which was that the house was designedly burnt, to afford a pretence for removing the ambassador to Somerset House (where he was afterwards accommodated), which lying on the banks of the Thames, any person might have more private access to him by water. Others said that the Pretender came over with the ambassador, and had private interviews with the queen and some of her ministers; but that his residence here being suspected, the house was fired to favour his escape in the confusion."

The house was insured; but the French king's dignity would not permit him, it is said, to suffer a fire-office to pay for the neglect of the domestics of his representatives,* and it was accordingly afterwards rebuilt magnificently, at his majesty's cost. Northouck describes it, in 1773, as having long been tenanted first by Lord Chancellor Hardwicke, and then occupied by the Spanish ambassador. He adds: "It stands back from the street, is fronted with stone in a majestic style; eight lofty Corinthian pilasters reach to the entablature over the first storey, which supports the attic storey, which has been censured as out of proportion; and the house stands greatly in need of wings, to render it complete." The same is the opinion of the author of the "New Critical Review of the Public Buildings," already quoted. The following additional details of Powis House we glean from Mr. P. Cunningham's "Handbook:"—"The front was surmounted on the coping by urns and statues. Over the street door was a phoenix, still standing (but without the head) in the tympanum of the pediment of the house, No. 51. The ornament above the capitals of the pilasters was the Gallic cock. The staircase was painted by Giacomo Amiconi, a Venetian painter of some reputation in this country. He chose the story of Holofernes, and painted the personages of his story in Roman dresses. On the top was a great reservoir, used as a fishpond and a resource against fire. The house was taken down in 1777." There is a large engraving of the mansion by Thomas Bowles, dated 1714, the year after the destruction of the first building by fire.

A large house on the north side, No. 45, now the Working Men's College, was during the last century the residence of Lord Chancellor Thurlow. The house is chiefly noticeable for its deep bay-windows, and its old-fashioned iron railings on each side of the steps leading to the doorway. Within, most of the rooms are large and lofty, and the principal staircase is broad and spacious.

---

* *European Magazine* for June, 1804, p. 429.

Under an arched recess upon the staircase there stood formerly a bust of Lord Thurlow. It was from this house, on the night of the 24th of March, 1784, the day before the dissolution of Parliament, that the Great Seal of England, one of the emblems of the supreme authority of the occupant of the woolsack, was stolen. The story of the theft is thus told by Mr. Cunningham:—"The thieves got in by scaling the garden-wall and forcing two iron bars out of the kitchen window. They then made their way up to the chancellor's study, broke open the drawers of his lordship's writing-table, ransacked the room, and carried away the Great Seal, rejecting the pouch as of little value, and the mace as too unwieldy. The thieves were discovered, but the seal, being of silver, had got into circulation through the melting-pot, and patents and other important public documents were delayed until a new one was made." In another version of the tale it was stated that the thieves effected their escape without having been heard by any of the family; and though a reward was offered for their discovery they could never be traced, nor was the Great Seal ever recovered. A Cabinet Council was immediately called, and a new seal was ordered to be made, and such expedition was used, that by noon the next day the new Great Seal was finished in a rough fashion, and was used as a makeshift until another was prepared, which it took the artist a whole year to complete. An accident similar to the above befell Lord Nottingham, Lord Chancellor in the year 1577, when the official mace was stolen. The story of its recovery, quite a romance of its kind, is told by Hone, in his "Year Book."

Many good stories are told about the haughty and eccentric Lord Thurlow, a few of which we offer to our readers.

When, by the death of his publisher, Mr. Payne, of Pall Mall, George Crabbe found himself poor and unknown in London, reduced to the necessity of asking assistance, he applied, among other great men, to Lord Thurlow, to whom he wrote more than once. "To the first letter, which enclosed a copy of verses," writes the poet's son, "Lord Thurlow returned for answer a cold and polite note, regretting that his avocations did not leave him leisure to read verses. The great talents and discriminating judgment of Lord Thurlow made Crabbe feel this repulse with double bitterness; and he addressed to his lordship some strong but not disrespectful lines, intimating that in former times the encouragement of literature had been considered as a duty appertaining to the illustrious station which he held. Of this effusion the lord

chancellor," adds the filial biographer, "took no notice whatever." It is satisfactory to learn from the same source that a year later—not, however, till he had found a friend in Edmund Burke—Crabbe received from Lord Thurlow an invitation to breakfast at his house in Great Ormond Street, when the latter apologised to the poet for his neglect, and placed in his hands on leaving a sealed letter containing a bank-note for £100, with a promise of further aid of another kind as soon as he should enter holy orders.

Lord Thurlow's personal appearance was often the subject of amusing and laughable remarks. It is asserted that he was singularly ugly; so ugly that when his portrait was shown to Lavater, the physiognomist, he observed—"Whether that man is on earth or in another place that should be nameless, I know not; but wherever he is, he is a born tyrant, and will rule if he can." The Duke of Norfolk had, at Arundel Castle, a fine breed of owls, one of whom, from its excessive ugliness, he named Lord Thurlow; and it is said that great fun was caused by a messenger coming to the duke in a lobby of the House of Peers with the news that "Lord Thurlow had just laid an egg."

For the following anecdote, relative to Lord Chancellor Thurlow, whilst living in Great Ormond Street, we are indebted to Mr. Cradock's amusing "Memoirs:"—

"Soon after Mr. Thurlow was made Lord Chancellor, he addressed his brother, the Bishop of Durham, in the following words:—'Tom, there is to be a drawing-room on Thursday, where I am obliged to attend; and as I have purchased Lord Bathurst's coach, but have no leisure to give orders about the necessary alterations, do you see and get all ready for me.' The bishop, always anxious to obey the *sic volo, sic jubeo*, of his brother, immediately bestirred himself, and everything was considered as completed in due time; but when the carriage came to the door, the bishop found that Lord Bathurst's arms had never been altered. Knowing his brother's hasty temper, he happily hit immediately on the only expedient to prevent a storm: the door was held open till the Lord Chancellor arrived, and as soon as he was seated and had fully examined the interior, he stretched out his hand, and most kindly exclaimed, 'Brother, the whole is finished entirely to my satisfaction, and I thank you.' The same expedient, as to the door, was resorted to again at his return from St. James's, and of course no time was lost to remedy all defects." Doubtless, the very next day the arms and crest of the Bathursts were superseded by those which Garter King of Arms had assigned to

Lord Thurlow; for, being the first gentleman of his race, he probably inherited none.

Lord Thurlow, it is well known, was rough and plain-spoken to a degree, not to say occasionally wanting in common courtesy; and yet sometimes, when the fit took him, he could unbend, much like Dr. Johnson, who, by the way, was himself an

carriage, and saw them safely to their lodgings in what was then the fashionable street of Church Row. The circumstance being related to Lord Thurlow, the Lord Chancellor took an early opportunity of calling on the young man, to thank him in person, and finding him at breakfast, sat down and joined him at his morning meal, where he

LORD THURLOW.

occasional guest here with his lordship. Mr. Cradock, in his "Memoirs," for instance, records a slight incident which shows him in an amiable light. Though there never was a Lady Thurlow, yet he had two daughters, of whom he was fond and proud. One evening, as they were coming away from the Assembly Rooms at Hampstead, there was a slight riot in Well Walk among the servants in waiting. The young ladies being alarmed, a young officer stepped forward and offered his assistance and protection, which they were glad to accept. He handed them to their

made himself particularly agreeable. It was not till after his lordship was gone that the young man found out that he had been entertaining a lord chancellor unawares.

Notwithstanding his eccentricity, Lord Thurlow will ever be looked upon as a great lawyer and magistrate. When he last offered in the House of Lords to deliver a judgment in a divorce case, the whole house rose in honour to his years and learning. Dr. Johnson said he was a splendid fellow; and Sheridan declared that "no man was half so wise as Thurlow looked."

QUEEN SQUARE, 1810.

The Working Men's College, of which we now proceed to speak, had its origin in a very humble manner. In 1848, a barrister of Lincoln's Inn, Mr. John Malcolm Ludlow, proposed to the then newly-appointed chaplain of Lincoln's Inn, the Rev. F. D. Maurice, that some district near should be taken in hand by the lawyers whom Mr. Ludlow could get together, for the purpose of holding educational classes, Bible readings, &c., among the working classes. This was in a building in Little Ormond Yard, not far from the present college. In course of time this party of gentlemen, with some others, formed "The Society for Promoting Working Men's Associations," and built the Hall of Association, under the workshops of the Tailors' Association, in Castle Street. Here were begun classes and lectures, to both of which women were admitted. In 1854 Mr. Maurice drew up a lengthy plan for the formation of a College for Working Men, in which it was agreed "that the education should be regular and organic, not taking the form of mere miscellaneous lectures, or even of classes not related to each other." It was also agreed that the teachers, and, by degrees, the pupils, should form an organic body, so that the name of "college" should be at least as applicable to the institution as to University College or King's College. And it was also determined that the college should, in some sense or other, immediately or ultimately be self-governed and self-supported. Mr. Maurice's plan having been duly discussed, a circular was distributed, setting forth the nature and objects of the college. In the meantime a house —No. 31, Red Lion Square—had been taken; and the infant establishment consisted of a principal, a council of teachers, and students. The first "term" opened on October 31, 1854, the candidates for admission as members numbering upwards of 100, Mr. Maurice filling the presidential chair. Many other names of men of note have since been added to the lists. In 1856 the college became "affiliated" to the London University. In the following year —the lease of the house in Red Lion Square having expired—the College took up its quarters in Great Ormond Street. In course of time, owing to the increase in the number of students, and for other reasons, the adjoining house, No. 44, was purchased, and added to the College property; and in 1870, partly out of funds contributed by friends, and partly by money advanced on loan, some large additional buildings were erected at the end of the grounds in the rear of the house, to serve as class-rooms, lecture-hall, museum, &c. There is also an excellent library, and a room set apart for general sociable conversation among the members.

In 1874 the college was incorporated, under the name of the "Working Men's College Corporation," under the provisions of an Act of Parliament, and thus permanently settled its status; and the debt which arose from taking the present house, and also by the erection of the additional buildings, was nearly extinguished by the "Maurice Memorial Fund" having been placed at the disposal of the council as a Domus-fund. Professor Maurice, the founder, continued to be the Principal of the College till his death, in 1872, when he was succeeded by Mr. Thomas Hughes, and he by Sir John Lubbock in 1883. Besides the College proper, here are also the Working Men's College Adult Evening School and the International Collegiate School.

One or two doors westward is the Hospital of St. John and St. Elizabeth. This is a Roman Catholic charity for the relief of the sick poor of the metropolis. The church connected with the institution is a large and handsome building, and was erected by Sir George Bowyer, as a knight of the Order of St. John. The hospital was founded in 1856, and was for some time under the direction of the late Cardinal Wiseman. Considerable alteration was subsequently made in the building, and it was re-opened in 1868.

The house lately standing at the corner of Powis Place, and incorporated into the Hospital for Sick Children, was the last home of Dr. Richard Mead, the celebrated physician and "archiator" of King George II., who died there in 1754. Born at Stepney in 1673, Dr. Mead lived to become the friend of Drs. Radcliffe, Garth, and Arbuthnot, and he had sufficiently established his reputation as a physician as to be called in consultation to the sick room of Queen Anne, two days before her death. On the accession of George II. Dr. Mead was appointed Physician in Ordinary. He had in the meantime held several important positions, including the post of Physician to St. Thomas's Hospital. The doctor's last, and perhaps the most useful, of all his works is his "Medical Precepts and Cautions."

Dr. Mead, no less celebrated as a patron of artistic and literary genius than in his own walk of life, was one of the first collectors of a private gallery, which he threw open freely to art-students and to private amateurs. His house, indeed, may be said to have been the first academy of painting in London. At the bottom of the garden at the back of his house the doctor had constructed a museum, in which was brought together a large collection of pictures and antiquities, besides which he had an extensive and valuable library. His doors were always open to the poor and indigent for advice; men of intellect were sure of finding from Dr. Mead all help and aid. He kept continually in his pay a number of scholars and artists of all kinds, who were continually at work for him, or, rather, for the public. No foreigner of taste and learning came to London without being introduced to him, and being asked to dine at his table. His library was open to every one who wished to consult it, and he allowed his books to be borrowed by the studious. Dr. Mead's library, medals, and pictures were sold by auction and dispersed after his death, in 1754.

The Hospital for Sick Children was established in the year 1852 in the above-mentioned old-fashioned mansion, with its spacious garden behind. The retrospect, in looking back over the time during which the hospital has existed, shows a marvellous progress. At its first opening only one child—a little girl—came to be admitted as a patient, and at the end of a month only eight in-patients and twenty-four out-patients had applied. For some years there was a struggle, not only for funds, but for existence, on the part of the new institution. Happily, some influential people took up the children's cause. The Bishop of London, Lord Carlisle, and Lord Shaftesbury said many a good word for it. Charles Dickens, as brilliant as he was large-hearted, advocated it by tongue and pen. Who, having read "Our Mutual Friend," will have forgotten "Little Johnny's" removal to "a place where there are none but children; a place set up on purpose for children; where the good doctors and nurses pass their lives with children, talk to none but children, touch none but children, comfort and cure none but children?" Notwithstanding all that was said and written in its favour, little money at first seemed to be forthcoming, but much sympathy and kind encouragement also, the best impetus that can be given to a really good cause, aware of its own value —publicity. In course of time the first annual report appeared, announcing as patroness of the Children's Hospital the most exalted mother in the realm—the Queen, and then definitely stating the objects. These were—" 1. The medical and surgical treatment of poor children. 2. The attainment and diffusion of knowledge regarding the diseases of children. 3. The training of nurses for children." It had above thirty beds, and in the first five years of its existence had given out-door and in-door relief to above 50,000 children, when want of funds threatened to arrest its merciful work. A public dinner was arranged at the Freemasons' Hall; Charles Dickens undertook to preside. From his speech on the occasion we

get a picture of the hospital, drawn in his own masterly manner. After some preliminary remarks, he proceeded: " Within a quarter of a mile of this place where I speak stands a courtly old house where once, no doubt, blooming children were born, and grew up to be men and women, and married, and brought their own blooming children back to patter up the old oak staircase which stood but the other day, and to wonder at the old oak carvings on the chimney-pieces. In the airy wards into which the old state drawing-rooms and family bed-chambers of that house are now converted are such little patients, that the attendant nurses look like reclaimed giantesses, and the kind medical practitioner like an amiable Christian ogre. Grouped about the little low tables in the centre of the rooms are such tiny convalescents, that they seem to be playing at having been ill. On the dolls' beds are such diminutive creatures, that each poor sufferer is supplied with its tray of toys; and, looking round, you may see how the little, tired, flushed cheek has toppled over half the brute creation on its way to the ark, or how one little dimpled arm has mowed down (as I saw myself) the whole tin soldiery of Europe. On the walls of these rooms are graceful, pleasant, bright childish pictures. At the beds' heads are pictures of the figure which is the universal embodiment of all mercy and compassion, the figure of Him who was once a child Himself, and a poor one. Besides these little creatures on the beds, you may learn in that place that the number of small out-patients brought to that house for relief is no fewer than 10,000 in the compass of one single year. In the room in which these are received you may see against the wall a box on which it is written that it has been calculated that if every grateful mother who brings a child there will drop a penny into it, the hospital funds may possibly be increased in a year by so large a sum as forty pounds." That night added £3,000 to the resources of the hospital, and Dickens afterwards read publicly for the same charitable purpose his " Christmas Carol." Year by year the number of out-patients increase enormously, whilst the in-patients are still limited by the want of sufficient funds. Nevertheless, as the list of subscribers swells, and one or two legacies fall in, the number of tiny beds is added to by twos and threes. In an article in Dickens' *All the Year Round* (1863), we read :—" Steadily as it has advanced, generously and wisely as it has been supported, it is yet but the small beginning of a work of duty. In the first five of its ten years of existence, it received into its beds more than 1,100 children seriously and dangerously ill, and gave the best help of medicine to 30,000 who were nursed at home. In the second half of its life, nearly 2,000 sick children have been sedulously tended in the little beds of the hospital, and almost 50,000 have received, as out-patients, gratuitous advice and medicine. The help is gratuitous; need of help is the sole recommendation necessary."

Since the above period the work of the hospital has become increasingly well known, and its borders have expanded along with its sphere of usefulness. First came the purchase of the house and garden adjoining that in which the hospital had been established; then came the addition of a room for convalescents; then the admission of women to be trained as nurses, and the institution of lectures on the diseases of children. The children who were recovering were sent to Brighton or to Mitcham for the fresh air they needed; and Cromwell House, at Highgate, has been occupied as a convalescent home for the children leaving the hospital.

In 1875, a further extension of the hospital was completed by the erection of a magnificent block of buildings in the rear of the old house, from the designs of Mr. E. M. Barry, R.A. It is an imposing brick-built structure, decorated with terra-cotta, and flanked by octagonal towers, which are made to play an important part in the fulfilment of the sanitary requirements of the place. Immediately facing the entrance—which is in Powis Place—is a beautifully decorated chapel, with walls of polished alabaster, and a roof supported by columns of alabaster and marble. This chapel was the gift of an anonymous donor, and it has been set apart, without actual consecration, for the religious services of the house, the services being conducted by the ladies who undertake the administration of the hospital, and the congregation consisting of the nurses and such of the little patients as are able to attend. On either side of the entrance, on the ground floor and on the first floor, is a spacious ward, each one being named, by special permission, after some member of the royal family. On the upper floor there are a number of smaller wards, to afford quiet to single patients after operations, or to admit of the separation of infectious disease (if it should accidentally break out) from the main body of the hospital. This new building affords space for 112 beds, and upon its construction the best architectural and sanitary knowledge has been brought to bear. It may be well to record here that the nurses are under the supervision of trained ladies, who are called "sisters," who reside in the hospital and are provided with board, but whose services are otherwise gratuitous. There is a "sister"

to each ward, and one to the out-patient department, and under the sisters there are paid nurses, in the proportion of at least one to every ten patients. These nurses, however skilful in their calling, are engaged upon probation, and are not retained unless they are found to possess tact and aptitude in the management of children—a circumstance, it has been remarked, which renders it curious and interesting to observe that they are all little women.

In 1882 Dr. Mead's house was pulled down, in order to complete the rebuilding of the Hospital according to the original plan and design of Mr. Barry. This charity, being unendowed, is dependent entirely on voluntary contributions for its support and maintenance.

On the west side of Powis Place is a large and handsome stone building, called the Homœopathic Hospital. In what is now the east wing of the edifice (then No. 50) the family of the Macaulays were living in the early part of the present century. It was then occupied by Zachary Macaulay, and in it his celebrated son, the future essayist, orator, and historian, Lord Macaulay, spent some portion of his early manhood.

Mr. G. O. Trevelyan, in his "Life of Lord Macaulay," draws a most pleasant picture of the interior of this house, when the younger brothers and sisters of the future essayist were still in the school-room, the fun and mirth of the week days, however, being softened down by the regular visit on Sundays to St. John's Chapel, Bedford Row, to sit under the ministry of Daniel Wilson. "It was round the house in Great Ormond Street that the dearest associations of the family were gathered," writes Mr. Trevelyan, who tells us how his mother, Lord Macaulay's sister, drove thither when dying to look once more on its well-known walls. Here the family lived very quietly, Mr. Z. Macaulay having met with reverses in business; and here he was living when the "Essay on Milton," contributed by his son, the future Lord Macaulay, to the *Edinburgh Review*, made him at once the "talk of the town." "The family table in Bloomsbury," writes Mr. Trevelyan, "was at once covered with cards of invitation from every quarter of London."

At No. 27, on the south side of the street, are the offices of the United Kingdom Benefit Society, one of the oldest and best conducted societies of the kind in the metropolis. It was instituted in 1839, and was originally located in Castle Street, Long Acre, but removed to Great Ormond Street about 1865. The society, which was formed for the purpose of affording relief to its members in case of sickness, and of an allowance to the family in case of death, is enrolled agreeably to Act of Parliament, and has upon its books a very large number of members.

Addison, in the *Spectator* (No. 9), lets us into the character of this street in his time. He writes in a tone half serious and half jesting :—" There are, at present, in several parts of this city, what are called street clubs, in which the chief inhabitants of the street converse together every night. I remember, upon my inquiring after lodgings in Great Ormond Street, the landlord, to recommend that quarter of the town, told me there was at that time a very good club in it. He also told me upon further discourse with him, that two or three noisy country squires, who were settled there the year before, had considerably sunk the price of house-rent, and that the club (to prevent the like inconvenience for the future) had thoughts of taking every house that became vacant into their own hands, till they had found for it a tenant of a sociable nature and good conversation."

In New Ormond Street is an institution called the Workhouse Visiting Society. It was established to promote the moral and spiritual improvement of workhouse inmates (of whom there are upwards of 117,000 in England and Wales), and to provide a centre of communication and information for all persons interested in that object. The society is in connection with the National Association for the Promotion of Social Science. It was founded in 1858, and has already enlisted a large number of persons in its interests, who labour among the various classes which are to be met with in our workhouses. The objects of this society are being carried out in all parts of England, and the work has been extended to Ireland. Besides the work of visiting carried on by the members, a scheme has also been started by them for the formation of workhouse libraries. The society has also a Home for Incurable and Infirm Women, which was opened in 1861. The occupation of those in the home consists of housework, cooking, and laundry-work, for a month in turn, with needlework, and two hours of instruction in the evening : they also assist the nurse in attendance on the aged patients in the infirm ward. Two girls also, for a month at a time, are attached to the infant nursery of the Children's Hospital in Great Ormond Street. There is a considerable degree of liberty allowed to the girls in the Home, as it is desired to treat them and trust them as they will have to be trusted in situations.

Guilford Street, into which we now pass, runs parallel with Great and New Ormond Streets, and extends from Russell Square to Gray's Inn Road.

"Its site," says Malcolm, "was formerly a path, which led from Gray's Inn Lane by the Foundling Hospital, the gardens of Great Ormond Street, and the back of Queen Square, to Baltimore House (afterwards inhabited by the Duke of Bolton and the Earl of Roslyn), and it was generally bounded by stagnant water at least twelve feet lower than the square." In the first half of the present century, however, the street had become the residence of a large number of the most successful barristers, and even of several members of the judicial bench. In it lived, long after he had attained the dignity of Lord Chief Baron of the Exchequer, the late Right Hon. Sir Frederick Pollock. Here, too, lived Sir Edward Sugden (afterwards Lord St. Leonard's, and Lord High Chancellor of England) whilst in the full tide of his professional success. At No. 71, two doors off, resided Mr. Serjeant Wilde, another Chancellor in embryo, the future Lord Truro.

A great part of the north side of Guilford Street—in fact, the whole space between Brunswick and Mecklenburgh Squares—is occupied by the grounds surrounding the Foundling Hospital, of which institution we shall speak in a future volume. We may, however, mention here that a small inn, named the "Boat," in the then open fields to the rear of the hospital, was the rendezvous of Lord George Gordon and the other ringleaders of the mob of "No Popery" zealots who, in the year 1780, set half London on fire, and caused a panic of a week's duration.

Both Brunswick and Mecklenburgh Squares are of comparatively modern growth, and are highly respectable, but not in any way fashionable. Macaulay more than once contrasts with Holland House and West-end society "the quiet folks who live in Mecklenburgh and Brunswick Squares." In Brunswick Square, as one of them tells us, the great historian would pace up and down with his sisters Margaret and Hannah for a couple of hours at a time, talking incessantly on politics and literature, or "deep in the mazes of the most subtle metaphysics." John Leech, the well-known artist, and contributor to *Punch*, was at one time living in this square ; and Mecklenburgh Square has numbered among its residents Lord Kingsdown and Mr. G. A. Sala. The house-fronts of Brunswick Square have been described as "brick walls with holes in them," as is the case with the majority of the squares in this neighbourhood ; it is blocked up on the east side by the grounds of the Foundling Hospital, which form, on the other hand, the west boundary of Mecklenburgh Square. The east side of the latter is architecturally embellished, and the enclosure contains some very fine trees.

HOSPITAL FOR SICK CHILDREN, GREAT ORMOND STREET. (*See page* 562.)

CHAPTER XLIV.

RUSSELL AND BEDFORD SQUARES, &c.

"Fountains and trees our wearied pride do please,
Even in the midst of gilded palaces;
And in our towns the prospect gives delight,
Which opens round the country to our sight."—*Spratt.*

The Site of Russell Square at the Beginning of the Present Century—Statue of Francis, Fifth Duke of Bedford—General Appearance of the Square—Bolton House—A Pair of Eccentric Peers—Lord Chancellor Loughborough—Other Distinguished Residents—Bedford Place—Montagu Place—Keppel Street—Bedford Square—Lord Eldon and the Prince Regent—The "Princess Olivia of Cumberland"—Gower Street—The Toxophilite Society—Jack Bannister, the Actor—The Eccentric Henry Cavendish—University College—Flaxman's Models—The Graphic Club—University College Hospital—Dr. Williams' Library.

ON the demolition of Bedford House, the adjoining lands were laid out for building purposes, and Russell and Bedford Squares were erected about the year 1804, and were named after the Russells, Earls and Dukes of Bedford. For some time previously—as we have already shown in our account of Bloomsbury Square, Great Ormond Street, and other places in the locality—many of the houses in the immediate neighbourhood were very extensively inhabited by judges and successful lawyers; and on the building of the above squares the houses were so largely taken up by members of the legal profession, on account of their nearness to Lincoln's Inn, that in course of time the epithet of "Judge-land" came to be applied to this particular

part of Bloomsbury, in much the same manner as in late years Pall Mall and its neighbourhood came to be called "Club-land."

Russell Square, which we enter at the western end of Guilford Street, occupies part of what in 1720 was called Southampton Fields, but what in later times became known as Long Fields. At the beginning of the present century, Long Fields lay waste and useless. There were nursery grounds northward; towards the north-west were the grounds of the Toxophilite Society; Bedford House, with its lawn and magnificent gardens planted with lime-trees, occupied the south side; whilst Baltimore House, which later on came to be called Bolton House, stood on the east side, at the corner of Guilford Street. This square is one of the largest in the metropolis; in fact, it is the next largest to Lincoln's Inn Fields. The houses are of brick, with the lower part in some cases cemented. Something of an architectural character is given to a block on the west side, between Montagu Place resting on a plough, while in the other he holds some ears of corn. There are four emblematical figures at the corners of the pedestal, which is adorned in bas-relief with various rural attributes. The statue—a very fine specimen of Sir Richard Westmacott's best style—was erected in 1809.

SIR THOMAS LAWRENCE'S HOUSE, RUSSELL SQUARE. (*See page* 566.)

and Keppel Street, but the majority of the houses are better inside than out. On the south side of the central enclosure, looking down Bedford Place, and facing the monument to Fox in Bloomsbury Square, is a statue which recalls to mind one of those illustrious statesmen of ancient Rome, whose time was divided between the labours of the Senate and those of their Sabine farms. The statue represents that eminent and patriotic agriculturist, Francis, the fifth Duke of Bedford, with one hand

A writer in the *St. James's Magazine* thus speaks of this locality : " Russell Square is, under ordinary circumstances, a very nice place to walk in. If those troublesome railway vans and goods wagons would not come lumbering and clattering, by way of Southampton Row, through the square, and up Guilford Street, on their way to King's Cross, 'La Place Roussell' would be as cosy and tranquil as 'La Place Royale' in Paris. It has the vastness of Lincoln's Inn Fields without its dinginess."

The handsome mansion on the south-east side of the square, at the corner of Guilford Street, was built, in 1759, for the eccentric and profligate Lord Baltimore; and, as we have already stated, it was at first called Baltimore House. Hither his lordship decoyed a young milliner, Sarah Woodcock, and was prosecuted for having caused her ruin, but acquitted. He died in 1771 at Naples, whence his remains were brought to London, and lay in state, as we have mentioned, at Exeter Change. The house was subsequently occupied by the equally eccentric Duke of Bolton, whose name was then given to it. Northouck remarks, wittily and truly, that "it was either built without a plan, or else has had very whimsical owners; for the door has been shifted to different parts of the house, until at last it is lost to all outward appearance, being now (1776) carried into the stable-yard!"

The Duke of Bolton, who was, of course, known as Lord Henry Powlett during his elder brother's life, served in early life in the navy, in which, however, if we may believe Sir N. W. Wraxall, "he had gained no laurels." He was supposed generally to be the Captain Whiffle so humorously described by Smollett in his "Roderick Random." His mother was Miss Lavinia Fenton, an actress in her day (well known for her impersonation of "Polly Peachum").

Bolton House was afterwards occupied by Lord Loughborough when Lord Chancellor, as also by Sir John Nicholl and Sir Vicary Gibbs.

On the 21st of June, 1799, George III., with the Queen and several members of the Royal Family, assembled at Bolton House, when occupied by Lord Loughborough, and after partaking of a cold collation, proceeded to view the Foundling Hospital. Lord Loughborough, though an Erskine by birth, was a "paltry and servile politician," according to Lord Holland. He died soon after his elevation to the Earldom of Rosslyn, and George III. pronounced his funeral oration by declaring that "he had not left a greater rogue behind him."

When the square was laid out for building, Bolton House was the only mansion standing, and this was incorporated into the rest of the square, though somewhat incongruously; and though it is now divided into two large residences, it still retains its name of Bolton House.

Passing to the other mansions in the square, we may state that Sir Samuel Romilly lived and died (by his own hand) at No. 21; Chief-Justice Abbot (Lord Tenterden) at No. 28; Mr. Justice Holroyd at No. 46; Mr. T. (afterwards Lord) Denman at

No. 50; and at No. 12, Mr. W. Tooke, F.R.S., the writer on currency and political economy, M.P. for Truro in 1835-7.

At No. 67 lived for some time the lawyer, poet, philanthropist, and man of letters, Sir Thomas N. Talfourd, a judge of the Court of Common Pleas, who died suddenly, in 1854, in the court-house at Stafford, while addressing the grand jury.

A person no less distinguished, though in quite another way, Sir Thomas Lawrence, the courtly painter, and President of the Royal Academy, resided at No. 65 for a quarter of a century. He died there in 1830, after a very short illness. Concerning the residence of Sir Thomas Lawrence, there is a note in the *Gentleman's Magazine* for January, 1818, by the Rev. John Mitford, which says:—"We shall never forget the Cossacks, mounted on their small white horses, with their long spears grounded, standing as sentinels at the door of this great painter, whilst he was taking the portrait of their general, Platoff."

Bedford Place, connecting Russell Square with Bloomsbury Square, was built between 1801 and 1805 on the site of Bedford House. Here, at the house of Mr. Henry Fry, died, in 1811, Richard Cumberland, the author of *The West Indian*. In Upper Bedford Place, on the opposite side of Russell Square, in 1826, and for some years later, lived Mr. Richard Bethell, afterwards Lord Chancellor and Lord Westbury.

At No. 4, Montagu Place, between Russell and Bedford Squares, in 1841, lived the late Sir John T. Coleridge, father of Lord Coleridge; he had previously resided in Torrington Square, and afterwards in Park Crescent, Regent's Park. To the north-west of Russell Square are Woburn and Torrington Squares, in the latter of which was the residence of Sir Harris Nicolas, editor of Nelson's Despatches and Letters, and a distinguished antiquary and genealogist. He died at Boulogne in 1848.

Running parallel with Montagu Place, and with Store Street, forming a communication with Tottenham Court Road, is Keppel Street. This is chiefly noticeable as containing a chapel for Anabaptists.

Bedford Square, on the west side of the British Museum, stands on a part of the Bedford estate, and covers some considerable portion of the old "rookery" of St. Giles's; it is about six acres in extent, or exactly half the size of Lincoln's Inn Fields. In the reign of George IV. and William IV. it was extensively occupied by lawyers who had climbed to the top of their profession, and also by very many of the judges, among whom were Chief Justice Sir Nicholas Tindall, Sir John Richardson,

Mr. Justice Burrough, Mr. Justice Bayley, Mr. Justice Littledale, Baron Graham, Baron J. A. Park, and Mr. Justice Patteson. No. 7 was for many years occupied by Sir Robert Harry Inglis, the venerable M.P. for Oxford University.

At No. 6 lived Lord Chancellor Eldon from 1804 down to 1816; and here occurred the memorable interview between his lordship and the Prince Regent, afterwards George IV., which has been so often told, though it will bear telling here again in the words of Mr. Peter Cunningham :—"The Prince came alone to the Chancellor's house, and upon the servant opening the door, observed that as his lordship had the gout, he knew he must be at home, and therefore desired that he might be shown up to the room where the Chancellor was sitting or lying. The servant said he was too ill to be seen, and that he had also positive orders to show in *no one*. The Prince then asked to be shown the staircase, which he immediately ascended, and pointed first to one door and then to another, asking, ' Is that your master's room ? ' The servant answered ' No,' until he came to the right one, upon which he opened the door, seated himself by the Chancellor's bedside, and asked him to appoint his friend Jekyll, the great wit, to the vacant office of Master in Chancery. The Chancellor refused—there could be no more unfit appointment. The Prince, perceiving the humour of the Chancellor, and that he was firm to his determination not to appoint him, threw himself back in the chair and exclaimed, ' How I do pity Lady Eldon ! ' ' Good God ! ' said the Chancellor, ' what is the matter ? ' ' Oh, nothing ! ' answered the Prince, ' except that she will never see you again, for here I remain until you promise to make Jekyll a Master in Chancery.' Jekyll, of course, obtained the appointment."

In March, 1816, during the riots at the West-end on account of the rejection of the Corn-Law Alteration Bill, some portion of the mob proceeded to Bedford Square, and broke the windows of the house of the unpopular Tory Lord Chancellor.

In Alfred Place, Bedford Square, was living in 1820 Olivia Serres, *née* Wilmott, when she came forward before the world to claim royal rank and precedence as "the Princess Olivia of Cumberland," declaring that she was the legitimate daughter of Henry Frederick, Duke of Cumberland, youngest brother of George III., who had created her, by a somewhat informal document in his own hand-writing, Duchess of Lancaster. Her claim to this title was discussed more than once in the House of Commons, and was revived after her death by her children; but it was finally negatived by a decree

of the Court for Divorce and Matrimonial Causes, in June, 1866. The "Princess" died in 1834, and was buried in the churchyard of St. James's, Piccadilly.

Gower Street, which runs from the north-east corner of Bedford Square into the Euston Road, is a broad thoroughfare, nearly a third of a mile in length, but dull and monotonous in appearance. Mr. James Grant, in his "Travels in Town," is not far from the mark when he describes this as "a street which scarcely exhibits any signs of being an inhabited place. . . . . Here and there," he writes, "you see a solitary pedestrian, or perchance a one-horse chaise. The stranger in passing along this street feels an emotion of melancholy come over him, caused by its dulness and unbroken monotony, and wonders how people can betray so entire a disregard of the truth as to represent the metropolis as a place of business and bustle, of noise and din."

"This street," observes a writer in *Once a Week*, in 1867, "was still so perfectly free from smoke forty years ago that grapes were ripened by the sun in the open air in the garden of one at least of the houses. Lord Eldon used often to speak of the fine fruit which he raised in his garden here, and also mentioned in Court the sad effect of the smoke upon it. A still more extraordinary fact is that even so late as the year 1800, Mr. William Bentham, of Upper Gower Street, had nearly twenty-five dozen of the finest and most delicious nectarines, all fit for the table, gathered off three trees in his garden, and that the same plot of ground continued, even long after, to produce the richest-flavoured celery in great abundance."

In 1791 the Toxophilite Society began to hold its meetings in grounds on the eastern side of Gower Street, under lease from the Duke of Bedford; and they continued here till 1805, when they were driven away westwards, the land being "required for building purposes." We shall meet with them again when we come to the Regent's Park.

Gower Street in its time has numbered among its residents a few remarkable men. At No. 65, Jack Bannister, the actor, lived and died. " In the drama," as we learn from a memoir in the *Mirror*, " he was affecting, because he was natural and simple ; in society, he was distinguished by the same characteristics. His unaffected hilarity in conversation, the flexibility of his mind in adapting itself to every subject which arose, and the almost puerile good humour with which he recalled and recited the incidents of his earliest life and observation, formed altogether a picture equally singular and interesting. In these moments he showed himself to the greatest advantage; his animated countenance displayed at once the intelligence of a man, the sweetness of a woman, and the innocent sportiveness of a child. His social virtues will never be forgotten; they assured to him the respect and the esteem of all; he enjoyed upon earth full reward of his talents and good qualities, while his hopes of an hereafter were cherished with a warmth and confidence resulting from a true and lively faith."

A house at the corner of Montagu Place and Gower Street was for some years the town residence of the eccentric philosopher, the Hon. Henry Cavendish, who was well known for his chemical researches. Few visitors were admitted there, but some found their way across the threshold, and have reported that books and apparatus formed its chief furniture. For the former, however, Cavendish set apart a separate mansion in Dean Street, Soho. Here he had collected a large and carefully-chosen library of works on science, which he threw open to all engaged in research; and to this house he went for his own books, as one would go to a circulating library, signing a formal receipt for such of the volumes as he took with him. Cavendish, it is asserted, lived comfortably, but made no display; and his few guests were treated on all occasions to the same fare, and it was not very sumptuous. A Fellow of the Royal Society reports that "if any one dined with Cavendish he invariably gave them a leg of mutton and nothing else." Another Fellow says that Cavendish "seldom had company at his house, but on one occasion three or four scientific men were to dine with him, and when his housekeeper came to ask what was to be got for dinner, he said, 'A leg of mutton!' 'Sir, that will not be enough for five.' 'Well, then, get two,' was the reply."

Dr. Thomas Thomson writes of Cavendish:— "He was shy and bashful to a degree bordering on disease. He could not bear to have any person introduced to him, or to be pointed out in any way as a remarkable man. One Sunday evening he was standing at Sir Joseph Banks's, in a crowded room, conversing with Mr. Hatchett, when Dr. Ingenhousz, who had a good deal of pomposity of manner, came up with an Austrian gentleman in his hand, and introduced him formally to Mr. Cavendish. He mentioned the titles and qualifications of his friend at great length, and said that he had been particularly anxious to be introduced to a philosopher so profound and so universally known and celebrated as Mr. Cavendish. As soon as Dr. Ingenhousz had finished, the Austrian gentleman began to speak,

assuring Mr. Cavendish that his principal reason for coming to London was to see and converse with one of the greatest ornaments of the age, and one of the most illustrious philosophers that ever existed. To all these high-flown speeches Mr. Cavendish answered not a word, but stood with his eyes cast down, quite abashed and confounded. At last, spying an opening in the crowd, he darted through it with all the speed of which he was master, nor did he stop till he reached his carriage, which drove him directly home."

Sir Humphry Davy, in addition to the eloquent eulogium passed on Mr. Cavendish soon after his death, left this less studied but more graphic sketch of the philosopher amongst his papers:— "Cavendish was a great man, with extraordinary singularities. His voice was squeaking, his manner nervous, he was afraid of strangers, and seemed, when embarrassed, even to articulate with difficulty. He wore the costume of our grandfathers; was enormously rich, but made no use of his wealth. He gave me once some bits of platinum for my experiments, and came to see my results on the decomposition of the alkalis, and seemed to take an interest in them; but he encouraged no intimacy with any one. . . . He lived latterly the life of a solitary, came to the club dinner, and to the Royal Society, but received nobody at his own house. He was acute, sagacious, and profound, and, I think, the most accomplished British philosopher of his time." He died in 1810.

On the east side of Gower Street is University College, which was founded in the year 1826, for the purpose of affording "literary and scientific education at a moderate expense;" divinity being excluded. The credit of the idea of a university for London, in which the ancient languages should be taught, free from those artificial restrictions which bound Oxford and Cambridge so tightly, has generally been given to Lord Brougham and the other Whig politicians of his time. Cyrus Redding, however, in his "Recollections," claims the praise for Tom Campbell, the poet, who certainly took an active part in its foundation, and even journeyed—indolent as he was by nature— to Berlin in order to observe with his own eyes the professional system of Prussia, and to mature a plan for the government of the university. Testimony to the same effect was eventually borne by Lord Brougham himself.

The foundation-stone of the college was laid on Monday, the 30th of April, 1827, by H.R.H. the Duke of Sussex, who had long been associated with the leaders of the Whig party. The architect was Mr. William Wilkins, R.A., the designer of the National Gallery. The Duke of Sussex, on laying the stone, said, "May God bless this undertaking which we have so happily commenced, and make it prosper for honour, happiness, and glory, not only of the metropolis, but of the whole country." He also expressed a hope that the undertaking would excite the old universities to fresh exertions, and force them to reform abuses. An " oration," or prayer, was then offered up by the Rev. Dr. Maltby, afterwards Bishop of Durham. The ceremony was followed by a dinner at Freemasons' Hall, nearly all the chief Whigs of the day being among the guests.

The building was opened on the 1st of October in the following year, under the title of the University of London. Its constitution then was that of a joint-stock company, and the original deed of settlement provided for a dividend not exceeding four per cent. on the share capital—a dividend which, as a matter of fact, was never paid, inasmuch as from the first the expenditure of the college absorbed all that portion of the receipts in which it was supposed the dividend would be found. Thomas Campbell, then in the height of his celebrity, was appointed Lecturer on Poetry on the first opening of the institution. As the title of " University " was nothing more than a title, conveying with it none of the privileges we are accustomed to associate with the name, not even the power of granting degrees, the House of Commons in 1836 prayed for a charter of incorporation conferring such privileges and power. In answer, the Government of the day founded what is now known as the University of London, and proposed to the old institution to take the name of University College. To this proposal the proprietors, on the recommendation of the council, agreed, only stipulating that their college—as they had hoped would be done for their university—should be incorporated by royal charter. The idea seems to have been that by this means would be extinguished all the pecuniary rights of the proprietors. As this, however, was not effected, the charter, indeed, not referring to the subject at all, and as it was thought that from these rights there might at some future time arise inconvenience to the college, a private Act of Parliament was applied for with a view to settle the matter once and for all. This was obtained in 1869, and had not only the result desired, but also the effect of considerably enlarging the powers of the institution in several directions—among others, in the education of women, and instruction in the Fine Arts.

The governing body of the college consists of a council, elected by its members, who in their turn comprise the Governors, the Fellows, and the Life Governors, the first of whom, as representing the registered proprietors of the original shares, although, as we have said, all their pecuniary rights have been abolished, retain the privilege of nominating their successors. The Council itself consists of a President, Vice-President, and Treasurer, and not more than twenty-one or less than sixteen other members, six of whom, eligible to re-election, retire every year. The powers of this body are very wide—comprising, indeed, the sole and entire management of the college, both in the financial and educational departments, and also the government of the hospital to the same degree. There is, however, a subordinate body known as the Senate, and consisting of the professorial staff, which, having no voice in the government of the College, and no existence, indeed, under the Act of Parliament, is yet empowered to advise with the council on various subjects of management, especially of the libraries and museum, and has, moreover, a good deal to say to any contemplated addition or alteration in its own numbers. In connection with the larger establishment is a school, which stands to it in the light of a feeder, a considerable number of well-instructed pupils yearly passing up into the ranks of its students. The head master stands in all respects on the same footing as the professors of the college, and, like them, is subject to the regulations and control of the council. There are three faculties in the college—of arts and laws, of science, and of medicine—besides a department of civil and mechanical engineering. In the first two faculties are numbered thirty-one professorships, and of the eleven scientific chairs therein included, but one is endowed, the chair of physiology, although the professor of geology receives a yearly sum of £31 from the Goldsmid Fund.

The college comprises a central façade and two wings, and has a total length of about 400 feet. In the centre, which looks to the west, is an immense Corinthian portico, formed by twelve columns supporting the pediment, and elevated on a lofty plinth, approached by numerous steps effectively arranged. Behind the pediment is a cupola, with a lantern light, and in the great hall beneath it are placed on view the original models of the principal works of John Flaxman, which were presented to the institution some ten years after the death of the sculptor by his sister-in-law, Miss Denman, to whom, with the late Miss Flaxman, belonged the remaining works of the great

English sculptor—in the shape of drawings, models in plaster and wax, and other interesting relics—which were disposed of by public auction in April, 1876, and realised a sum of more than £2,000. In the vestibule of the college is Flaxman's restoration of the Farnese Hercules; beneath the dome is his grand life-size group of "Michael and Satan;" and around the walls are his various monumental and other bas-reliefs. In an adjoining room was placed Flaxman's "Shield of Achilles" and other works.

In the ground-floor are lecture-rooms, cloisters for the exercise of the pupils, two semi-circular theatres, the chemical laboratory, and museum of *materia medica*. In the upper floor, besides the great hall above mentioned, are museums of natural history and anatomy, two theatres, two libraries, and other rooms set apart for the purposes of the college. The principal library is richly decorated in the Italian style; it is large and valuable, containing upwards of 68,000 volumes and 16,000 pamphlets, to which has lately been added a fine collection of works on mathematics, physics, and astronomy, the gift of the late Mr. J. T. Graves. The laboratory, completed from the plan of Professor Donaldson in 1845, is stated to combine all the recent improvements of our own schools with that of Professor Liebig, at Giessen.

At University College the Graphic Club, composed of artists, painters, and engravers, used to hold their monthly meetings for the purpose of interchange of thought on matters connected with the fine arts. The club was originally established by the late Mr. John Burnet and his friends; and it numbered among its members J. M. W. Turner, Prout, Landseer, Clarkson Stanfield, and other departed worthies.

On the opposite side of Gower Street, facing the college gates, is the North London, or University College Hospital. It was founded soon after the college itself, under the presidency of Lord Brougham, for the relief of poor sick and maimed persons, and the delivery of poor married women; and also for furthering the objects of the college, by affording improved means of practical instruction in medicine and surgery to the medical students of the college under the superintendence of its professors. The building, which was erected from the designs of Mr. Alfred Ainger, affords accommodation for 160 beds, fourteen of which, in two separate wards, are devoted exclusively to the use of children under twelve years of age. The total number of persons relieved yearly is about 20,000, at the cost of £15,000; whilst the income from subscriptions and other sources amounts to not

quite half that sum, thus leaving a yearly deficit of nearly £8,000 to be provided for.

In Grafton Street East, and nearly opposite the hospital, is the Dissenters' Library, which was originally founded in Cripplegate,* in the year 1711, by Dr. Daniel Williams, a Presbyterian minister, for the use of the Presbyterian, Independent, and Baptist persuasions, with a salary for a librarian and housekeeper. In pursuance of his will, a building was erected in Redcross Street, with space for 40,000 volumes (though the original collection did not comprise more than 16,000 volumes), and an apartment for the curator. In the library was also a register in which Dissenters might record the births of their children. When the premises in Redcross Street were required for the extension of the Metropolitan Railway, in 1865, the library was temporarily transferred to a hired house in Queen Square, Bloomsbury, where it remained for eight years, until a home was found for it here. The site of the new library cost £4,000, and the new building in which it is lodged £7,000 more. It is a plain and substantial Gothic building. The basement includes, besides offices, strong rooms for the custody of manuscripts. On the ground floor are the entrance-hall, committee-rooms, waiting-rooms, &c. The library occupies the whole first floor, which is lofty and well lighted. The upper portion of the building is occupied by the librarian. The architect was Mr. T. Chatfield Clarke, and the structure is as nearly fireproof as possible.

The library, a very rich collection of theological works, and especially of Nonconformist literature, was first actually opened in 1729, and the new library was completed and opened in September, 1873. It now comprises about 30,000 volumes, among which are various editions of the Bible, also the first folio edition of Shakespeare; but there are no Caxtons or Wynkyn de Wordes. The library is open to respectable persons of every class daily throughout the year, excepting during the month of August and in Christmas week; on Good Friday and Whit Monday it is also closed. Books are allowed to be taken out under proper restrictions. Upon the walls of the library are portraits of Richard Baxter, by Riley; of Matthew Henry, of Wm. Tyndale, of Joseph Priestley, by Fuseli; of John Milton, and of Isaac Watts. The trustees, twenty-three in number, must all be Presbyterians; and it may be added that each trustee makes a present of books to the library.

Of Dr. Williams's ministerial career we have already spoken in our account of Redcross Street;

---

* See Vol. II., p. 239.

UNIVERSITY COLLEGE, GOWER STREET. (*See page* 568.)

but it may be added that he was one of the friends and fellow-workers of Baxter, and an advocate of what was known as "occasional conformity." He lived very frugally, but having married two rich wives, was able to lay by money towards his favourite scheme. He bequeathed money to the University of Glasgow for the support of eight students for the ministry, besides other sums in aid of the maintenance of poor ministers and their widows. He took care that his library should be open to persons of all denominations. Dr. Williams was among those who urged the Nonconformist body to refuse the concessions offered to them in conjunction with the Roman Catholics, and became one of the firmest supporters of the House of Brunswick.

A portion of Dr. Williams's estates, bequeathed for 2,000 years, was appropriated to the following objects :—The formation of a library; exhibitions at Glasgow University, and divinity scholarships; also to the establishment of schools for poor children in various parts of England and Wales; to the payment of poor Dissenting ministers; Christian teachers in Ireland, the West Indies, and New England; and to the distribution of the Doctor's own works among suitable persons.

CHAPTER XLV.

GORDON AND TAVISTOCK SQUARES, &c.

"Lucus in urbe fuit mediâ, gratissimus umbrâ."—Virgil, Æn., i.

Gordon Square—The "Catholic and Apostolic Church"—A Scene in the Chapel of the "Irvingites"—Memoir of the Rev. Edward Irving—University Hall—Tavistock Square—Dickens' Amateur Theatricals at Tavistock House—Tavistock Place—The "Building in which the Earth was Weighed—St. Andrew's Chapel—Great Coram Street—The Russell Literary and Scientific Institution—Thackeray and Dickens—Burton Street and Crescent—John Britton, the Topographer—Robert Owen, the Socialist—Major Cartwright, the Champion of Parliamentary Reform—Mr. Burton, the Builder—Judd Street—Sir Andrew Judde—Regent Square—Argyle Square—The New Jerusalem Church—Liverpool Street—The Cabinet Theatre.

GORDON SQUARE was so called after Alexander, fourth Duke of Gordon, whose daughter, the Lady Georgiana Gordon, married, as his second wife, John, sixth Duke of Bedford, whose first wife was a daughter of the noble house of Torrington.

The south-west corner of Gordon Square is occupied by a very large and noble Gothic building, the Metropolitan Church or Cathedral of the "Catholic and Apostolic Church," as the followers of Edward Irving style themselves. It was built about the year 1850, from the designs of Mr. R. Brandon and Mr. Ritchie. The exterior is of Early-English design, and the Decorated interior has a triforium in the aisle-roof, after the manner of our early churches and cathedrals. The ceilings are highly enriched, and some of the windows are filled with stained glass; the northern doorway and porch and the southern wheel-window are very fine. A beautiful side chapel has been added on the south, styled a "Lady Chapel;" but the name is inappropriate, as devotion to the Virgin Mary forms no part of the Irvingite creed. Grouped around the church are some Gothic houses, with projections and gables, pointed-headed windows, and traceried balconies.

Previous to the building of the Catholic and Apostolic Church, the "Irvingites" had their headquarters for some years in a chapel in Newman Street, which, as we have already stated, had previously served as Benjamin West's studio.

"The scene in this chapel," writes Mr. James Grant, in his "Travels in Town," "was one which might well have made angels weep. I myself have repeatedly, in the course of one morning's service, witnessed no fewer than from four to seven exhibitions, in the way of speaking with tongues [he means, of course, 'unknown tongues']. There was one young lady who . . . spoke three different times in this way in less than an hour; and sounds more wild or more unearthly than those she uttered it has never been my lot to hear." The writer, however, whilst regretting Mr. Irving's novel and strange views, defends him zealously from the charge so frequently brought against him in his life-time, of aiding in an imposture, certifying to his single-heartedness and honesty. He adds that the late Mr. Henry Drummond, of Albury, M.P. for Surrey, and a son of the Prime Minister Spencer Perceval, were among those who frequented this chapel, and that Mr. Irving himself, as the "minister" of it, was styled its "angel."

Irving first propounded or exhibited the strange doctrine which became associated with his name in the parish of Row, and the town of Port Glasgow, in Scotland; but afterwards settled in London, preaching first in a chapel in Hatton Garden, and afterwards in the Scotch Church in Regent Square, which was built expressly for him. Here, we are informed, "the religious services were interrupted by the harangues of the inspired; women started up and in strange tones poured forth a jargon of words which none could understand, but which were assumed to be inspired by the same power that had imparted the gift of tongues on the day of Pentecost; even the lame were commanded to walk, and the dead to rise to life by those confident thaumaturgists, who were astonished at the non-compliance of their patients, and in whom, want of faith alone, they declared, had been the cause of the failure. And of all the deluded none exceeded Mr. Irving himself, whose morbid intellect it inspired with fresh activity, and to whose eloquence it furnished a new and exciting theme. The latter days, he declared, had come; the miraculous powers of the Church were restored; the millennium itself was at hand. But the Church of Scotland could no longer tolerate the unsoundness of his preaching and the extravagant displays of his congregation; and in 1830 he was deposed from his local cure, as minister of the Scots Church in Regent Square, by the presbytery of London, and finally, in the year 1833, from his standing as an ordained minister, by the presbytery of his native Annan. For these exclusions, however, Mr. Irving cared little, surrounded as he was by prophets and prophetesses, who were of higher account with him than presbyteries and general assemblies; and on his expulsion from Regent Square he betook himself to a building in Newman Street, which his people had fitted up as a place of worship, and where he organised his congregation into a separate and distinct Church. They were now placed under a fourfold ministry of apostles, prophets, evangelists, and pastors, Mr. Irving himself being ordained as the 'angel' of the Church in Newman Street. In 1834 he died, at the age of forty-two, worn out by a life of intellectual excitement and by the feverish labours of his latter years in supporting and propagating the doctrines of his new system."*

Irving's oratorical powers, and the novelty of the doctrines promulgated by him, "drew" immense congregations, and he became the "observed of all observers." We are told that his figure, air, costume, and uncapped head attracted the gaze, if not the admiration, of the young and old. He was a tall, gaunt figure, with dress of unusual cut, with his hat generally in his hand; a head of black hair, starting in all directions like the projecting quills of the "fretful porcupine;" lank cheeks, and eyes apparently directed to the two sides of the street rather than to his pathway, which was usually in the middle of the road.

Mr. Grant, in his "Travels in Town," tells us that the Irvingite body, in spite of having diminished in numbers since the death of its founder, has seven churches in the metropolis besides its central place of worship, in allusion, doubtless, to the "Seven Churches" of the Book of Revelation.

On the west side of Gordon Square, and in the rear of University College, is University Hall. It was designed by Professor Donaldson in 1849, and was built for the purpose of instructing such young men as chose to reside there in theology and moral philosophy, subjects which are excluded from the college curriculum. The architecture is Elizabethan or Tudor, in red brick and stone, and the grouping of the windows is effectively managed.

Tavistock Square, which lies on the east side of Gordon Square, is named from the Duke of Bedford's second title, Marquis of Tavistock. Tavistock House, long the residence of James Perry, editor of the *Morning Chronicle* during its palmiest days, became in later times the abode of Charles Dickens, who took possession of it in October, 1851, having removed hither from Devonshire Terrace, Marylebone. Here he almost immediately set to work upon the first number of "Bleak House," which he had long been meditating. Here his children's private theatricals were commenced on Twelfth Night in 1854, being renewed annually till the actors ceased to be children any longer. They were often aided by Mr. Mark Lemon, Douglas Jerrold, and Mr. Planché, and among the audience were Sir Edwin Landseer, Clarkson Stanfield, and the other friends of "Boz" in his early days. But it was not only at Christmas that Dickens delighted in his private theatricals. In the summer of 1855, for instance, he threw open his little theatre to several gatherings of a larger and outer circle of friends, amongst whom were Lord Campbell, Peter Cunningham, Lord Lytton, William M. Thackeray, and Thomas Carlyle. He described himself on his play-bills as "Lessee and Manager, Mr. Crummles;" his poet was Wilkie Collins, "in an entirely new and original domestic melodrama;" and his scene-painter was Clarkson Stanfield. The performances included "The Lighthouse," by Mr. W. Collins; and it may be recorded here that the scene of the Eddystone Lighthouse in this little play, afterwards carefully framed, and hung up in the hall at Gad's Hill, near Rochester, Dickens' last home, fetched a thousand guineas at the sale of the great novelist's effects. It was at supper, after one of these performances, that Lord Campbell told the company that he would rather have written "Pickwick" than be Lord Chief Justice and a Peer of Parliament.

"The best of the performances," writes Mr. John

Forster, "were 'Tom Thumb' and 'Fortunio,' in 1854 and 1855, Dickens himself now first joining in the revel, and Mark Lemon bringing into it his own clever children, and a very mountain of child-pleasing fun in himself. Dickens had become very intimate with him, and his merry, genial ways had given him unbounded popularity with the young ones, who had no such a favourite as 'Uncle' Mark. In Fielding's burlesque he was the giantess Glumdalea, and Dickens was the Ghost of Gaffer Thumb, the names by which they appeared respectively being the 'Infant Phenomenon' and the 'Modern Garrick.' But the youngest actors carried off the palm. There was a Lord Grizzle, at whose ballad of Miss Villikins, introduced by desire, Thackeray rolled off his chair in a burst of laughter that became absurdly contagious. Yet even this, with hardly less fun from the Noodles, Doodles, and King Arthurs, was not so good as the pretty, fantastic, comic grace of Dollalolla, Huncamunca, and Tom. The girls wore steadily the airs which are irresistible when put on by little children; and an actor, not out of his fourth year, who went through the comic songs and the tragic exploits without a wrong note or a victim unslain, represented the small helmeted hero." There is, it may be added, a most amusing paper in *Macmillan's Magazine* on these "Amateur Theatricals at Tavistock House," written by one who had been a member of the juvenile company. In the getting-up of these amusements Dickens was happy to secure the help of Mr. J. R. Planché in costume, and the "priceless help" of Clarkson Stanfield in his scenery.

Southward of the square is Tavistock Place, which has had among its residents some men of note in their day. At No. 9 lived John Pinkerton, the historian. "Here," says Mr. Peter Cunningham, "his depraved mode of life was the cause of continual quarrels with abandoned women." No. 34 was for some time the residence of Francis Douce, the antiquary, the author of a "Dissertation on the Dance of Death," and "Illustrations of Shakespeare and of Ancient Manners." John Galt afterwards resided in the same house. Here he wrote his autobiography and many other literary works, including a "Life of Byron." No. 37, more recently the residence of Sir Matthew Digby Wyatt, is worthy of a note, as having been the residence of Francis Baily, President of the Royal Astronomical Society, and also the spot where, in 1851, the weight of the world was ascertained by him. With reference to this building, Sir John Herschel writes: "The house stands isolated in a garden, so as to be free from any material tremor from passing carriages. A small observatory was constructed in the upper part. The building in which the earth was weighed, and its bulk and figure calculated, the standard measure of the British nation perpetuated, and the pendulum experiments rescued from their chief source of inaccuracy, can never cease to be an object of interest."

Close by is St. Andrew's Chapel, which was for some time famous for the antics of the musical "Archdeacon" Dunbar. At the time of its erection, early in the present century, this chapel was considered a prodigy of Gothic art and beauty.

Parallel with Tavistock Place, on the south side, and extending from Woburn Place to Brunswick Square, is Great Coram Street, so named after Captain Coram, the founder of the Foundling Hospital. In this street is a building of some architectural pretensions, the centre having a handsome portico with four pillars. It is called the Russell Literary and Scientific Institution, and is somewhat similar in plan to the London Institution, though on a smaller and less ambitious scale. The house was erected on speculation for the purpose of holding assemblies and balls, and was purchased in the year 1808 from Mr. James Burton, the builder, by the managers of the institution. There is here an extensive and valuable library, consisting of the most useful works in ancient and modern literature; and the reading-room is well managed and attended.

In 1837, Thackeray, then newly married, took up his residence in this street, where he lived for two years, occupying himself with his literary contributions to *Fraser*, and an occasional illustration. It was while residing here that he one day called on Dickens, with an offer to illustrate "Pickwick"—an offer which was "declined with thanks," and possibly turned the course of his life into a different channel. Had his offer been accepted, he probably would have become an artist, and possibly an R.A.; but "Vanity Fair" would never have been written.

On the north side of Tavistock Place are Burton Street and Burton Crescent. In the former, at No. 15, lived Mrs. Davidson, who, as Miss Duncan, attained high repute on the stage by her performances in *The Honeymoon* and other dramas, but who lived to see her fame decline. Often would she walk to and from the theatre twice a day, to rehearsal and performance, in wet and cold weather, whilst her husband was either in bed or at a gaming-table.

In this street, as Mr. Grant tells us in his "Travels in Town," there was formerly one of the chapels of the sect founded by Emmanuel Swedenborg, called the New Jerusalem Church.

At Burton Cottage, Burton Street, lived John Britton, F.S.A., the topographer, antiquary, and man of letters, who has already been briefly mentioned in our account of Red Lion Street, Clerkenwell.* John Britton was a native of Kington St. Michael, Wiltshire, where his father was a small farmer and kept a village shop. At an early age he came to London, and, as we have said, was apprenticed to a wine-merchant. At that time, and even on reaching manhood, his education was very imperfect; he, nevertheless, formed the acquaintance of various persons connected with the humbler walks of literature, and was induced to embark in a small way on authorship himself, by compiling some common street song-books, &c. Becoming acquainted with Mr. Wheble, the publisher of the *Sporting Magazine*, for which he had prepared some short notices, he obtained his introduction into the career which he so long and honourably pursued. Wheble, whilst residing at Salisbury, had issued the prospectus of a work to be called the "Beauties of Wiltshire," but was not able to carry it on; but now, finding that Britton was a native of that county, Wheble proposed to him to compile the work he had announced. Among Britton's acquaintances was a young man named Brayley, of about his own age, but somewhat better taught; they had assisted each other in their studies, and they now entered upon a sort of literary partnership. In due time the "Beauties of Wiltshire" was completed, and at the invitation of the publishers the joint authors immediately afterwards set to work on the "Beauties of Bedfordshire." Eventually the "Beauties" of all the other counties of England were published, in twenty-six volumes, but only the first nine were written by the original authors. In 1805, Mr. Britton produced the first part of a more elaborate work, the "Architectural Antiquities of England," which in the end formed five splendid volumes. From this time Mr. Britton's course was one of laborious and persevering authorship in the path which he made for many years in a special manner his own—that of architectural and topographical description. Of the many works of this character which he produced, the most important is the "Cathedral Antiquities of England." Mr. Britton died in 1857, at an advanced age.

No. 4, Crescent Place, which intersects Burton Street, was for some years the home of Robert Owen, the Socialist. Like Mr. Britton, Owen was of humble origin. He was for some time a successful cotton-spinner at Lanark, in Scotland,

during which period he attended with benevolent care to the welfare of the persons employed and to the education of their children. He here introduced many improvements, since adopted in other schools, so as to make instruction at once attractive and useful; and founded, if not the first, one of the earliest of the infant schools. About this time he published his "New View of Society, or Essays on the Formation of Human Character," and subsequently a "Book of the New Moral World," in which he developed a theory of modified Communism. In 1823, this eccentric philanthropist went to North America, where he attempted, but unsuccessfully, to found a settlement. The latter years of his life, which were spent in England, were devoted to various objects, all more or less visionary, "the foretelling of the millennium on earth; the establishing of a system of morality, independent of religion; and a vindication of his claims to be able to hold conversations with the spirits of the dead, particularly with the late Duke of Kent." He died in 1858, at his birthplace in North Wales.

Burton Crescent is only noticed in the "Handbook of London" as containing "a statue of Major Cartwright, by Clarke, of Birmingham, which is a disgrace to art." This Major Cartwright was one of the earliest advocates and champions of Parliamentary reform. In "A Book for a Rainy Day" it is stated that he was born at Marnham, Nottinghamshire, in 1740. "In the year 1758 he entered the naval service, under the command of Lord Howe; was promoted to a lieutenancy in September, 1762, and continued on active service until the spring of 1771. Then retiring to recruit his health, he remained at Marnham till invited by his old Commander-in-chief, in the year 1775 or 1776; but not approving of the war with America, he declined accepting the proffered commission. About the same time he became major of the regiment of Nottinghamshire Militia, then for the first time raised in that county, in which he served seventeen years. When George III. arrived at the year of the Jubilee, a naval promotion of twenty lieutenants to the rank of commanders took place, and the name of J. C. standing the twentieth on the list, he was commissioned as a commander accordingly. In the year 1802 he published 'The Trident,' a work in quarto, having for its object to promote that elevation of character which can alone preserve the vital spirit of a navy, as well as to furnish an inexhaustible patronage of the arts." The major, who often distinguished himself at the Covent Garden hustings, lived to a ripe old age, and was much esteemed by all who knew him.

* See Vol. II., p 323.

He died at his residence in Burton Crescent in the year 1824.

Burton Street and Burton Crescent preserve the name of the builder, who may be regarded as the creator of all this district, James Burton, of whom Mr. Britton thus writes in his "Autobiography:" —"The career of Mr. Burton was like that of many other ardent and speculating persons. In his first undertaking of building Russell Square, Bedford Place, Upper Bedford Place, &c., he was eminently successful, and might have retired from the working world with a handsome fortune; but he was tempted to embark in further speculations by engaging to cover a large tract of ground belonging to the Skinners' Company: this proved a failure, and he sustained serious losses. During this time he became connected with John Nash, the sycophant architect and companion of the Prince Regent and after King. That architect, like Mr. Burton, was an active, speculating man; and among other plans for the improvement of London, his designs for Regent Street, the Regent's Park, St. James's Park, and Buckingham Palace, were accepted and acted upon. Mr. Burton was intimately connected with Nash in carrying into effect much of the New Road, and also the Regent's Park, in the latter of which he built a handsome villa for himself, where he resided some years. At a previous time he had embarked in gunpowder works in Kent, and built a country seat near Tunbridge. Soon afterwards he ventured on the perilous task of building and forming the new town of St. Leonard's; to convey occupants to which he established coaches to run between that place and the metropolis. These were hazardous and losing schemes, and the very worthy but daring builder was, consequently, involved in ruin. Amongst a large family, his son, Decimus Burton, was eminently successful as an architect, and designed many handsome buildings in London.

To the east of Burton Crescent, and connecting Brunswick Square with the Euston Road, is Judd Street. Sir Andrew Judd, or Judde, after whom the street was named, was a native of Tunbridge in Kent, and was Lord Mayor of London in 1551. He bequeathed a large part of his wealth towards founding and endowing a public school in his native town. Among the lands so bequeathed were certain "sand-hills on the back side of Holborn," then let for grazing purposes at a few pounds a year, but now covered with houses, and bringing in an income of several thousands a year. Sir Andrew Judde lies buried in St. Helen's, Bishopsgate, and his school now flourishes among the best grammar schools in the kingdom.

On the east side of Hunter Street, behind the Foundling Hospital, is Regent Square, which is chiefly noticeable for containing the Scotch Presbyterian Church, where, as we have already stated, the Rev. Edward Irving and his peculiar doctrines and "tongues" attracted large and fashionable congregations in the early part of this century. The church, which stands at the corner of Compton Street, is Gothic in style, and was built in 1824-25, by Mr. (afterwards Sir William) Tite, the architect, who adopted as his model the principal front of York Minster; the twin towers are 120 feet in height. On the east side of the square is St. Peter's, commonly called Regent Square Church. Here, too, is a charitable institution, wholly dependent upon voluntary contributions; it is called the Home of Hope, and has been established "for the reception of such young women, before they become mothers, as are unfitted, from their previous good character and position, for the general wards of a workhouse."

Passing in the direction of King's Cross, by a few streets of little or no importance, we arrive in Argyle Square, which, with its trees and greensward, has quite a refreshing appearance after escaping from some of the narrow streets which surround it. Here is the New Jerusalem Church, which was opened in 1844 for the followers of Swedenborg, whom we have mentioned above. The church is in the Anglo-Norman style of architecture, and was built from the designs of Mr. Hopkins; it has two towers and spires, each terminating with a bronze cross; the intervening gable has a stone cross, and a wheel-window over a deeply-recessed doorway. The interior of the church has a vaulted roof; the altar arrangements are somewhat peculiar, and there is an organ and choir.

Liverpool Street, Sidmouth Street, and a few others in the neighbourhood, were named after the Ministers in office at the date of their erection. In Liverpool Street, a little to the eastward of Argyle Square, is a small building which has been occasionally used for amateur theatrical performances. It was originally an auction-room, but has since been turned into the King's Cross, or, as it is sometimes called, "Cabinet Theatre."

Having now arrived at King's Cross, which has been already fully described in these pages,* we shall in the succeeding chapters travel over the outlying portions of London, on the south-west and west frontier of the great metropolis, commencing our journey anew at Hyde Park Corner.

* See Vol. III., p. 539.